W9-CES-463

SECOND EDITION

OUR SOCIETY

Human diversity in Canada

EDITED BY PAUL U. ANGELINI

Sheridan College

THOMSON

NELSON

Australia   Canada   Mexico   Singapore   Spain   United Kingdom   United States

THOMSON

—★—™

NELSON

Our Society: Human Diversity in Canada, 2nd Edition

Edited by Paul Angelini

Editorial Director and Publisher:
Evelyn Veitch

Executive Editor:
Joanna Cotton

Acquisitions Editor:
Brad Lambertus

Director of Marketing:
James Rozsa

Developmental Editor:
Edward Ikeda

Production Editor:
Natalia Denesiuk

Production Coordinator:
Helen Jager Locsin

Copy Editor:
Dawn Hunter

Creative Director:
Angela Cluer

Interior Design:
Ken Phipps

Cover Design:
Johanna Liburd

Cover Images:
Lower left: Serena Siqueland/
PhotoDisc
Centre left: SW Productions/
PhotoDisc
Top centre: EyeWire Collection
Right: PhotoDisc
Bottom centre: FPG International

Compositor:
Computer Composition

Indexer:
Edwin Durbin

Printer:
Transcontinental

National Library of Canada Cataloguing in Publication Data

Main entry under title:

Our society : human diversity in Canada / edited by Paul U. Angelini. — 2nd ed.

Includes bibliographical references and index.
ISBN 0-17-622316-9

1. Pluralism (Social sciences)—Canada. 2. Canada—Social conditions—1991– . I. Angelini, Paul Ubaldo, 1962– .

HN103.5.O97 2002   306'.0971
C2002-903231-8

CONTENTS

Preface

The second edition of *Our Society: Human Diversity in Canada*, like the first, was written for students who have had little or no exposure to the issues surrounding diversity in Canada. As an introductory, topic-oriented text, *Our Society* is designed to give readers a panoramic view of diversity in Canada framed within the dominant theoretical paradigms of the day. For readers who have already examined diversity, this second edition provides up-to-date statistics, analyses of recent events, and a bibliography that covers a wide variety of issues in each subject area.

All postsecondary schools and high schools have at least one course that attempts to explain life in Canada. Courses range from the general, such as Introduction to Canadian Studies, to the specific, such as Race and Ethnic Relations in Canada. Increasingly, students have demanded more comprehensive analyses of life in Canada. For example, the course I teach has evolved from one dealing exclusively with race and ethnicity to one dealing with many issues in Canadian life, including regionalism, gender, and social stratification. This course, renamed Human Diversity and Interactions in Canada, better reflects the interests of my students.

This text focuses on human diversity in Canada. Diversity in simple terms refers to the differences that set people apart from each other. Therefore, in introducing students to the diversity of Canadian life, the text addresses the following questions: How do Canadians differ from each other? What are the scope and range of each difference? How have differences evolved over time? How do we as Canadians view diversity? Rather than encouraging uniformity, the authors intend, through careful analysis, to promote tolerance and understanding and to show that differences can and do bring Canadians together. In the end, students will appreciate the differences that characterize Canadian life and will have a fuller understanding of what it means to be Canadian. The more we understand about ourselves and the more comfortable we become with this understanding, the more likely we are to accept others without prejudice. After all, difference should be celebrated, not lamented.

The reasons for completing the second edition of this book are the same as those for the original undertaking in 1997. First, students were vocal in their demands for more comprehensive courses dealing with the differences that characterize and shape life in every corner of Canada. The text, therefore, is student driven.

Second, few texts dealing with this subject matter are written for the target audience of postsecondary and high-school students. Several features make this book uniquely suited for this target audience.

- The text is learning centred, meaning that the concerns of students come before those of teachers. The writing style, organization, and level of analysis are introductory, with only the most important conceptual jargon included. Reading this text does not require specific prior knowledge.

- The book is student friendly. Important terms are bolded and featured in an end-of-text glossary for easy reference. In each chapter, boxes highlight important or complementary information. In addition, each chapter includes five to six critical thinking boxes that ask students to answer questions critically and constructively.

- The topics covered are truly inclusive. We tried, as much as possible, to include both those topics demanded by students and those that instructors believed were necessary.

- The text is unabashedly Canadian! It provides students with a balanced introduction to life in Canada.

All students—at college or university or in high school—are at a time in their lives when they begin to make definitive assessments about the world around them. We hope the treatment of the subjects covered in will make their decisions informed and responsible ones.

ACKNOWLEDGEMENTS

The work involved in putting together the second edition was no less arduous than the work required for the first. Again, without the guidance and support of many people, this text would still be just an idea. As a group we would like to thank the reviewers: Thomas Fleming (Seneca College), Fiona Angus (UBC), Don MacKenzie (St. Lawrence College), Ken Smith (retired), and Rick Holmes (Mohawk College).

We would also like to thank a number of people at Nelson for helping to make the second edition a reality. We owe a great debt to executive editor Joanna Cotton for her sound advice, expert counsel, and never-ending support. A similar debt is owed senior developmental editor Edward Ikeda, whose cogent editing, knowledge of copyright issues, and exceptional organizational skills kept this project on course and on time! We also appreciate the assistance of Brad Lambertus, Karen Howell, and Natalia Denesiuk.

I would like to thank Paul Saundercook for originally convincing me that a project of this nature was both viable and needed. His understanding of the postsecondary marketplace is second to none. I would also like to thank Hopie Palmer and Victor Montgomery for their research and graphic assistance.

Paul U. Angelini
Hamilton, Ontario
August 2002

I

An Overview of
Diversity in Canada

PART I

Part I takes a macro approach to diversity in Canada. Using the analogy of a house, these first two chapters are the building blocks, the foundation, the walls, and the roof. Together they provide a structure—they "frame" the discussions that take place in Part II.

Chapter 1 looks at regionalism. It begins with a definition of regionalism and then briefly outlines the different regions in Canada. It finishes by examining how the federal government in Ottawa has increased the tensions between regions and by assessing the actions taken by the same government to lessen regional inequality.

Chapter 2 introduces the reader to the study of demography in Canada. In addition to outlining the terms necessary for the study of demography itself, this chapter examines specific demographic trends critical to understanding developments in Canadian diversity.

Regionalism in Canada: the Forgotten Diversity

Paul U. Angelini

Two things hold this country together. Everybody hates Air Canada coffee and everybody hates Ontario.
— late New Brunswick Premier Richard Hatfield

Regions usually have some concrete, physical foundation…. But to some extent regions are also a state of mind.
— Political scientist Rand Dyck

Objectives

After reading this chapter, you should be able to

- define regionalism

- appreciate the role of regionalism in Canadian social life

- outline briefly some of the suspected causes of regionalism

- understand the sociopsychological component to regionalism

- understand the role of the federal government in creating and attempting to lessen regional differences and appreciate the aspects of our political system that intensify regional differences

INTRODUCTION: HOW IS REGIONALISM A FORM OF DIVERSITY?

The purpose of this chapter is three-fold: (1) to outline what is meant by **regionalism,** (2) to briefly explain some of the suspected causes of regionalism, and, most important, (3) to make the case that there is an important sociopsychological component to regionalism that is seldom acknowledged. Simply put, people have a profound effect on their region and on the world around them.

Let us stress that our purpose here is not to attempt to find the causes of regionalism. These attempts usually are bogged down in theoretical and ideological debates that, in the end, tell us little about the people living in these areas. We will, however, briefly outline what some other writers and researchers consider the causes of regionalism. You will have to assess for yourselves which make the most sense. When in doubt you always have the option of doing more research.

Canada is a country characterized by difference. From coast to coast there are differences in physical terrain, climate, population, distribution of natural resources, percentage of people living in urban areas, ethnicity, religion, occupation, and income. These are real and identifiable differences—but what about "subjective" differences? How do people living in each region feel about themselves, their region, and their fellow inhabitants? What influences how people answer these questions? These are important considerations because the answers to these questions help us more fully understand what is meant by regionalism, and they help bring the "human" aspect to this study. After all, regions are made up of people and people make regions.

WHAT IS REGIONALISM AND WHY STUDY IT?

Regionalism examines the people living in different areas in Canada and the different feelings they have regarding themselves, the people living in other areas, and the federal and provincial governments. Regionalism, therefore, is most of all an attitude. We can define regionalism as an attitude that reflects a long, deep, certain feeling held by the citizens of a particular geographical area that they have their own, unique identity. Often they feel that they have not been given adequate recognition for their hard work and sacrifices. Their dissatisfaction is focused in three specific areas:

1. They believe that people in the federal and provincial governments have not accurately recognized their contribution to the life of their region.

2. They believe they have not been given due recognition for their contribution to building this country called Canada.

3. They believe that their interests have not been adequately represented by the government in Ottawa and that this is one of the principal reasons that some regions receive far more money from the federal government than do others; over the years this has meant that economic differences in regional development have been made worse.

In short, although Ontario and Quebec, the central region of Canada, receive almost everything, the Western and Atlantic regions receive very little. Ontario and Quebec get much of the recognition for building Canada; in comparison, the Western and Atlantic provinces get very little. Before continuing, however, we must address three problems with regional analysis.

PROBLEMS WITH REGIONAL ANALYSIS

Three central problems exist in discussing regionalism:

1. How are geographical regions defined?
2. Are provinces necessarily regions?
3. Are regions the appropriate tool to study the people living in Canada?

How Are Geographical Regions Defined?

Some dispute exists concerning what physical characteristics should be used to designate a region. Historically, we in Canada have used geography to designate four regions (see Figure 1.1).

Perhaps the best example of dispute is over what is commonly referred to as the "West." Geographically, British Columbia is radically different from the three Prairie provinces because of the Cordilleran mountain system (the Canadian Rockies). As a result, many people in British Columbia do not believe that they should be included in the "Western" region. This belief is reinforced by the fact that the economies of these four provinces are also different: The B.C. economy is not based on farming, but the economies of Manitoba and Saskatchewan are. British Columbia has a huge forest industry and a significant fishing industry, whereas Alberta is the centre of Canada's oil and natural gas industries. Similar economic and physical differences exist within the other regions of Canada, too.

Figure 1.1 Regions of Canada

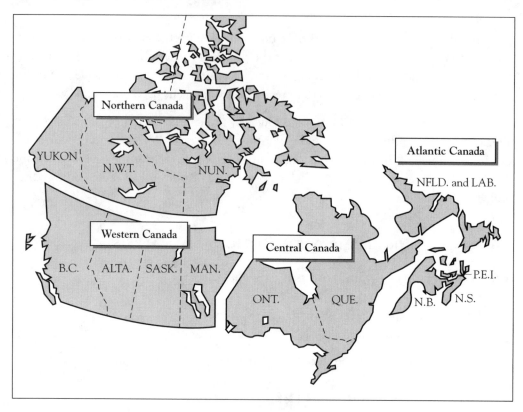

Are Provinces Necessarily Regions?

Questions arise about the belief that a province is a region. Within provinces there tend to be different regions that share certain characteristics that make them distinct from other parts of the province. The best examples of such differences are those between Northern Ontario and Southern Ontario and between Northern Quebec and Southern Quebec. In the case of Ontario, the northern part has always differed with respect to economic growth (much slower, if at all), unemployment, per capita income, and types of jobs. Unemployment is one area in which the differences are very visible. Northern Ontario has traditionally experienced higher unemployment rates than the rest of Ontario, in large part because of the resource focus of industry in Northern Ontario, the seasonal nature of such work, and the existence of one-industry towns—when that industry closes, the town shuts down. It is not uncommon for unemployment in Northern Ontario to be double the provincial average.

In short, the economic prosperity of Ontario is usually only experienced in Metropolitan Toronto, other parts of the **Golden Horseshoe**, which stretches along the coast of Lake Ontario from Niagara Falls to Oshawa, and some parts of south-central Ontario. A survey by Statistics Canada shows that six of the top ten cities according to median employment income in Canada are located in Southern Ontario; eight of the top ten are located in Ontario (see Table 1.1).

Are Regions the Appropriate Tool to Study the People Living in Canada?

Because so many questions surround what constitutes regions, issues have arisen regarding the use of regions as an explanatory tool. A wide variety of other tools could be used to explain social life in Canada, including social class, occupation, elites, ethnicity, economic

Table 1.1   Median Employment Income of Selected Canadian Cities, 1999

	Income ($)
Oshawa, Ontario	29 700
Ottawa-Hull, Ontario	28 200
Toronto, Ontario	26 700
Windsor, Ontario	27 700
Hamilton, Ontario	26 800
Kitchener, Ontario	26 800
Calgary, Alberta	25 400
Thunder Bay, Ontario	25 200
London, Ontario	24 700
Regina, Saskatchewan	24 500
Victoria, British Columbia	24 400
Vancouver, British Columbia	24 300
Halifax, Nova Scotia	23 500
Edmonton, Alberta	23 400
Quebec City, Quebec	23 300
Montreal, Quebec	22 800
Winnipeg, Manitoba	22 400
Canada	**22 400**

Source: Statistics Canada, *The Daily*, Catalogue No. 11-001E, August 15, 2001.

development, and individual choice. Marxists and neo-Marxists stress that analyzing social class and power will best explain the reality of living in Canada. Other writers, such as Richard Simeon, dismiss the use of regions as an analytical tool altogether.[1]

PROVINCES AS REGIONS

With questions surrounding the use of regions as a tool for understanding the Canadian experience, and if provinces are not necessarily regions, can we realistically treat physically and economically different provinces as regions? Our belief is that we can. Specifically, it is important to realize that since 1945, provincial governments have consistently increased their own control over their populations and have continued to challenge the authority of the federal government with respect to the economic and political leadership of their citizens. It is possible that provinces possess the political tools and the will to create a shared regional identity.[2] Our approach does not deny that different regions exist within provinces, and it does recognize provinces as a vital part in the life of the people living in them. As we will see in the section dealing with government actions, Canadian history is full of attempts on the part of the federal government to address provincial demands and to try to bring economic development and prosperity to different parts of the country, with varying degrees of success.

THEORIES ABOUT THE CAUSES OF REGIONALISM

Many explanations have been offered for the causes of regionalism, for why some regions have prospered and others have not, and for the effect this has had on the people who live there. The following is a brief sketch of some of the more prominent of these explanations.[3]

The Natural Resources Approach

The natural resources approach is more often referred to as "staples theory."[4] Generally, this theory asserts that the key to economic prosperity is the availability of natural resources. A short list of such resources includes oil, natural gas, fish, lumber, fur (beavers), coal, and various minerals.

This approach comprises two critical beliefs. The first asserts that some areas in Canada prosper while others do not because of the availability and marketability of their natural resources. In short, how much of a particular resource does your region possess, and does your region have companies or other countries prepared to buy that resource? The second critical belief concerns the external limits on developing your resource. Specifically, how is your resource affected by the fluctuations in price caused by changes in the international marketplace? Some examples will help make this point. How do the oil-producing countries located primarily in the Middle East (e.g., Saudi Arabia, Kuwait, Qatar, and Bahrain) affect the price of oil extracted from oil fields in Alberta? How do changes in world grain prices affect grain growers in Saskatchewan? In large part the prices are beyond the control of the people who produce the product. This helps explain why Western grain farmers and Atlantic fishermen demand compensation and assistance from the federal government in Ottawa to offset international price changes.

To conclude, the staples approach asserts that economic prosperity is largely determined by the availability of natural resources. The problem with this approach is that there is a tendency to exaggerate the likelihood that a region will prosper economically if natural resources are located there in extremely large quantities. Some regions in Canada have an abundance of natural resources yet have not experienced the economic prosperity that the theory would predict. As Ralph Mathews has written, Southern Ontario, for example, has no strong natural resource base, yet it is wealthy. Meanwhile, although the Atlantic provinces have a rich base of iron ore, coal, gold, forests, fish, and hydroelectric power, they have remained poor throughout most of the period since Confederation.[5]

Market Approaches

Market approaches assert that some regions are more prosperous than others because of interference, usually by governments, in the local market that results in market failure. Types of government interference include subsidizing companies that need help to survive and subsidizing the wages of employees.

Market approaches emphasize that for economic development to take place, governments must not interfere with the way the free market functions. Wages should be allowed to fall, taxes collected from companies should be minimal, labour (workers) should move to where jobs are, and money (capital) should not be restricted or penalized if and when it decides to relocate—when companies decide to stop operations, lay off workers, and set up shop elsewhere.

In the 1980s and 1990s market approaches were quite popular as solutions to the problem of regional differences in economic development and as solutions to the economic problems of countries as a whole. The United States and the United Kingdom have vigorously pursued these policies. In Canada, the Progressive Conservative premier of Alberta, Ralph Klein, and the Progressive Conservative former premier of Ontario, Mike Harris, were both fiercely committed to allowing the free market to operate unmolested by their respective governments.

Interventionist Approaches

Generally, interventionist approaches are based on the belief that some regions have prospered while others have not because of the many political (politicians and government) and economic (the development strategies of companies) forces that have historically favoured some regions at the expense of others.[6] As a general solution, these interventionist approaches regard government involvement as absolutely essential to overcoming regional problems.

Interventionist approaches differ from the staples and market theories in two specific respects. First, staples theory regards regional differences in economic prosperity as natural; interventionist approaches do not. Second, market theories see problems as avoidable if, in large part, governments simply allow the free market to operate. Interventionist approaches do not see the problems as avoidable.

In the post–World War II era, the Canadian federal government has practised interventionism quite extensively. The most visible forms of this intervention are federal government **transfer payments** (worth billions of dollars each year) to the provinces to help the poorer regions of the country (see Table 1.2).

Marxist Approaches

From a Marxist perspective, regional economic inequality is a natural outcome of the class and power differences in a society dominated by capitalism, because the driving force of capitalism is the accumulation of profit. Accumulating profit includes maximizing the value of your company for the shareholders who buy and sell shares in your company and exploiting the people, places, and things used during the production of the goods or services.

Marxism regards regional economic differences as "functional" (i.e., beneficial) to the operation of capitalism for three reasons. First, capitalism uses workers in poorer regions as reserve or surplus labour to hire and lay off whenever the capitalist sees fit. In other words, when times are good, workers from poor regions travel to more prosperous ones to work; when times are bad, these same workers are simply let go, and they return to the region from which they came. Second, underdeveloped regions provide raw materials that are processed in more developed regions. In this way money (capital) is drained from the poor regions to the richer ones. Third, poorer regions provide a market for the goods and services produced in the more developed regions.[7]

Capitalists exploit poorer regions in another way that is usually implicit in Marxist analysis and needs to be reinforced here: capitalists use the existence of poorer regions as a threatening tool to get concessions from workers (e.g., to accept less money and fewer benefits) and governments (e.g., to collect less tax money) in wealthier regions. Just as companies threaten to move their operations (including jobs) to the developing world (e.g., Mexico) if unions, workers, and governments do not provide concessions to them, so too do companies threaten to do the same within Canada. In 1995 the premiers of both Alberta and New Brunswick were accused of encouraging such behaviour in an attempt to lure business out of other provinces and to their own.

Table 1.2 Major Transfers to Provinces and Territories (Millions of Dollars)

Province / Territory	1994–95	1996–97	1999–2000	2000–01
Newfoundland	1 484	1 512	1 518	1 545
Prince Edward Island	316	323	350	371
Nova Scotia	1 932	1 949	2 025	2 175
New Brunswick	1 610	1 632	1 725	1 854
Quebec	11 446	11 096	11 703	12 529
Ontario	10 530	9 653	11 125	11 833
Manitoba	2 039	2 032	2 141	2 298
Saskatchewan	1 411	1 450	1 173	1 104
Alberta	2 525	2 313	2 827	3 014
British Columbia	3 573	3 291	3 901	4 132
Northwest Territories	74	68	525	591
Nunavut	—	—	546	597
Yukon	34	32	350	355
Total	**36 974**	**35 351**	**39 909**	**42 398**

Note: The 1994–95 figures comprise Equalization, Established Program Financing, and the Canada Assistance Plan. The 1996–97 figures comprise the new Canada Health and Social Transfer and Equalization Payments, as projected in the 1995 budget, and are estimated entitlements. The 1999–2000 and 2000–01 figures comprise the Canada Health and Social Transfer and Equalization Payments as contained in the 2001 budget.

Sources: The 1994–95 figures: *Budget, 1995*, Table 1. The 1996–97 figures: available online at <www.fin.gc.ca/toce/1995/buddoclist95-e.html>, accessed 8 February 2002. The 1999–2000 and 2000–01 figures: Department of Finance Canada, *Federal Transfers to Provinces and Territories*, February 2002, available online at <www.fin.gc.ca/activty/fedprov-e.html>, accessed 8 March 2002.

To conclude, in the above four ways Marxists regard regional imbalance as a normal outcome of capitalism.

FACTORS THAT INTENSIFY REGIONALISM

The Canadian political system operates in ways that intensify regional feelings and economic differences. Two of the most important are federalism and our electoral system.

Federalism

When the Dominion of Canada was created in 1867, a time we refer to as Confederation (see Box 1.1), the politicians who wrote the *British North America Act* (since 1982 the *Constitution Act of 1867*) decided that there should be two levels of government to govern

---

CRITICAL THINKING BOX 1.1

....

Which theory do you believe best explains regionalism in Canada? Would Canadians in other provinces share your belief? If so, why? If not, why?

---

the Canadian people. The first level is federal and refers to the national government located in Ottawa. The second level is provincial and refers to the provinces and territories and their governments.

These same politicians outlined what level of government would be responsible for what area of social life. Section 91 of the Constitution outlines federal responsibilities and section 92 outlines provincial ones. Historically, when disputes arose over a new policy area, such as atomic energy or aviation, the Supreme Court decided which level of government assumed the responsibility for that particular policy area. The federal government was given control of the armed forces, and provincial governments were given control over health care and education. **Federalism** can be defined as a system of government that divides responsibilities between two levels of government, with each level being unable to abolish the other. The two levels of government must cooperate with each other. For roughly the past twenty years, this cooperation has taken the form of meetings between the provincial premiers, their key cabinet ministers and advisers, and the prime minister along with his or her key cabinet ministers and advisers. The making of political decisions and policies jointly by federal and provincial cabinet ministers, senior bureaucrats, premiers, and prime ministers is called **executive federalism**.

Executive federalism creates problems. Senior members of government and the bureaucracy make important decisions, and many of those members have the interests of specific regions or other interests at heart, not the interests of Canada as a whole. This is of greater concern when decisions are made behind closed doors without properly informing Canadians of what is going on and without providing Canadians with opportunities for criticism, revision, and input. The **Meech Lake Accord** (1987) was an example of this type of decision making. The prime minister, Brian Mulroney, had thought it would all be a matter of simply "rolling the dice." Canadians were so upset at having been shut out of the negotiations that few tears were shed when the accord did not receive the necessary provincial approval in Manitoba and Newfoundland to be adopted by the government in Ottawa.

Executive federalism compounds the problems associated with regionalism when some regions feel they are not being represented in Ottawa and when some provinces feel other provinces have too much influence there. This has certainly been the case regarding

---

BOX 1.1

Confederation in Chronological Order

....

Date and Province or Territory	Seat of Government
1 July 1867	
Ontario	Toronto
Quebec	Quebec City
Nova Scotia	Halifax
New Brunswick	Fredericton
15 July 1870	
Manitoba	Winnipeg
Northwest Territories	Yellowknife (originally Winnipeg)
1 July 1871	
British Columbia	Victoria
1 July 1873	
Prince Edward Island	Charlottetown
13 June 1898	
Yukon Territory	Whitehorse
1 September 1905	
Saskatchewan	Regina
Alberta	Edmonton
1 April 1949	
Newfoundland	St. John's
1 April 1999	
Nunavut	Iqaluit

---

perceptions of Ontario and Quebec. Both the Western and Atlantic provinces have always claimed that the two central provinces have far too much representation in Ottawa. Historically, members of Parliament from Ontario and Quebec have dominated important key cabinet positions, such as foreign affairs, finance, justice, and international trade, as well as senior positions in the bureaucracy and government agencies.

The Western provinces have always believed that the citizens of Ontario and Quebec have not adequately recognized their sacrifices and contributions to building Canada. They also believe that their interests have not been vigorously represented in Ottawa. This was especially true during Pierre Trudeau's years as prime minister (1968–79 and 1980–84). For the better part of fourteen years, Trudeau's Liberal governments did not have one member elected to Parliament west of the city of Winnipeg, leaving Saskatchewan, Alberta, and British Columbia with virtually no federal political representation in government for almost 15 years! Consider how Ontario and Quebec would react should they ever experience the same lack of representation.

Before the First Minister's Conference in Victoria, British Columbia, on 1 August 2001, Newfoundland Premier Roger Grimes complained loudly about the return of a per capita funding formula to federal transfers to the provinces. In 1999, at the urging of then Ontario Premier Mike Harris, Ottawa's Canadian Health and Social Transfer (CHST) was calculated using a per capita formula; such a formula benefits the more populous provinces. Premier Grimes put forward the idea that the Atlantic provinces were being asked to put more money into the CHST so that Ontario could expand the services it offered its citizens, which were already beyond what was being delivered in the Atlantic provinces. In effect, the poorer provinces ended up subsidizing the richer ones!

Our Electoral System

The electoral system in Canada contributes to making regionalism worse. Canada's electoral system is a single-member plurality system or what some call "first past the post." In this system a party receives one seat for every riding it wins. The number of seats in each province depends on its population—the provinces with the most people receive the most seats. We call this **representation by population**. Therefore, the party that wins the most seats wins the election. However, the candidate who wins the riding does not necessarily need more than 50 percent of the votes. To win, a candidate simply needs more than anyone else running against him or her. An example will better illustrate this point. Candidate X receives 46 percent of the votes, and Candidate Y receives 30 percent, while Candidate Z receives 24 percent. Candidate X wins, with only 46 percent of the votes (which is not a majority) and in spite of the fact that 54 percent of the people (the total votes of Candidates Y and Z) voted against Candidate X. Now, if this scenario is repeated

CRITICAL THINKING BOX 1.2

How would you feel if your province were not represented in the federal government for almost fifteen years? What might be the sociopsychological consequences of such an experience? How did the citizens of Saskatchewan, Alberta, and British Columbia feel and act during Pierre Trudeau's years as prime minister?

in riding after riding, the party that Candidate X belongs to will win the election, even though in the election more people voted for other parties. The 1995 Manitoba election was an excellent example of this. The Conservatives won the election with 43 percent of the popular vote and therefore were given thirty-one out of fifty-seven seats in the legislature. The New Democrats were given twenty-three seats in return for 33 percent of the popular vote. The Liberals, however, won only three seats, in spite of the fact that they received 24 percent of the popular vote! The November 2000 federal election is another good example (see Box 1.2).

Our electoral system contributes to regionalism when the party that wins the election wins because it has won more seats than any other party in Ontario and Quebec. Other regions of the country lose when they do not vote for the same party that wins the most seats in Ontario and Quebec. Of the 301 seats contested in the federal election held 27 November 2000, 178 belong to Ontario (103) and Quebec (75). The winning political party, therefore, will spend a lot of time, effort, and money pleasing the people and monies interests that elect them. This is inevitable, because the majority of Canada's financial, banking, and manufacturing interests are overwhelmingly concentrated in these two provinces, especially in Ontario. A leisurely drive on the major highways that lead to and from Metropolitan Toronto (highways 401, 403, 407, and the Queen Elizabeth Way) will certainly confirm this fact.

BOX 1.2

Federal Election, 27 November 2000

Party	Elected Members	Percentage of Popular Vote
Liberal	172	40.8
Canadian Alliance	66	25.5
Bloc Québécois	38	10.7
New Democratic Party	13	8.5
Progressive Conservative	12	12.2
Other	0	2.3
Total	301	100.0

Source: Adapted from the *Parliament Internet Website*, available online at <www.parl.gc.ca/Information/…p/PartyElect.asp>, accessed on 8 March 2002.

THE REALITY OF REGIONALISM AND ITS OUTCOMES

Perhaps the most visible signs of regionalism and, therefore, of the discontent felt by people living in some regions, are the political parties that were created to represent the interests of a particular region. These parties are a vivid representation of the concerns, expectations, attitudes, and fears of an entire region. Some examples include the rise of the Bloc Québécois in Quebec, the Reform Party (now the Canadian Alliance) in Western Canada, and the Confederation of Regions Party in New Brunswick. These parties were created for at least two reasons. The first concerns the basic similarity between the Liberal and Progressive Conservative parties in terms of ideology, policies, and organization. If the two main parties look the same and sound the same, then the concerns of some people are not being addressed. Starting your own party overcomes these problems. Second, belonging to these new parties is a way of protesting the two other parties—it is a protest against the traditional way of doing things. Joining a new party is a way of saying "if you don't listen to us, we will find other ways to voice our discontent and push forward our interests." If you are electorally successful, the other political parties must take you seriously. The Canadian Alliance/Reform Party is an excellent example of this.

The Case of Western Canada

Western Canada has always held the belief that its interests are continually undervalued and sometimes simply ignored by the government in Ottawa. The growth of the Reform Party (now the Canadian Alliance) is directly linked to this belief. Some of the more prominent examples will demonstrate this point.

The first example goes back to the implementation of the **National Policy** in 1879. The National Policy of Prime Minister John A. Macdonald was an attempt to build a country out of many different geographical regions and to change the very nature of the Canadian economy from one based on extracting natural resources to one based on manufacturing and other nonresource activities.[8] The tool used to begin this change was the *tariff*. A tariff is applied to goods imported into Canada, making them more expensive for Canadians who want to buy them. The result of applying a tariff on imported goods was that they became more expensive than similar goods produced in Canada. The purpose of the tariff was to protect Canadian manufacturing companies, which were located primarily in central Canada. The practical consequence, however, of the National Policy was that, for example, Western farmers had to buy their manufactured goods, such as tractors and combines, from more expensive producers in central Canada because the cheaper ones, produced in the United States, were made even more expensive when the tariff was applied to them. This cost Western farmers huge amounts of money, and they have never forgotten it. Generally, Westerners believe that they have contributed enormously to Ontario's economic development and prosperity.

The second example concerns the financial institutions, primarily banks, which are located overwhelmingly in Ontario. By jacking up interest rates to control inflation, the actions of these financial institutions have penalized those who live and work outside Ontario. In the 1980s the Bank of Canada attempted to control inflation in Ontario's Golden Horseshoe region by hiking interest rates regardless of how these higher interest rates would negatively affect economic growth in other parts of Canada. This meant that Western grain farmers, Atlantic fishermen, and people outside the Golden Horseshoe would have to pay more, because of the higher interest rates, to work and live (see Figure 1.2). In the early part of the 1980s interest rates climbed to more than 20 percent! Would you want to borrow money to buy a new tractor or fishing boat at that rate of interest? Compare that rate with interest rates in 2002.

The third example concerns the multimillion-dollar maintenance contract for Canada's high-technology CF-18 fighter aircraft. In 1987 three companies submitted bids: Bristol Aerospace of Winnipeg, IMP of Halifax, and Canadair of Montreal. Originally the contract was awarded to Bristol Aerospace of Winnipeg because it was more technologically capable of handling the sophisticated aircraft and because the bid was between 8 and 12 percent cheaper. When Canadair began to publicly complain and when members of Parliament from Quebec began to put huge pressure on Prime Minister Brian Mulroney by reminding him that Quebec had voted overwhelmingly for his Progressive Conservative party in the federal election of 1984, Mulroney reversed the decision and awarded the contract to Canadair. The pressure of Quebec MPs was especially intense because another election was just around the corner in 1988. The prime minister believed it was more important to keep Quebec happy than Manitoba because Quebec has seventy-five seats in Parliament whereas Manitoba has only fourteen. The people of Manitoba were punished once again when the federal Liberals announced in 1995 that Air Force Headquarters would be moved from Winnipeg to Ottawa in 1996. In fact, during World War II, Industry Minister C.D. Howe established almost 50 crown corporations in Ontario and Quebec. These industries continued to benefit both economies long after the war ended.

Perhaps no issue in the new millennium will have a greater impact on Western Canada than what can only be called "the farm crisis." It is virtually unknown outside farming communities and has been consistently ignored by federal and provincial governments. This crisis has hit Western farming communities particularly hard. Put simply, international price fluctuations leading to low commodity prices, corporate agribusiness mergers, high production costs, and poor weather conditions have contributed to a steady decline in the number of farm families and has returned net farm income to Depression-era levels.[9] The case of Saskatchewan is particularly illuminating. Agriculture and Agri-Food Canada (AAFC) projected annual realized net income for Saskatchewan farmers to be just $1783 per farm in 1999 for a provincial total of only $96 million; levels have not been this low since 1938.[10] In fact, annual realized net farm income has fallen to

Figure 1.2   Western Perceptions of Their Contribution to Canadian Development

Central
Canadian Banks

Depression-era levels for grain and hog producers in Alberta, Ontario, and across Canada.[11] Canadian farmers face the prospect of operating twenty-first-century farms with Depression-era net incomes.[12]

Another example is similar in context to the ones above but concerns the Atlantic provinces. The opening of the St. Lawrence Seaway in 1957 was greeted with great fanfare in Ontario and Quebec. The same could not be said of New Brunswick and Nova Scotia. To these provinces the opening of the St. Lawrence Seaway was simply another way that economic interests in central Canada took business away from the entire Atlantic region, especially the port cities of Saint John and Halifax.

Our Northern Experience

No region of Canada has been more universally ignored and misunderstood than the land above the sixtieth parallel, collectively known as Canada's North. Our northern reaches are so far removed from our daily consciousness that we lack a basic understanding of the land and the people who live there. Here is a quick quiz; the answers are in Box 1.3 on page 20. What is the name of the territory than came into existence on 1 April 1999? What is its capital city? How big is the newest territory? What is the name of the dominant ethnic group that lives there? What language do they speak? What does the name of the territory mean in their language? Why is the new territory important to its inhabitants?

Since two-thirds of Canadians live within 320 km of the Canada–U.S. border, any location beyond 320 km is considered "up north." For inhabitants of Winnipeg, Edmonton, and Regina, any journey north is considered to be heading "up north," yet it would take days (depending on the mode of transportation) to reach the sixtieth parallel, let alone the borders of Nunavut, Yukon, or the Northwest Territories. Perhaps the best example of this southern centrism is found in southern Ontario. For the inhabitants of the Golden Horseshoe, especially Toronto, driving to cottages located in the Muskoka and Kawartha lakes is considered going "up north." In fact, some consider Barrie (located in central Ontario) to be "up north." Few Ontarians have any understanding of cities anywhere north of the Golden Horseshoe. Here is another quick quiz. These answers you must find for yourself. What college is located in Barrie? What are the names of colleges located in the cities of Thunder Bay, Sault Ste. Marie, Sudbury, Timmins, and North Bay? Are there universities located in any of these cities? If so, what are their names? What industries dominate the lives of people living in the northern reaches of Ontario, Quebec, Manitoba, Saskatchewan, Alberta, and British Columbia? What is the meaning and significance of a "one-industry town"? (See Box 1.4 on page 21.)

As Canadians we must make a concerted effort to have an awareness and appreciation of those living in our country's northern reaches.

CRITICAL THINKING BOX 1.3

What are the logical consequences of the farm crisis for Canadians? Why is this issue not at the top of all government agendas? Why have the media essentially ignored this issue?

THE ACTIONS OF THE FEDERAL GOVERNMENT

The federal government has always recognized that regionalism does exist. Since Confederation it has spent much time and billions of dollars attempting to reduce the gap between the economically prosperous regions of Canada and those that are not so well off. The federal government has historically attempted to accomplish this in three distinct ways: (1) by reducing physical distances, (2) by instituting programs (spending money), and, perhaps most significant, (3) by concentrating on sociopsychological phenomena (i.e., attitudes and people's perceptions of each other and of other regions).

Reducing Physical Distances

The early attempts to reduce regional differences and isolation were physical in nature. The first was the construction of the Canadian Pacific Railway (CPR) by Canada's first prime minister, John A. Macdonald. The purpose of the railway was to unite the different and far-off regions from the Atlantic Ocean to the Pacific Ocean. Building the CPR was also a precondition for British Columbia joining Confederation; without the railway, there is much doubt that British Columbia would have joined.

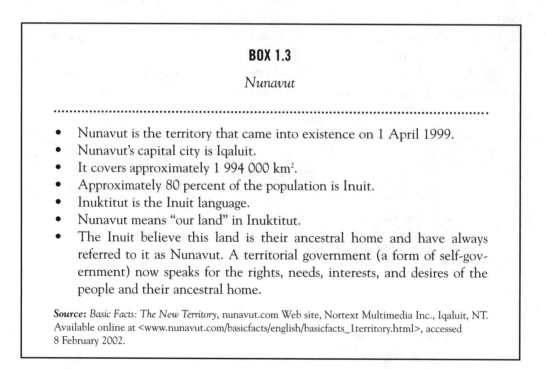

BOX 1.3

Nunavut

....

- Nunavut is the territory that came into existence on 1 April 1999.
- Nunavut's capital city is Iqaluit.
- It covers approximately 1 994 000 km^2.
- Approximately 80 percent of the population is Inuit.
- Inuktitut is the Inuit language.
- Nunavut means "our land" in Inuktitut.
- The Inuit believe this land is their ancestral home and have always referred to it as Nunavut. A territorial government (a form of self-government) now speaks for the rights, needs, interests, and desires of the people and their ancestral home.

Source: *Basic Facts: The New Territory*, nunavut.com Web site, Nortext Multimedia Inc., Iqaluit, NT. Available online at <www.nunavut.com/basicfacts/english/basicfacts_1territory.html>, accessed 8 February 2002.

BOX 1.4

One-Industry Towns

....

This is the term applied to Canadian communities whose economic activity is dominated by one particular industry, such as logging, mining, or fishing. The prosperity of each town is directly linked to the prosperity of its major employer. When these companies experience economic troubles or close their doors, the surrounding community suffers accordingly. Can you name any "one-industry towns"?

The next noteworthy attempt came with the creation of Trans Canada Airlines (TCA) in 1937, later renamed Air Canada. The creation of TCA was based on the realization by the government that air travel would be the quickest and most efficient way to service the large, outlying, and sparsely populated regions of Canada, in addition to linking the larger metropolitan areas. Private airline companies, it was believed, would not fly to these remote areas because it would not be profitable. This remained the rationale for Air Canada until it was privatized (sold to private investors—the government no longer owns it) in 1989. However, many would argue that Air Canada ceased to operate according to its original mandate long before it was privatized.

Other examples of attempting to physically link the people of Canada were the construction of the Trans-Canada Highway and the creation of Via Rail, a Crown corporation to run railway passenger service, in 1977–78. The vicious budget cuts to Via Rail carried out by the Progressive Conservatives during the mid- to late 1980s disproportionately penalized Atlantic Canada more than any other region of the country. Protests to these cuts were widespread, and many believed them to be based on poor research and intentional attempts by the federal government, which continually portrayed Via Rail in a negative fashion, to justify the cuts.[13]

Spending Money

Economically, the federal government has provided money, in many different ways, to the ten provincial governments to help minimize economic differences.[14] In large part the federal government accomplishes this through the use of transfer payments. Transfer payments take place when the federal government collects money through taxation, such as personal income tax, and then hands over or "transfers" a certain percentage of the money collected, as agreed to by the provinces, to the provincial governments. The provinces use this money to help pay for programs such as health care and education. As already mentioned, federal transfer payments are worth billions of dollars each year. It can be argued that transfer payments are more important to the poorer provinces than to the richer ones. A brief look at Table 1.3 shows that on a per capita basis, the poorer provinces receive a greater proportion of transfer payments than the more prosperous ones do. In 2000–01 Newfoundland received a total transfer payment in excess of $1.5 billion. This accounts for 42 percent of Newfoundland's estimated revenues (almost twice the national average) and works out to be $2867 per person, the highest of any province. Ontario received a total transfer payment of $11.8 billion, which works out to only $1016 dollars per person and accounts for only 19 percent of Ontario's estimated revenues. On a per capita basis, Alberta's $3 billion transfer payment translates to $1007 dollars per person, the lowest in Canada. In spite of federal government attempts to reduce spending by transferring less money to the provinces, transfer payments are still worth billions of dollars.

The federal government has also formed and used government departments and agencies, as well as legislation, to study and to help stimulate economic growth in poorer regions. Some of the more notable examples include the *Agricultural and Rural Development Act* (1965), the Fund for Rural Economic Development (1966), the Department of Regional Economic Expansion (1969), the Department of Regional Industrial Expansion (1982), the Department of Industry, Science, and Technology (1987), the Atlantic Canada Opportunities Agency (1987), Western Diversification (1987), Enterprise Cape Breton (1987), Canadian Polar Commission (1991), Canadian Rural Partnership (1998), and the First Nations and Inuit Health Branch of Health Canada (2000).

In 1995 regional representation can be seen in the names given to three federal government departments: Public Works and Atlantic Canada Opportunities Agency, Indian Affairs and Northern Development, and Finance (with responsibility for Quebec regional development).

Promoting Understanding among Canadians

The final way the federal government has tried to minimize the differences between regions is by promoting understanding between Canadians. Because of Canada's large physical size (9 970 610 km^2) and small population (approximately 31.7 million, see Box 1.5 on page 24) the federal government has taken responsibility for connecting distant regions to each other, emotionally and attitudinally. Specifically, by emphasizing what it meant, or means, to be "Canadian" and by educating Canadians about Canada itself, our history, people, places, and attitudes.

The federal government in Ottawa has attempted to educate and inform Canadians about each other by using new technology as it became available (radio and TV) and by the use of **royal commissions**.

Table 1.3 Federal Government Transfer Payments to the Provinces, 2001–2002

Province	Amount	Per Capita
Newfoundland	$1.5 b	$2 867
Prince Edward Island	$371 m	$2 675
New Brunswick	$1.9 b	$2 452
Nova Scotia	$2.2 b	$2 312
Manitoba	$2.3 b	$2 003
Quebec	$12.5 b	$1 700
Saskatchewan	$1.1 b	$1 078
British Columbia	$4.1 b	$1 018
Ontario	$11.8 b	$1 016
Alberta	$3 b	$1 007

Source: *Major Federal Transfers to Provinces and Territories*, <www.fin.gc.ca/fedprov/mtpe.html>. Reproduced with permission.

In response to new radio technology, the federal government formed the Canadian Broadcasting Corporation (CBC) in 1932. CBC Radio provided an opportunity for Canadians to talk to each other and learn about each other. It also provided Canadian musicians, social commentators, sports broadcasters, newsreaders, and talk show hosts an opportunity to develop their creative talents. Hockey was first broadcast on CBC Radio. In fact, hockey play-by-play commentator Foster Hewitt coined one of the most well-known phrases in all of sport when he described a goal being scored as simply, "He shoots, he scores!" The CBC later did the same when television technology evolved, and in 1952 it formed CBC Television. The purpose of CBC Television was or is to emphasize things that are "Canadian" and to connect people to their community and region. Over the years this has resulted in Canadian programs such as *The Beachcombers*, *Hockey Night in Canada*, *Road to Avonlea*, and *Rita and Friends*. CBC television also gave birth to the regionally oriented newscasts that usually follow the national news.

Before TV, the federal government was already involved in the making of films and documentaries. In 1939 it created the National Film Board (NFB). For decades now NFB documentaries and short films have been seen across Canada, especially in schools. Canadians everywhere are familiar with the thirty-second NFB vignettes broadcast between programs on the CBC. The work of the NFB has been awarded many international honours. Overall, the purpose of the CBC and NFB has been to educate and inform Canadians, and the federal government has spent hundreds of millions of dollars over the

---

BOX 1.5

Canada in a World Perspective

Country	Area (km^2)	Population (2001 estimated)	Population (per km^2)
Russia	17 075 400	145 000 000	8.5
Canada	**9 970 610**	**31 700 000**	**3.1**
China	9 556 100	1 328 000 000	136.0
United States	9 529 100	250 000 000	29.9
Brazil	8 511 965	173 900 000	20.3
Australia	7 628 300	19 600 000	2.5

---

years to promote this education. There is no better example of this, and perhaps no more ambitious, than the 2001 CBC documentary *Canada: A People's History*. It was an immediate hit with Canadians, averaging 2.5 million viewers for the first six episodes.[15] But CBC-TV producer Mark Starowicz could only entice one company to buy advertising time.[16] CBC proceeded to make the $25 million series in spite of corporate Canada's indifference. It seems Canadians do want to know about each other!

The federal government's heavy involvement in radio, TV, and film is based in part on the belief that what Canadians think, feel, and believe about each other differs from region to region and that this has an important impact on Canadian unity. This belief has prompted the federal government to investigate specific problems in Canada or the likely effects some government policies might have on some regions. The tool used by the federal government to do this is the royal commission. A person appointed by the federal government heads royal commissions. They utilize the expertise of people who work in the public sector or the private sector, academics, and, if necessary, experts outside Canada. Royal commissions do not implement policy, they simply advise the government of the day.

The purpose of royal commissions is to investigate and suggest directions for policy. Royal commissions, therefore, study, investigate, and accumulate information on important issues or matters of government policy. In the past there have been two royal commissions that were concerned with certain aspects of regionalism as they travelled across Canada. The first was the 1937 Royal Commission on Dominion–Provincial Relations, which produced an in-depth study of federal–provincial financial relations—how the federal government transferred money to the provincial governments. The second was the 1981–85 Royal Commission on the Economic Union and Development

Prospects for Canada. This commission was important because it came out in favour of free trade with the United States, in spite of the fact that some experts who presented before the commission concluded that free trade would be harmful to the poorer regions of Canada, especially the Atlantic provinces.

It is not uncommon for the Federal government to ignore the recommendations of royal commissions. In 1997, *The Royal Commission Report on Aboriginal Peoples* tabled almost 500 recommendations. The principal recommendation was to increase spending immediately and commit new resources to Aboriginal life in Canada. The Commission suggested spending an average of almost $2 billion per year for the next 20 years. This extra spending would be in addition to the $5 billion to $7 billion already spent annually. Ottawa has yet to implement this principal recommendation. In January 1998, Ottawa announced a $350 million program to deal with the mental and physical damage caused by the residential school program established and partly administered by the federal government (see Box 1.6 on page 26).

Royal commissions are popular with the federal government, and it is common for one to last several years. Since 1867 there have been approximately 400 royal commissions.[17] This is an average of three per year!

THE SOCIOPSYCHOLOGICAL DIMENSION TO REGIONALISM: THE REALITY

Clearly profound economic and social differences exist among the regions in Canada. It is equally clear that there are sociopsychological differences as well. That is, people in different regions do think and feel differently about each other and about the federal government in Ottawa.

What does the **sociopsychological dimension to regionalism** mean? It means more than economic differences between regions with respect to money, companies, investment, income, government policy, elections, and federalism. The sociopsychological dimension is concerned with how individuals living in different regions feel about themselves, their community, other regions, and the federal government. Regional differences in these areas are commonly thought to exist, say, only between the French-speaking majority of Quebec and the English-speaking majority of Quebec and the rest of Canada. Differences, however, go much further than just language and culture. Every year, public opinion polls, quality-of-life surveys, government surveys, and other forms of research indicate that Canadians have different beliefs, opinions, and attitudes about living in Canada and about who benefits the most from government policy. Generally, Ontario and Quebec are considered to be the big winners and Atlantic Canada the big loser. These beliefs have generated much envy. The most recent manifestation of this envy (some would say anti-

Ontario attitude) appeared in national headlines before the First Ministers Conference held in Victoria, British Columbia, on 1 August 2001. Nova Scotia Premier John Hamm suggested that the equalization formula be redesigned to put more money in Atlantic coffers. Former Ontario Premier Mike Harris responded by comparing the Nova Scotia Premier to a welfare cheat! University of Moncton Professor Donald Savoie, one of Canada's leading authorities on regional issues, believes the Atlantic provinces received a raw deal with Confederation and that "the region is not doing well because of federal government policy."[18] In fact, Savoie believes that equalization payments are designed to ensure Atlantic Canadians have enough money to buy goods made in Ontario and Quebec—in short, the Atlantic provinces have been kept poor by central Canada.

It is not surprising that people living in different parts of Canada have different attitudes concerning the Canadian experience. These differences are largely because the region you live in, the job you do, and the language you speak all affect the way you think and feel. Our socialization and life experiences have a profound influence on the way we come to understand each other, the federal government, and ourselves. Two examples will illustrate this point. The first concerns the 1995 fishing dispute between Canada and Spain, and the second concerns the cross-Canada contempt for central Canada and Metropolitan Toronto.

The 1995 Fishing Dispute

The 1995 fishing dispute centred on Canadian claims that Spanish fishing vessels waited just beyond Canada's 200-mile (about 320-km) boundary and fished to excess using illegal

---

BOX 1.6

Residential Schools

Between 1867 and 1945, Native children were legally obligated to attend residential schools. While attending these schools, Native children were

- forbidden to speak their native language. In some schools they were physically punished for attempting to do so.
- forbidden to wear native clothing.
- geographically separated from their parents. The distances were so great and costs of travelling so high that children seldom saw their parents.
- told their culture was backward and inferior.

---

nets and taking even the smallest turbot (a species of fish). Earlier, in an attempt to allow fish stocks to replenish themselves, the federal government had banned cod fishing (before the 1992 election), and later it drastically reduced the turbot quotas for Canadian fishermen. Ottawa believed Spanish fishing would eventually lead to the complete collapse of turbot stocks. When Canadian Coast Guard vessels arrested two Spanish fishing vessels, the citizens of the Atlantic provinces, particularly Nova Scotia, were celebrating everywhere, organizing support rallies, carrying signs, and just plain being happy. Finally, the federal government was seen by them as acting on their behalf. The important point here is that the same happiness and pleasure was not shared to the same degree by people living in Toronto, Calgary, Saskatoon, Dryden, Laval, or other cities that do not depend on fishing or fish processing for their livelihood. The CBC, CTV, *Maclean's*, the *Toronto Star*, and *The Globe and Mail* all reported extensively on the dispute. This attention was heartening for many living in the Atlantic region during these tough times. Barbara Nees from the sociology department of Memorial University in St. John's remarked that it gave people a positive sense of community and a feeling that they were not suffering alone.[19]

The issue for this century for the Atlantic provinces may turn out to be the bulk sale of fresh water to markets in the United States. Atlantic province governments look at water as another resource to be exploited, another commodity to be sold in the international marketplace where demand is high, especially in the American southwest. Newfoundland Premier Roger Grimes is at the forefront of this push. The federal government, however, is under increasing pressure from the general population and many environmental groups to do the opposite. With economic uncertainty still plaguing the Atlantic fisheries, the bulk sale of fresh water has taken on new importance.

The Contempt for Central Canada, Especially Metropolitan Toronto

Perhaps nowhere is the sociopsychological dimension to regionalism more evident than with respect to the contempt felt by most Canadians for central Canada and Metropolitan Toronto. Rivalries certainly exist between the big cities in Canada, but although there may be intraprovincial rivalries between cities like Calgary and Edmonton or Regina and Saskatoon, and there may be rivalries across provinces between cities like Halifax and Saint John, what all these cities have in common—along with all other cities across Canada—is that they resent the privileged position of Toronto. This resentment is primarily based on central Canada's virtual dominance of economics, politics, and social life.

Economic Dominance

The economic dominance of central Canada, especially Metro Toronto, is evident in the overwhelming presence of the head offices of the most dominant corporations in Canada. According to the *Financial Post*, in a 1989 ranking by sales or operating revenues, 365 of

Canada's largest 500 companies (73 percent) have their head offices in Ontario or Quebec.[20] In fact, the first non-Ontarian to occupy the office of minister of finance was Jean Chrétien, a Quebec native, in 1979. Since then, only one finance minister has come from outside Ontario or Quebec. Can you name him and his province of origin?

In the June 2001 *Report on Business*, 32 of the top 50 corporations (in terms of profit) were located in Ontario and Quebec: 18 in Toronto, 11 in Montreal, and 1 each in Laval, Waterloo, and Aurora. Of the remaining 18, 14 are located in Calgary and 1 each in Edmonton, Winnipeg, Burnaby, and Vancouver. Of the top 100 corporations, 58 are located in Ontario and Quebec, 40 throughout the rest of Canada and 2 in the United States. A simple mention of "Bay Street" brings to mind huge office towers, money, and economic power. Again, the economic dominance of the Golden Horseshoe region of Ontario is clearly visible with a simple drive along the highways that run through it: the Queen Elizabeth Way (QEW), the 401, 403, 407, and 427.

Political Dominance

Politically, Ontario and Quebec virtually dominate Canada in terms of representation in Parliament, with 178 out of 301 seats and appointments to key cabinet posts such as the departments of finance, foreign affairs, justice, and international trade. The trend has been for the federal government to choose a finance minister who is a lawyer from Bay Street (who must first be elected, of course). Usually, this lawyer returns to a job on Bay Street at the conclusion of his or her political career.

Cultural and Social Dominance

Culturally, the media outlets of the CBC, Baton Broadcasting, Global TV, and City TV are all located in Metro Toronto. Canada's "national" newspapers, *The Globe and Mail* and the *National Post*, and Canada's largest circulation daily, the *Toronto Star*, are located in Metro Toronto. Metropolitan Toronto is also the centre of publishing and, along with Montreal, it is the centre of fashion, entertainment, and the arts. In particular, Metro Toronto is the home of Maple Leaf Gardens, the Air Canada Centre, SkyDome, the CN Tower, Ontario Place, the Canadian National Exhibition, the Hummingbird Centre, Canada's Wonderland, Caribana, the Royal Ontario Museum (ROM), the Royal Alexandra Theatre, the Pantages Theatre, Roy Thomson Hall, and countless other sites and exhibits. For all the reasons mentioned, it is little wonder that the different regions of Canada envy and resent central Canada and Metro Toronto in particular.

CRITICAL THINKING BOX 1.4

Have the Western provinces received their share of recognition for helping to build this country? What about the Atlantic provinces? Have Ontario and Quebec received too much?

CONCLUSION

Regionalism is an important diversity in Canada, so important, in fact, that examining the nature of regionalism is critical if we are to have a complete understanding of social life in Canada. Canadians from different regions are diverse in so many ways. From a regional perspective, for example, Canadians find themselves different in the areas of geography, climate, income, ethnicity, social class, and attitudes toward each other and toward the federal government. The last two differences confirm for us that regionalism does have an important sociopsychological component.

What does the future hold for these regional differences? Probably much of the same. It is extremely unlikely that the nature of the Canadian political system will change any time soon, if at all. This is especially true of federalism and our electoral system, two key elements that intensify regional feelings and differences. As a consequence, it is highly unlikely that the behaviour of the federal government will change. It is equally unlikely that the nature of capitalism will change. As the saying goes, "Money will go

CRITICAL THINKING BOX 1.5

To what extent does regionalism make Canadians different from each other? Are regional differences more or less important than other differences such as language, social class, gender, sexual orientation, family structure, race, and ethnicity? List what you consider the five most important differences. Why did you choose the differences you did? Would a student in another province choose the same ones? Why or why not?

CRITICAL THINKING BOX 1.6

···

How do you explain and reconcile the paradox that the federal government created vast regional disparities (economically and sociopsychologically) and later committed itself to reducing the disparities it had created?

where it will get more money." That means money (and jobs) will travel indiscriminately between regions, within regions, and, when necessary, even outside Canada.

These two developments, or lack thereof, do not say much for the future of Canada. As Canadians, we must be vigilant and insist that all levels of government treat all Canadians living in all regions fairly and equally. If any level of government fails to behave in this manner, it should be reminded that the ballot box is never more than a few years away.

CHAPTER SUMMARY

Regionalism is important to understanding life in Canada. There are economic, political, and sociopsychological components to regionalism. To understand regionalism in its entirety, we must pay particular attention to the sociopsychological component because it is usually not addressed in the traditional literature. There are many different theories dealing with the causes of regionalism, and it is up to you to decide which of the four dominant theories presented here best explains the growth of regionalism. The federal government has a role both in creating and attempting to minimize regional differences. Finally, we must be aware of and appreciate that certain aspects of our political system—federalism and our electoral system—can and do intensify regional differences.

KEY TERMS

executive federalism, p. 12
federalism, p. 12
Golden Horseshoe, p. 7
Meech Lake Accord, p. 12
National Policy, p. 16
regionalism, p. 4

representation by population, p. 14
royal commission, p. 22
sociopsychological dimension to
 regionalism, p. 25
transfer payments, p. 10

DISCUSSION QUESTIONS

1. What is *regionalism*? Why is regionalism important to understanding the Canadian experience?
2. Briefly outline four theoretical explanations for regionalism. Which do you think makes the most sense? Would Canadians from different provinces choose different explanations? If so, why? If not, why not?
3. How do federalism and our electoral system compound and intensify regional differences?
4. What do we mean by the *sociopsychological dimension* to regionalism?
5. What role(s) has the federal government played in both creating and helping to reduce regional differences? Can you think of any current examples?
6. Is the idea of regionalism "real" to you? If so, why? If not, why?

NOTES

1. See Richard Simeon, "Regionalism and Canadian Political Institutions," in *The Canadian Political Process*, R. Schultz et al., eds. (Toronto: Holt, Rinehart and Winston, 1979).
2. See Harry H. Hiller, *Canadian Society: A Macro Analysis* (Scarborough: Prentice-Hall, 1991), p. 11.
3. The explanations of these approaches draw heavily from the following: Ralph Mathews, "Understanding Regionalism as Effect and Cause," in *Social Issues: Sociological Views of Canada*, 4th ed. (Scarborough: Prentice-Hall, 1988), pp. 60–72; Ralph Mathews, *The Creation of Regional Dependency* (Toronto: University of Toronto Press, 1983), pp. 37–55; Janine Brodie, *The Political Economy of Canadian Regionalism* (Toronto: Harcourt Brace Jovanovich, 1990), pp. 21–36; and Donald J. Savoie, *The Canadian Economy: A Regional Perspective* (Toronto: Methuen, 1986), pp. 9–24. The names of some approaches have been altered.
4. This approach is drawn from Mathews, "Understanding Regionalism," pp. 64–65, and Mathews, *The Creation of Regional Dependency*, pp. 45–46.
5. Mathews, "Understanding Regionalism," p. 65.
6. This explanation is based on the one provided by Brodie, *The Political Economy of Canadian Regionalism*, pp. 27–34. The explanation includes Keynesianism, regional science, and developmental approaches.
7. Mathews, "Understanding Regionalism," p. 69.
8. For an excellent explanation of the National Policy, see Desmond Morton, *A Short History of Canada* (Edmonton: Hurtig, 1983), pp. 92–105. This brief history of Canada is both readable and enjoyable. We highly recommend it to anyone interested in the development of Canada.
9. Darrin Qualman, *The Farm Crisis and Corporate Power*, Canadian Centre for Policy Alternatives, April 2001, p. 13.
10. Ibid., p. 6.

11. Ibid.
12. Ibid., p. 13.
13. For a disturbing account of the decimation of Via Rail see Jo Davis, ed., *Not a Sentimental Journey: What's Behind the Via Rail Cuts, What You Can Do About It* (Toronto: Gunbyfield Publishing, 1990).
14. For an explanation of the evolution and different types of transfer payments, see Garth Stevenson, *Unfulfilled Union: Canadian Federalism and National Unity*, 3rd ed. (Toronto: Gage, 1988), pp. 124–50.
15. Linda McQuaig, "Just One Sponsor, but Canadians Love CBC *People's History*," 21 December 2000. Available online at *Straight Goods.com*, <http://goods.perfectvision.ca/ViewFeature.cfm?REF=23>, accessed 8 February 2002.
16. Ibid.
17. Keith Archer et al., eds., *Parameters of Power: Canada's Political Institutions* (Toronto: Nelson, 1995), p. 287.
18. "Maritimes Kept Poor by Ontario," *The Hamilton Spectator*, 30 July 2001.
19. "Conflicting Emotions," *Maclean's*, 27 March 1995.
20. David Kilgour, "Ending Regional Favouritism," *Policy Options* 12(9), (November 1991): 3–7.

Demographic Trends in Canada

Michelle Broderick

Except in the case of vaccination against small pox…it is unlikely that immunization or therapy had a significant effect on mortality from infectious diseases before the twentieth century.
— T. McKeown, *The Modern Rise of Population*

In technologically advanced human societies, virtually every female now survives to reproductive age. This is a biologically novel situation.
— F. Fenner, "Foreword," in *The Structure of Human Populations*

Objectives

After reading this chapter, you should be able to

- understand what the field of demography entails

- identify what kinds of information are used in the demographic study of populations

- understand the methods used by demographers

- appreciate that demographic variation can often account for social, cultural, and economic diversity within a population

- recognize that the study of the demographic history of Canadian populations touches on a wide variety of subjects, from illegitimacy to epidemics

Demography: An Introduction

Demography is the scientific study of human populations. It focuses on the size and composition of a population, which depend on such factors as fertility, nuptiality, mortality, and migration. Demography demonstrates how social and economic factors affect these demographic parameters and, hence, human behaviour. Variations in demographic characteristics can be observed at many different levels, for example, township, city, province, or nation, and they are often linked to social and economic features of these population units. Unique demographic histories experienced by populations in different regions are often the main cause of social, cultural, and economic diversity observed today. By studying the history of populations, we not only learn how they have diversified over time, but also, because of the greater time depth (several generations), find it easier to link social and economic factors to demographic patterns. This chapter will examine and define the variables used in demography, followed by some examples of contemporary and historical studies on Canadian populations.

Some Important Definitions: Demographic Variables

A **variable** is a characteristic that differs or varies among groups, such as age and religious affiliation. In demographic research, the variables examined are those that affect the growth of a population: fertility, nuptiality, mortality, and migration.

Fertility

Fertility refers to the number of **live births** occurring in a population within a specific period (either one year or aggregates of years). Fertility differs from **fecundity**, which is the maximum number of children that a woman can produce during her lifetime, that is, the potential of childbearing. The figure for fecundity is based on the length of the female reproductive period, usually defined as between the ages of 15 and 44, during which time a woman can produce a maximum of 15 to 20 children; however, few women ever reach this potential because of the biological and social factors that reduce fertility. For instance, the length of the reproductive period can be affected by the age at which a woman marries—if reproduction does not occur outside of marriage. If a woman marries and has her first child at the age of 25, her reproductive period will be approximately 19 years. During this time she could produce on average 13 children. If that same woman married and had her first child at the age of 35 instead of 25, her reproductive period would be shorter, and the number of children she could produce would be considerably lower. Other factors affecting female fertility are the use of contraceptives and abortifacients; by preventing or terminating unwanted births, fewer children are born. Social attitudes toward reproduction can also affect fertility. For instance, if a woman's role in society is that of homemaker, where childbearing is seen as a valuable contribution, then women will tend to have more children. Illness and disease can also limit fertility, by either preventing fertilization or by inducing spontaneous abortions (miscarriages).

Several methods are used to calculate fertility. The easiest method is the **crude birth rate**, which is the number of live births in a given population (see Figure 2.1). This method is "crude" in the sense that it is based on the entire population, not just the women who are capable of reproducing; therefore, this figure can be misleading because the number of women between fifteen and forty-four years of age can vary among populations. A more refined and accurate method is the use of the **fertility rate**, which is based on the number of women of reproductive age (fifteen to forty-four years).

Nuptiality

Nuptiality, or marriage, is an important variable for two reasons: (1) marriage is related to fertility, in that the age at which marriage occurs can define the length of the female reproductive period and (2) the timing of marriage is affected by social and economic factors.

Figure 2.1 Crude Birth Rate in Canada, 1996 (live births per 1,000 population)

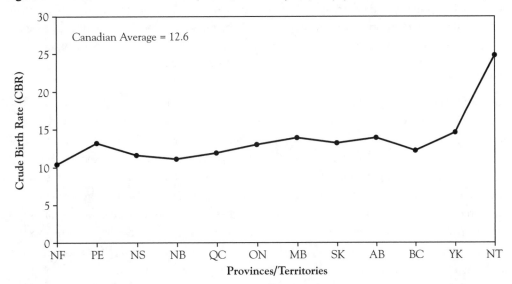

The pattern of fertility is not uniform across Canada. The lowest birthrate was recorded in Newfoundland and the highest in the Northwest Territories.

Source: Adapted from Statistics Canada Internet site, <www.statcan.ca/english/Pgdb/People/Health/healthdemo04a.htm>, accessed 7 August 2001.

For example, patterns of economic activity, such as farming, coupled with religious restrictions, such as Lent, have in the past resulted in a seasonal pattern of marriage, with most marriages occurring between October and December (i.e., after the harvest but before religious festivals). Today, this pattern is no longer observed in Canada. It is also common for people to delay marriage until they have achieved economic independence from their parents. The examination of nuptiality not only includes looking at those individuals who marry, but also at those who do not. For instance, if the majority of men and women in a population marry, the potential for population growth through births increases; however, if a large portion of the adult population do not marry, and, hence, may not reproduce, then population growth will be slowed. The incidence of **celibacy**, the proportion of individuals in a population who never marry, is often related to economics, especially to inheritance practices. For example, in Ireland farmers traditionally passed on their wealth (land) to one son only. The other children (both sons and daughters) either remained on the homestead and did not marry, or they left to seek their fortunes elsewhere.[1] Such a practice would also influence emigration and, hence, the size of the population.

Typical methods used to measure marriage include the **crude marriage rate**, which is the number of marriages recorded in a population, and the **age-specific marriage rate**, based instead on the number of single individuals, who never married, in a given age interval (see Figure 2.2). **Age at first marriage** can also be calculated and provides, as already mentioned, information on the length of the female reproductive period (see Figure 2.3). This particular measure has been found to be highly sensitive to economic factors.

Mortality

Mortality refers to the number of people in a population dying in a given period. Two important aspects of mortality are life span and life expectancy. **Life span** refers to the maximum age that a human has ever lived. This figure is currently 122 years: Jeanne Louise Calment was born in Arles, France, on 21 February 1875 and died on 4 August 1997.

As with fecundity, very few humans reach this potential. The **life expectancy** is the age to which most humans can expect to live and is based on the average age at death. In Canada, this figure is seventy-five years for males and eighty-one years for females.[2] A variety of biological and social factors can affect mortality. For instance, exposure to disease and toxic substances (such as pollution), nutrition, physical labour or exercise, stress, and access to health care can all affect mortality in a population.

Mortality is measured in a variety of ways, such as the **crude death rate**, which is the number of deaths in a given population (see Figures 2.4 and 2.5). Again, this is a crude method and does not reveal details of the mortality experience. A more detailed picture is achieved by examining mortality in different age groups, that is, **age-specific mortality rates,** and it helps to identify major risk factors affecting different segments of the popu-

Figure 2.2   Crude Marriage Rate in Canada, 1996 (marriages per 1,000 population)

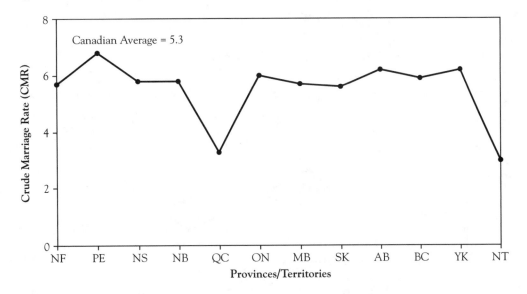

Quebec and the Northwest Territories deviate the most from the Canadian marriage pattern.

Source: Adapted from Statistics Canada, *Marriages*, Catalogue No. 84F0212XPB, 1996, page 4, Table 4.

lation. One of the most useful age groups in which to study mortality is of those aged less than one year, that is, the **infant mortality rate** (see Figure 2.6). This measure is extremely useful as an indicator of the general health status of the population because infants are more susceptible to environmental factors, such as food consumption, medical care, and public sanitation. In other words, the infant mortality rate reflects the standard of living in a population. Infant mortality is also associated with life expectancy. When infant mortality is low, life expectancy is high, and vice versa. For instance, in developed countries life expectancy is much higher than in developing countries, and this reflects the standard of living. Analysis of infant mortality is sometimes divided into two age groups: under six months of age and between six and twelve months of age. Death under six months of age tends to be associated with problems that a child was born with, whereas death between six to twelve months of age is usually related to external or environmental factors, such as disease or nutrition.

Morbidity, the incidence of particular diseases in a population, is also of interest because this is related to both the social and physical environments. For instance, in Canada we enjoy a temperate climate with warm summers and cold winters. As a result many microorganisms and disease-causing parasites cannot survive year-round. Therefore,

Figure 2.3   Average Age at First Marriage in Canada, 1996

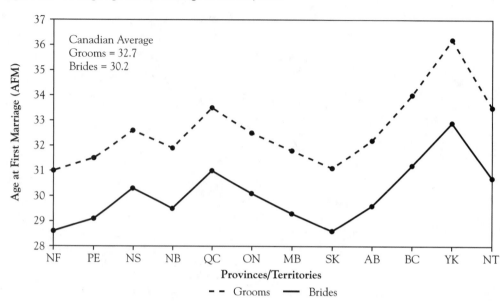

The Canadian pattern of age at first marriage is not unique. It is common to find that men marry at slightly older ages than do women. Variation is observed across Canada, with people marrying at younger ages in New Brunswick and Saskatchewan and at older ages in Yukon, British Columbia, and the Northwest Territories.

Source: Adapted from Statistics Canada, *Marriages*, Catalogue No. 84F0212XPB, 1996.

we do not experience high rates of certain diseases that are seen elsewhere (e.g., malaria). The age profile of a population will also influence morbidity. In Canada the proportion of the population over the age of sixty-four almost tripled between 1921 and 1996, increasing from 4.8 percent to 12.2 percent[3] (see Figure 2.7 and Critical Thinking Box 2.1). This increase is in part the result of lower fertility (fewer children are being born) and of higher life expectancy or survivorship (more people are living longer). Because we have a larger portion of older individuals, we also have an increase in diseases associated with aging, such as cancer and degenerative bone diseases.

Migration

Migration refers to the movement of people into and out of specific geographical areas. There are two types of migration, **immigration**, which is the movement into a specific area, and **emigration**, which is the movement out of a specific area. Both forms of migration occur at the same time. Factors affecting migration can be grouped into three general

Figure 2.4 Crude Death Rate in Canada, 1996 (deaths per 1,000 population)

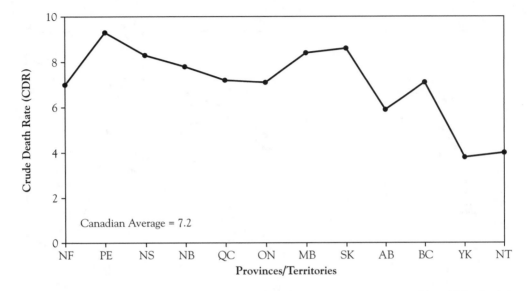

The crude death rate varies across Canada. The highest death rate occurs in Prince Edward Island, while the lowest occurs in Yukon.

Source: Adapted from Statistics Canada, *Births and Deaths*, Catalogue No. 84F0210XPB, 1996, Table 2.4.

categories: (1) economic, meaning the search for economic opportunities; (2) political, such as the persecution of a particular group of people and social institutions such as slavery; and (3) environmental, such as earthquakes, floods, and famines. In examining the factors affecting migration, you must remember that push and pull factors occur at the same time, that is, some factors pull people toward an area while others push them away. For instance, an urban setting generally offers a higher frequency and wider variety of jobs; therefore, it attracts people. However, the cost of living in an urban setting tends to be much higher than in a rural area and acts as a deterrent. Migration can also be viewed as either voluntary or involuntary. Voluntary migration occurs when the decision to move or not is up to the individual. For example, if you were offered a well-paying job in Calgary, the decision to move would be entirely yours. Migration is involuntary when the individual is forced to move or stay (see Critical Thinking Box 2.2) as was the case during World War II, when many people were forced to flee Europe, while others were prevented from doing so by the Nazi regime.

Several measurements of migration are commonly used. The in-migration or **immigration rate** consists of the number of people entering an area. The out-migration or **emigration rate** consists of the number of people leaving an area. The **gross migration rate**

Figure 2.5   Sex-Specific Mortality Rates in Canada, 1996 (deaths per 1,000 males and females in the population)

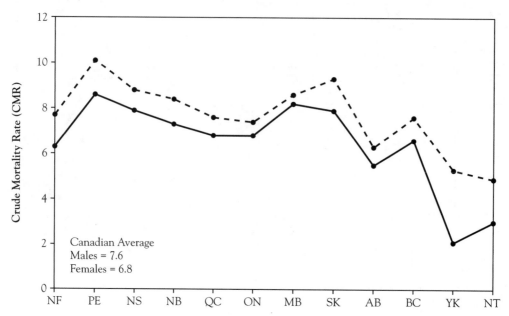

By comparing the crude mortality rates between the sexes, you can see that males are dying at a higher rate than females. This pattern is reflected in their life expectancies, which are 75 years for males and 81 years for females.

Source: Adapted from Statistics Canada, *Births and Deaths*, Catalogue No. 84F0210XPB, 1996, Table 2.4.

reflects the total number of people who both enter and leave an area. The **net migration rate** is the annual increase or decrease in the size of a population, based on the number of people entering an area minus the number who leave. Migration is often the single most important factor affecting the size—growth or decline—of a population, and it can play an important role in the spread of disease. For example, during the nineteenth century Canada suffered repeated epidemics of cholera, which were introduced by infected migrants.[4]

Migration can involve internal and external migrants. **Internal migrants** are those who move within a specific area. **External migrants** are those who move from outside a specific area. These areas can be defined at many different levels, such as a neighbourhood, province, or nation. For instance, in a sample from the 1996 Canadian census,[5] it was found that during the previous year 71.2 percent of migrants moved within the same province, 16.2 percent moved into a different province, and 12.6 percent immigrated from outside Canada (see Figure 2.8). These figures are not substantially different from those several decades ago. In 1976, 68.1 percent of migrants moved within the same province,

CRITICAL THINKING BOX 2.1

....

The Aging of Canada's Population

The **dependency ratio** reflects the proportion of the population who are under the age of 15 and above the age of 64. This group is viewed as being dependent on society, directly or indirectly. The aged are directly supported by our society through the government pension plan and discounted services, whereas children are only indirectly supported, because it is the responsibility of their parents to care for them.

Whereas the dependency ratio has decreased over time, from 64.43 in 1921 to 48.56 in 1996, the contribution of those over the age of 64 has increased more than threefold, from 12.2 percent to 37.4 percent. This increase reflects the fact that our Canadian population is aging. This trend is likely to continue, and as a result we run the risk of increased poverty and illness among the aged, as our society may not have the resources to support those services needed by the elderly.

Can we begin to plan for this contingency today?

Source: Data from Statistics Canada, *Population by Selected Age Groups and Sex for Canada, Provinces and Territories, 1996 Census*, available online at <www.statcan.ca/english/census96/canprov.htm>; accessed 7 August 2001.

17.8 percent moved into a different province, and 14.0 percent immigrated from outside Canada.[6] It is important to note, however, that the rate of migration from outside Canada is under strict management with yearly quotas, whereas no such formal constraints exist on internal migration. Management of external migration can dictate the occupational, ethnic, age, gender, and political profiles of migrants. It can also severely limit their choices of an ultimate destination (see Critical Thinking Box 2.3). The majority of external migrants originate from Asia (57.0 percent) and Europe (19.0 percent), and the remainder come mainly from the United States (2.8 percent), the Caribbean and Bermuda (5.5 percent), Africa (7.3 percent) and Central and South America (7.3 percent).[7]

SOURCES OF DEMOGRAPHIC INFORMATION

Numerous sources of information (data) are used in demography. All births, deaths, and marriages that occur in a population are usually recorded in vital registries. Two sources of registries are available: (1) **civil registries,** which are compiled by government, and

Figure 2.6   Infant Mortality Rate in Canada, 1996 (deaths per 1,000 live births)

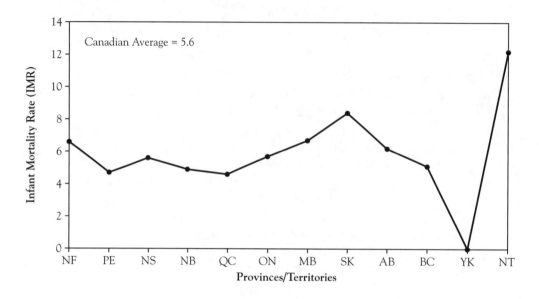

The infant mortality rate also displays a certain amount of variation across Canada. It is at its lowest in Yukon and at its highest in the Northwest Territories.

Source: Adapted from Statistics Canada, *Births and Deaths*, Catalogue No. 84F0210XPB, 1996, Table 2.4.

(2) **ecclesiastical registries**, which are compiled by individual religious groups. The amount or detail of information recorded in these sources varies. For instance, a birth record usually includes the name of the child, the date of birth or baptism (depending on the source), the names of the parents, and the place of birth or baptism. Other information that may be included is the occupations of the parents, the place of birth, and religious affiliation. Death records typically record the name of the deceased, place of death, cause of death, and age at death. Other information sometimes available includes occupation and place of residence. Marriage records generally include the names of the bride and groom, the date of their marriage, their marital status, the place where they were married, their occupation, age, and religious affiliation. On occasion, their place of birth and the names of their parents are also recorded.

Censuses, compiled by government, are also an important source of information. A **census** is a list of all people who reside in a particular geographical area during a specific period. The first Canadian census after Confederation was taken in 1871, although censuses were recorded before Confederation (the earliest of these dates to 1666). The **decen-**

CRITICAL THINKING BOX 2.2

....

Slavery and the Arrival of Black People in Nova Scotia

The first black people in Canada arrived here as slaves. The institution of slavery was formally acknowledged through numerous royal proclamations, beginning in Quebec in 1689, and continued well into the early nineteenth century. Black people were imported in large numbers into Nova Scotia primarily as a source of labour in the construction of the city of Halifax. The next major wave of black immigrants into Nova Scotia came after the American Revolution and the War of 1812.

Although many slaves fled from the United States to Canada via the *underground railway*, between 1787 and 1800 they also fled from Canada into New England, where slavery had already been abolished. It was not until 1833 that slavery was abolished in Canada and the rest of the British Empire, and many now believe that this was more in the nature of an economic decision than a moral one, that is, related to the high monetary cost of maintaining slavery.

Black people, like many other ethnic groups who either voluntarily or involuntarily migrated to Canada, have made important contributions to our country. Why is their early presence in Canada downplayed at best or ignored at worst?

Source: T. Johnson, "The Canadian Black Population and Immigration," *Anthropos* 73 (1978): 588–92; S.E. Williams, "Two Hundred Years in the Development of the Afro-Canadians in Nova Scotia, 1782–1982," in *Two Nations, Many Cultures: Ethnic Groups in Canada*, 2nd ed., J.L. Elliott, ed. (Scarborough: Prentice-Hall, 1983).

nial census, that is, a census taken every tenth year, was first established while Canada was still under British rule.[8] Information usually recorded in a census varies considerably, both over time and across space, but usually includes household or dwelling, name, age, sex, relationship to the head of the household (e.g., wife, son, niece, boarder), religious affiliation, and occupation. From census records we can examine household composition and formation. A **household** is a group of individuals who live together; this need not be a family, and it can include hired servants and boarders. When combined with vital registries, census records can be used to reconstruct individual families, that is, to create **genealogies**.

Other sources that can complement those already mentioned are cemetery data, voters' lists, military records, wills, and personal journals, to name but a few. The type of

Figure 2.7   Proportion of the Population over the Age of 64 Years, 1951 and 1996

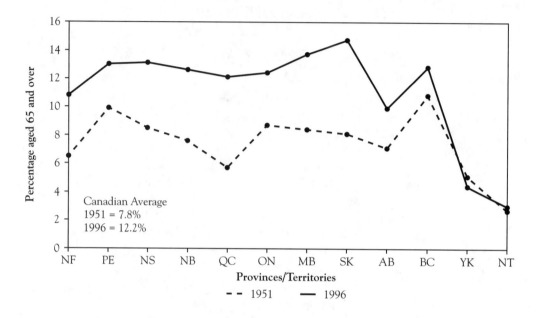

Regional variation in the proportion of the population over the age of 64 is marked. In most cases, an increase in the number of seniors is also noted over time. This variation across time and space is related to changes in fertility, mortality, and migration.

Source: Adapted from Statistics Canada, *Age, Sex, and Marital Status*, Catalogue No. 93-210, Nation Series, 1996 Census of Population, Table 1, pages 6 to 18 (1951 data) and the Statistics Canada Internet site at <www.statcan.ca/english/census96/canprov.htm> (1996 data).

sources used will often depend on the topic of research and the availability of records. For instance, if you want to study fertility, you would need access to birth registries, either civil or ecclesiastical; if possible the use of both sources is recommended as this provides a check on the accuracy of the data. However, both the government and ecclesiastical institutions can restrict access to **nominative records**, which list names. Therefore, you might not be able to reconstruct the fertility experience of specific women; instead, you would generalize about fertility based on the number of women aged fifteen to forty-four in a given population and the number of births registered within a specific period of time.

Problems with Sources of Demographic Information

Numerous problems exist with using the mentioned sources. First, these sources were collected for reasons other than demographic research, therefore, they may contain hidden biases. **Crosschecking** the data, that is, using as many sources as possible, can minimize

Figure 2.8   Mobility in Canada, 1996

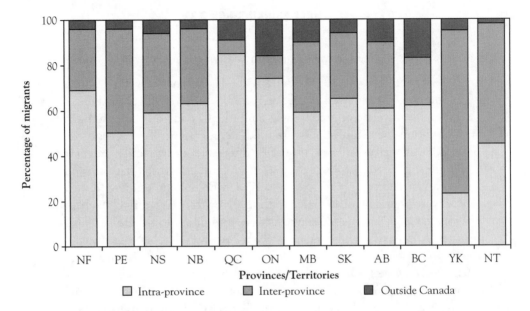

In most cases, the majority of migrants (individuals in this case who have migrated in the previous year) are moving within the same province. Exceptions are in Yukon and the Northwest Territories, where most migrants come from other provinces. Migrants from outside Canada tend to congregate in provinces that have a more diverse economy, such as Ontario, Manitoba, Alberta, British Columbia, and Quebec.

Source: Adapted from the Statistics Canada Internet site <www.statcan.ca/english/census96/apr14/mob2.htm>.

biases. For example, linking individuals from death records to both birth and census records will allow you to check the accuracy of the initial information, such as age, spelling of name, and so on. When linking various sources, there are often problems, many of which are related to the fact that the spelling of people's names and place names changes over time. Second, the quality of the data often varies because of errors in copying the initial information, level of literacy, method of initial data collection, and falsification of data (e.g., age is often misreported in censuses). Third, problems can also be related to changes in geographical boundaries, both ecclesiastical and civil. Therefore, a change in fertility might only be an artifact; that is, it might have been caused by the loss or gain in the number of communities included in a given parish or district.

Because of the variety of limitations associated with sources of demographic information, several techniques have been developed to assess them. In small populations

CRITICAL THINKING BOX 2.3

....

Chinese Immigration to Western Canada

Chinese immigration to Western Canada began with the British Columbia gold rush of 1858. Between 1881 and 1885 large numbers of Chinese men were recruited to help build the Canadian Pacific Railway. Immigration of Chinese was limited demographically because the Canadian government was primarily interested in attracting migrant labourers, not settlers. As such, restrictive immigration policies created an unusual demographic profile among Chinese communities, that is, they were predominantly male. With the growth of organized labour in Western Canada, numerous policies were introduced that were designed at first to discourage new migrants (e.g., British Columbia introduced a $50 tax on each new Chinese immigrant), then to end the arrival of Chinese migrants. (The *Chinese Immigration Act* of 1923 was in effect until it was repealed in 1947; between those years, no Chinese migrants could legally enter Canada.) These policies were in response to a perceived threat to organized labour of cheap Chinese labour.

Can we trust government policymakers to have enough insight into the effects of their policies concerning immigration, or will they create irrevocable damage to individuals, cultures, and societies?

Source: J.L. Elliott, "Canadian Immigration: A Historical Assessment," in *Two Nations, Many Cultures: Ethnic Groups in Canada*, J.L. Elliott, ed. (Scarborough: Prentice-Hall, 1983); P.S. Li, "Chinese Immigrants in the Canadian Prairie, 1910–47," *Canadian Review of Sociology and Anthropology* 19(1982): 527–40.

with, say, fewer than one hundred **vital events**—births, marriages, and deaths—each year, a comparison of baptisms to marriages can be used. If this ratio is seven or eight to one, then it is possible that marriages were underregistered, because this ratio should be between four and five to one. The sex ratio of baptisms can also be used. If this ratio exceeds 110 over several years, then female baptisms are underregistered, because the ratio of males to females should be around 105 at birth. When examining large populations, those with hundreds of vital events (or more) recorded each year, you can use one of three methods to evaluate the quality of the data. The **documentary method** involves using the expertise of other researchers who have worked with those same sources—in other words, others may be able to attest to the accuracy and completeness of the records.

The **expectation method** involves calculating expected proportions of vital events based on such factors as economic conditions, marriages, and migration. The **comparative method** entails calculating trends of vital events based on data from nearby populations. Overall, the more intimately researchers come to know their populations, the better they will be able to identify and assess any discrepancies.

ANALYZING DEMOGRAPHIC INFORMATION

The population is the focus of demographic research. Each **population** can be defined based on four aspects: (1) biological, involving shared genes; (2) ecological, involving shared environment; (3) social, involving a common cultural heritage; and (4) demographic, meaning shared time and space.[9] For instance, ethnicity is often used as a social factor defining a population. In 1996 the bulk of the Canadian population (53.0 percent) consisted of those of British, French, or European origin. The remainder identified their ethnic origin as Asian, Arab, or African (12.5 percent); Aboriginal (2.6 percent); Latin, Central and South American, Pacific Islands, or Caribbean Islands (2.3 percent); and Other (29.6 percent—note that a new category, Canadian, was included with "Other")[10] (see Figure 2.9). Once the population has been identified, the data are collected, which often involves thousands of entries (births, marriages, deaths, and census entries). Therefore, before analysis can proceed, the data must be reduced to make them more manageable. This usually involves **aggregating** the data, that is, summarizing observations either over specific geographical areas, time periods, or both. For instance, obtaining an average age at marriage for each decade over the study period reduces the data and makes comparisons easier.

In analyzing the data, two approaches are available: longitudinal or cross-sectional. **Longitudinal analysis** involves following a birth or marriage cohort through time. A cohort is a group of people who share the timing of a vital event—for example, all individuals in a population who were born in 1890. **Cross-sectional analysis** involves dividing data into nonoverlapping age categories to make demographic inferences about segments of the population who are at different stages of life (e.g., child versus adult). For instance, to examine fertility patterns using the longitudinal approach, you would take all of the population born in a specific period and follow them from birth to death; using the cross-sectional approach, you would group your population into different age groups, using these different groups to represent the patterns experienced over a lifetime. Of the two, the cross-sectional approach is the quickest and easiest, because it is not necessary to collect demographic information (e.g., births) over a long period; however, the longitudinal approach is potentially the most accurate, because you can examine the cumulative effects of social and environmental factors on the same group of people over time.

Figure 2.9 Ethnic Origin of Canada's Population, 1996

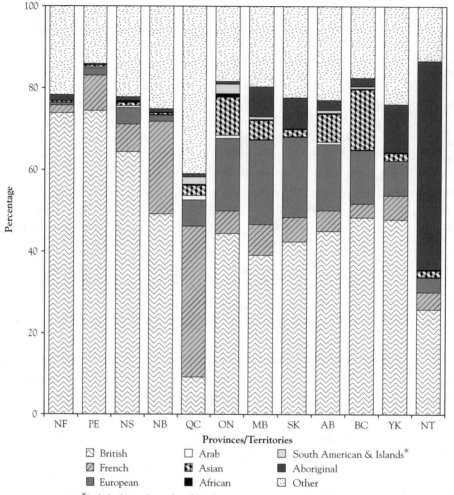

Legend:
- British
- French
- European
- Arab
- Asian
- African
- South American & Islands*
- Aboriginal
- Other

*Includes Latin, Central, and South America, and the Pacific and Caribbean Islands.

A great deal of variation exists across Canada regarding ethnic origin. A particular ethnic group domi-nates Newfoundland, Prince Edward Island, Nova Scotia, Quebec, and the Northwest Territories. Those of British descent dominate in the east, ranging from 74% in Newfoundland to 49% in New Brunswick. In Quebec, individuals of French descent make up 37% of the population, while in the Northwest Territories, 51% of the population are of Aboriginal descent. Due to the variation in its ethnic makeup, each province has a unique cultural mosaic.

Source: Statistics Canada Internet site <www.statcan.ca/english/Pgdb/People/Population/demo28a.htm>.

Biological Inferences

One of the goals of demographic research is to make inferences about the genetic structure of a population. This is achieved by either looking at marriages or looking at births and deaths.

Choosing a Marriage Partner

Marriage, which infers reproduction and, hence, the passing on of genes, can be either random or nonrandom. In most populations, humans included, the selection of a mate is **nonrandom**—that is, a distinct preference in the choice of a mate is evident. This preference can be related to physical or socioeconomic characteristics, such as physical attractiveness, age, religious affiliation, socioeconomic status (social class), and ethnicity. Individuals tend to choose mates who share the same sociocultural background as they do. This preference may be related to a conscious decision not to marry outside of one's group (e.g., Jews and Catholics), or it may simply be the by-product of geographical and social segregation of subgroups in a population. In other words, individuals belonging to a particular economic and ethnic group often live in the same general area and interact socially more within their group than outside it; therefore, the potential mates each is exposed to are in a sense "preselected" and share the same social background.

The task of the demographer is to identify these preferences in a population. Several methods are used to assess the frequency of nonrandom mating: genealogical analysis, isonomy, and kinship coefficients. **Genealogical analysis** requires years of effort, depending on the size of the population in question, because it involves reconstructing individual families. **Isonomy** is a faster method that involves looking at the frequency of marriages occurring between individuals who share the same surname (e.g., John Martin marrying Susan Martin). Of course, this method involves several assumptions, not the least of which is that similar surnames have the same origin (e.g., all Martins ultimately descended from one family of Martins). **Kinship coefficients** are similar to isonomy in that surnames are also used; they differ in that they do not focus on marriages but simply look at the proportion of surnames in a population, calculating the probability that the individuals are related. Each method attempts to identify the existence of preferences in the exchange of mates between families; the demographer working with kinship coefficients is trying to determine whether individuals in certain families choose their marriage partners from specific families or whether they marry someone irrespective of that individual's family.

Evolution by Natural Selection

The disappearance of the dinosaurs and the appearance of anatomically modern humans are generally what come to mind when people think of evolutionary change. But **evolution** can also occur on a microlevel that involves small changes in the gene frequency of a population. **Natural selection** refers to the preferential survival and reproduction of individuals in a population by virtue of possessing a genetic characteristic that gives them an advantage. For instance, if a certain blood type protected an individual from a deadly disease, then those who shared that blood type would be more likely to survive than others and have a higher probability of successfully reproducing. The result would be that future generations would increasingly possess the advantageous blood type. The net result, when comparing generations, would be a change in gene frequency (e.g., an increase in individuals with blood type A and a decrease of those with blood type O—which has been tentatively associated with exposure to the bubonic plague).[11] Such a change can be referred to as "evolution." When this change results from the genetic adaptation to an environmental stress, we term it natural selection.

Natural selection is not easily detected in human populations.[12] The main reason for this is the length of the human generation, which is approximately twenty-five years. Therefore, we would need to study many generations in detail before we could detect natural selection. This is not possible, because researchers would not live long enough to complete their research, and it is unlikely that funding could be obtained for a project of such a long duration. The use of historical populations is also limited in this regard, because we are not able to obtain genetic samples (e.g., blood samples). However, a method has been developed that measures the potential for natural selection in human populations. This method is called **Crow's Index of Selection**. Crow's index takes into account both deaths and births—mortality and fertility—and focuses on whether differences occur in subgroups of the population; subgroups can be defined using a variety of social factors, such as ethnicity, religious affiliation, and socioeconomic status. If differences do occur, then the potential for natural selection exists, that is, a change in the frequency of a gene or genes that results because a segment of the population became genetically adapted to an environmental stress.[13]

HISTORICAL DEMOGRAPHIC ANALYSIS OF CANADIAN POPULATIONS

Common sources of demographic information include written documents, such as birth, death, and marriage registries. When focusing on historical sources in Canada, the time depth is limited to the arrival of people from Europe, Asia, and Africa. At the very best, some information is available as early as the fifteenth century. Early sources are geographically limited to what was referred to as New France and to several British colonies, such as New England and Rupert's Land; some of these areas were later known as Upper and Lower Canada. What follows is a survey of the types of demographic research on Canadian populations. Although excluded from this chapter because of space constraints, it is important to note that a subfield of demography, **paleodemography**, focuses on nonwritten sources, such as skeletal remains, to study patterns of birth, death, and migration in prehistoric populations.

Regional Survey

Most demographic research in Canada has focused on Quebec and Ontario, with relatively less work done on other provinces and territories. This focus on central Canada is partly because of the availability of records; the majority of immigrants arrived and lived in central Canada, and thus this area has the longest time frame of demographic sources.

An exhaustive and complete survey of historical demographic studies of Canadian populations is not possible here. Instead, the intention is to introduce the topic of demography. It is hoped that interested readers will pursue specific areas in more depth (see the Selected Bibliography at the end of the book for names of journals that regularly feature a broad range of articles on Canadian historical demography). What follows is a brief examination of historical demographic studies of Canadian populations.

The study of migration in historical Canada is one of the most common types of research, which is easily explained by the fact that, except for North American Aboriginals (see Critical Thinking Box 2.4), Canada was settled by migrants. Such studies often focus on the contributions of particular ethnic groups, such as the Arabs,[14] Irish,[15] Ukrainians,[16] Italians,[17] and Armenians,[18] to name but a few. Others take a more general approach, focusing on trends over a wider area and including several ethnic groups.[19] Considerably less attention has been given to emigration from Canada.[20] Research on the growth of urbanism and urban centres in Canada is also of interest, and it often relates directly to patterns of immigration.[21]

Research on fertility and nuptiality examines such issues as birth control and abortion,[22] illegitimacy,[23] and changes in fertility patterns over time and across space.[24] In many cases, fertility is linked to a variety of economic factors. In some instances, marriage and fertility patterns are described for specific ethnic groups, which is useful in identifying sociocultural differences affecting these and other demographic variables.[25] A related focus of Canadian research is family and household composition, both of which are strongly influenced by local economic patterns.[26]

Studies of historical patterns of mortality often focus on epidemics, such as cholera,[27] smallpox,[28] typhoid,[29] and influenza.[30] This type of research not only examines the mortality associated with these diseases, but also looks at the sociocultural effects they caused. Other methods examine the more general patterns of mortality.[31] Again the importance lies in the comparisons with other populations to identify the role of human behaviour in the spread of disease, for example, the role of food preparation techniques, method of water storage, or crowding.

These studies illustrate the diverse nature of the Canadian population. Each geographical region has experienced a unique demographic history, which, in turn, has affected local, social, and economic conditions; it is important to note that this interaction continues to this day. We are dealing with an inherently dynamic system, and we can expect that the legacy created by past demographic behaviour will continue to affect future populations. By understanding this phenomenon we will be better equipped to identify future trends and to plan for potential problems, such as the stress on local economies when 50 percent of our population consists of people over the age of 64.

CRITICAL THINKING BOX 2.4

The First People in North America

The first people to arrive in North America were the ancestors of today's Aboriginal population, who crossed from the Old World via a land bridge that linked northeastern Siberia to Alaska. This land bridge, called **Beringia**, was last in existence between 27 000 and 11 000 years ago. The Aboriginals are thought to have arrived in North America sometime between 20 000 and 15 000 years ago; we have evidence from archaeology that humans had reached central Mexico about 11 000 years ago. It seems likely that people crossed the land bridge in pursuit of migrating herds of animals, such as mammoths, caribou, and bison.

The archaeological record indicates that the North American Aboriginals had diversified into a variety of cultural groups, some of which attained complex levels of sociopolitical organization, that is, tribes and chiefdoms. However, the arrival of Europeans disrupted Aboriginal cultures, in some instances irrevocably. Today, many descendants of these early migrants are in the process of resurrecting their rich cultural heritage.

Because we are all immigrants to this country, and if length of residence has any meaning, then why are the land claims of North American Aboriginals not given precedence over our own?

Source: B.M. Fagan, *People of the Earth*, 7th ed. (New York: Harper Collins, 1992).

CONCLUSION

Demographic research can be useful in demonstrating the importance of social and economic factors on human behaviour. By looking at fertility, nuptiality, mortality, and migration, the effects of numerous variables, such as resource exploitation, patterns of occupation, and social class, can be uncovered. This information can then be combined with other sources, not only to build a profile of life in the past, but also to help us understand the dynamic nature of human populations today. Understanding the interrelationship between the biological and social aspects of human groups can have important implications for a variety of policies directed at living populations, ranging from the effective delivery of community health care to the development and introduction of population control measures. Such information can also contribute to our understanding of the interrelationship between human populations and their physical environments. Knowledge of complex systems may enable us to more effectively deal with, and perhaps avoid, a variety of crises—most of which are created by humans—such as the emergence and spread of new and virulent diseases.

CHAPTER SUMMARY

This chapter introduces the major concepts used in demography. Sources of information on populations vary and include records compiled by government, such as birth registries, ecclesiastical institutions, such as church marriage registries, and individual people, such as wills, journals, or diaries. However, because no source of demographic information is perfect, care should be taken to identify biases in the information. The methods used by demographers are sometimes dictated by the nature of the data. For instance, if researchers do not have access to data over a long period, they are necessarily limited to performing cross-sectional analyses.

Some sources and methods used in demographic analysis are examined by focusing on four key areas: fertility, nuptiality, mortality, and migration. Fertility and mortality affect the natural growth or decline in a population's size; the ratio between the two determines whether a population increases, decreases, or remains stable. Nuptiality, or marriage, influences fertility in several ways. For instance, the timing of marriage can define the length of the female reproductive period, and variation in the proportion of the population who marry, or do not marry, can affect fertility by limiting or increasing the number of couples who are in a position to produce children—assuming that reproduction outside of marriage is low. Migration is one of the most important factors affecting the growth or decline of a population; if more individuals enter an area than leave it, the size of the population will increase. The reverse is also true; if more individuals leave an area than enter it, the size of the population will decline. Each of these four variables (fertility, nuptiality, mortality, and migration) varies within and among populations. Over time they define the unique demographic nature of a population, and they are ultimately responsible for generating the degree of diversity that is currently observed, regardless of how that diversity is defined (e.g., culturally, politically, or economically).

This chapter briefly surveys the types of demographic research on historical Canadian populations. These include studies of immigration and emigration, birth control, illegitimacy, households, and epidemics. In most cases the aim of such research is not only to describe events in the past, but also to link them to social, economic, and (when possible) biological factors. The ultimate aim of such research is to understand the factors that can affect a population's demographic profile. This information may then be applied to current issues and problems, such as overpopulation and the spread of deadly viruses.

KEY TERMS

age at first marriage, p. 36

age-specific marriage rate, p. 36

age-specific mortality rates, p. 36

aggregating, p. 47

Beringia, p. 52

celibacy, p. 36

census, p. 42

civil registries, p. 41

comparative method, p. 47

crosschecking, p. 44

cross-sectional analysis, p. 47

Crow's Index of Selection, p. 50

crude birth rate, p. 35

crude death rate, p. 36

crude marriage rate, p. 36

decennial census, p. 42

demography, p. 34

dependency ratio, p. 41

documentary method, p. 46

ecclesiastical registries, p. 42

emigration, p. 38

emigration rate, p. 39

evolution, p. 49

expectation method, p. 47

external migrants, p. 40

fecundity, p. 34

fertility, p. 34

fertility rate, p. 35

genealogical analysis, p. 49

genealogies, p. 43

gross migration rate, p. 39

household, p. 43

immigration, p. 38

immigration rate, p. 39

infant mortality rate, p. 37

internal migrants, p. 40

isonomy, p. 49

kinship coefficients, p. 49

life expectancy, p. 36

life span, p. 36

live births, p. 34

longitudinal analysis, p. 47

migration, p. 38

morbidity, p. 37

mortality, p. 36

natural selection, p. 50

net migration rate, p. 40

nominative records, p. 44

nonrandom mate selection, p. 49

nuptiality, p. 35

paleodemography, p. 51

population, p. 47

variable, p. 34

vital events, p. 46

DISCUSSION QUESTIONS

1. If you were going to reconstruct your own family history (genealogy), what types of information would you need? Which sources would provide you with this information? What potential problems might arise the further back in time you proceeded?

2. Which factors might affect the timing of marriage today (age at marriage)? Would these factors be similar to or different from those affecting marriage in the past? What effect could these factors have on fertility?

3. To meet the needs of a changing economy (new technology) our population needs to become more educated. What effects could increased educational attainment, that is, spending more time in school, have on age at marriage and fertility?

4. Until the twentieth century, the growth of the Canadian population was not the result of natural growth (births exceeding deaths) but primarily the result of immigration. Which factors do you think might have attracted these early migrants? Which factors might be attracting immigrants today?

5. Compare and contrast the mortality experience of the Canadian population over a 100-year period. Obtain the information you need from Statistics Canada. Look at the different categories of causes of death (e.g., infectious disease, degenerative disease). Are there any differences between the sexes regarding the mortality experience? Are there any differences in the mortality experience among the provinces? If so, what might account for these differences? Has the pattern of mortality changed over time? If so, explain how (and perhaps why) it has changed.

NOTES

1. K.H. Connell, *The Population of Ireland 1750–1845* (Oxford: Clarendon Press, 1950), p. 47.
2. Statistics Canada, Table 1.4.3.1, "Life Expectancy—Abridged Life Table, at Birth and Confidence Interval, by Sex, Canada, Provinces, Territories, and Health Regions, 1996," available online at <www.statcan.ca/english/freepub/82-221-XIE/00601/tables/htmltables/P1431.htm>, accessed 7 August 2001.

3. Statistics Canada, "Population by Selected Age Groups and Sex for Canada, Provinces and Territories, 1996 Census," available online at <www.statcan.ca/english/census96/canprov.htm>, accessed 7 August 2001.

4. G. Bilson, *A Darkened House: Cholera in Nineteenth-Century Canada* (Toronto: University of Toronto Press, 1980), p. 23.

5. Statistics Canada, available online at <www.statcan.ca/english/census96/aor14/ mob2.htm>, accessed 7 August 2001, Cat No. 93F0028XDB96016.

6. Statistics Canada, *Population: Demographic Characteristics—Mobility Status* (Ottawa: Supply and Services Canada, 1978), p. 1.

7. Statistics Canada, "Immigrant Population by Place of Birth, Showing Periods of Immigration 1981–1990 and 1991–1996, for Canada, 1996 Census, available online at <www.statcan.ca/english/census96/nov4/imm2c.htm>, accessed 7 August 2001.

8. Statistics Canada, *1996 Census Handbook* (Ottawa: Industry Canada, 1997).

9. G.A. Harrison and A.J. Boyce, "Introduction: The Framework of Population Studies," in *The Structure of Human Populations*, G.A. Harrison and A.J. Boyce, eds. (Oxford: Clarendon Press, 1972), pp. 3–4.

10. Statistics Canada, available online at <www.statcan.ca/english/Pgdb/People/Population/demo028a.htm>, accessed 7 August 2001, Cat. No. 93F0026XDB96002. These figures are based on those who listed a single origin.

11. A.K. Roychoudhury and M. Nei, *Human Polymorphic Genes: World Distribution* (Oxford: Oxford University Press, 1988).

12. T. Dobzhansky, "Natural Selection in Mankind," in *The Structure of Human Populations*, G.A. Harrison and A.J. Boyce, eds. (Oxford: Clarendon Press, 1972), p. 232.

13. J.F. Crow, "Some Possibilities for Measuring Selection Intensities in Man," *Human Biology* 30 (1958): 1.

14. B. Abu-Laban, "Arab Immigration to Canada," in *Two Nations, Many Cultures: Ethnic Groups in Canada*, J.L. Elliott, ed. (Scarborough: Prentice-Hall, 1979), p. 372.

15. A.G. Brunger, "Geographical Propinquity Among Pre-famine Catholic Irish Settlers in Upper Canada," *Journal of Historical Geography* 8 (1982): 265.

16. V.J. Kaye and C.W. Hobart, "Origins and Characteristics of the Ukrainian Migration to Canada," in *Persistence and Change: A Study of Ukrainians in Alberta*, C.W. Hobart et al., eds. (Toronto: Ukrainian Canadian Research Foundation, 1978), p. 25.

17. R.F. Harney, "Men Without Women: Italian Migrants in Canada 1885–1930," *Canadian Ethnic Studies* 11 (1979): 29.

18. I. Kaprielian, "Immigration and Settlement of Armenians in Southern Ontario: The First Wave," *Polyphony* 4 (1982): 14.

19. See for example J.L. Elliott, "Canadian Immigration: A Historical Assessment," in *Two Nations, Many Cultures: Ethnic Groups in Canada*, J.L. Elliott, ed. (Scarborough: Prentice-Hall, 1979), p. 289; W. Parker, "The Canadas," in *Studies in Overseas Settlement and Population*, A. Lemon and N. Pollock, eds. (New York: Longman, 1980), p. 267; J.C. Weaver, "Hamilton and the Immigration Tide," *Families* 20 (1981): 197; G. Wynn, "Ethnic Migrations and Atlantic Canada: Geographical Perspectives," *Canadian Ethnic Studies* 18 (1986): 1.

20. See for example A.A. Brookes, "The Golden Age and the Exodus: The Case of Canning, Kings County," *Acadiensis* 11 (1981): 57; R. Crawley, "Off to Sydney: Newfoundlanders emigrate to industrial Cape Breton 1890–1914," *Acadiensis* 17 (1988): 27; Y. Lavoie, *L'Émigration des Québécois aux États-Unis de 1840 à 1930* (Quebec: Editeur officiel du Québec, 1979).

21. See for example C.M. Gaffield, "Boom and Bust: The Demography and Economy of the Lower Ottawa Valley in the Nineteenth Century," *Canadian Historical Association. Historical Papers* (1982): 172; M.B. Katz, M.J. Doucet, and M.J. Stern, "Population Persistence and Early Industrialization in a Canadian City: Hamilton, Ontario, 1851–1971," *Social Science History* 2 (1978): 208; P. Matwijiw, "Ethnicity and Urban Residence: Winnipeg, 1941–1971," *Canadian Geographer* 23 (1979): 45; Weaver, "Hamilton and the Immigration Tide," p. 197.

22. P. Gossage, "Absorbing Junior: The Use of Patent Medicines as Abortificants in Nineteenth-Century Montreal," *The Register* 3 (1978): 1; A. McLaren, "Birth Control and Abortion in Canada, 1870–1920," *Canadian Historical Review* 59 (1978): 319–40.

23. R.D. Sharna, "Premarital and Ex-nuptial Fertility (Illegitimacy) in Canada 1921–1972," *Canadian Studies in Population* 9 (1982): 1.

24. H. Charbonneau, "Jeunes femmes et vieux maris: la fécondité des mariages précoces," *Population* 35 (1980): 1101; E.M.T. Gee, "Early Canadian Fertility Transition: A Components Analysis of Census Data," *Canadian Studies in Population* 6 (1979): 23; E. Roth, "Historic Fertility Differentials in a Northern Athapaskan Community," *Culture* 2 (1982): 63; J.E. Veevers, "Age Discrepant Marriages: Cross-National Comparisons of Canadian–American Trends," *Social Biology* 31 (1984): 118.

25. See for example J. Keyes, "Marriage Patterns Among Early Quakers," *Nova Scotia Historical Quarterly* 8 (1978): 299.

26. A.G. Darroch and M.D. Ornstein, "Family and Household in Nineteenth-Century Canada: Regional Patterns and Regional Economies," *Journal of Family History* 9 (1984): 158; F.K. Donnelly, "Occupational and Household Structures of a New Brunswick Fishing Settlement: Campobello Island, 1851," in *Labour in Atlantic Canada*, R. Chanteloup, ed. (Saint John: University of New Brunswick, 1981), p. 55; P.S. Li, "Immigration Laws and Family Patterns: Some Demographic Changes Among Chinese Families in Canada, 1885–1971," *Canadian Ethnic Studies* 13 (1980): 58; S. Medjuck, "The Social Consequences of Economic Cycles on Nineteenth-Century Households and Family Life," *Social Indicators Research* 18 (1986): 233; D.A. Norris, "Household and Transiency in a Loyalist Township: The People of Adolphustown, 1784–1822," *Social History* 13 (1980): 399.

27. Bilson, *A Darkened House*, p. 23.

28. J.R. Gibson, "Smallpox on the Northwest Coast, 1835–1838," *BC Studies* 56 (1982): 61.

29. S. Lloyd, "The Ottawa Typhoid Epidemics of 1911 and 1912: A Case Study of Disease as a Catalyst for Urban Reform," *Urban History Review* 8 (1979): 66.

30. J.D.P. McGinnis, "The Impact of Epidemic Influenza: Canada, 1918–1919," *The Canadian Historical Association, Historical Papers* (1977): 121.

31. R. Bourbeau and J. Légaré, *Évolution de la mortalité au Canada et au Québec, 1831–1931: Essai de mésure par génération* (Montreal: Les Presses de l'Université de Montréal, 1982); H. Charbonneau and A. LaRose, eds., *The Great Mortalities: Methodological Studies of*

Demographic Crises in the Past (Liège: Ordina Éditions, 1979); R.W. Fogel et al., "The Economics of Mortality in North America, 1659–1910: A Description of a Research Project," *Historical Methods* 11 (1978): 75; Y. Landry, "Mortalité, nuptialité et canadianisation des troupes française de la guerre de Sept Ans," *Social History* 12 (1979): 298; B. Osborne, "The Cemeteries of the Midland District of Upper Canada: A Note on Mortality in a Frontier Society," *Pioneer America* 6 (1974): 46.

The Many Faces
of Diversity

PART II

Part II takes a micro approach to diversity in Canada. Chapters 3 to 9 each examine a particular kind of diversity. The topics range from "traditional" diversities such as race, ethnicity, social inequality, and gender, to less traditional ones, including sexual orientation, the family, and disabilities.

Continuing with our house analogy, if Part I is the structure of the house, then Part II is the details of the interior. The text moves from the general, in Part I, to the specific, in Part II, as reflected in the title of Part II, "The Many Faces of Diversity."

Chapter 3 looks at social inequality in Canada. It introduces the reader to the inequalities of income and wealth and to the social structure in Canada. It reviews the major theories of inequality and stratification and examines their strengths and weaknesses.

Chapter 4 explores race and ethnicity in Canada. It outlines the major determinants of personal and group identity, the factors that influence societal interaction, and the problems of prejudice, discrimination, and racism. It also briefly outlines the history of immigration to Canada and the meaning of "race."

Chapter 5 looks at Aboriginal peoples. It vividly illustrates the heterogeneous nature of Aboriginal peoples, cultures, and languages. It also examines the deep historical presence of Aboriginal peoples in Canada, allowing you to better understand contemporary native issues and circumstances. Finally, this chapter points out that the legal circumstances of Aboriginal peoples are much different from those of other Canadians.

Chapter 6 deals with disability. After briefly looking at the history of disability in Canada, it explores the roles of several institutions in the lives of disabled people, including the government, religious organizations, schools, and the family. The chapter ends with a look at important social policy issues for disabled Canadians.

Chapter 7 examines the issue of gender. It defines the reality of gender identity and makes it clear that men and women occupy different spheres in society. It also outlines a number of social and biological theories that explain why men and women are socialized the way they are. Finally, it addresses the question of whether gender divisions are positive or negative, both for society and for the individual.

Chapter 8 looks at sexuality. It focuses primarily on the evolution of and variation in human sexuality. In dealing with variation, it points out that sexual diversity involves more than homosexuality—the heterosexual world is also diverse. In considering the evolution of sexuality, the chapter provides some historical background, which allows you to assess recent studies.

Chapter 9 analyzes diversity in Canadian families. It challenges the notion of the traditional family, redefining the word *family* to help explain the different types of families that exist in Canada today. This chapter also looks at the changing pattern of Canadian families and of family relations.

Social Inequality and Stratification in Canada

Eddie Grattan

Men are by nature unequal. It is vain, therefore, to treat them as if they were equal.
— James Anthony Froude, "Party Politics"

We hold these truths to be self-evident, that all men are created equal.
— Thomas Jefferson

Objectives

After reading this chapter, you should be able to

- describe the degree of social inequality in Canada

- present a summary of the major theories of social inequality

- detail the impact of social inequality on our daily lives

- list the variety of forms of social inequality

- describe the social class system of Canada

INTRODUCTION

All societies are characterized by social inequality and **stratification. Social inequality** is the varying degree to which different people have access to and control over valued resources, such as money, wealth, status, and power. In Canada, access and control are severely restricted by a person's social background, sex, and race or ethnicity. The differing degrees of access to and control over valued resources serve to divide Canadian society into recognizably distinct and unequal groups, or strata. Canada is a stratified society.

Let me provide an example from a personal experience. During the 2002 National Hockey League playoffs, I attended a hockey game at the Air Canada Centre. Although the game was quite exciting, having to sit in the so-called cheap seats (at $60 each!) often made the game difficult to follow. Spectators in the most expensive seats (the "platinums"), however, appeared to experience the event more intensely and personally: they could hear the players shouting to one another and see more clearly the players' expressions, as well as the hits, saves, and goals.

The difference between my experience and that of the people in the more expensive seats may appear to be an issue of little significance. Nevertheless, if I have a relatively low income, it is unlikely I will be able to afford a "gold" seat; if, however, my income is relatively high, it is likely I will be able to purchase a more expensive ticket and thus increase my enjoyment of the game.

It is evident that these differing (or unequal) experiences reflect wider patterns of inequality (in this case, income differences) in society.

BOX 3.1

Who Can Afford Tickets for Sports Events?

Over the past ten years, ticket prices for major sporting events have increased dramatically. Single tickets for the 2002 NBA All-Star game, for example, ranged in price from US$950 to US$4950! And tickets for the 2001 Grey Cup in Montreal started at C$58 for bronze, increasing to as much as C$185 for platinum. Regular season tickets for the Toronto Blue Jays range from C$16 to C$35, and the Toronto Argonauts of the CFL offer tickets ranging from C$12 to C$42. The availability of many of these tickets, however, is limited, as the vast majority of seats in most arenas and stadiums belong to season-ticket holders, most of whom renew their seats annually.

CRITICAL THINKING BOX 3.1

....

How does the amount of income affect the types of sport a person will play?

The ability to pay is, of course, dependent largely on income level. The amount of income a family earns determines many aspects of its existence, including the types of food it consumes, where (or, indeed, if) to travel on vacation, where, and for how long, the children will attend an educational institution, as well as many of the family's values and beliefs.

In some instances, the ability (or inability) to pay literally can determine whether one lives or dies. This reality is illustrated by the sinking of the ocean liner *Titanic* in 1912, when about 1500 of the 2300 passengers lost their lives. Passengers in the more expensive, upper-deck cabins had a greater chance of survival than those in the cheaper, lower-deck cabins:

> Of those holding first-class tickets, more than 60 percent were saved, primarily because they were on the upper decks, where warnings were sounded first and lifeboats were accessible. Only 36 percent of the second-class passengers survived, and of the third-class passengers on the lower-decks, only 24 percent escaped drowning. On board the *Titanic* class turned out to mean much more than the quality of accommodations: it was truly a matter of life or death.[1]

In Canada, social inequality is strongly associated with a person's social background, race or ethnicity, and sex. Canadians born into families with low incomes will generally receive less education and, thus, find it difficult to obtain high-income positions. Immigrants to Canada, particularly those with little education, generally face greater obstacles to finding employment. Women, although sharing similar levels of education as men, on average earn significantly less than men do.

INEQUALITIES OF INCOME AND WEALTH IN CANADA

Inequality of Income

In everyday conversation the terms "income" and "wealth" are used interchangeably; however, although closely related, an important distinction exists between them. **Income** is the *flow* of money received over a specified period, usually a year. Ms. Smith, for example, when asked her income, will most likely reply X dollars per year. The largest part of income for most Canadians is received in the form of wages and salary. A smaller part derives from government financial assistance, such as unemployment and welfare bene-fits—although for some, one of these is a significant portion of total income.

Other, less identifiable, forms of income are also important. These include gifts, money received as from cashing in an insurance policy, and capital gains (for example, money received from selling shares of stock at a price higher than their initial cost). It is often difficult to calculate precisely how much these contribute to the average income of Canadians, as the necessary information is difficult to obtain.

Canada is a wealthy country. In terms of per capita income, it ranks among the top in the world. Yet within Canada, marked inequalities of income and wealth persist. In 1999, the average income of Canadian families was $68 818 (see Table 3.1).

Average income, however, disguises significant income differences among fami-lies. An informative way of looking at these differences is to split all Canadian families into five equal groups, each referred to as a *quintile*. The groups are assembled in the fol-lowing way. Imagine that all families are placed in a line, a family's place being determined by its income level. The poorest family is placed at the front of the line, followed by the next poorest, and so on, until the last family, with the highest income, is placed at the end. Next, the line is split into five equal groups. The first group, or quintile, is composed of the first 20 percent of the line. Obviously, this group will consist of the poorest people. The next group consists of the next 20 percent. A similar process occurs in selecting the

Table 3.1   Average Total Income (in Constant 1999 Dollars) in Canada of Families and Unattached Individuals

	Families ($)	Unattached Individuals ($)
1995	58 592	25 634
1996	59 451	25 414
1997	60 772	25 431
1998	63 247	26 289
1999	63 818	27 058

Source: Adapted from Statistics Canada, "Average Total Income by Selected Family Types" from *Income in Canada*, Catalogue No. 75-202, 1999.

third, fourth, and fifth groups. The fifth group, of course, comprises those families with the highest incomes.

Table 3.2 reveals that people in the first, or lowest, quintile receive only 23.4 percent of their income from wages and salaries. Consisting of the poorest families in Canada, many of whom live below the poverty line, the majority of income received by families in this quintile is in the form of government transfer payments—for example, welfare benefits, children's benefits, or employment insurance. Single-parent families, as well as recently arrived immigrants, make up a large proportion of these families.

As income levels increase from the lowest to the highest quintiles, so does the proportion of income received from wages and salaries. The highest quintile, for example, consisting of those families with the highest incomes, receives 79.8 percent of its income from wages and salaries. Only 3.3 percent of its income derives from transfer payments.

A more revealing look at income inequality is provided by Table 3.3, which indicates that income inequality has not changed significantly since 1987. Of the total income received by households in Canada in 1996, the lowest quintile received only 5.0 percent. If Canada were an equal society, this quintile, composed of 20 percent of the population, would receive 20 percent of the total income. So, with only 5 percent of total income, it obtains only a small percentage of what it would receive in a perfectly equal society. The fourth and fifth quintiles, consisting collectively of the top 40 percent of

Table 3.2 Sources of Income of Canadian Families and Unattached Individuals within Income Quintiles, 1997

Sources of Income	Lowest Quintile	Second Quintile	Middle Quintile	Fourth Quintile	Highest Quintile
			(Percentage)*		
Wages and salaries	23.4	42.4	66.1	77.9	79.8
Net income from self-employment	2.5	5.2	5.7	5.2	6.7
Transfer payments	66.2	37.7	16.2	8.1	3.3
Investment income	2.3	3.9	3.0	2.5	3.7
Other money income	5.5	10.9	8.9	6.3	4.5

* Percentages do not all total 100 percent because of rounding.

Source: Adapted from Statistics Canada, *Income Distribution by Size in Canada*, Catalogue No. 13-218, April 1999.

Table 3.3 Distribution of Total Income in Canada by Quintiles for All Households (in Percentage*)

Sources of Income	Lowest Quintile	Second Quintile	Middle Quintile (Percentage)*	Fourth Quintile	Highest Quintile
1987	5.1	10.9	17.3	24.5	42.2
1992	5.0	10.8	17.1	24.7	42.4
1996	5.0	10.4	16.7	24.6	43.4

*Percentages do not all total 100 percent because of rounding.

Source: Adapted from Statistics Canada, *Household Facilities by Income and Other Characteristics*, Catalogue No. 13-218, March 1998.

income-earners in Canada, received a combined 68.0 percent of total income. This compares with 15.4 percent for the bottom 40 percent of income-earners.

The past ten years have seen a widening of the disparity in income levels. Most markedly, the percentage of low-income earners increased for the first time in twenty years, rising from 10 percent in 1989 to 13.3 percent in 1997.[2] A major reason for this shift is the reduction in government transfers through the 1990s. Such reductions affect those at the lower end of the income scale much more severely than those at the top. This contrasts with the period of the early 1980s and mid-1990s, when income levels in Canada remained virtually stationary. Before this, from about 1920 to 1980, incomes in Canada quadrupled, with Canadians in 1980 being able to purchase four times as many goods and services as in 1920. The change since 1980 has forced many Canadians, particularly those entering the labour market, to adjust their expectations with the awareness that their level of income will be substantially below that of their parents and grandparents.

Of the top 1 percent (about 76 000 families) of Canadian income-earners in 1993, average income was $295 300. Much of this income, an average of $68 000 per family, was received in the form of investment income. Also, the majority of high-income earners worked in similar areas of the economy, mainly in managerial, administrative, medical, and health-related occupations. More specifically, of all physicians, surgeons, and dentists in Canada in 1993, more than 25 percent belonged to the top 1 percent of income-earners.

Inequality of Wealth

Wealth is the accumulation of assets, such as a house, car, savings, cottage, land, jewellery, and art objects. As already mentioned, there is a close relationship between wealth and income, since only those with a substantial income can accumulate wealth. Those with high incomes accumulate wealth because of excess **disposable income**—income above that required for necessities, such as food, clothing, and accommodation. For many others, especially those living near or below the poverty line, it is often difficult, if not impossible, to accumulate wealth because little disposable income remains after purchasing necessities.

Sociologist Alf Hunter provided a more detailed illustration of this in his classic work on social inequality in Canada.[3] Writing in 1981, Hunter noted that workers earning about $25 000 per year possess average wealth of half ($12 500) that amount; those earning more than $50 000 annually have wealth double ($100 000) that amount; and those earning more than $100 000 possess wealth more than ten times ($1 000 000) that amount. So, if a person's income increases by $75 000 ($25 000 to $100 000) his or her wealth could increase by almost one million dollars! These large increases in wealth, resulting from relatively small increases in income, emerge from the increasing amounts of disposable income available as income increases. A relatively small increase in income can have extraordinary effects on wealth accumulation.

Table 3.4 shows that inequalities of net worth are more extreme than inequalities of income. This is not surprising, as data on income do not reveal financial assets such as investments in stocks and RRSPs and property ownership. As Table 3.5 reveals, in recent years there has been a widening disparity in net worth. Between 1984 and 1999, the top 20 percent of all family units experienced a 39 percent increase in net worth and the second quintile a 2 percent increase. The inability of lower-income Canadians to accumulate wealth is evident in data on retirement savings. In 1999, of those reporting an income of less than $20 000, only 15 percent contributed to an RRSP or employer-sponsored registered pension plan (RPP). This contrasts with 6 percent for those earning between $20 000 and $39 999, and 92 of those reporting incomes of more than $60 000.[4]

ASCRIPTION AND INEQUALITY

The inequalities of income and wealth discussed here reflect the stratified nature of Canadian society. Important in this respect are racial and ethnic relations, male and female relations, and a person's social background. Our ethnicity and race, sex, and social background have fundamental effects on our lives, often restricting our ability to achieve desired educational, occupational, and financial goals. We possess no control over our racial or ethnic identity, over whether we are male or female, or over our social background. For this reason, these factors are called **ascribed statuses.**

Increasingly, attention is being given to the role of age and physical or mental disability in affecting social inequality. Although these factors have traditionally been viewed as having less of an impact on inequality than ethnicity and race, sex, and social

Table 3.4   Distribution of Net Worth in Canada by Decile, 1999

Deciles*	Total Net Worth (%)	Median Net Worth ($)
All family units	100	81 000†
Lowest 10%	0	–2 000
Second 10%	0	3 100
Third 10%	1	14 300
Fourth 10%	2	35 500
Fifth 10%	3	64 700
Sixth 10%	5	101 500
Seventh 10%	8	152 600
Eighth 10%	11	220 800
Ninth 10%	17	338 100
Tenth 10%	53	703 500

* Family units ranked by net worth.

† Median net worth means that one half of Canadian families have a net worth of more than $81 000 and one half have a net worth of less than $81 000.

Source: Adapted from Statistics Canada, *The Assets and Debts of Canadians: An Overview of the Results of the Survey of Financial Security*, Catalogue No. 13-595, March 2001, p. 11.

Table 3.5   Change in Median Net Worth from 1984 to 1999, by Net Worth Quintile

| | Median Net Worth (Constant 1999$) | | Change from 1984 to 1999 (Constant 1999$) | |
	1984 ($)	1999 ($)	($)	(%)
All family units	58 400	64 600	6 200	11
Lowest 20%	0	–600	–600	0
Second 20%	12 200	12 500	300	2
Third 20%	58 400	64 600	6 200	11
Fourth 20%	124 400	157 500	33 100	27
Fifth 20%	291 200	403 500	112 300	39

Source: Adapted from Statistics Canada, *The Assets and Debts of Canadians: An Overview of the Results of the Survey of Financial Security*, Catalogue No. 13-595, March 2001, p. 30.

background, recently they have been shown in several instances to contribute significantly to social inequality.

Ascribed statuses affect our chances of success in society. Because education is essential to occupational and financial success, those ascribed statuses that hinder educational success are important in understanding inequalities of income and wealth. A close link exists between number of years of schooling and a person's occupation and income. Of the many factors involved in determining a person's occupation (especially her or his first), the most important is education. However, the type and amount of education a person receives is itself strongly determined by ascribed statuses.

Ethnicity and Race

Canadians of Asian, black, British, and Jewish ancestry have the highest average years of schooling; Indians, Inuit, and Italians tend to have the lowest.[5] This would, on the surface at least, suggest that ethnicity corresponds positively with income level. That is, British, Asians, blacks, and Jews will earn the most, Indians, Inuit, and Italians the least. Evidence suggests this is partially correct.[6] In 1985 men of Jewish ancestry earned the highest average income ($47 000). Men of British ancestry, surprisingly, made average incomes of between only $30 000 and $36 000, ranking about halfway. Blacks earned approximately $25 000, and Asians slightly more than $20 000. Those with the least education—Inuit, Métis, and Natives—also ranked near the bottom, between $23 000 and $25 000.

Data for 1991 suggest that the situation may be changing slightly. Although there continue to be marked differences in the income earned by nonvisible and visible minorities, some nonvisible ethnic groups, such as Italians, Portuguese, and Poles, received average incomes in 1991 about equal to that of the British.[7]

Blacks and Asians, despite their high average levels of postsecondary education, do not earn incomes equivalent to their educational credentials. Of Asian and black immigrants arriving in Canada between 1981 and 1991, 22 to 28 percent held university degrees, almost double the rate of the Canadian population. However, compared with the Canadian population, a greater proportion of Asians and blacks have education levels less than Grade 9.

Even if the high number of Asians and blacks with less than a Grade 9 education is taken into account, the low average earnings of the groups remain largely unexplained. This may be the result of several related developments.[8] First, more than other ethnic groups, blacks and Asians are the targets of racist and discriminatory employment and hiring practices. Second, having only recently arrived in Canada, immigrants are employed, like most new workers, at the lower end of business organizations. It may take several years for many of them to reach the upper levels of business organizations.

Furthermore, although these ethnic and racial groups may eventually succeed in achieving a significant degree of occupational, and hence financial success, it is unlikely that even a few will ever secure a position within the economic elite in Canada. Since the nineteenth century, the Canadian economic elite—the owners and controllers of the major corporations and banks—has been overwhelmingly of British origin.

By establishing control early in Canadian development, this elite has been able to consolidate its dominant position and prevent other ethnic groups from gaining access to top positions. In 1972, 86.2 percent of the economic elite was of British origin, compared with a British-origin population in Canada of 44.7 percent. People of French origin make up 28.6 percent of the population, and in 1971 they constituted only 8.4 percent of this elite. Canada's economy is in the hands of a relatively small group of men of British origin, who continue to pass on their privileges and positions of power to their children, in the process excluding others from elite positions. As the sociologist Wallace Clement observed,

> Top decision making positions in the economy…in Canada are dom-
> inated by a small upper class…. This…provides them with a life style
> much different than that experienced by the vast majority of
> Canadians and the privileges that accrue to them are passed on to
> their children…. Canada has not fulfilled its promise as a society with
> equal opportunity. As long as corporate power is allowed to remain in
> its present concentrated state, there is no hope for equality of oppor-
> tunity or equality of condition in Canada.[9]

Clement also illustrates the changing *class* origins of the Canadian economic elite. In 1951, 50 percent of the economic elite had class origins in the upper class. By 1972, this figure had increased to 59.4 percent. In 1951, 32 percent of the economic elite had class origins in the middle class. This figure had increased to 34.8 percent by 1972— changing only slightly over the period. The most significant change is in the proportion of the economic elite with working-class origins—*decreasing* from 18 percent to 5.8 percent from 1951 to 1972.

Social Background

Social background is an important determinant of education levels. Working-class men and women have lower levels of postsecondary schooling than their counterparts in the middle class. This occurs for at least two reasons: (1) lower incomes mean working-class students have more difficulty financing the cost of postsecondary education; (2) education and studying are not a major part of working-class life and culture. Middle-class parents are more likely to have books around the house and encourage their children's

CRITICAL THINKING BOX 3.2

....

Should wealthy families in Canada be made to redistribute their wealth?

schooling. Working-class parents, on the other hand, are less involved in educational concerns, preferring to defer to the knowledge of the teacher and the school system.

Sex

Men and women in Canada have similar levels of education. Only at the highest levels of the education system (master and doctorate) do men outnumber women, although this is changing. Despite similar education levels, however, men have higher average incomes than women, even in cases where they perform the same jobs. Despite evidence of an increase in weekly wages of full-time female workers in the early 1990s and a levelling of the earnings of male workers,[10] in 1995, employed women in Canada made roughly 65 percent of the average earnings of employed males.[11] There are several reasons for this discrepancy.

First, men occupy most management and ownership positions, and they make the decisions on the appropriate incomes for employees. Traditionally regarded as the second income earner, out to supplement the main income of the husband, women have generally been paid substantially less. This discriminatory practice, although slowly changing, makes it difficult for many women, in particular single mothers, to provide a satisfactory standard of living for themselves and their families.

Second, and related, women are disproportionately employed in occupations viewed as an extension of their household duties, such as teaching, nursing, and social work. The cultural perceptions surrounding such occupations reflect those of the "home-maker," someone who is nurturing, caring, sensitive, efficient, and emotional. Although such stereotypes are also slowly being modified, many women remain in occupations traditionally regarded as "women's work." Elementary-school teachers and nurses, for example, are overwhelmingly women. Furthermore, women who strive to build a career are often treated and viewed differently from men with similar ambitions. Women who prefer not to marry or have children in the hope of pursuing a career are frequently depicted as selfish, greedy, and "unfeminine."

Third, many women find themselves in what is called a "double-ghetto." This occurs when a woman both works for a wage and undertakes housework, including looking after the children and the needs of her husband.

Fourth, over the past twenty-five years the number of single-parent families in Canada headed by women has almost doubled. However, the proportion of single mothers in the workforce has fallen slightly, from 32 to 26 percent. As Susan Crompton, a sociologist, noted, this shift has occurred for several reasons.[12] First, the tremendous increase in the number of working wives has essentially displaced single mothers from certain occupations. Second, as the educational requirements of jobs have increased, single mothers have found it increasingly difficult to obtain these necessary qualifications. The difficulties and expense of raising a child, or children, frequently make it financially infeasible for many single mothers to seek employment (see Box 3.2). Many mothers receive no child support from the fathers and so are forced to live almost wholly on government assistance. This situation is partly responsible for the **feminization of poverty** over the past two decades.

Age

Increasingly, attention is being paid to the importance of age in promoting inequality. Many observers have focused particularly on the financial plight of our senior citizens. It has been pointed out that, over the course of the twentieth century, the number of people age 65 and over has steadily risen and will rise even more markedly this century. Improved medical technologies, healthier lifestyles, and the large number of births between the years 1945 and 1965 are responsible for this increase.

As individuals, living well past the traditional retirement age of 65 may appear to be a happy prospect; but as a society, it is becoming apparent that there are many difficulties associated with a greying population. First, partly because most elderly people do not do paid work, they are stereotyped as lazy, mentally slow, traditionally minded, and incapable of contributing to society. Second, as more and more people live well into their retirement years, many quickly find themselves spending whatever savings they may have accumulated over their working lives. This forces many seniors to live in poverty. Indeed, outside of children and youth, the elderly—most of whom are women—constitute the largest group in poverty in North America. For example, according to Statistics Canada,[13] in 1997, an estimated 49.1 percent of unattached women and 33.3 percent of unattached men over the age

CRITICAL THINKING BOX 3.3

Should lone, or single, mothers be given greater government financial assistance in light of the difficulties they face?

of 65 lived below the poverty line. In those instances when seniors are physically able to work, they generally find themselves in low-prestige, minimum-wage jobs.

With a growing senior population, the Canadian government faces increased pressure to improve the financial situation of those entering retirement. At the same time, however, government cutbacks and continued public demand to reduce spending on the unemployed, welfare recipients, and seniors (in the form of an income security system), suggest that the situation of the elderly in this century may deteriorate further.

BOX 3.2

Left Behind: Lone Mothers in the Labour Market

....

The stagnating employment situation of lone mothers is not for lack of willingness to work. Many lone mothers currently outside the labour force want to work; those who are working are more likely than wives to be employed full time, and a substantial proportion of those working part time would rather have full-time jobs. However, wives are older and better educated and have more work experience. Moreover, having another adult to help with childcare arrangements can only make it easier for married mothers to look for and retain a job. Faced with competition from a large pool of better-educated women, ... it is not surprising that many lone mothers have difficulty establishing themselves in the job market.

But a "hierarchy of success" can also be found in the population of lone mothers. Separated or divorced mothers are "ex-wives" who occupy a more advantageous position in the labour market than never-married women because they have more education and more work experience. Much of the labour market disadvantage of never-married lone mothers may be attributable to their lower educational attainment, which raises the question of whether pregnancy outside marriage increases the likelihood of interrupting formal education and delaying the acquisition of work experience. It is certainly clear that two distinct types of women, with considerably different demographic and socioeconomic characteristics, are merged under the rubric "lone mother." It seems a disservice to both groups to ignore the differences between them.

Source: Statistics Canada, *Perspectives on Labour and Income*, Catalogue No. 75-001, Summer 1994.

Disability

Historically, people with physical or mental disabilities have generally been excluded from participating in mainstream society, particularly in the workforce. More recently, however, through the lobbying efforts of organizations representing the disabled, as well as a variety of employment equity programs, many people with disabilities now find themselves participating actively and fully in work and social activities. Nevertheless, people with disabilities continue to confront stereotyping, prejudice, and discrimination. People with disabilities, as a group, suffer severe social inequality, experiencing high levels of unemployment and welfare.

VIEWS OF INEQUALITY

The existence of inequality does not tell us whether it is good or bad, positive or negative, moral or immoral. Does inequality of income and wealth, for example, contribute to a more peaceful and stable society? Does it provide greater financial rewards to those who work the hardest? Or, does it serve to further the exploitation and oppression of one section of society by another? Responses to these types of questions have been numerous, but it is possible to classify them into two basic positions.

Structural–Functionalism: Inequality Is Good, Necessary, and Inevitable

The first position, **structural–functionalism**, argues that inequality is positive and necessary for the proper functioning of society. Writers adopting this position view society as operating in a manner similar to the human body. Just as the different parts of the body— skin, muscles, bones, organs, and so on—collectively function to maintain the operation and survival of the whole body, the different parts—the structure—of society together function to promote the overall peace and stability of society.

Everything that exists in society serves a function. Prostitution, for example, although illegal and commonly regarded as a major problem, is seen as serving the important function of allowing men, and women, to vent their sexual frustrations. Without prostitution, according to structural–functionalists, it is likely that rape and other sexual assaults would increase, along with the rate of divorce. Prostitution, then, according to this view, simultaneously functions to reduce violent sexual assaults and maintain intact the important role of the family unit.

Inequality is viewed in a similar manner. Structural–functionalists consider inequality both unavoidable and desirable. The existence of inequality in all societies, past and present, indicates that it must serve a positive function. But how does inequality contribute to the stability and functioning of society? Inequality, in the form of different income levels, in this view, provides an incentive for the most able people in society to work the hardest to attain those jobs considered by society to be the most functionally important. Doctors, lawyers, dentists, and so on, earn substantial incomes because of their great importance to the stability and continuing operation of society.

If a doctor and a bus driver, for example, received similar incomes, few people would want to endure the years of education and hard work required to qualify as a doctor. Not only would there arise a critical shortage of doctors, but it is also likely this shortage would lead to the acceptance into medical school of many unsuitable applicants. It is necessary, therefore, that a differential reward system exist, whereby those performing the most important jobs receive higher incomes and more prestige than those in occupations considered less important. Without differential rewards, the most talented would have no incentive to pursue the functionally most important jobs. Inequality, then, as an essential and inherent feature of the economic structure of society, is vital to the proper functioning of the whole society. For this reason, those making this argument are referred to as structural–functionalists.

Some Problems with Structural–Functionalism

To their credit, structural–functionalists emphasize the need for some form of incentive to ensure that the most talented attain those jobs requiring extensive knowledge and training. It is unlikely that in a society in which everyone receives the same level of income, regardless of occupation, the most talented would seek to undertake the most important occupations.

There are several problems, however, with the structural–functionalist position. First, the emphasis on individual talents and abilities suggests that those with the most talent and ability will succeed and that those less able and less intelligent will be less successful. To structural–functionalists, a person's degree of success should be determined solely by individual effort. Consequently, everyone should have an equal chance to succeed—there should be **equality of opportunity**. This involves equal access to education and the elimination of sexual and ethnic discrimination in employment and hiring practices. This type of argument fails to satisfactorily analyze the impact of ethnicity, class, and gender on the creation and continuation of inequalities in society. Many ethnic groups, the poor, and women face severe impediments to educational and occupational success. "The point to stress," as sociologist Edward Grabb noted,[14] "is that established structures tend to define the prospects and life chances of people in most instances." As a society, we may want everyone to be given an equal opportunity, but it is apparent that many people cannot overcome major obstacles that have been put in their way, thus preventing them from moving ahead.

Second, are occupations financially rewarded based on their functional importance to society? Not always, it seems. For example, what is the functional importance of professional athletes and entertainers? Jaromir Jagr, Alex Rodriguez, and Shania Twain may annually earn millions of dollars, but are they crucial to the functioning of society?

A less obvious example relates to the functional importance of doctors. Are they more important than, say, garbage collectors? According to structural–functionalists, garbage collectors receive lower incomes than doctors do because of their lesser importance to the overall functioning of society. But there is little evidence to back this up. Indeed, it could strongly be argued that as a society we could do without doctors more readily than without garbage collectors. On the one hand, the elimination of garbage collectors would result in mountains of rotting garbage and the epidemic outbreak of potentially fatal diseases. Without doctors, on the other hand, more people would undoubtedly die and at an earlier age, but it is unlikely that society would suffer serious damage.

Another example is provided by the recent arguments made by feminists and many others regarding the value of housework. Although unpaid in financial terms, such work is obviously important, if not crucial, to the overall functioning of society.

Third, some people are motivated by factors other than money. Bryan S. Turner, in his book *Equality*, noted the nonmonetary motives that are traditionally associated with the nursing profession: "A number of social roles such as nursing may be regarded as socially important despite their low income and persons who occupy such roles are typically motivated by moral or religious arguments where a direct monetary reward is absent."[15]

Fourth, structural–functionalists emphasize the importance of individual hard work and perseverance in determining occupational and financial success. This assumes that movement from one class to another, both up and down, is largely a consequence of individual strengths or weaknesses and pays little attention to the role of inherited wealth in preserving economic inequalities and class differences over time. The majority of Canada's wealthiest families, as already noted, are of Anglo-Saxon origin and the beneficiaries of inherited wealth.

CRITICAL THINKING BOX 3.4

Are some workers, such as nurses and teachers, less motivated by money and more by a desire to help people?

Conflict Theory: Inequality Is Bad, Avoidable, and Unnecessary

The second position, **conflict theory**, relates inequality to conflict in society. Conflict theorists view inequality as both a cause and an effect of exploitation, conflict, and oppression. There are many different types of conflict theorists, with disagreement centring on the precise form conflict takes and how it can be reduced or eliminated. Some conflict theorists view class inequality and conflict as central, whereas for others gender or race is more important.

Karl Marx

One of the most important conflict theorists was Karl Marx (1818–83). Marx argued that all societies are divided between those who possess wealth and power and those who do not. In modern society, the major division, or inequality, is between the **capitalist class**, or bourgeoisie, and the **working class**, or proletariat. Capitalists are those who own the factories, land, machinery, and other materials used for the production of goods and services. Marx termed these materials the **means of production**—they are, simply, the means to produce goods and services. Workers, on the other hand, do not own property, and to survive they must sell their labour power to capitalists.

To Marx, the relationship between capitalists and workers is based on a fundamental conflict of interests. Capitalists are motivated by profit, and workers are interested in obtaining as much income as possible. But because higher wages mean less profit, workers and capitalists have different, and conflicting, interests and objectives. According to Marx, capitalists exploit workers by paying them less than the real value of their work. For example, suppose I work as a bartender for eight hours one day, at $6 an hour. At the end of the day, I receive $48 ($6 × $8). However, the amount of money I have in the cash register is considerably more, let us say $98. It is apparent, then, that I am paid $50 ($98 − $48) less than the amount I collected. Of this $50, my boss, the owner of the bar, will be required to pay business expenses, such as hydro, food, mortgage, and so on. Of the $50, then, my boss may make a profit of only $20. Nevertheless, this is money that I worked for, not my boss. To Marx, this $20, the difference between what I am paid and the value of my work, represents the degree to which I am exploited. Marx termed this difference—in this case, $20—surplus value, or profit.

The greater the amount of surplus value the greater the level of **exploitation**. For example, if my boss's profits increase each year and my wages remain unchanged, the profit, and hence the level of exploitation, increases. During Marx's lifetime, this is indeed what occurred, as most workers were unable to survive without the aid of charity of some kind. Many starved to death as capitalists increased their share of income and wealth.

Figure 3.1 From Class to Cash Consciousness

Marx referred to the process of increasing inequality and poverty as the *immiseration* of the working class. He hoped it would force workers into recognizing the exploitative nature of the system in which they lived and the need to overthrow the capitalist class and institute a new, more equal, society.

But Marx was unsure whether workers would recognize their real interests and revolt. He observed that the capitalist class, as a consequence of its ownership of all institutions in society, including the media, was informing workers that their poverty resulted not from exploitation, but from their own personal failings: they simply did not work hard enough. This made most workers feel responsible for their own poverty. Marx referred to this outlook on the part of the working class as *false consciousness*: workers essentially believed it was not the system of capitalist exploitation that was to blame, but themselves.

The increasing exploitation of the working class, Marx believed, would lead eventually to conflict between capitalists and workers (see Figure 3.1). Workers would rid themselves of their false consciousness and recognize their shared experience: exploitation. Marx referred to this shared experience as class consciousness. It would eventually result in an organizational effort to overthrow the capitalist class and to the establishment of a new—communist—society, based on equality and freedom.

In communism, exploitation would no longer exist, as all goods and services would be produced by and for the whole population. There would no longer be a division between owners and workers; all property would be owned by the whole population, not by one class or group of people. Goods and services would no longer be distributed based on a person's ability to pay but instead based on need: "From according to his ability, to each according to his need" (Marx).[16]

Some Problems with Marx's Theory

Marx presented an accurate depiction of nineteenth-century society; however, at the time of Marx's death in 1883, major changes were occurring in the societies of Europe and North America. Consequently, today we consider many of his predictions about the development of Western society to be somewhat misplaced or greatly in need of revision.

First, Marx's assumption of property ownership as constituting the central source of conflict within society has not proven wholly correct. Many observers argue that other factors, such as gender, race, ethnicity, and national identity have generated greater conflict and tension.

Second, Marx predicted increasing income disparities between capitalists and workers; however, two developments have occurred to prevent this. The first is the growth, starting about 1880, of a large middle class. The growth of government services over the past hundred years has created a large group of clerical (white-collar) workers, who tend to view themselves as distinct, in prestige and status, from the working class.

CRITICAL THINKING BOX 3.5

Most workers may be exploited, as Marx argued. Do you believe that most workers feel exploited?

Also, and related, in the twentieth century all workers experienced significant increases in their standard of living. Compared with the nineteenth century, poverty levels have declined sharply, and average incomes have risen dramatically. Consequently, many workers feel little animosity toward their employers.

Third, governments over the past century or so have assumed control of increasingly more areas of society. Although this has arguably lessened individual freedom, as will be discussed shortly, it has also enabled governments to maintain greater control of the economy in an effort to avoid major economic crises, such as the Great Depression of the 1930s, that provide the preconditions for worker unrest.

Although they have lessened over the course of the twentieth century, substantial income and wealth inequalities still exist in Canada—inequalities that have widened over the past two decades; a growing number of low-income families and individuals are living below the poverty line. This suggests that Marx's analysis of society as comprising the haves and have-nots still provides insight into the workings of modern society.

Max Weber

Max Weber (pronounced Vayber) (1864–1921) accepted Marx's assertion of the importance of the ownership or nonownership of property as a major source of inequality and as a potentially important source of conflict. However, Weber highlighted the other sources of potential conflicts, as well as offering a more complex system of stratification.

Weber agreed with Marx that class, ownership or nonownership of property, is a central feature of modern society. Capitalists possess great amounts of wealth, power, and prestige. However, argued Weber, often the possession of business property is not accompanied by power and prestige. Social prestige, or status, as the degree of positive evaluation by members of society, often derives from a person's level of education, income, and occupation. Doctors, lawyers, dentists, university professors, and so on, enjoy high status in large part because of their income level and the education they possess. Wait staff, shop attendants, and bartenders experience low status or prestige because of their low incomes and the limited education requirements of their jobs.

Political power is the degree of political influence a group has. Some unions, for example, acting on behalf of workers, often exert extensive pressure on employers, including the government, in an effort to increase salaries and improve working conditions. But because not all unions have the same degree of influence, some workers are more politically influential than others. Furthermore, other groups in society, such as those sharing a common lifestyle, similar income levels, and so on, possess greater prestige and political power than many business property owners. To Weber then, differences in social prestige (status) and access to and control of the political system have important effects on the degree of income and wealth inequalities and on the nature of the stratification system.

Because Weber viewed inequality as stemming from a variety of sources and conceived of stratification as a complex phenomenon, he talked about social class and status groups rather than simply about class, the ownership or nonownership of property as defined by Marx. Furthermore, Weber contended that frequently there is no necessary relationship between economic (class), prestige (status), and political (power) rankings. For example, university professors, who have long rejected unionization, tend to have a low power ranking but a high status ranking. In addition, the economic ranking of professors tends to be significantly lower than suggested by their high status. Some manual workers, on the other hand, ranking low in terms of status, earn higher incomes (have higher economic ranking) and often have greater power than professors.

The aristocracy in Britain also serves to illustrate the often-wide discrepancies among economic, status, and political rankings. The British aristocracy, based on heredity, for centuries has enjoyed great prestige. Politically, however, its strength has been declining and no longer matches its high status ranking. The British aristocracy has also been declining economically, with many families forced to sell valuable assets in an effort to maintain their traditional lifestyle and status ranking.

Although recognizing the importance of the ownership or nonownership of property, Weber believed society to be more profoundly affected by the growth of bureaucratic institutions, such as government and large businesses. He believed these limited individual freedom. Workers may indeed be exploited, conceded Weber, but it is unlikely that this will provoke conflict with the capitalist class, and it will certainly not bring about a new—communist—society. Furthermore, even if workers were to overthrow the capitalist class and establish a new society, communism would require an even larger bureaucracy and so further restrict individual freedom. The new leaders would establish themselves as a bureaucratic ruling class, and the workers would simply be trading in one set of rulers for another.

Weber's emphasis on status as an important indicator of social class provides a more accurate representation of the class structure of modern society. The growth of the middle class, and its desire to purchase consumer products such as cars, houses, televisions, and designer clothes, symbolizes its concern with status and prestige. Also, it is apparent that growth in the number of government departments has reduced individual freedom: more and more areas of our life are controlled by rules and regulations, requiring little individual expression or decision making.

THE SOCIAL CLASS STRUCTURE OF CANADA

Depending on the theoretical perspective you adopt, you can define the nature and number of social classes in Canada in several ways. Nevertheless, this section presents a brief description of what are commonly viewed as the major social classes in Canada: the upper class, middle class, working class, and subworking class.

The Upper Class

The **upper class** in Canada comprises those who own substantial amounts of wealth, about 4 or 5 percent of the population. Within the upper class a distinction is often made between those possessing wealth passed down from generation to generation (inherited wealth) and those acquiring wealth through recent business successes ("new money"), such as Bill Gates and Donald Trump. The Eaton's department stores, for example, established in the late nineteenth century, were until recently owned continuously by the Eaton family of Toronto. Having inherited wealth over several generations, this type of family is often referred to as bluebloods, or the upper-upper class. It is estimated that at least half the wealthiest families have benefited to some degree from inheritance.[17]

Members of the upper-upper class characteristically attend expensive private schools and universities, at home and abroad. These institutions serve to teach the values, beliefs, manners, and ways of looking at the world that are exclusive to this class (see Figure 3.2).

The other members of the upper class earn income from well-paying occupations or investments. These "new money" capitalists make up the bulk, between 70 and 80 percent, of the upper class. They are often prohibited from socializing with "old money" families through the many private clubs and associations, as well as social events, established exclusively by and for those with inherited wealth. Bluebloods also prefer avoiding the publicity and media attention frequently craved by new money capitalists such as Donald Trump.

The Middle Class

Members of the **middle class** in Canada own some property—usually a house, one or two cars, and perhaps a cottage. They have relatively high-paying, secure occupations, pro-

Figure 3.2 Lifestyles of the Wealthy

viding a degree of satisfaction and feeling of accomplishment. Many of these occupations are in the public sector, and they offer generous benefit allowances, for example, sick, dental, and maternity benefits, privately established pensions, and, until recently, long-term job security. This situation is changing, though, with governments across Canada cutting public sector jobs and lowering pay levels.

The Working Class

The working class comprises those who own little or no wealth and are employed in low-paying and generally insecure occupations, such as most of those within the service sector. It is largely because of limited education—most working-class people have not progressed beyond high school or community college—that members of the working class face limited, and typically low-paying, employment opportunities.

The Subworking Class

The subworking class is made up of those, around 20 percent of the population, with the lowest or no incomes—the homeless, welfare recipients, the unemployed, single-parent families, the aged, and those in extremely low-paying occupations. Life for this class tends to be very unstable, both financially and emotionally. Families have limited, or no, savings as nearly all income is required for the purchase of necessities.

Members of the subworking class often live in a separate area of a town or city, and their cultural environment—values, beliefs, attitudes, behaviour, and social activities—tends to be distinctive.

SOCIAL MOBILITY IN CANADA

In North America, especially the United States, it is commonly suggested, particularly by structural–functionalists, that economic success is achieved through individual hard work and determination. This idea implies that movement up and down the social class structure occurs frequently and primarily because of personal effort and initiative. This view of social mobility is ritually portrayed and celebrated in television programs and Hollywood movies: obstacles to personal success reside solely within the individual.

How accurate is this portrayal? How many people actually move up the class ladder? How many fall down? What is the pattern of social mobility in Canada? What is the likelihood, for example, of the daughter or son of a steelworker eventually becoming a member of the middle class?

The social class structure of Canada has remained relatively stable for several decades. The number of people within each class has remained constant, although many

CRITICAL THINKING BOX 3.6

....

Can you provide an example of a middle-class family experiencing upward social mobility?

of those within each class have changed. A study conducted in 1986 revealed that close to 40 percent of men and women experienced some form of upward mobility, and a similar figure moved downward.[18]

The degree of social mobility in Canada is greater than that of most other Western countries. Nevertheless, as pointed out earlier, ascribed statuses continue to affect movement up and down the social and occupational hierarchy. In Canada, as Joanna Naiman concluded, "the very top and the very bottom of the status hierarchy remain relatively closed, and most occupational mobility is mainly small movement in the middle."[19]

An important element of upward mobility is level of education. As already mentioned, studies indicate a close relationship between a person's first job and their education level. However, it would appear that this may be changing as the educational requirements of jobs increase and the Canadian economy, like economies in the rest of the industrialized world, experiences major structural changes. Free trade, the growth of service industries, and the shrinking of industrial production suggest that the mobility and social class patterns of the past forty or fifty years may be undergoing a fundamental restructuring.

CHAPTER SUMMARY

This chapter has examined several aspects of social inequality in Canada. (1) There is inequality of income and wealth in our society. Although both income and wealth are unequally distributed, historically inequality of wealth has exhibited greater extremes. (2) Two major theories, structural–functionalism and conflict theory, each provide insight into the nature of social inequality, although neither is without problems. (3) Social inequality pervades nearly all aspects of our lives. Social class, race and ethnicity, sex, age, and physical and mental ability all have an impact on social inequality. (4) Canada has four major social classes. (5) In recent years structural changes in the global economy have increased social inequality in Canada and elsewhere, and in the future, this is unlikely to change.

KEY TERMS

ascribed status, p. 67

capitalist class, p. 77

conflict theory, p. 77

disposable income, p. 67

equality of opportunity, p. 75

exploitation, p. 77

feminization of poverty, p. 72

income, p. 63

means of production, p. 77

middle class, p. 82

political power, p. 80

social inequality, p. 62

stratification, p. 62

structural–functionalism, p. 74

upper class, p. 82

wealth, p. 66

working class, p. 77

DISCUSSION QUESTIONS

1. To explain social inequality, which of the ascribed statuses (social class, race and eth-nicity, sex, age, disability) do you consider the most important? Provide evidence.
2. Which theory do you believe more adequately explains social inequality—conflict theory or structural–functionalism?
3. Why are single women more likely to be living below the poverty line?
4. Provide reasons why you believe the Canadian government should or should not attempt to reduce the degree of income and wealth inequality in Canada.
5. As a person grows older, which ascribed statuses do you think become more signifi-cant in his or her life?

NOTES

1. John J. Macionis, Juanne Nancarrow Clarke, and Linda M. Gerber, *Sociology* (New Jersey: Prentice-Hall, 1993), p. 243.
2. G. Picot and A. Heisz, "The Labour Market in the 1990s," in *Canadian Economic Observer*, February 2000, Statistics Canada, Cat. No. 11-010-XPB (Ottawa: Statistics Canada, 2000), pp. 312, 315.
3. Alfred A. Hunter, *Class Tells: On Social Inequality in Canada* (Toronto: Butterworths, 1981), p. 99.
4. *Infomat, A Weekly Review.* "Likelihood of Saving Increase with Income." 20 July 2001, Cat. No. 11-002E.
5. Ibid., p. 132; Macionis et al., *Sociology*, p. 337.

6. Jane Badets and Tina W.L. Chui, *Focus on Canada: Canada's Changing Immigrant Population*, Statistics Canada, Cat. No. 96-311E. (Ottawa and Scarborough: Statistics Canada and Prentice-Hall, 1994), p. 79.

7. Anton L. Allahar and James E. Cote. *The Structure of Inequality in Canada* (Toronto: James Lorimer and Company Ltd. 1998), p. 63. Using data for 1990, Feng Hou and T.R. Balakrishnan reach the same conclusion in "The Economic Integration of Visible Minorities in Contemporary Canadian Society" in *Social Inequality in Canada: Patterns, Problems, Policies*, 3rd ed., James Curtis, Edward Grabb, and Neil Guppy, eds. (Scarborough: Prentice Hall Allyn and Bacon Canada, 1999), p. 223.

8. Macionis et al., *Sociology*, p. 337.

9. Wallace Clement, *The Canadian Corporate Elite: An Analysis of Economic Power* (Ottawa: Carleton University Press, 1986), pp. 192, 364–65.

10. Picot and Heisz, "The Labour Market," p. 312.

11. Graham S. Lowe, "Labour Markets, Inequality, and the Future of Work," in *Social Inequality in Canada: Patterns, Problems, Policies*, 3rd ed., James Curtis, Edward Grabb, and Neil Guppy, eds. (Scarborough: Prentice Hall Allyn and Bacon Canada, 1999), p. 123.

12. Susan Crompton, "Left Behind: Lone Mothers in the Labour Market." *Perspectives* (Summer 1994): 23.

13. Statistics Canada, *Income Distributions by Size in Canada, 1997*, Catalogue No. 13-207-XPB, 1999.

14. Edward G. Grabb, *Theories of Social Inequality: Classical and Contemporary Perspectives* (Toronto: Holt, Rinehart, and Winston, 1990), p. 190.

15. Bryan S. Turner, *Equality* (London: Tavistock Publications, 1986), pp. 40–41.

16. This quotation appears in *Critique of the Gotha Programme*, by Karl Marx (Moscow: Progress Publishers, 1970).

17. James B. Davies, "The Distribution of Wealth and Economic Inequality" in *Social Inequality in Canada: Patterns, Problems, Policies*, 3rd ed., James Curtis, Edward Grabb, and Neil Guppy, eds. (Scarborough: Prentice Hall Allyn and Bacon Canada, 1999), p. 72.

18. Gillian Creese, Neil Guppy, and Martin Meissner, *Ups and Downs on the Ladder of Success* (Ottawa: Statistics Canada, 1991).

19. Joanne Naiman, *How Societies Work: Class, Power, and Change in a Canadian Context*, 2nd ed. (Toronto: Irwin Publishing, 2000), p. 224.

Race and Ethnicity: The Obvious Diversity

Paul U. Angelini and Michelle Broderick

We kept the blacks out and we did it in a peculiarly Canadian fashion—by pretending publicly that our immigration laws did not discriminate against anyone by reason of race, creed or colour while at the same time preventing all Negroes from crossing the border into Canada.

— Pierre Berton, *Why We Act Like Canadians*

We are all immigrants.

— common Canadian saying

Objectives

After reading this chapter, you should be able to

- sketch the diverse history of Canadian immigration

- outline the major determinants of personal and group identity and clarify the meaning and implications of the term "multiculturalism"

- analyze the most important factors that influence societal interaction

- appreciate the nature and seriousness of the problems and issues in race and ethnic relations in Canada

- talk about who you are in a manner that develops a positive self-image and acceptance of racial and ethnic differences

INTRODUCTION

Few issues can raise temperatures to such heights, with relative ease, as the issue of race and ethnic relations in Canadian society. Discussions inevitably lead to debates concerning what it means to be Canadian and how one becomes Canadian. From its very beginnings, Canada has been a multicultural and multiracial society. Sadly, this fact is frequently omitted from school curricula. As a result, Canadians tend to be largely ignorant of the history of immigration in Canada. It is assumed that British and French settlers "founded" Canada, irrespective of the Native Peoples who already occupied much of what we call North America. In fact, people from many parts of the world arrived on Canadian shores expecting to begin a prosperous life in a new land. People arrived from all over Europe, Asia, and the United States; people from all walks of life, including slaves and free people of colour. With so many different people arriving from so many different parts of the world, it is little wonder that Canada has experienced and is experiencing all the growing pains of so many different people living together. This does not mean we should accept some of the problems as "normal"; it simply means we should acknowledge them (past and present) and deal with them directly in the hope of not repeating what we have done in the past or are doing now. History does not repeat itself—human beings do!

The purpose of this chapter is to introduce students to the history of immigration to Canada, multiculturalism, identity, and the factors that affect interaction in Canadian society. The hope is to help students come to understand the challenges facing them in developing a society tolerant and accepting of cultural and racial differences.

A BRIEF HISTORY OF IMMIGRATION TO CANADA

Discussions concerning the merits of immigration to Canada are never far from debates on Canadian identity—what is a Canadian, who is a Canadian? One of the most widely held myths in Canada is the belief that Canada has always been a "white" British and French country; from its very beginnings, Canada has been multiethnic (see Box 4.1). A historical analysis of Canadian immigration patterns is essential if we are to have a thorough understanding of race and ethnic diversity in Canada.

In 1970 the Royal Commission on Bilingualism and Biculturalism outlined four distinct phases to Canada's immigration history.[1] Let us look briefly at each of these phases.

Stage 1: The Beginnings to 1901

Immigration to Canada before 1901 was slow. People came to Canada possessing many different skills and with quite different experiences: fishermen, farmers, merchants, traders, soldiers, adventurers, slaves, and fugitives. French and British immigrants were dominant

BOX 4.1

An Insidious Myth

··

The myth that Canada was and is a "white" country has no foundation in fact, yet it is part of our national consciousness. Writer Adrienne Shadd refers to this as an "insidious" myth. People tend to forget that Native Peoples were here first: black slaves were among the earliest to arrive in Canada during the seventeenth and eighteenth centuries; the Chinese presence in Canada dates back to the nineteenth century. A wide variety of races and nationalities helped to build Canada. This truth, however, is not properly reflected in school curricula.

Source: Carl E. James, *Seeing Ourselves: Exploring Race, Ethnicity and Culture*, 2nd ed. (Toronto: TEP, 1999), p. 160.

in terms of their numbers, cultural influences, and power, but they were not the only ones to arrive. Before 1800 or so only 10 percent of Canada's population was not British, French, or Native. More than half of all immigrants who arrived to Canada during the nineteenth century, however, were of German origins. Germans settled in New France and Nova Scotia, where fifteen hundred of them founded the Lunenburg settlement between 1750 and 1753. Germans also settled in other parts of the Maritimes and in what is today Quebec. German sectarians, including Mennonites, Moravians, and Tunkers, predominantly from the United States, came to Canada from about 1780 until well into the 1800s. In the middle of the nineteenth century, some of them settled in Ontario, especially in Waterloo County.

About 10 percent of the United Empire Loyalists who came to Canada after the American Revolution were black.[2] Some of these blacks were slaves that white owners brought with them. Contrary to popular myth, slavery did indeed exist in Canada (see Box 4.2). Moreover, between 1815 and 1860, forty- to sixty-thousand fugitive slaves and free people of colour arrived.[3] The Dutch and the Scandinavians were the only other large groups who came, accounting for less than 1 percent of the total immigration population at this time.

The extinction of the Native inhabitants of Newfoundland, the Beothuk, is almost universally forgotten. The tribe died out by the 1820s due to a combination of starvation (not having free access to their traditional fishing grounds), tuberculosis (which took a heavy toll), and being hunted for sport by the European settlers![4]

BOX 4.2

Slavery in Canada, Part I

....

TO BE SOLD,

A BLACK WOMAN, named
PEGGY, aged about forty years ; and a
Black boy her ſon, named JUPITER, aged
about fifteen years, both of them the property of the
Subſcriber.

The Woman is a tolerable Cook and waſher woman
and perfectly underſtands making Soap and Candles.

The Boy is tall and ſtrong of his age, and has been
employed in Country buſineſs, but brought up prin-
cipally as a Houſe Servant—They are each of them
Servants for life. The Price for the Wowan is one
hundred and fifty Dollars—for the Boy two hundred
Dollars, payable in three years with Intereſt from the
day of Sale and to be properly ſecured by Bond &c.—
But one fourth leſs will be taken in ready Money.

PETER RUSSELL.

York, Feb. 10th 1806.

Source: Daniel G. Hill, *Human Rights in Canada: A Focus on Racism* (Ottawa: Canadian Labour Congress, 1977), p. 3.

Stage 2: 1880–1918

Stage 2 is characterized by Europeans leaving Europe. So many left for the New World that these years have been described as "the mightiest movement of people in modern history."

As European society continued its evolution from a rural one to an urban one and as its population continued to grow, millions and millions decided to leave, hoping to find better opportunities for themselves elsewhere. Many went to the United States, South America (especially Argentina and Brazil), and, beginning in the late 1890s, Canada. By this time the federal government had decided to settle the empty Canadian West and was encouraging migration there.

CRITICAL THINKING BOX 4.1

··

Why is the existence of slavery in Canada not a well-known fact? Why is the existence of slavery in Canada not a standard part of high-school curricula? Did you know slavery existed in Canada? If so, where did you receive this information? If not, why?

Other factors, too, brought immigrants here: the closing of the American frontier, the Yukon gold rush, huge construction projects like the transcontinental railway, and new developments in farming technology all made Canada more attractive.

In 1913 alone more than 400 000 immigrants arrived, the largest number in any single year. Between 1896 and 1914 more than three million came to Canada. Of these, about 1 250 000 were from the United Kingdom and approximately one million from the United States. The important feature of this period was the arrival of people from Central and Eastern Europe, including Ukrainians, Poles, Hungarians, Romanians, and Russians. By 1921, 15 percent of Canada's population was neither of French nor of British origin.

The increased numbers for those groups already settled in Western Canada were nothing short of amazing. The population of German origin went from 46 800 in 1901 to 148 000 in 1911, and by 1931, 242 000 Germans were living in the Prairies. The Scandinavian population went from 17 300 in 1901 to 130 000 in 1921. The Ukrainian population increased almost twenty-fold, from 5600 in 1901 to 96 000 in 1921, and the population of Polish origin experienced similar growth, from 2800 in 1901 to 32 000 in 1921.

In the rest of Canada other groups also saw their numbers rise dramatically. The Italian population went from 11 000 in 1901 to 67 000 in 1921, and the Jewish from 16 100 to 126 000 in 1921. Other arrivals included Greeks, Syrians, Lebanese, and Armenians. Like the Italians and Jews, these immigrants preferred to settle in the cities of central Canada rather than the farming communities of the West.

Stage 2 also saw the imposition of the head tax on Chinese immigrants. (The racist treatment of Asian immigrants was to be repeated during World War II; the only difference was the target—this time it was Japanese-Canadians.) The head tax was intended to slow the arrival of Chinese. In 1885 it was set at $50. In 1900 it was set at $100. This tax, however, did not slow the influx of Chinese so the tax was increased to $500 per person, or head, in 1903.

The racist workings of the Canadian immigration policy did not stop there. In 1908 the government attempted to limit East Indian immigration by requiring that

CRITICAL THINKING BOX 4.2

....

Every immigrant entering Canada since 1995 must pay an "administrative fee" of $975. Since this is a flat tax, all must pay regardless of their ability to pay it. A refugee family of two adults and two children must pay $1950 in landing fees. If this same family makes their own way to Canada, they will have to pay an additional nonrefundable processing fee of $500 per adult and $100 per child. Is this fee really a head tax? Is it fair to ask immigrants to pay such a fee? What are the benefits and weaknesses of asking immigrants to pay such a fee? List three benefits and three weaknesses.

Source: Andrew Brouwer, "Protection with a Price Tag: The Head Tax for Refugees and Their Families Must Go," Caledon Institute of Social Policy, available online at <www.caledoninst.org/maytree/full03.htm>, accessed 18 February 2002.

anyone arriving from India had to do so by coming to Canada directly without stopping. This became known as the "direct passage" stipulation. In 1914, 376 Sikhs arrived from India directly—they did not stop at any other site during their voyage. Their ship, the *Komagata Maru*, was made to wait in Vancouver harbour for three months—before it was shamelessly turned away.[5]

In 1907, more than 8000 Japanese immigrants arrived in Canada, particularly in British Columbia. This heightened anti-Asian sentiment in B.C. and led to tighter restrictions on immigration. These feelings culminated in racial riots in September of that year. By 1921, 16 000 Japanese were living in Canada, 15 000 of them in B.C.

Chinese immigrants are always credited with having made a huge contribution to the building of Canada's railways. This accolade, however, often masks the exploitative and often brutal treatment they received during the building itself. Pierre Berton and others have remarked that there is one dead Chinese worker for every mile of rail laid. By 1921, there were 40 000 Chinese in Canada, 24 000 of them in British Columbia.

Stage 3: 1918–1945

Between World War I and II, immigration continued, but it never reached the explosive numbers of Stage 2. Between 1914 and 1939 the United States severely reduced the number of immigrants it would take, and this made Canada the favoured destination. But Canada, too, began to put restrictions on immigration. Whereas the United States chose to adopt a system based on quotas, Canada decided to make lists of countries that were

---

BOX 4.3

Slavery in Canada, Part II

....

Slavery did indeed exist in Canada. The first slave was brought to New France in 1628 from Madagascar. During and after the American Revolution, United Empire Loyalists brought slaves with them. At least six of sixteen members of the first Parliament of Upper Canada owned slaves.

Source: Daniel G. Hill, *Human Rights in Canada: A Focus on Racism* (Ottawa: Canadian Labour Congress, 1977), p. 7.

Slavery in Canada, Part III

....

In 1734, Marie-Joseph Angelique, a black female slave, burned down part of the city of Montreal after she was informed of her owner's intention to sell her.

Source: Carl E. James, *Seeing Ourselves: Exploring Race, Ethnicity and Culture*, 2nd ed. (Toronto: TEP, 1999), p. 161.

"preferred" or "nonpreferred." These categories usually excluded Chinese immigrants, for example, and severely limited others from Asia.

Stage 3 saw the campaign against Japanese and Chinese immigrants known as the campaign against the "Yellow Peril." A Chinese exclusion law was passed banning poor Chinese immigrants: it was not repealed until 1947.[6] By 1931 there was an increase of 19 000 Asians in Canada, bringing the total to 85 600, but the census of 1941 showed the number had declined to 74 000.

During the 1920s blacks also suffered from the racist nature of Canada's immigration policy. In the middle of the decade the government decided that a "British subject" would be defined as a citizen of a Commonwealth country whose population was predominantly white.

In the meantime, other ethnic groups continued to arrive. Between 1923 and 1930, 20 000 Swedes, 19 500 Norwegians, and 17 000 Danes immigrated to Canada.

The Great Depression essentially stopped immigration to Canada. Between 1931 and 1941 only 140 000 immigrants arrived. Some groups saw their numbers decline. The populations of German, Russian, and Asian origin in Canada declined by 9000, 4000, and

---

BOX 4.4

Maroons

....

Maroons were slaves originally stolen from Africa who escaped slavery and their British masters in Jamaica. The Maroons established settlements in the central mountains and hills of Jamaica and subsequently fought two wars against the white colonists. At the conclusion of the second war in 1795, many Maroons were deported to Nova Scotia and Sierra Leone.

Source: Harry Harmer, *The Longman Companion to Slavery, Emancipation and Civil Rights* (Toronto: Pearson Education Ltd., 2001), pp. 158, 168, and 203.

---

10 500, respectively. Throughout the war, Canada was reluctant to accept the victims of terror from Nazi Germany.

Stage 4: 1945–1974

Large numbers of people came to Canada after World War II. Between 1945 and 1961, 2 100 000 arrived. This was the most prolonged period of immigration in Canadian history. It was also the most diverse in terms of social class, ethnicity, and occupation. Large numbers of Italians, Germans, Poles, Jews, and Dutch came. Immigrants from Britain, however, accounted for the largest number—one third of the total.

Canada at this time began to experience all the benefits and problems associated with an advanced, industrialized, urban country. Not surprisingly, immigrants began to settle in cities and towns. Toronto became the favourite destination. By 1961, 42 percent of Toronto's population and one third of Metro Toronto's were not born in Canada. In fact, 29 percent of those living in Toronto and one third of those living in Metro Toronto arrived there between 1946 and 1961.

The largest wave of immigration in Stage 4 occurred between 1951 and 1960. In just nine years more than 250 000 Italians, for example, entered Canada. Like the Greeks and Portuguese, many of them left rural areas to settle in Canadian cities. These immigrants shared many other characteristics. They were largely unskilled, had no experience with city living, and had low levels of formal education. These three groups headed mostly for Toronto, where today they live in large recognizable communities.

The case of Italians living in Toronto is especially interesting. The Italian population of Metro Toronto now is estimated at more than 400 000, making it the largest Italian community outside of Italy.

This period is also remembered for its racist and brutal treatment of Japanese-Canadians. At the end of World War II, 4000 Japanese-Canadians were forced to leave Canada under a "repatriation" program. More than half had been born here, and more than two-thirds were Canadian citizens! How would it feel to know that your birthplace and citizenship mean nothing if the government decides to deprive you of your basic human rights? The story of Japanese-Canadians sent to internment camps, most of them in British Columbia—with only what they could carry and the remainder of their belongings being confiscated and sold by the government—now form an integral part of discussions of Canada and the war years. When released after the war was over, most of the internees left British Columbia, and, by 1961, 8000 Japanese-Canadians were living in Metro Toronto.

Although the Bilingualism and Biculturalism Report on Immigration ended its analysis in 1974, immigration to Canada did not. We can add a fifth stage to Canadian immigration history, largely as a result of the 1974 change in Canadian immigration policy away from seeking those with specific skills to satisfying the demands of the Canadian economy. As the economy changes, so do the skills demanded of immigrants.

Stage 5: 1975 to the Present

The dominant feature of Stage 5 is emigration from countries in the developing world. Low levels of economic development characterize these countries and the overwhelming majority of their populations are not white. The arrival of these people, who form racial minorities in Canada, has had a profound effect. With new immigrants arrive new challenges; this is especially true for their preferred destination, Metro Toronto.

The most reported origins of immigrants between 1991 and 1996 were Chinese, East Indian, Filipino, Sri Lanka, Polish, and Vietnamese[7] (see Table 4.1). In fact, between 1991 and 1996, almost 1 039 000 immigrants arrived in Canada: 57 percent were born in Asia.[8] Nearly a quarter of all immigrants arrived from Eastern Asia (Hong Kong, People's Republic of China). The next largest group was Southern Asia (Indian subcontinent). European immigrants accounted for 19 percent of the 1991–96 total, down significantly from 90 percent in the years before 1961. Before 1961, European immigrants arrived mainly from the United Kingdom, Italy, Germany, and the Netherlands (see Table 4.2). Between 1991and 1996, most European immigrants came from East European countries such as Poland, Romania, and Russia. Canada's mosaic is definitely becoming more colourful and educated (see Box 4.5).

Since the 1951 Census, immigrants have consistently composed approximately 16 percent of the Canadian population.

ETHNICITY, RACE, AND SOCIOLOGICAL THEORY

We will now examine three dominant theoretical approaches to society and how they differ with respect to what constitutes society, its development, and the various issues and problems about society that need to be discussed and debated.

Symbolic Interaction Theory

Interactionists believe that relations in society can be viewed by examining the communication and manipulation of symbols. Understanding race and ethnic relations and dealing with conflicts in society must be done by examining how each individual defines the situation he or she is in and how this definition is influenced by culture, race, and ethnicity. Interactionists ask questions such as how do members of different groups define the world around them? What role does language play in helping define the situation? Why do symbols play such an important part in race and ethnic relations?

Table 4.1 Top Ten Countries of Birth for Recent Immigrants to Canada, 1991–1996*

Country	Immigrants	
	Number	Percentage
1. Hong Kong	108 915	10.5
2. People's Republic of China	87 875	8.5
3. India	71 335	6.9
4. Philippines	71 325	6.9
5. Sri Lanka	44 235	4.3
6. Poland	36 964	3.6
7. Taiwan	32 140	3.1
8. Viet Nam	32 060	3.1
9. United States	29 020	2.8
10. United Kingdom	25 425	2.4
Total immigration from top 10 countries	539 294	52.1
Total immigration for this period	1 038 995	100.0

* Includes only the first four months of 1996.

Source: Statistics Canada, *The Daily*, available online at <www.statcan.ca/Daily/English/971104/d971104.htm>, accessed 18 February 2002.

Table 4.2 Top Ten Countries of Birth for All Immigrants to Canada, before 1961

| | Immigrants | |
Country	Number	Percentage
1. United Kingdom	265 575	25.2
2. Italy	161 730	15.3
3. Germany	107 270	10.2
4. Netherlands	88 810	8.4
5. Poland	57 820	5.5
6. United States	45 050	4.3
7. Hungary	33 215	3.1
8. Ukraine	27 640	2.6
9. Greece	21 555	2.0
10. People's Republic of China	17 545	1.7
Total immigration from top 10 countries	826 610	78.3
Total immigration for this period	1 054 930	100.0

Source: Statistics Canada, *The Daily*, available online at <www.statcan.ca/Daily/English/971104/d971104.htm>, accessed 18 February 2002.

Conflict Theory

Conflict theorists believe that power is the key to understanding interaction in society. Power, they argue, comes primarily from the ownership of those things necessary to produce goods in society, such as land, resources, buildings, machines, technology, and knowledge. Different groups in society, those who own things and those who do not, compete for power. Some groups attempt to change the status quo, whereas others work to preserve it. Conflict theorists ask questions such as why do some ethnic groups have more power than others? Do government policies such as multiculturalism and employment equity (affirmative action in the United States) really address the power imbalance in society, or, are they simply superficial modifications to prevent real changes to the distribution of power? Generally, conflict theorists believe a radical reorganization of the power structure in society is a prerequisite for stable race and ethnic relations.

Structural–Functionalist Theory

Structural–functionalists emphasize the importance of maintaining social order. In their analysis of race and ethnicity, they concentrate on the manner in which policies such as

---

BOX 4.5

The Brain Gain

....

Independent immigrants arriving in Canada must meet education and occupation-related criteria. In 1998, 72 percent of the skilled workers selected had university degrees. Even when their dependents 15 years of age and over are included, the number drops only slightly to 59.6 percent. This rate is more than four times the rate of university graduates among Canadian-born households (13.3 percent).

Source: Andrew Brouwer, "Immigrants Need Not Apply," Caledon Institute of Social Policy, available online at <www.caledoninst.org/maytree/full04.htm>, accessed 18 February 2002.

---

multiculturalism and affirmative action contribute to social order. Do stereotypes and prejudice have a negative effect on society? How do race and ethnic relations in Canada promote or destroy social order? These are common questions that a structural–functionalist might ask.

THE SOCIAL MEANING OF CULTURAL IDENTITY

Socially, a person's cultural identity comprises many different elements, including race, ethnicity, class, sex and gender, religion, region, occupation, language, country of origin, and sexual orientation. We will discuss two of the most crucial of these elements of identity: ethnicity and race.

Ethnicity

Your perception of your ethnicity is one of the most important elements of your identity. Many definitions of **ethnic groups** exist, and most of them have three common elements: (1) an ethnic group shares a common ancestry and history, (2) an ethnic group shares many norms, values, and traditions, and (3) an ethnic group is considered a group by those others who do not share the first two elements. We can define ethnic groups, therefore, as those who share several norms, values, and traditions; have a common ancestry and history; and are considered distinct by the rest of society because they share these elements.

Language is essential to the identity of any ethnic group, although not all ethnic groups require their members to share the same language. Without question language is the most crucial aspect of identity. It is the symbolic mode of communication we use to transmit ideas, information, and history from one generation to the next and to socialize the young. As the well-known sociologists Peter and Brigitte Berger put it: "Language provides the lifelong context of our experience of others, of self, of the world … it provides the most powerful hold that society has over us."[9] It is not surprising that language is such an important component of ethnicity.

Race

Race is the second major component of identity. Race is also one of the most misused and misunderstood words in the field of diversity. It has two separate meanings: (1) a biological meaning and (2) a sociological one.

From a biological perspective, we all belong to the same race—the human race. This simply means that all humans belong to one species. Therefore, all humans, regardless of which population they belong to, are genetically compatible. This in turn means that they can reproduce and produce viable (that is, fertile) offspring. As an example, a person of Inuit descent can produce fertile offspring with an individual of Australian Aboriginal descent. If humans were not compatible genetically, we would belong to different species and, therefore, be unable to reproduce fertile offspring. A horse and a donkey belong to different species and their offspring, known as a mule, is sterile and cannot reproduce. Because we all belong to the same species, we can reproduce regardless of what other humans we decide to have children with.

The meaning of the term "race" has three problems. First, race refers to subspecies. Most traits used to define subspecies, or races, vary along a continuum. But when we attempt to divide people into different races, we do so in a completely subjective and arbitrary way. Suppose we divide people according to skin colour and type of earwax (wet versus dry), inevitably some people would share both these traits and some would not. So how would we be able to divide people into specific racial categories?

The second problem with the question of race concerns interbreeding between populations. Humans are and always have been, even before the development of mass trans-

---

CRITICAL THINKING BOX 4.3

Which sociological theory do you believe best explains race and ethnic relations in Canada? List at least three reasons for your choice and explain each in detail.

BOX 4.6

Protection of the French Language: Bill 101 (1977) and Bill 178 (1988)

....

With the intention of protecting Francophone identity, successive Quebec governments have gone to great lengths to ensure the use and survival of the French language in Quebec and, ultimately, in Canada.

In 1977 the Parti Québécois government introduced Bill 101. Bill 101 reaffirmed that French would be the language of business and labour and restricted English-language schooling to two groups of people: (1) those whose parents were educated in English and (2) those who were already attending English-language schools. The target of Bill 101 was the immigrants arriving in Quebec who were sending their children to English schools and not to French ones.

In 1988 the Liberal government of Quebec introduced its own language bill, Bill 178. Known as the "sign law," it restricted the use of English-language signs in two ways: first, by not allowing English on outside signs and second, by legislating that the letters on French signs inside stores be three times larger than English ones.

---

portation, a very mobile species. This means it is virtually impossible to accurately assess the amount of interbreeding that has taken place between human populations. As a consequence of this, there are no true "pure" human races, and there probably never have been.

Finally, the third problem with the question of race has to do with its origins—where did this term come from? The concept of race is associated with a history of exploitation. When Europeans started to travel to new lands, the economic benefit of exploiting others became the driving force of European colonization. It was easier to exploit and abuse a population if they were viewed as less than human. Systems of classifying people that were developed hundreds of years ago arranged populations into a hierarchy with the best ("closest to God") being white and the less human ("furthest from God") being darker skinned—the darker the skin the further away from God. Sadly, this kind of thinking persists, even in the field of education, where researchers assert that some populations are not as intelligent as others are by virtue of their genes (genetic makeup).

Sociologically, our differing physical features are symbols that are accompanied by emotionally charged meanings. In short, physical features influence the way people see themselves and the way people interact. As Carl E. James has written: "Race is significant as long as groups are determined by selected physical traits, and as long as people act upon these meanings. However, we must bear in mind that race is largely based on its social meaning."[10]

It is important to understand the emotionally charged nature of physical symbols. Sociologically, race is part of everyone's life. Whites in Canada tend to take their skin colour for granted while at the same time they identify others by the colour of their skin.[11] Indeed, white people in Canada are in large part socially ignorant of the benefits of being white in a white-dominated society. Whites in Canada (the dominant group) define what is good, acceptable, excellent, and successful. In short, they have the power to define the standards by which all members of society are judged. "Whiteness" is generally associated with good and "blackness," with few exceptions, is associated with negativity, gloominess, pessimism, hostility, and evil[12] (see Box 4.7).

Over the years, many non-white students have identified incidents and situations where they have experienced different treatment when compared with white students of the same age. Students have sarcastically referred to these experiences as "special" treatment (see Box 4.8). Some common experiences of non-white students include being watched more closely when shopping in malls, being accused of public loitering when conversing in groups, having change slapped down on the counter rather than being handed

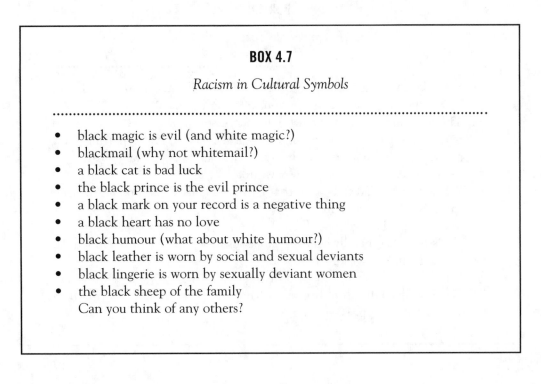

BOX 4.7

Racism in Cultural Symbols

- black magic is evil (and white magic?)
- blackmail (why not whitemail?)
- a black cat is bad luck
- the black prince is the evil prince
- a black mark on your record is a negative thing
- a black heart has no love
- black humour (what about white humour?)
- black leather is worn by social and sexual deviants
- black lingerie is worn by sexually deviant women
- the black sheep of the family
  Can you think of any others?

the change, being accused of being drug dealers when carrying pagers, and being served last in restaurants and bars.

To conclude, when we speak of identity, the social meaning of race takes precedence over the biological meaning. Biologically speaking, race is an outmoded and archaic concept.

ATTITUDES AND BEHAVIOURS THAT AFFECT SOCIAL INTERACTION

Many factors play a negative role in social interaction, including prejudice, discrimination, racism, and ethnocentrism.

Prejudice

Prejudice is the attitude of prejudging people based on statements and beliefs that do not hold up to rational or critical scrutiny. Prejudice occurs when, in spite of evidence to the contrary, a person still holds negative feelings and opinions toward other people and

---

BOX 4.8

Other Examples of "Special" Treatment

- Schools teach the history of British and French people in Canada but ignore the history and contributions of other people.
- The few minority members who are successful in the field of television news are concentrated in sports, weather, and traffic reporting. Few minorities are prime-time anchors for national news programs.
- Politicians in Canada are usually white.
- White people tend to believe that there is a "black" culture but no such thing as a "white" culture.
- Many people believe that all blacks in Canada are from Jamaica.
- White people generally believe that people from the subcontinent (India, Pakistan, and Bangladesh) are poor.

For a similar but more focused discussion see Peggy McIntosh, "White Privilege: Unpacking the Invisible Knapsack," in *Peace and Freedom* (July/August 1989), pp. 10–12.

CRITICAL THINKING BOX 4.4

How many events of "white privilege" have you witnessed or experienced recently? Why are whites largely ignorant of such "privileges"? Give at least three reasons.

groups. Prejudgments are seldom based on experience. Carl E. James has written, "The tendency to make prejudgments may be seen as necessary, as the human mind needs to organize the stimuli with which it is bombarded."[13] In many respects prejudging is accepted and expected in a world where the amount of knowledge understood by the human race is said to double every five years. Prejudging seems to make a complicated world easier to deal with. It is not surprising, therefore, that prejudice is a universal phenomenon and a common problem in social interaction.

The human tendency to put things into groups or categories is clearly visible when we speak of **stereotypes**. A stereotype can be defined as a collection of generalizations about a group of people that are negative, exaggerated, and cannot be maintained when subjected to critical analysis. Some common stereotypes include the following:

- All Italians belong to the Mafia.
- All blacks are criminals.
- All Aboriginals are drunks.
- All Sikhs drive taxis.
- All Pakistanis own corner stores.
- All Jews are cheap.

The key feature that explains the attractiveness of stereotypes is that they are overly simplistic. Minority groups have continually complained of their stereotypical treatment by the mass media.

Discrimination

Prejudice is the attitude, and **discrimination** is the action. Discrimination can be defined as the unequal or unfavourable treatment of people because of their perceived or actual membership in a particular ethnic group that restricts their full participation in Canadian society. When discrimination is carried out based on race (people who share physical characteristics) and when common behaviour is assumed (that people who share certain physical characteristics behave in a certain way), we call this **racism** (see Box 4.9). Many regard the denial of Aboriginal land claims and self-government as a form of racism. Land claims and self-government are crucial to Aboriginal identity and survival—to regain control over their traditional land, including access to all resources, especially hunting and fishing rights. Others point to the 1999 Nisga'a agreement as a model for future agreements with Aboriginal people (see Box 4.10). The treatment of the Nisga'a contrasts sharply with Ottawa's treatment of the Mi'kmaq.

There are two types of discrimination, individual and institutional. **Individual discrimination** is perhaps the most common type, but, as we will see, it may not be the most damaging. Examples of such individual actions include refusing to sit next to or associate with members of minority groups while in public places; giving or receiving poor or slow service in restaurants and stores; refusing to date people from outside your ethnic or racial group; and, finally, discouraging your children from developing friendships with people from outside your ethnic or racial group. Sometimes individual discrimination takes the form of what Daniel Hill called "nice guy" discrimination.[14] This means people will act in a discriminatory manner and justify it according to the potential for negative reactions from others. So, for example, you don't hire members of minority groups for fear that other workers may "rebel" and not accept them.

The second type, **institutional discrimination**, occurs daily and limits the full participation of minority groups in the political, economic, and educational institutions in Canada. Some debate exists about the racist nature of this form of discrimination. The consensus seems to be that the intent is not racist but the outcomes certainly are. This is especially true of the people who work in these institutions—they are usually unaware of the outcomes of their institutional policies and practices.

An example of this form of discrimination is hiring practices. In 1989, racial minorities composed only 4 percent of the Metro Toronto Police Force.[15] These officers were highly concentrated in the ranks of cadets, constables, or in training; only three held the rank of inspector.[16] By 1998, gains by racial minorities were insignificant: Only three

CRITICAL THINKING BOX 4.5

Are jokes based on racial and ethnic stereotypes "just jokes," or do they reinforce negative attitudes and beliefs and in the process destroy self and group esteem? Why are these jokes so popular? Give at least three reasons and explain them.

BOX 4.9

Racism in the Canadian Justice System

....

The existence of racism in the Canadian Justice System was acknowledged by the minister of state for multiculturalism and citizenship in 1990, the Law Reform Commission of Canada in 1992, and the Law Reform Commission on Systemic Racism in the Ontario Criminal Justice System in 1995. The report of the latter concluded that blacks constitute just less than 3 percent of the population of Ontario but 15 percent of the prison population.

The same is true for Aboriginal Peoples who compose about 3.7 percent of the Canadian population and 2 percent of the adult general population, yet composed 17 percent of the federal prison population in 1998.

Sources: Frances Henry et al, *The Colour of Democracy: Racism in Canadian Society*, 2nd ed., (Toronto: Harcourt Brace, 2000), p. 147; "Prison Population and Costs," *Juristat*, 1997/1998, released 6 April 1999.

---

held the rank of staff inspector, only three were senior police officers, and only 7.4 percent of all uniformed employees were racial minorities.[17] Yet, by 2005, racial minorities will compose well over 50 percent of Metropolitan Toronto's population.

Another example of institutional discrimination includes textbook selection in schools, marketing, advertising, minimum levels of education for hiring, and cultural biases in aptitude or qualification tests. During the 1970s, the reading texts for the primary grades in Ontario schools were the *Mr. Mugs* series. The series centred entirely on a white, middle-class family. Small wonder that in 1971 a report on the study of four hundred textbooks in Ontario, entitled *Teaching Prejudice*,[18] painted an unflattering picture of textbooks used in Ontario schools (see Box 4.11).

Ethnocentrism

Ethnocentrism is the attitude whereby an individual views the world from the point of view of his or her own culture. There are two variations of ethnocentrism: (1) the assumption that what is true of your culture is true of other cultures and (2) the belief in the superiority of your culture in comparison with other cultures. The most common form of ethnocentrism is the first. It is embodied in statements that question why certain cultures do not behave or do things in the same manner as your own culture does. Statements of this nature would include variations of: "Why don't they do it like this ... [meaning, like we do]?" "That's a strange way of doing things." "They're weird." Ethnocentric attitudes

---

BOX 4.10

The Nisga'a Treaty, 2000

....

In 1999, the Nisga'a of the Nass Valley signed a historic agreement with the government of British Columbia that was greeted with great applause in Aboriginal communities across Canada. The Nisga'a were granted limited rights to self-government, including the ability to make laws (provided those laws do not supersede the laws of Parliament). In the areas of language and culture, Nisga'a laws will supersede provincial ones. They were also awarded

- 1930 km^2 of land
- a share of the catch of the Nass River
- fishing and forestry rights outside the Nass Valley
- $200 million as a financial settlement
- $40 million for road building in and around the Nass Valley
- the right to deliver federal and provincial social services
- the right to establish an Aboriginal government, police, and judicial system but not to pass laws that supersede Parliament

---

definitely influence social interaction, and, furthermore, many ethnocentric attitudes and beliefs are held unconsciously.

THE MEANING AND IMPLICATIONS OF MULTICULTURALISM

Multiculturalism is one of the most used and most misunderstood words in the field of ethnicity. It has many definitions and explanations; some focus on the concept of culture, some on the ideology on which it is based, and still others refer to it in terms of government policy.

Multiculturalism is commonly associated with the idea of the "Canadian mosaic"—the view that different cultural groups come to Canada, retain their language and culture, and still become Canadian. It is not uncommon to consider yourself a hyphenated Canadian: French-Canadian, Greek-Canadian, Ukrainian-Canadian, Jamaican-Canadian, and the like. The concept of hyphenated citizenship is at odds with what has prevailed in the United States, where people are expected to abandon their heritage culture and assimilate into the dominant one. Thus, U.S. society is termed a "melting pot."

BOX 4.11

Teaching Prejudice in 1971

....

Non-white groups were frequently referred to as bloodthirsty, primitive, cruel, and savage, in contrast with saintly and refined Europeans. With only a few passing exceptions, Aboriginals, blacks, and Asians who contributed to Canadian development in significant and positive ways were omitted from reference. In addition, major events in the sad history of Canada's mistreatment of minorities—the extinction of the Beothuk, the treatment of Japanese-Canadians during World War II, the abuse of Métis and Indians throughout Canada—were barely touched, if at all.

Source: From *Teaching Prejudice*, as quoted in Daniel G. Hill, *Human Rights in Canada: A Focus on Racism* (Ottawa: Canadian Labour Congress, 1977), p. 15. Reproduced by permission.

Perhaps one of the best attempts to define this complicated word is provided by Fleras and Elliott. They combine the cultural and ideological components with the reality of government policy for an all-inclusive definition. According to Fleras and Elliott, multiculturalism is "a doctrine that provides a political framework for the official promotion of cultural differences and social inequality as an integral component of social order."[19]

Multiculturalism is based on the ideology of **pluralism**, which is the belief that ethnic diversity and conflict remain central features of modern industrial societies and that ethnicity continues to be an essential aspect of individual identity and of group behaviour. The implications of the acceptance of pluralism are threefold. First, pluralism recognizes that cultural and racial conflict is inevitable and unavoidable; at best we can only hope to

CRITICAL THINKING BOX 4.6

....

How do, or did, your high-school and postsecondary school texts compare with the standards of *Teaching Prejudice*? What about the newspaper you read, the news programs you watch, or the movies you see at the theatre and rent at the video store?

manage and mitigate this conflict as opposed to pursuing some fantasy of eliminating it. Second, pluralism recognizes that people hold on to their cultural heritage with much passion and commitment; therefore, to better manage cultural conflict, we must openly acknowledge and accept cultural differences. Third, pluralism is the belief that pursuing a multicultural policy is beneficial to Canadian unity, for it strengthens Canada and enriches the Canadian experience, especially in the fields of literature and the arts. In addition, pluralism lets Canadians know that they are part of a larger global community where we all must communicate and cooperate with each other if we are to survive.

Pluralism is the opposite of **assimilation**. Assimilation is the process by which immigrants adopt the language, values, norms, and worldview of the host culture. All immigrants experience some degree of assimilation. Immigrant cultures cannot totally insulate or isolate themselves from the influences of the host society—this is especially true of immigrant children, because children must attend school. The education system is perhaps the single most persuasive assimilationist force that immigrants are exposed to. While in school, immigrant children are socialized to the complete worldview of the host culture: its history, accomplishments, values, norms, customs, biases, and prejudices. Some assimilation on the part of immigrants is an inevitable fact of immigration and, thus, never completely avoidable.

The Purpose of Multiculturalism

The response of the federal government to the history of immigrant experiences with prejudice, racism, discrimination, stereotyping, and the like has been to officially recognize the racial and ethnic diversity in Canada and to support and encourage Canadians to learn more about the people of Canada and the country itself. For decades the federal government has encouraged the acceptance of different cultures through various policies and initiatives broadly labelled as "multicultural." In 1988, Parliament officially enacted the *Multiculturalism Act*. The Act pledges federal government assistance "in bringing about equal access and participation for all Canadians in the economic, social, cultural and political life of the nation."[20]

To achieve these goals the Act outlines ten specific objectives (see Box 4.12). The objectives have much consistency; we can narrow the list to three general goals:

1. The promotion of both official languages. The federal government declares that multiculturalism will be pursued within a bilingual, English and French, framework.

2. A commitment to help all members of cultural groups to overcome barriers that limit their full participation in Canadian society.

3. The promotion of understanding among different groups and the acceptance of cultural differences.

Multiculturalism is not the only government initiative designed to promote equality and equity. Other initiatives of the federal and provincial governments include the introduction of a *Charter of Rights and Freedoms* with the repatriated Constitution of 1982, human rights commissions, and employment equity programs (see Box 4.13).

With these ideas in mind, Canadians need to come to consensus concerning the purpose of multiculturalism. Too many people believe, with encouragement from the media, that multiculturalism is supposed to cure all problems in society that are a result of numerous different cultures living in close proximity to each other. Nothing could be further from the truth. The reality of multiculturalism, as government policy, is about the *management* of racial and ethnic conflict. It is not about the *elimination* of such conflict, which is unrealistic. Cultural conflict can be better managed if all groups share the same degree of cultural freedom. The more all groups feel they are free to live in and promote their culture; the more they will respect the culture of other members of society.

Employment Equity in a Multicultural Society

In 1986 the federal government introduced the *Employment Equity Act*. It affects all employees of the federal government and federally regulated industries. The purpose of the Act is to promote the equality of opportunity for four groups of workers: racial minorities, Native Peoples, women, and people with disabilities. The Act is based on the reality that these groups have historically been discriminated against in the labour market. Section 15.2 of the *Charter of Rights and Freedoms* protects employment equity.

Employment equity programs are considered by many to be the most effective way of reversing at least a century of discriminatory hiring practices that favoured white males. The dominant group has vigorously opposed such programs. Some of the more popular reasons cited for resisting such programs include that equity programs are reverse discrimination, that they ignore the merit principle, and that they ignore the belief that fairness is best achieved by treating everyone the same[21] (see Box 4.13). Yet, as Tator et al. point out, each of these reasons cannot stand up to critical scrutiny.[22] First, are such programs really reverse discrimination or urgently necessary to correct at least a century of preferential treatment of the dominant group, especially white males? Are white males the *only* qualified applicants? Second, do they really ignore the merit principle or simply choose to disregard personal characteristics that do not affect job performance, such as cultural background, skin colour, gender, and family/friendship networks? Third, does treating everyone fairly translate into equal treatment? Or does ignoring and refusing to accommodate ultimately lead to discrimination?[23]

Although employment equity programs are important, it is highly unlikely that they can achieve their goals without the implementation of other measures, such as institutions making individuals accountable for discriminatory and racist behaviour; sanctioning

BOX 4.12

Objectives of the Canadian Government's Policy of Multiculturalism

1. Recognize and promote the understanding that multiculturalism reflects the cultural and racial diversity of Canadian society and acknowledges the freedom of all members of Canadian society to preserve, enhance, and share their cultural heritage.
2. Recognize and promote the understanding that multiculturalism is a fundamental characteristic of Canadian heritage and identity and that it provides an invaluable resource in the shaping of Canada's future.
3. Promote the full and equitable participation of individuals and communities of all origins in the continuing evolution and shaping of all aspects of Canadian society and assist them in the elimination of any barrier to such participation.
4. Recognize the existence of communities whose members share a common origin and their historic contribution to Canadian society, and enhance their development.
5. Ensure that all individuals receive equal treatment and equal protection under the law, while respecting and valuing their diversity.
6. Encourage and assist the social, cultural, economic, and political institutions of Canada to be both respectful and inclusive of Canada's multicultural character.
7. Promote the understanding and creativity that arise from the interaction between individuals and communities of different origins.
8. Foster the recognition and appreciation of the diverse cultures of Canadian society and promote the reflection and the evolving expressions of those cultures.
9. Preserve and enhance the use of languages other than English and French, while strengthening the status and use of the official languages of Canada.
10. Advance multiculturalism throughout Canada in harmony with the national commitment to the official languages of Canada.

Source: *The Canadian Multiculturalism Act: A Guide For Canadians* (Ottawa: Multiculturalism and Citizenship Canada, 1990), pp. 13–15.

those who behave in unacceptable ways; and being committed to devoting significant resources to combating discrimination and racism even in difficult economic times.[24]

CONCLUSION

Race and ethnicity are powerful determinants of identity in Canadian society, and it is important to understand the nature and depths of the problems associated with developing stable relations in a society characterized by racial and ethnic difference. The nature and composition of Canada is changing. New immigrants are arriving from the developing world, especially from Asia and the Indian subcontinent. Like those who came between 1991 and 1996, they settle primarily in the urban areas of Ontario, Quebec, Alberta, and British Columbia.

Canada is not the same country today that it was fifty years ago—nor will it be the same fifty years from now. The challenge is to ensure that the social institutions that serve our society reflect the people they serve. This must be done in a manner that accepts the cultural, linguistic, and racial diversity of all Canadians—it will be difficult. Prejudice, racism, and discrimination seem to be part of every society, and it may be naive to think that we can eliminate them. We must, however, work to manage them in a productive manner so that all Canadians can develop a positive self-image and a more complete understanding of our country.

CHAPTER SUMMARY

It is almost impossible to overstate the importance of race and ethnic relations in Canada. An analysis of Canadian immigration history is crucial for a complete understanding of Canadian society and to destroy prevalent myths. Canada has never been just a purely British and French, white society—Aboriginal peoples were here, and other people arrived and continue to come from all over the world. In the early nineteenth century this included black slaves and in later decades Chinese and Japanese people as well. Immigrants from the developing, non-white world continue to arrive in Canada in large numbers—the Canadian mosaic is becoming ever more colourful.

Race and ethnicity are important components of individual and group identity. Meanwhile, prejudice, racism, stereotyping, ethnocentrism, and discrimination continue to have a strong negative impact on social interaction. Therefore, a policy of official multiculturalism has been enacted to help manage social interaction in Canada.

BOX 4.13

Employment Equity and Toronto Firefighters

....

In the 1990s, more than 90 percent of the employees of the Toronto Fire Department were white males. To help the department better reflect the community they serve, the personnel committee of the Toronto City Council recommended that the department give preference to thirteen *qualified* women and racial-minority candidates, ahead of white men who scored slightly higher during the qualification process. The chief of the department protested vigorously even though the thirteen candidates were drawn from a total pool of 140 fully qualified candidates selected from four-thousand applicants; all candidates had passed the physical, health, and aptitude tests. The motion to hire these candidates was defeated by city council. The Ontario Human Rights Commission filed a complaint, claiming that the Toronto firefighters' union was blocking the proposal and creating a "poisoned work environment."

Source: Frances Henry et al., *The Colour of Democracy: Racism in Canadian Society*, 2nd ed., (Toronto: Harcourt Brace, 2000), p. 364.

KEY TERMS

assimilation, p. 108

discrimination, p. 103

ethnic groups, p. 98

ethnocentrism, p. 105

individual discrimination, p. 104

institutional discrimination, p. 104

multiculturalism, p. 106

Multiculturalism Act, p. 108

pluralism, p. 107

prejudice, p. 102

race, p. 99

racism, p. 104

stereotypes, p. 103

DISCUSSION QUESTIONS

1. What stage of immigration is known as "the mightiest movement of people" in modern history? What accounted for this mass movement of people?
2. What is the significance of the fifth stage (1975 to the present) of Canadian immigration history?

3. Define prejudice and discrimination. What is the difference between them?
4. What do we mean by race and ethnicity? Why are these ideas so important to Canadians? Provide some examples.
5. How does conflict theory account for the existence of racism and discrimination?
6. How would structural–functionalism interpret Canada's policy of multiculturalism?

NOTES

1. "Report of the Royal Commission on Bilingualism and Biculturalism, Book IV, The Contributions of other Ethnic Groups," in *Immigration and the Rise of Multiculturalism*, Howard Palmer, ed. (Toronto: Copp Clark, 1975), pp. 1–16. Unless otherwise noted, all statistics and examples of historical events are drawn from these pages.
2. Adrienne Shadd, "Institutionalized Racism and Canadian History: Notes of a Black Canadian," in *Seeing Ourselves: Exploring Race, Ethnicity and Culture*, Carl E. James, ed. (Toronto: TEP, 1999) pp. 159–62.
3. Ibid.
4. Ninette Kelly and Michael Trebilcock, *The Making of the Mosaic: A History of Canadian Immigration Policy* (Toronto: UTP, 1998), p. 36
5. Daniel G. Hill, *Human Rights In Canada: A Focus On Racism* (Ottawa: Canadian Labour Congress, 1977), p. 10.
6. Harry Hiller, *Canadian Society: A Macro Analysis* (Toronto: Prentice Hall, 2000), p. 174.
7. Statistics Canada, *The Daily*, available online at <www.statscan.ca/Daily/English/971104/d971104.htm>, accessed 18 February 2002.
8. Ibid.
9. Peter Berger and Brigitte Berger, *Sociology: A Biographical Approach* (New York: Basic Books, 1971), p. 75.
10. Carl E. James, *Seeing Ourselves: Exploring Race, Ethnicity and Culture* (Toronto: TEP, 1999), pp. 41–42.
11. Ibid., p. 42.
12. P. Essed, *Everyday Racism: Reports from Women of Two Cultures* (Claremont, CA: Hunter House, 1990).
13. James, op. cit., p. 133.
14. Hill, *Human Rights in Canada*, p. 13.
15. Frances Henry et al., *The Colour of Democracy: Racism in Canadian Society*, 2nd ed. (Toronto: Harcourt Brace, 2000), p. 105.
16. Ibid.
17. Ibid.
18. Hill, op. cit., p. 13.
19. Augie Fleras and Jean Leonard Elliott, *Multiculturalism in Canada: The Challenge of Diversity* (Scarborough: Nelson, 1992), p. 272.
20. *The Multiculturalism Act*, 21 July 1988.
21. Henry et al., op. cit., pp. 364–65.

22. Ibid., pp. 364–66.
23. R. Abella, *Report of the Commission on Equality in Employment* (Ottawa: Supply and Services Canada, 1984), p. 3.
24. Henry et al., op. cit., pp. 366–75. An excellent discussion.

Aboriginal Peoples

John Steckley

Several years ago in a sociology class on social problems, I recall wondering if anyone else was poor, because the professor repeatedly referred to Native people as statistical examples of poverty.... Not for one moment would I make light of the ugly effects of poverty. But if classroom groups must talk about Indians and poverty, then they must also point out the ways in which Native people are operating on this cancer. To be sure, the operations are always struggles and sometimes failures, but each new operation is faced with more experience, more skill, more confidence and more success.

— Métis writer Emma LaRoque, "Three Conventional
Approaches to Native People" (1993:212)

Objectives

After reading this chapter, you should be able to

- understand better the diversity of Canadian Native culture

- understand the historical background and development of Native issues and contemporary circumstances

- understand the extent to which Natives are in different legal circumstances than are other Canadians

- understand the negative impact on Natives of official policies in the areas of education, religion, and the justice system

- understand some of the strengths and challenges of a Native-run justice system

INTRODUCTION

Knowing about Native Canadian people takes years. There is so much to learn, so little of which can be presented in a short chapter. First, we need to appreciate the incredible length of time that Native people have been in Canada—that is the key to understanding a lot. Not all Natives are the same, be that in terms of traditions and such cultural features as language, housing, and food preferences, or in other ways. There are rich Natives and poor ones. There are Native alcoholics, but also those who have never had a drink or who just have a couple of beers "with the guys," like most other Canadians. Some Native people adhere to traditional religious ways, and others make Christianity a "traditional" Native belief system. There are Native hunters and trappers, and Native computer programmers, too.

Much, however, is held in common. Native people share a genetic heritage, an identity, and a complex set of legal regulations that both serve and restrict them. Abolishing those laws—basically one law, the **Indian Act**—or keeping them as they are will not create solutions. Redefining these laws is the only answer, but it will be difficult. The question is not one of giving Native people a separate status, but of taking the separate status that now exists and changing it for the good of Native people—and for all Canadians.

BEGINNINGS: IT ALL STARTED LONG AGO

No one knows how long ago the Native people of Canada first walked on these lands. Anthropologists say that people came across to the Americas from Asia, sometime when the last Ice Age lowered the water level of the oceans so much that there was a land bridge, some thousand kilometres wide, connecting Siberia to Alaska. Native traditions tell us that they were placed here by the Creator and that they lived nowhere else before. Either way, Canada's Native peoples are First Nations. The great length of time that Native people have been here means that they have very deep roots in this country. From these roots have grown their sense of the sacredness of the land, their feeling of being its primary caretakers.

Many feel that Native people have been in the Americas for at least 20 000 years. If this hypothesis is accurate, then 95 percent of Canadian history is the history of Native people before contact, for the first Europeans to visit Canada (the Vikings) came here only about 1000 years ago. Picture in your mind what 95 percent looks like by imagining Canadian history as taking one year. If Native people arrived here just after the clock struck twelve on New Year's Eve, then Europeans did not get here until 12 December, around dinnertime. Permanent European settlement did not begin in Canada (in Newfoundland and Quebec) until about four hundred years ago—in our historical year that would make the time of such settlement late in the afternoon of 23 December.

THEORY

What is the place of Native people in Canadian history since contact? This question can be answered from several different theoretical positions. One is the structural–functionalist position of looking just at how Natives helped this country develop. Take the example of the fur trade. During the first two centuries of postcontact history, the fur trade was the biggest industry in Canada, and Native people played a key role in it, as both suppliers and intermediaries. Furthermore, the newcomers needed to learn how to survive here. Natives enabled them to travel by providing canoes, snowshoes, and directions. Natives taught the newcomers how to feed themselves, instructing them in how to grow Native crops that were new to Europeans—corn, beans, and squash—and by showing them which berries and other wild foods were edible. They instructed the Europeans in how to hunt animals that were unfamiliar to them, such as moose and raccoon. In the wars of the seventeenth and eighteenth centuries Native allies helped to ensure that whoever governed Canada, first the French and then the British, could stave off the forces from what is now the United States. In the War of 1812, the role of Aboriginal nations such as the Mohawk, Ojibwa, and Wyandot was critical to the survival of the colony that was to become Canada. And in the twentieth century, in both world wars, Natives were proportionately among the highest groups represented in our armed forces.

To stop here would be to paint too rosy a picture of the interaction of Natives and newcomers. A conflict theory approach would emphasize that although the role of Natives in the fur trade often started between equals, exploitation of the Natives eventually developed, particularly with the introduction of alcohol in the trade. At the Hudson's Bay Company (HBC) trading post of York Factory, on the west side of Hudson Bay, the amount of rum traded per year hit a peak of 3928 litres by 1753. Between 1720 and 1774, the HBC traded 98 346 litres of rum from that post alone. Conflict theorists would denounce the clear manipulation of the treaties and the other "legal" but morally questionable means by which Natives were removed from their lands, the cultural prejudice that led to the banning of traditional ceremonies from late in the nineteenth century until 1951, and the destructive effects of the residential schools, a feature of the twentieth century.

DIVERSITY: THE MANY TONGUES OF NATIVE CULTURES

At the time of first contact with Europeans, Native cultures in Canada were very diverse. This diversity can be seen, for example, in the foods the different peoples ate and in the size of their houses. Although all the Native peoples hunted, fished, and gathered foods to a certain extent, some, along the St. Lawrence River and in southern Ontario, also engaged in agriculture. They cultivated and had as the greater part of their diet corn, beans, and squash. Some Native peoples lived in single-family dwellings such as the familiar wigwams, tepees, and igloos. Others, however, in British Columbia and Ontario, lived in long, narrow buildings, some of which stretched more than 100 metres long and served as multihousehold "apartment buildings" for very extended families. Maquinna, a powerful Nootka (a west coast nation) leader early in the nineteenth century, had a house that was forty-five metres long, perhaps nearly twelve metres wide, and about forty-three metres high. Around one hundred people were said to call that house their home.

Language is a good tool with which to illustrate the diversity of Native culture in Canada. Today roughly fifty Native languages still have people who can speak them, although this number is decreasing. Native languages in Canada have a greater diversity than in Europe: Canadian Native languages form eleven separate groups; eight are **language families** or groupings of related languages, and three are **language isolates**, with no known relatives. Europe has only two language families (Indo-European and Finno-Ugric) and one language isolate (Basque).

The largest language family is Algonquian, which has languages in every province. The family includes two widespread languages with a good number of speakers. Ojibwa (including Saulteaux, Mississauga, Algonquin, and Odawa) is spoken by thousands of speakers from Quebec to British Columbia. Cree, from which two provinces take their names (Saskatchewan, "fast-flowing water," and Manitoba, "spirit strait") likewise has thousands of speakers, and they live from Quebec to Alberta. The other languages are more regionally restricted, with Mi'kmaq spoken in the Atlantic provinces and Quebec (which means "it narrows" in Mi'kmaq), Maliseet in New Brunswick, Innu (Montagnais and Naskapi) in Labrador and Quebec, Blackfoot (Blackfoot, Blood, and Peigan) in Alberta, Abenaki in Quebec, and Delaware in Ontario.

A feature unique to this family is the distinction between **animate** and **inanimate**, which roughly approximates the distinction alive and not-alive, but with distinct cultural twists (e.g., in Blackfoot, Ojibwa and Delaware, strawberries and leaves are inanimate, but ice and kettles are animate). This feature touches almost every word in the language, affecting primarily noun plurals and verb endings (see Box 5.1).

Athabaskan languages are found in the four western provinces, the Northwest Territories and Yukon Territory and include Beaver, Carrier, Chilcotin, Chipewyan, Dogrib, Han, Hare, Kaska, Gwich'in, Sarcee, Sekani, Slavey, Tagish (now extinct), Tahltan, and Tutchone.

The Eskimo-Aleut family, which includes the various distinctive dialects of Inuktitut in Canada, is found across the North, in all three territories, and in Labrador and Quebec.

The Iroquoian family, whose languages gave Canada its name (meaning "village" in the extinct language of St. Lawrence Iroquoian), as well as the names for its most populous province (Ontario, "it is a large lake" in Huron) and city (Toronto, "poles in water" in Mohawk) comprises the languages of the six nations of the Iroquois Confederacy (Mohawk, Oneida, Onondaga, Cayuga, Seneca, and Tuscarora), which are spoken in Ontario and Quebec.

The Siouan family, distantly related to Iroquoian, includes two languages spoken in the Prairies, Nakota or Assiniboine and Dakota.

British Columbia has the greatest Native language diversity in Canada. Found in that province but no other are the Salishan languages (Bella Coola, Comox, Halkomelem, Lillooet, Okanagan, Pentlatch, Sechelt, Semiahmo, Shuswap, Squamish, Straits, and Thompson), the Wakashan languages (Haisla, Heiltsuk, Kwakwala, Nitinat, and Nootka), the two Tsimshian languages, and language isolates Haida, Kutenai, and Tlingit (which is spoken also in Yukon).

DEMOGRAPHICS

Historical Picture

The number of Native people in Canada at the time of first contact is estimated to have been between five hundred thousand and two million. Canada was "full" of people then. All parts of the country were lived in or used. The areas of greatest population were where Canada's three largest cities of Vancouver, Toronto, and Montreal are now. The Pacific coast, with its rich forests and rich marine resources of fish, seals, sea otters, shellfish, and whales, had the largest groups, perhaps totalling some two hundred thousand people in what is now British Columbia. Groups in southern Ontario and the area along the St. Lawrence River in Quebec, where Native people grew crops, fished, and hunted deer, were next largest, numbering probably more than sixty thousand.

Why, then, did so many eighteenth- and nineteenth-century European writers refer to the great open "empty" lands of Canada? Much of the country had been emptied by disease. Europeans who came to Canada carried with them, unknowingly, diseases that they had endured for centuries. But Natives had not experienced these afflictions before, and their bodies had not built up immunities with which to combat them. Native people became easy victims of smallpox, influenza, scarlet fever, whooping cough, typhus, measles, and tuberculosis. With deadly efficient regularity, most of a Native nation would die within a few years of first contact with Europeans.

BOX 5.1

Animate and Inanimate: A Unique Characteristic of Algonquian Languages

In East Cree (spoken in Quebec), animate plurals end with *-ak*, while inanimate plurals end with *-a*. The following are examples:

awasis	child	*awasisak*	children
eskan	antler	*eskanak*	antlers
maskisin	shoe	*maskina*	shoes
kaapaashtepaich	dryer	*kaapaashtepaicha*	dryers

Verb endings are affected as well:

Milwasisiw awasis	(S)he is a good child
Milwasin maskisin	It is a good shoe
Niwapamaw awasis	I see a child
Niwapahten maskisin	I see a shoe

The greatest killer was smallpox. It swept west gradually, but relentlessly, killing people in unbelievably high numbers. In the 1630s it hit the Montagnais, Algonkian, and Huron. The Huron lost perhaps two thirds of their population in just four years. During the 1770s Prairie Natives were mowed down like so much wheat. In 1776–77 the victims included such peoples as the Cree and the Assiniboine. The explorer Simon Hearne claimed in 1781 that 90 percent of the Chipewyan had fallen prey to disease. In 1862–64 smallpox found British Columbia. Coastal groups such as the Tsimshian, and interior peoples such as the Chilcotin, suffered high casualties. Some historians have claimed that one third of all Native peoples in the British Columbia area died during those two years. In 1870 smallpox returned to the Prairies and killed as many as 3500 Natives.

The Contemporary Picture

How many Native people are there in Canada today? This number is not easy to determine. There are registered Indians, Inuit, and Métis. Who is "Indian" and who is not is a complicated legal matter. The *Indian Act* of 1876 enshrined a sexist definition by stating that an "Indian" was any man of "Indian blood" reputed to belong to a particular band, any child of such a man, or any woman who is or was married to such a man. Under this Act, a man would keep his status, no matter whom he married; a woman, however, would lose her status if she married someone not legally an Indian and her children would share

CRITICAL THINKING BOX 5.1

There has been a "sudden rise" in the number of registered Indians over the past ten years. Why is this?

that fate. Adding insult to injury, a white woman who married an Indian man would gain Indian status. This discriminatory law was in force until 1985.

In 1881 there were 108 547 "status Indians." By 1984, before the change in the *Indian Act*, this number had risen to roughly 349 000. **Bill C-31** was passed in 1985, enabling people who had lost their Indian status through marriage or through the marriage of their mother to apply to be reinstated. More than 100 000 successfully did so, pushing the current number of "**registered Indians**" (the term that replaced "status") to well over 600 000.

These "registered Indian" cards are one reason that people have applied to regain Indian status. Perhaps you have worked as a salesperson at a store when someone presented you with an "Indian card," which meant that the person did not have to pay provincial taxes on what you were selling. This is because the land that Native people are living on is technically "outside the province," federal land. Some people resent this, taking the view that Native people are receiving special privileges. The Native peoples' response to this is that they have prepaid these taxes many times over with the treaties that cost them their lands.

Inuit

Often someone asks why the people are called Inuit now and not "Eskimo." The answer is that the Inuit never called themselves "Eskimo," which comes from a Mi'kmaq word meaning people who eat blubber and other animal products raw. The Inuit and the Mi'kmaq fought for a long time, so you can well imagine that the name "Eskimo" had negative connotations. The word "Inuit" is a plural noun in the Inuktitut language that literally translates as "men." The singular form is Inuk.

Inuit differ from Indians in being in Canada for a shorter time, somewhere between five and ten thousand years. Inuktitut is distantly related to the Siberian language Chukchi, making it the only Native Canadian language related to an Asian language. Culturally, the Inuit developed objects—such as the kayak and igloo—unlike anything found among other Native people in Canada.

Not until 1939, when Canada wanted to assert territorial claims in the Arctic, did the federal government take official responsibility for the Inuit. Each Inuk was given a metal disk with a number that was used as a token of their status. Today, about 60 percent of Inuit have disk numbers.

Since "joining Canada," much has happened that has been harmful to the Inuit. Southerners involved with various projects in the Arctic in the 1940s and early 1950s killed off sufficient caribou to make the Inuit who lived off that animal disappear as a people. In 1953 the federal government forced the people of Inukjuak (Port Harrison) in Northern Quebec to move some 3200 kilometres north to uninhabited Ellesmere Island. Ottawa claimed that this was for the betterment of the people, as local natural resources were depleting and Ellesmere Island was untouched. A darker interpretation is that this forced move was made primarily to guarantee Crown rights to that contested territory and that the government officials did not know or care that the kinds of resources in the two areas were very different. In the 1950s and 1960s the Inuit had the highest rate of tuberculosis in the world.

Inuit status has taken on a new nature for some since the territory of Nunavut ("Our Land") came into being on 1 April 1999 in the eastern two thirds of the Northwest Territories. More than 80 percent of Nunavut's population of about 25 000 is Inuit. They own 18 percent of the land (almost all the rest being Crown land), have subsurface rights to oil, gas, and other minerals for about 2 percent of Nunavut, and will receive royalties from the extraction of those minerals from the rest of the territory. They do not require a licence to hunt or fish to meet their basic needs.

Métis

The term **Métis** is used in two ways. One, typically written with a lowercase *m*, refers to anyone who is of mixed genetic heritage: part Native and part white. The second one, with an uppercase M, usually refers to the descendants of French fur traders and Cree women. Beginning in the late eighteenth century these latter Métis developed a culture that effectively combined European and Native features. They spoke Michif, which had nouns that were usually French and verbs that were mostly Cree. They lived for part of the year in river-lot farms in the Winnipeg area, but their main annual activity was the buffalo hunt. From the hunt came pemmican (buffalo jerky), a key Métis contribution to the fur trade. It supplied much-needed, well-preserved food for the men who paddled the canoes and carried the huge loads transported in the fur trade.

The Métis came to think of themselves as a nation. They had earned this sense through battle, especially with the Hudson's Bay Company (HBC). The "Bay" owned most of the Prairies and about half of present-day Canada, through a 1670 charter given by English King Charles II, who little knew what he was signing away. Charles II also granted the HBC a trading monopoly. In 1811, a senior HBC official placed settlers in the middle of Métis territory, not concerned that people already lived there. In 1814 the

BOX 5.2

False Image of the Inuit: Leaving the Elders on the Ice

In a recent (2001) Canadian introductory sociology textbook the following story appears:

> Shantu and Wishta fondly kissed their children and grandchildren farewell. Then sadly, but with resignation at the sacrifice they knew they had to make for their family, they slowly climbed onto the ice floe. The goodbyes were painfully made as the large slab of ice inched into the ocean currents. Shantu and Wishta would now starve. But they were old, and their death was necessary, for it reduced the demand on the small group's scarce food supply.
>
> As the younger relatives watched Shantu and Wishta recede into the distance, each knew that their turn to make this sacrifice would come.[1]

It is an image of the traditional Inuit that has been taught for generations: Inuit elders being abandoned for the good of the family or community because resources are low. It also paints a distorted picture of traditional Inuit culture, one seen more in textbooks than in real life. It is like teaching that murder–suicide is a regular part of contemporary Canadian family life because the rare occasions in which it has happened have been over-communicated in the media. Documented instances Inuit abandonment of Elders are rare, and they appear to have been desperate solutions for desperate circumstances. Contact with white visitors such as whalers and traders are strongly implicated in the creation of such circumstances.

It is an image that has served a variety of purposes. In sociology textbooks, it has been used an example of Emile Durkheim's notion of "altruistic suicide," committed when the rules of society compel individuals to kill themselves.[2] The image has often been used in sociology and anthropology textbooks to teach about cultural relativity, of how what is considered "normal" in one society is considered "deviant" in another. Extreme examples have helped to teach that lesson. By portraying the Inuit as such an extreme, textbook writers (and teachers) have done them an injustice.

governor of these settlers declared that the Métis could not trade in pemmican, as the HBC had a monopoly. This led in 1816 to a struggle at Seven Oaks, near the junction of the Red and the Assiniboine rivers. The resulting Métis victory became a symbol of their nationhood, celebrated in song.

In 1849 the Métis beat the HBC again. Pierre-Guillaume Sayer, charged with illicitly trafficking in furs, was released—even though he was convicted. Perhaps the judge had been influenced by the armed presence of two hundred to three hundred Métis outside the courtroom.

In 1867 the HBC started negotiating with Canada to sell its land, and the federal government moved to set up a colony in Manitoba. Métis rights to the land were not considered. The Métis took action. Led by 25-year-old, college-educated Louis Riel, the Métis achieved a military takeover in 1869 and set up an independent government to negotiate with Ottawa. Initially, events went well for them.

In 1870 most HBC land was transferred to Canada, and the *Manitoba Act* of 1870 established the province of that name with a legal recognition of Métis rights. This took the form of "scrip," a certificate declaring that the bearer could receive payment in land, cash, or goods. But government officials and land speculators ensured that the Métis would not receive what they were due. They were "legally" cheated—the laws changed eleven times in twelve years—of their land, so that only a few remained on the coveted river lots. Most Métis simply moved west. But in 1885, with their rights ignored again, and again led by Louis Riel, the Métis set up an independent government in Saskatchewan. They were suppressed by federal Canadian forces, and Riel was hung for "treason."

As a separate people, the Métis almost disappeared. However, during the 1930s, Alberta Métis pushed for the creation of communal settlements similar to reserves. In the words of Métis leader Adrian Hope: "We've had enough of negotiable scrip … to buy booze…. What we are asking for is land we cannot sell, cannot mortgage, but land to which we can belong."[3] In 1938 eight Métis "colonies" were formed. Unfortunately, the Alberta government controlled them. The Métis could only advise or recommend. From 1969 to today the colony Métis have been engaged in a legal fight for two basic rights: (1) They want the colony to have the political power of a municipality; for the most part, that was granted during the 1980s. (2) They want more say concerning economic development. In this they have not been as successful. The colony Métis have tried to obtain royalty payments for gas and oil extracted from their land, but this has been a bitter and unrewarding fight. Any economic plans that the colony Métis make are still subject to provincial veto. Beyond the colonies, there are the Métis National Council and provincial organizations in Ontario and in the Prairie provinces; these suffer from difficulties of legal definition and lack of recognition.

How many Métis are there in Canada? Estimates vary from 500 000 to 1 000 000.[4]

How many Natives, then, are there in Canada? That depends on how you define "Native." If you go by legal definition, then you start with more than 600 000 registered Indians and add some 20 000 disk-carrying Inuit and 4000 Métis "colonists" to that. That is one definition. Self-identification is another. If every Canadian with Native genetic background were to be counted, they would number more than two million. French-Canadian biologist Jacques Rousseau established that more than 40 percent of the French-speaking population in Canada has at least one Native ancestor.[5]

TREATIES

What is a **treaty**? It is difficult to determine what the original meaning of any treaty was for those on either side of the negotiating table. The government felt that Natives would eventually disappear, so the wording involved might not have been so important to them. Native people had no precedent for giving away land forever. Today's Natives tend to feel these treaties are international agreements between "nations." They consider treaties to be statements of recognition of their sovereign or independent status, made necessary by the Royal Proclamation of 1763. This key document contained two statements of significance to Native issues in Canada.

First, land not part of New France and not owned by the Hudson's Bay Company was declared to be Indian land. Second, Indian land could only be taken from them through "public purchase," that is, treaties. Most of Canada is covered by such treaties, but exceptions exist. British Columbia has a few treaties, but the province removed Natives from most of their land without public purchase. Quebec received its northern half on the understanding that Native land rights would be dealt with, but nothing was done until the James Bay Agreement. Newfoundland, separate from Canada until 1949, has no such treaties.

Generally, in treaties, the Natives involved would agree to give up their rights to a certain area of land. In return they would have a smaller area or areas reserved for their use, hence, the name **reserves** for these blocks of land. The calculation was typically a certain amount of land per family of five, say sixty-five hectares. The Natives would also receive a certain amount of money. In that sense, treaties were like land sales. They were

CRITICAL THINKING BOX 5.2

Why is it difficult to determine how many Native people there are in Canada?

different, however, in that the Natives could not get their hands on the money. It was held for them "in trust" by the government. From 1818 on, Natives also would receive annuities, or annual payments, usually involving a small sum per person, say three dollars a year. Often hunting and fishing rights were part of a treaty.

Literally hundreds of such small treaties exist. Most of Canada, however, was dealt with through a series of large land transfers beginning with the Robinson Treaties of 1850 that involved the land immediately to the north of Lakes Superior and Huron. Built on the same model were the "numbered treaties," 1 to 11, signed between 1871 and 1921. These covered the territory from the eastern part of British Columbia and parts of Yukon Territory and the Northwest Territories in the west, across the Prairie provinces, to most of northern Ontario. Almost all treaties can be connected with the federal government wanting something, particularly mineral resources. The Robinson treaties were signed after the discovery of metals in northern Ontario. Treaty Number 8 was occasioned by the Klondike Gold Rush in the closing years of the nineteenth century, and oil found in 1920 led to Treaty Number 11.

Why do Natives make such a big deal about treaties? First, they hold the view that in the treaties they were recognized as sovereign nations. Second, there are few treaties in which the Native groups involved have not had some grievance concerning either verbal promises that were not written or written promises that were not fulfilled. For example, in 1818 in partial payment for giving up the "Mississauga Tract," land including in part what is now the city of Mississauga, the King's representative did "hereby promise and agree to pay to the said Nation of Indians inhabiting as above mentioned, yearly and every year for ever the said sum of five hundred and twenty two pounds ten shillings currency in goods at the Montreal price."[6] But forever lasted a short time, as these annuities were only paid for a few years.

Two years later, the Mississauga reluctantly agreed to give up their exclusive fishing rights to a few local creeks and rivers, as well as all their remaining land, "[s]aving and reserving, nevertheless, always to ... the people of the Mississagua [sic] Nation of Indians and their posterity for ever a certain parcel or tract of land containning [sic] two hundred acres."[7]

The Mississauga never signed away those two hundred acres (about eighty hectares), but they soon came to understand that without a land deed of the type that the settlers had, they had no hope of keeping that land, despite the written treaty promise. They left the area in the 1840s.

LAND CLAIMS

Typically, land claims are put forward by Native groups who are not covered by any treaties. They are based on the principle that people who have not signed away their rights to their land have Aboriginal rights that have not been extinguished or taken away. Sometimes, as with the Temagami Anishnabe (Ojibwa) of northeastern Ontario, land claims involve dispute over whether a people is included in a treaty. In the Temagami case, the band asserted that they never signed the Robinson–Huron Treaty of 1850. For more than a century, the Temagami pushed to sign an agreement so that they could obtain a reserve where they worked and lived. The position of the provincial governments over the same period remained that someone had already signed for the Temagami. The governments were very reluctant to give the Temagami a reserve in that pine- and tourism-rich area of the province. The courts ruled against the Natives, and the provincial government then made an offer that divided the band (only part of the community accepted the offer), creating a rift that remains.

More often, a land claim is made where no treaty applies. One famous case involves the Cree of James Bay. When northern Quebec was handed over to the province by the federal government in 1898 and 1912, it was stipulated that the Cree, Inuit, and Innu would have their rights dealt with through treaty. No Quebec government did anything until 1971, when Premier Robert Bourassa announced his plans for the James Bay Project, a grand scheme of constructing power dams on four large rivers. These dams would have flooded the homes and the hunting and trapping territories of the Cree. Bourassa had not even talked with the Cree, very few of whom spoke French, nor thought of negotiating with them concerning their rights to the land they had lived on for hundreds, maybe thousands of years. After nearly three years of verbal, legal, and public relations battles, the *James Bay and Northern Quebec Agreement* of 1975 was signed, with extensions north and east added in 1978 and 1984.

This agreement has been a mixed blessing. The Cree received a lot of money, although not as much as was promised. The Cree School Board has achieved a great deal more than their critics thought possible for a Native-run, Native-language, and culture-based system. Financially, some individuals have prospered, and some businesses have done well. Politically, the Cree have become a force to be reckoned with. They were able to stop the second phase of the project. During the Quebec Referendum of 1995, the Cree were prepared with legal documentation that could very well have won them the right to withdraw from a separate Quebec.

But there is a negative side too. Mercury, raised by the flooding, exists in dangerously high amounts in the fish, a major item in the local Cree diet. Communities that in the early 1970s were made up mainly of financially independent hunters and trappers have seen a good number of people forced onto welfare. Social problems such as substance abuse and suicide, unheard of before the James Bay Project, have reared their ugly heads.

A challenge to any Native group putting forward a land claim is to try to achieve the successes of the James Bay Cree, without paying the penalties.

The Nisga'a Treaty

The recently (2000) passed Nisga'a treaty has prompted much discussion, particularly in British Columbia, where a great deal of land "suddenly" became "Indian land." This is not a new land claim; the Nisga'a, a Tsimshian-speaking people, have been trying for more than a century to have their land claims resolved. They sent delegations to Victoria in 1881 and 1887. In the latter trip, they were told by the premier that "when the whites first came among you, you were little better than the wild beasts of the field."[8] The Nisga'a spoke to prime ministers in 1885 and in 1910. In the latter year, Prime Minister Wilfrid Laurier promised to resolve the land issue. The next year he was defeated at the polls, and his promise came to nothing. In 1909 and 1913, the Nisga'a sent representatives to Britain, with no success.

In 1927, the federal government made it difficult for the Nisga'a to try to get their land claims settled. Ottawa took away from Natives the democratic right to organize to discuss land claims. The Nisga'a did not give up. They and other British Columbia Native groups formed the Native Brotherhood of British Columbia in 1931, which discussed, in secret, how they could get their land claims settled.

In 1967, Nisga'a leader Frank Calder took the land question to court, seeking a declaration that his people had held Aboriginal title to the land before colonization and that their title had never been extinguished. The Nisga'a lost the decision in the B.C. court but appealed the decision, taking it to the Supreme Court of Canada. In 1973, in what is called "The Calder Decision," the appeal was lost in a split decision: the judges agreed that Aboriginal title had existed but disagreed as to whether that title continued to exist.

In 1976, the federal government and the Nisga'a began negotiations regarding finally settling their land claims under the new "comprehensive land claims policy." British Columbia did not join in the talks. They did not enter into the discussion until 1990, eight years after the Canadian *Constitution* recognized and affirmed Aboriginal title.

On 22 March 1996, the minister of Indian affairs, the B.C. Aboriginal affairs minister, and Nisga'a Tribal Council President Joseph Gosnell Sr. signed an Agreement-in-Principle for the first modern treaty in British Columbia. In 1999 Parliament, and on 13 April 2000, the Senate, passed the bill.

What did the Nisga'a get from the treaty? The 5500 Nisga'a received title to 1930 km^2 in their Nass valley homeland and \$487.1 million in benefits and cash. The treaty also gives them the right to make laws in several areas, including land use, employment, and cultural preservation (resembling jurisdictions such as municipal, provincial, and federal governments in that law-making capacity). They will own the forest and mineral resources on their land (as a private owner would) and have to manage them, like other owners, according to British Columbia's laws and standards.

What did the Nisga'a give up to get the treaty? They lessened their original claim by 25 percent and they gave up future claims on what amounts to more than 80 percent of their traditional territory. They gave up their tax exemptions.

Although the non-Native media, particularly in British Columbia, have presented this treaty as a step toward separation or the eventual breakup of Canada, it is closer to the mark to say that it puts the Nisga'a in a legal position similar to other Canadians.

BANDS

What is an Indian **band**? Just like "Indian," a band is something legally defined by the federal **Department of Indian Affairs (DIA)**. Bands can be created or done away with by the DIA. Typically, a band is made up of people of one cultural tradition with some historical connection with each other. They own land and funds in common and are governed in part by a band council headed by a chief. There are some 592 bands across Canada. The largest is the Six Nations, an Iroquois band in southern Ontario whose Web site declares that they have more than 20 000 members.[9]

Bands now face a problem that is dividing some communities. Membership is sharply rising, with no compensating increase in land or funds. Housing and postsecondary education money is handled by the band council. With the influx of "Bill C-31 Indians" the competition for such programs is tight. Many reserves are already crowded, and the problem is getting worse. There is tension in many communities.

A great frustration for chiefs and band councillors has long been their lack of power. They have less power than a municipality, which can raise funds through taxation (a band cannot), and which possesses an independence that a band would envy. The DIA has the power to veto any decision that a band council may make. Much of what bands do has to be sent to DIA for approval.

Native self-government is something that non-Natives tend to fear, thinking that the country will be divided into little separate nations across the land. Native groups differ as to what they think Native self-government is. Some just want the power that a comparably sized town or village has. Others desire the right to set up the structure of their choice, one that instead of having an elected chief and band council, has more traditional-style leaders, spokespersons for clans rather than one overall leader. For most Canadian Native groups, "the chief" was more a foreign creation than a traditional form of leadership. All bands want to be less controlled by the DIA. Native government is already distinct. Natives just want that distinction to be less of a powerless one.

BOX 5.3

The Division of Bill C-31

I was teaching in a summer program for Natives wanting to work as education counsellors. I remember two men of the same nation who were staying in the same house, usually seen together, sitting together in my class. Both were proud of their nation and its heritage. Both taught me significant aspects of that heritage. In one class, it came out that one of these men lived on the nation's reserve and had always had membership in the band, while the other was Bill C-31, and therefore had to live in a nearby town, although his heart was with the community that had no space for him. The first man made reference to his having a greater connection with his people and their heritage because he had always lived in the community of his nation. The other, who because his mother had lost her status through marriage had not been raised on the reserve, was hurt by what the first had said. He felt he was just as much a member of the nation as the "status Indian." Some harsh words were said, but owing largely to their ability to draw on the spiritual and conciliatory traditions of their people, peace between the two of them was finally achieved.

RESERVES

Students often ask me, with slightly hushed voices, "What is it like on a reserve?" It is as if they expected me to tell them stories of bizarre mystical rites and shape shifting. They are often disappointed when I say that many reserves look just like other comparable communities. They wonder, too, why Native people seem to cling to reserves even when some are overcrowded and violent. One answer is that for many Native people the reserve is their "home and Native land." There they are not a minority, subject to stares and discrimination.

The uncertainty that sometimes surrounds reserve status creates problems. One major reason that the 1990 confrontation at Oka (in Quebec) took place was because the people there did not have a reserve that could protect their burial grounds from a local golf course. They still don't. The tragedy behind the story at Davis Inlet in 1993, with Innu children suffering from serious substance abuse and attempting suicide, has a lot to do with the federal and Newfoundland governments forcing the people to move the reserve from the Labrador mainland to an island. This was done against the wisdom and the will of the local Innu, who knew they would have less access to the natural resources they valued, such as caribou. The move took a lot of the heart out of the people.

Reserves have a unique legal status. Technically, a reserve can be called federal rather than provincial land. It is owned by the band, but the federal government, through the DIA, has ultimate authority. Although people have their own houses and property lines, the land is held by the band in common. They do not pay municipal taxes, and housing is usually cheap. On the negative side, a family's part of the reserve cannot be used as collateral to get a loan from a bank.

Most Natives live on reserves. More than 60 percent of registered Indians live on reserves. Reserve patterns differ across Canada. In central and eastern Canada each band has only one reserve. Out West, a band is more likely to have more. In British Columbia, for example, there are fewer than two hundred bands but more than sixteen hundred reserves. Typically, there is a remoteness to reserves. In 1989 more than 60 percent were farther than fifty kilometres from a city or major town. A remarkable 18.6 percent were not connected to a city or major town by a year-round road.

A growing number of Native people work and live in towns and cities, however. Frideres and Gadacz (2001) estimate that in 1991, eleven Canadian cities had an Aboriginal population of at least 10 000. Edmonton, Montreal, Toronto, and Vancouver top the list, with an estimated 40 000 to 50 000 each.[10] These figures are probably a lot lower than the actual numbers. Estimates for Toronto's Native population are often given as more than forty thousand; it is sometimes called "the largest Indian reserve in Canada." This move to the city has been a trend of the past twenty-five years. In 1971 none of these cities had a reported Native population of more than five thousand.

Unfortunately for Natives, their greatest urban visibility is as the stereotypical "Indian drunk." In Toronto they are otherwise pretty much an "invisible minority." An Ojibwa student of mine told me that for years, when she worked in a bank in that city, customers would guess at her identity, asking her if she were Filipina, Chinese, or Korean. No one ever guessed it right.

As more Natives move to the city, there is a growing need for Native-run organizations to help them cope with urban life. These are appearing, usually starting with a Native Friendship Centre.

NATIVES AND THE JUSTICE SYSTEM

Natives do not fare well in the Canadian justice system. They are less likely than non-Natives to be put on probation and to be released on their own recognizance. Natives are more likely to be ordered to pay fines, and much more likely to be put in jail because they cannot pay the fines. They are more likely to serve their full sentence rather than having their sentence shortened by parole. Drinking in the same bar with non-Natives, and consuming roughly the same amount of alcohol, they are more likely to be picked up for being drunk around closing time. Natives are overrepresented in our prisons. Shock-value statistics abound, often doing more harm than good (see opening quote). Stories of what is happening and how solutions are being applied are less often presented and are more likely to improve the situation. The following are a few such stories and potential solutions.

Different Sides to Policing Natives

Starlight Tours in Saskatoon

Saskatoon has a population of about 200 000. Its Native population has been estimated at about 15 percent of that number, but the percentage of the poor in Saskatoon is almost double that at 30 percent. There is no detox centre in the city to which police can take intoxicated people they have picked up. The only public institution that they can take them to is jail.

In 1997, Brian Trainor, a veteran police officer, wrote a column in the *Saskatoon Sun* that told about a night on the beat for two fictional officers. In the story, they pick up a loud, verbally abusive drunk and take him on what is sometimes known as a "starlight tour," driving him outside town and leaving him there to walk back.

On the night of 27 January 2000, 33-year-old Darrell Night, an unemployed bricklayer and a big sturdy man at 1.9 m, 109 kg, got drunk. In the early morning hours he was arrested outside a friend's apartment by two officers, handcuffed, and put into a police cruiser. According to statements he would give later, he was then taken outside town and dropped off by Queen Elizabeth II Power Station south of the city, without a coat. The temperature had dropped to about –28°C. Darrell went to the station and got a night watchman to call him a cab. That may have saved his life.

He did not tell his story to anyone in legal authority at first. He was Cree, and the officers were white. Who would be more likely to be believed? It would take the report of two tragedies to make him tell his own story.

What made him tell his story was the discovery the next night of the body of a 25-year-old Cree man, Rodney Naistus, and, a few nights later, of a 30-year-old Cree student, Lawrence Kim Wegner. Both had been drinking. On 20 September 2001, the two officers who took Darrell Night in his starlight tour were convicted of unlawful confinement and were fired by the Saskatoon Police Service. An inquest into the deaths of Rodney Naistus and Lawrence Kim Wegner found no wrongdoing.

The Positive Side of the Saskatoon Police Service

It would be wrong to simply label the Saskatoon Police Service (SPS) as racist. Since 1994, with the creation of the Aboriginal Liaison Officer position, the SPS has developed several programs and events dedicated to creating a bridge between the police service and the Saskatoon Native community. In 1995, the SPS won the National Ivan Ahenakew Award for efforts in employing Aboriginal officers and in the development of cultural programs.

Perhaps the most successful elements of the SPS's efforts to connect with the Native community have come through the peacekeeper programs, which put officers together with Aboriginal at-risk youth, often under the guidance of Elders and other Native leaders. The programs include innovative cultural activities such as Project Firewood/Rocks. This involves Aboriginal youth and SPS officers travelling to northern Saskatchewan to load a semi-trailer with firewood and rocks to be taken to Saskatoon for the Elders. The Elders will use these materials in **sweat lodge** ceremonies (see Box 5.4), some involving both the youth and officers as participants.

Native Policing Services

Following the Manitoba Aboriginal Justice Inquiry of 1988–89 and the 1990 Oka confrontation, the federal solicitor general initiated in 1991 the First Nations Policing Policy. It operates on a principle of partnership involving First Nations, the federal government, and the provincial or territorial governments. These three enter into tripartite agreements for police services that fit the needs of the particular Aboriginal communities involved. Fifty-two percent of the funding for the agreements comes from the federal government, with the remaining 48 percent coming from the provincial or territorial government. By the end of 1999, there were 52 such agreements across the country. The following tells the story of one such agreement.

CRITICAL THINKING BOX 5.3

What problems do band leaders face that leaders of towns and cities do not?

BOX 5.4

The Sweat Lodge

....

The following is a general description of the sweat lodge as the Ojibwa (Anishinabe) use it in the context of the modern vision quest.[11] Sweat lodges differ both within the traditions of the Ojibwa people, and between them and other Aboriginal peoples.

The sweat lodge is typically constructed of 16 overlapping willow poles. It is shaped to resemble the sky world above that covers the earth like a dome. The entrance must face the east, where the sun rises.

A pit is dug inside the centre of the lodge where the grandfathers are received and where they meet mother earth. The grandfathers are stones that because of their great age hold the mysteries of the ages. Before the grand-fathers are brought into the lodge, they are placed at the bottom of a sacred fire in front of the lodge, joined to it by a pathway of cedar. Here they are heated until they become white hot. How long the vision quest seeker plans to sweat will determine how many stones will be called on to guide the indi-vidual in the sweat lodge.

The Elder and the participants to the fire throw tobacco into the fire and pray, giving thanks to the Creator. The Elder then tells how the sweat lodge came to be, a story that describes how a little boy was sent to the seven grand-father spirits in the star world during a time of great sickness and was given the gift of the sweat lodge to bring back to his people for healing. A water drum is placed inside the sweat lodge close to the entrance. This drum is called the Little Boy Drum in remembrance of the little boy who brought back the medicine teachings. The participants greet the drum as they enter. It has seven stones that surround the top, representing the seven grandfathers who first gave the little boy the teaching. When the sweat lodge is occupied, the Elder sings traditional ceremonial songs. The grandfathers are then brought in to the lodge and placed in the pit. The Elder throws water onto the grand-fathers, and the steam makes the lodge quite hot.

The Stl'atl'imx Tribal Police Case Study

On 20 December 1999, British Columbia received its first Aboriginal police service with full jurisdictional authority. The Stl'atl'imx (pronounced *Slat-lee-um*) Tribal Police (STP) force is responsible for ten First Nations communities, serving roughly 3150 people in southern British Columbia. Nine of the participating communities are the Lillooet ("Wild Onion") First Nation, the tenth is Shuswap, a closely related people.

Although the force dates back to 1988, it wasn't until 2 April 1992 that a tripartite agreement was signed. The STP is guided by the Stl'atl'imx Tribal Police Board (STPB), which has ten members, one from each of the participating communities. The STPB has more responsibility for managing and leading the STP than is found in most municipal police departments. The 1992 tripartite agreement included some dependence on the RCMP, with the latter providing assistance in the investigation of relatively serious cases.

The notion of a Native police service is new to non-Natives, easily interpreted by them as threatening, particularly, as in this case when the Native police service is asked to give assistance to provincial police off reserve. By May 1992, three petitions with 493 signatures were sent from the non-Native town of Lillooet to the B.C. attorney general with complaints of non-Natives being "harassed" by Native police.

The STP was reviewed in 1996 by the British Columbia Police Commission. At that time the STP had nine policing positions: a chief constable, a supervisor, three constables based in the community of Mount Currie, three in Lillooet (the Native community), and one in Seton Lake. The problems revealed in this review were typical of the fledgling Native police services across Canada: insufficient and often late year-to-year funding, difficulties in hiring experienced staff (particularly when contracts are a year long, rather than long term), inadequate training, the difficulties of policing a broad area of separated communities with few officers (making full-service, full-time shift work almost impossible), low morale, discontent with the authoritarian management style of the non-Native chief constable, and what can be called a clash of policing cultures.

The Police Board members were unanimous in wanting to have a police service based on the traditional Lillooet "watchman" system. The "watchman" was respected for his decision making. Traditionally, members of the community felt comfortable in approaching him to hear their cases whenever they felt that someone had committed a transgression. The majority of STPB members believed that the chief constable and the STP officers were not applying this philosophy but were following a more mainstream-culture policing approach. The officers themselves, most of whom were Native, were divided as to which philosophy or cultural style they preferred.

The culture of policing clash is one of the major challenges faced by all Native police services. It begs several important questions. How free are Native police services to innovate following traditional values? How might that freedom be restricted by the mainstream training their officers receive and the mainstream policing experiences of those who early on assume positions of leadership in these services? To what extent can Native police services reflect their traditional culture in trying to work with and get the respect of other, more established policing services and of provincial and federal funding administrators?

Despite some of the negative aspects of the review, the B.C. Police Commission noted that the Board and the STP were conscientious and dedicated to improving the quality of the service. This must have served to good effect, for three years after the review, the STP moved ahead to assume full jurisdictional authority. As Chief Constable Harry McLaughlin noted in the B.C. attorney general news release, "This occasion instills a new level of pride in our officers and a renewed sense of commitment to the Stl'atl'imx communities."[12]

Sentencing Circles

Sentencing circles provide alternatives to incarceration, through applying traditional notions of restorative justice. The circles typically involve community members such as Elders and Native social workers, lawyers, health care workers, and those affected by the crime, including the offenders, the victims, and their families. The circles are more informal than traditional courts. People sit in a circle. No judge is involved. Consensus is stressed in deciding what the sentence will be. The following is an example.[13]

In 1994, the United Chiefs and Councils of Manitoulin Justice Project began diverting cases from the courts to sentencing or justice circles. From 1 January 1998 to the end of June 1999, 77 justice circles were created, involving 110 members of the community. The kind of cases were typically property offences (i.e., vandalism, break and enter, and theft) and relatively minor instances of assault, but they did not include more serious crimes such as murder, manslaughter, sexual or spousal abuse, or impaired driving.

Sentences are referred to as "plans of action." These are traditionally based, but also creative and new. Public apologies are made by the "clients" not only to the victims involved, but also to the police and others affected by the harmful acts. Some of the apologies have aired on a local cable TV station.

Personal healing is a significant part of the plans of action. This healing has included referrals to drug and alcohol addiction treatment centres or mental health facilities, but it has also entailed traditional activities. The intent of these activities is to heal clients by raising their self-esteem and sense of identity through learning about their culture. Examples of the traditional activities recommended are helping to gather traditional medicines in the bush, participating in an arduous canoe trip around Manitoulin Island, and researching a family tree. Some clients have done more than was required of them, as they felt rewarded by the activity.

Since healing the community is a priority, the plans of action often require some form of community service. This has involved doing such things as cleaning up the results of vandalism, painting a new detox centre, and participating in a walk held annually to raise awareness of violence against women.

Making amends is also important. In one case, a woman had assaulted another woman, a long time neighbour. Had she decided to fight the charge, which was her initial intention, she probably would have been put on probation and told to stay away from the victim. Instead, with the apology, the two women have managed to remain on good terms, something that would be less likely to happen in the confrontation format of the courtroom.

An easy criticism of the Justice Project would be that people get off lightly. However, the clients speak of it being more difficult to face people you know than the anonymous strangers who are judge and jury.

There are difficulties. The workload is heavy. A lot of time is taken in putting together reports and proposals for the funding necessary to continue and to grow. Still, during the period studied (January 1998 to June 1999) no one had to return to the circle for noncompliance with their plans of action.

MEDICINE: AN EXAMPLE OF "NATIVE RELIGION"

What kind of religion do Native people have? There is no simple answer, no easy "-ism" as an explanatory label. Traditionally, the spiritual was connected with every aspect of life. Not separated into a single place like a room in a house, it was more like the air that circulates through every room. The current rebirth of Native spirituality continues the tradition of the interconnectedness of religion with other aspects of Native life. It is one of the most distinctive features of contemporary Native culture. One way to explain the nature of "Native religion" is through a discussion of the concept of medicine. No matter which Native language is involved, the word for medicine always strains the limits of accuracy of translation. It has a whole complex of meanings, many of which are not tied directly into the English-speaker's notion of a physical substance that one takes to feel better. It is holistic, incorporating elements from the spiritual, intellectual, and emotional, as well as the purely physical.

Take the "**medicine wheel**." It is not just a circle with four colours signifying the four directions. Each direction has associated characteristics, including an aspect of the self (e.g., spirit, mind, emotions, and body), a struggle of "positive" or "negative" emotions (e.g., sharing and envy for the east), an animal, one of the "four medicines," whose main function relates to what it does when burned, and more purely physical medicines. The

---

CRITICAL THINKING BOX 5.4

Why do many Native people feel that they need a "Native justice system"?

---

medicine wheel can be used as a way of comprehending the nature of humans and their relationship with all things around them. Native social workers and counsellors often successfully employ the medicine wheel as a therapeutic tool.

The four medicines are sweetgrass, tobacco, sage, and cedar. When burned, each has a medicinal function that goes beyond its mere physical properties. Sweetgrass, not a drug as the name might imply, is a sweet-smelling member of the grass family. When burned, it purifies the person and the immediate setting with its sacred smoke, much as incense does for Catholics and Hindus. People who fan the smoke over them are said to be "smudged." Smudging is a daily morning ritual for some.

Tobacco is often put in a fire, and the smoke communicates with the spirits. In Ojibwa culture, when people want to obtain a name in their own language, an increasing phenomenon for adults and children, they go to someone who is known to provide names, and give that person tobacco. The namer places the tobacco into a fire, and asks the Creator for help in finding the name in a vision.

Sage and cedar are believed to cleanse in both a physical and spiritual sense. Cedar is often used in a key element of contemporary Native medicine: the sweat lodge (see Box 5.4). The sweat lodge is like a sauna in a tent. In the centre are placed hot rocks that give off steam when water is thrown on them. Cedar is sometimes put into the water or directly on the rocks. People sing or pray, as the spirit moves them. Often they are taught there by an elder. The sweat lodge had been found to be profoundly effective in cleansing people spiritually and physically who are in Native drug or alcohol treatment centres and in prisons.

NATIVE EDUCATION

To understand about Native society in Canada today you must learn about **residential schools**, which were initiated in 1910. Unfortunately, the negative effects of this education are its prominent features. One tragically mistaken idea in these schools was the notion that to educate Native children, it was necessary to separate them from the "corrupting influence" of their language, their culture, and ultimately, their parents. About half the schools were Roman Catholic, the rest primarily Anglican and United Church. The religious groups received a grant of land and money and were left more or less to run the schools on their own. Although intentions were good, the results were horrifying. Schools were frequently hundreds of miles away from the homes of the students, who were forced to board in prisonlike buildings, often for ten months of the year. Students were sometimes dragged from their homes by police.

BOX 5.5

The Peace Pipe

....

An important medicinal function of tobacco is to create an atmosphere of peace and harmony through the smoking of a pipe. The "peace pipe" is used when people need to communicate, often in a situation of conflict. A personal experience can illustrate. I was teaching a summer course in northern Ontario. A Native teacher was working with me. We hadn't had much time to plan how we would teach the course. We had Native students who had had different instructors the year before, and we weren't particularly happy with what we were doing. The first week of classes was not satisfying for anyone.

We were living in the same house. Early one morning, my colleague knocked on my door and asked me to go to his room to smoke the pipe with him. He was a **pipe carrier**, which in Native culture signifies that he was respected and given a pipe because he had made a meaningful contribution to his people. He filled the pipe, offered it to the four directions, the sky and the earth, and then we smoked. As each of us held the pipe, we spoke of what our feelings were concerning the course. We both knew that what was being said would be honest, without being too critical of each other or the students. Our words were intended to work out our problems in such a way that harmony was achieved among all concerned. The atmosphere created by smoking the pipe together cleared the way for us to get past any ill feelings we might have had. We came to an understanding. I learned a lot.

Residential schools were not just bad educationally, with a simplified curriculum, undertrained teachers, hand-me-down educational materials, and with "learning a trade" often an excuse for exploiting students as unpaid farm and domestic labourers. These schools also harmed the Native family. Generally, strict teachers and principals were the only parental figures that the Native children experienced for most of the year. Abuse—physical, emotional, and sexual—occurred far too frequently. When the students became parents, they would often come to repeat the practices of their white role models. Brothers and sisters were kept apart in sexually segregated classes and residences, sometimes not getting an opportunity to talk with each other for months on end. One female Native student in a residential school stated: "I never did get to know my brothers. We were kept away from each other for too long. To this day I don't know much about my brothers. I just know that they are my brothers."[14]

When children left for residential school, often they knew only one language, the language of their home, community, and ancestors. But those who "spoke Indian" would be punished, usually with a severe beating.

The residential schools lasted until the 1960s. Their effects are still being felt. Many Native people are skeptical about education even when it is run by their own people. Still, increasingly Natives are taking over their own schools. In 1975–76, there were only 2842 pupils attending just fifty-three band-operated schools in reserves across Canada. That number shot up to more than 53 312 students in 372 band-operated schools by 1993–94.

Native students are staying in school much longer than they did before. The proportion of Native students living on reserve who remained in school until grade 12 was only 15 percent in 1970–71. This reached 47 percent by 1990–91. Similar figures appear for postsecondary schooling. In 1973 there were fewer than 1000 college and university students who were registered Indians. By 1987 that number had reached 14 000.

Taking charge of their own education is not an easy task for Native people. Good Native material is still in short supply, especially regarding language. Provinces carefully guard their curriculum as the standard of education, sometimes making it difficult for Native students to gain accreditation for grades and courses taken in band-run schools, when it comes to applying for transfer to any level of schooling from within the Native system. And the Department of Indian Affairs still controls the purse strings.

POWWOWS

A modern phenomenon seen every summer in a growing number of reserves is the **powwow**. What is a powwow exactly? First, and foremost, it involves drumming and dancing. Powwows open to the public usually involve dancing competition. My favourites are the athletic performances of the men in the fancy dances and the mesmerizing music of the women jingle dancing. The jingle comes from many little bell-like cones, "traditionally" made out of snuff-can lids. A good jingle dancer can make it seem like the dress has a life of its own. There are intertribal dances, with people moving to steps and songs that are shared between nations, helping to create a Pan-Indian culture.

The dances have a lot of meaning, particularly to the old people; during much of their lives, such Native dancing was illegal. The banning began with the potlatch, the most significant ceremony among nations such as the Haida, Kwakiutl, Tlingit, Tsimshian, Bella Coola, and Nootka of British Columbia. It is a celebration such as a birthday party, bar mitzvah, christening, mass, confirmation, or marriage. It is also the telling of a people's history. In a potlatch, people dance, sing, and wear masks and costumes that tell stories vital to understanding who a people are. Traditionally, a potlatch involved a great giving of gifts, saved up for a year or more by the family holding the ceremony and its clan. The next year they might attend a potlatch in which they are the guests and the receivers of equal gifts. The ceremonies could take days. Missionaries saw a potlatch as a "pagan ritual," government officials saw it as a "backward practice" that would prevent the Indians from becoming "civilized." So in 1884 a ban on the potlatch and on the similar spirit dance of the Salish was added to the *Indian Act*. The Act stated that anyone involved in such ceremonies "is guilty of a misdemeanour, and shall be liable to imprisonment for a term of not more than six nor less than two months in any gaol or other place of confinement, and any Indian or other person who encourages, either directly or indirectly, an Indian or Indians to get up such a festival or dance, or to celebrate the same, or who shall assist in the celebration of same is guilty of a like offense, and shall be liable to the same punishment."

In 1895 this ban also hit the Sun Dance of the Blackfoot, Blood, Piegan, Sarcee, Assiniboine, and Cree of the Prairies. Finally, in 1906, the ban was extended to all Native dancing. During the 1920s several Kwakiutl were charged and convicted under the "potlatch law." Their punishment was lessened by the fact that they "permitted" officials to take away the potlatch masks, priceless parts of their heritage, which ended up in museums and on the walls of private collectors who included the minister of Indian affairs. The dances continued underground. Not until 1951 was this part of the *Indian Act* repealed. The Kwakiutl set up a home for the masks when the museums returned most of them, but some remain lost to the people. Religious freedom did not exist for all Canadians during most of this century.

THE FUTURE

What is the future of Native people in Canada? Politically, it does not seem very bright. The federal government, concerned about debts not promises, is looking to divest itself of its responsibilities, either passing them down to the provinces or wiping the slate clean.

CRITICAL THINKING BOX 5.5

Why do you think the federal government banned the potlatch, the Sun Dance, and, eventually, all forms of Native dancing?

Both strategies are looked on with some suspicion by Natives. If you owe me one hundred dollars and you say that you have passed the debt on to someone who owes you money, how can I be sure I'll be paid? And if you say, "It is good not to have debts between friends, so let's clear the slate," can I trust you?

There is a brighter side. Native people, such as Elijah Harper, are saying that the answer to Native difficulties will not come from making governments face their responsibilities, but from Natives healing themselves and getting their own cultures in line. Strength, health, and purpose come from within, not without. And it extends beyond Native society. Native philosophy, rooted in the traditional but tested in the self-help, self-healing needs of Native life today, presents an alternative viewpoint for the rest of Canada to meet its challenges. Already, this is being seen in attitudes toward the environment. It could well guide us in justice and in other areas of life.

CHAPTER SUMMARY

In this chapter we have looked at a broad range of topics concerning Natives in Canada, especially with regard to four main points. (1) Diversity exists as well as sameness. Not all Natives are alike. We see this especially in language and other aspects of traditional culture, but it exists as well in adaptations to contemporary society. (2) Understanding any aspect of Native culture requires some knowledge of its historical roots, which often involve a very damaging prejudice and discrimination. In particular this is true concerning treaties, education, religion, and the justice system. (3) Native people are legally as well as culturally different from other Canadians. Native status brings with it different rights and limitations. And Natives are divided themselves into different legal classes: registered Indian, treaty Indian, Bill C-31 Indian, Métis, métis, and Inuit. (4) Native culture is vibrant and adaptive, not some dust-covered museum showpiece. As many Native people put it, "We're still here, and we will continue to be here."

KEY TERMS

animate, p. 118

band, p. 129

Bill C-31, p. 121

Department of Indian Affairs (DIA), p. 129

inanimate, p. 118

Indian Act, p. 116

language families, p. 118

language isolates, p. 118

medicine wheel, p. 137

Métis, p. 122

pipe carrier, p. 139

powwow, p. 140

DISCUSSION QUESTIONS

1. In percentage and in terms of "the year" of Canadian history, compare the length of time Natives and other Canadians have been living in this land.
2. Compare the diversity of Native languages in Canada to that of languages spoken in Europe.
3. How are the Inuit different from "Indians"?
4. Why are treaties of so long ago such an important political issue to Natives today?
5. How is the Native notion of medicine different from the usual mainstream Canadian idea of medicine?
6. What are the challenges faced by Native police services?

NOTES

1. James Henslin, Dan Glenday, Ann Duffy, and Norene Pupo, *Sociology, Canadian Edition: A Down-to-Earth Approach*, 2nd ed. (Toronto: Allyn and Bacon, 2001), p. 216.
2. Emile Durkheim, *Suicide: A Study in Sociology* (orig. 1951) trans. John A. Spaulding and George Simpson, eds. (French original, 1897; New York: Free Press, 1966).
3. In Donald Purich, *The Métis* (Toronto: Lorimer, 1988), p. 140.
4. James S. Frideres and René R. Gadacz, *Aboriginal Peoples in Canada: Contemporary Conflicts*, 6th ed. (Toronto: Prentice Hall, 2001), p. 37.
5. In Donald Smith, *Le Sauvage* (Ottawa: National Museum of Man, 1974), p. 88.
6. *Indian Treaties and Surrenders*, Vol. 1 (Toronto: Coles Publishing, 1971), p. 48.
7. Ibid., p. 52.
8. Premier William Smithe, 1887, as quoted in Alex Rose, *Spirit Dance at Meziadin: Chief Joseph Gosnell and the Nisga'a Treaty* (Medeira Park, B.C.: Harbour Publishing, 2000), p. 13.
9. Six Nations Council, "Six Nations of the Grand River," available online at <www.sixnations.ca/index.htm>, accessed on 27 February 2002.
10. Frideres and Gadacz, *Aboriginal Peoples in Canada*.
11. Adapted from Brian Rice and John Steckley, "Lifelong Learning and Cultural Identity: A Lesson from Canada's Native People," in Michael Hatton, ed., *Lifelong Learning: Policies, Programs, and Practices* (Toronto: Asian Pacific Economic Cooperation Publication, 1997), p. 226.
12. Chief Constable Harry McLaughlin, B.C. attorney general news release, available online at <http://turtleisland.org/news/news-policing.htm>, accessed 29 May 2000.

13. The United Chiefs and Councils of Manitoulin Justice Project, adapted from John Steckley and Bryan Cummins, *Full Circle: Canada's Native People* (Toronto: Prentice Hall, 2001), pp. 237–38.
14. R. Bell in Jean Barman, "Aboriginal Education at the Crossroads: The Legacy of Residential Schools and the Way Ahead," in D. A. Long and O. P. Dickason, eds. *Visions of the Heart: Canadian Aboriginal Issues* (Toronto: Harcourt Brace, 1996), p. 294.

Disability as Difference

Nancy Nicholls

[We make disability] in impersonal encounters, in school, on the job (and long before a job is gotten on), in the media, in human service agencies, within self-help groups, through governmental policy, within cultural belief (nurtured and displayed through all of the above and more), through technology, through sweeping societal changes, and even through the writings of observers of disability.

— Fine and Asch, as cited in Higgins, 1992

Objectives

After reading this chapter, you should be able to

• clarify the relationship of historical ideas and the history of disability in Canada

• appreciate the role institutions, especially government, church, education, and family, have on issues affecting people with disabilities

• know and analyze the different models and theories for studying disability

• explore the importance of the theory of "normalization" in the treatment of individuals with disabilities

• recognize critical social policy issues for people with disabilities in Canada

INTRODUCTION

When people used to talk about **inclusive societies**, it was assumed that they were refer-ring to issues of race and ethnicity. Increasingly, however, the notion of inclusivity also incorporates **disability**.

Disability is not a new phenomenon in Canada. To appreciate the issue of dis-ability in the twenty-first century and beyond, we will begin with some background dis-cussion about how people with disabilities were treated in the past. This historical perspective will (1) help shed light on the definition of disability; (2) outline the role institutions have played in the lives of those who have disabilities and in shaping the view others have of people with disabilities; (3) show how public interest has shaped the devel-opment of policies in the area; and (4) show how government has responded.

Not all disabilities affect all people the same way. We will look at the types of dis-abilities—physical, intellectual, and mental—and attempt to identify how differently they have been treated over time and how the various disabilities raise different issues for equality. We will highlight the major theoretical perspectives on the study of disability, with particular emphasis on the theory of "normalization."

HISTORICAL CONTEXT

The Early Years

Historically the view of those with disabilities was that they were being punished for their sins or those of their ancestors. Many felt that people with disabilities were possessed of "evil spirits." Often they were ridiculed and certainly they were ostracized by society—they were seen as outcasts and were unwelcome. In time, the view changed from a con-cern about evil spirits to one of seeing people with disabilities as weak, as less worthy, as persons in need of charity. Originally, the person's family was expected to provide this charity. The family was seen as the major institution to provide health, educational, and social care for all its members. In the early sixteenth century, people with disabilities were thought of as noncontributing members of society and as individuals who needed to be provided with only basic care (minimal food and shelter). If their families were unable to provide this care, then it would sometimes be provided by more fortunate members of society.

European settlers brought with them to Canada the views of individuals with dis-abilities that they had held in Europe. Individuals with disabilities were seen as weaker members of society in need of the protection of stronger members, and their family and friends were expected to care for them. For these settlers, life in the new land often involved physical hardship and physical strength; individuals who could not be adequately protected in the new country were sent back to Europe for care.

In Europe, the major provider of care outside the family had been the church, so it was natural, in terms of both culture and tradition, for the church to assume the same responsibilities in the new land. From about the mid-eighteenth century, as the population grew in New France (now Quebec), the Roman Catholic Church began to provide care for individuals requiring special assistance. Even after Britain assumed control of New France, the Roman Catholic Church maintained this role as the major institutional provider of care in Quebec. This lasted until the 1950s, when the provincial government assumed more responsibility and as the Quiet Revolution began to take root.

The Church provided care for individuals with mental disabilities. One of the earliest known institutions for the care of those with disabilities was a hospital founded by the Sisters of Charity (Grey Nuns) in Montreal. In the late eighteenth century, Quebec's Legislative Assembly authorized expenditures for the care of "insane" persons in Quebec, and a per diem rate was given to the Grey Nuns to provide care for the "insane" in their existing institutions in Trois-Rivières, Quebec City, and Montreal. This is the first example in Canadian history of government expenditure for people with disabilities.

Services were expanded in the nineteenth century, largely because of increased population growth. An example of this expansion is the establishment of a hospital for the "insane" in Saint John, New Brunswick.

It was very difficult for those with severe physical disabilities to survive the hardships and challenges of the new country, and those that did not return to Europe often died young. In the nineteenth century, in response to population growth but also because of two major epidemics of cholera and smallpox, services for the physically ill were also expanded. Similar medical crises, polio and the effects of thalidomide, had a major impact on the treatment of people with disabilities in the 1950s. Events such as these touched many lives and brought the issues of people with disabilities to the forefront.

Confederation and the *British North America (BNA) Act*

Pivotal to an understanding of the Canadian government's role in caring for people with disabilities is the *British North America Act*, now called the *Constitution Act*, of 1867. This Act established that health care and education, as well as what we now term "social services," are the responsibility of the provincial governments. It is important to note that the federal government retained the responsibility to provide health care to the Inuit populations and to veterans of the armed forces. Policy issues about the provision of services to people with disabilities often are entrenched in the division of powers as outlined in this Act.

New Services in the Nineteenth Century

An important player in the development of most services is the public. Without public pressure and interest, governments tend not to expand services. For people with mental disabilities, the public was satisfied with the government providing institutional care—citizens were not only concerned about the care given people with mental disabilities, but they were also equally, and some would argue more, concerned about the safety of the public. Institutional care provided in isolated areas, far from the public view, was considered best.

Public concern for people with physical disabilities, however, was growing, primarily for those who were deaf or blind. Sending such individuals back to Europe was no longer feasible or practical, as many of them were now a few generations removed from the "old country." In response to the pressure to provide special education to the deaf and the blind, asylums for the blind were funded in Halifax and Montreal, and the Ontario School for the Deaf was established in 1872 in Toronto. Alexander Graham Bell, who is well known for his invention of the telephone, was a major contributor both financially and in terms of public pressure to developing and influencing the provision of special education services to the deaf. This notion of education for individuals with physical disabilities influenced those concerned about other kinds of disabilities. In 1888 an institution was built in Orillia, Ontario, to provide education to the "**mentally deficient**."

It is sad to note that what started out as a movement for special education in many instances resulted in institutions that provided merely housing, often, in less than adequate conditions.

Along with public pressure for the government to provide services came an impetus from the public to offer volunteer services. Volunteer organizations were established, such as the Canadian Red Cross in 1896 and the Victorian Order of Nurses in 1898. Volunteer services both increased the provision of care to people with disabilities and had a significant impact on the quality of care provided. As more people worked with individuals with disabilities through these volunteer efforts, public awareness grew about the issues facing people with disabilities, as did public support of increased financial and moral support.

The epidemic outbreak of serious diseases has often been the impetus for demanding services; another major impetus is civilian disaster. In 1917 an ammunition ship, the *Mont Blanc*, exploded in the port of Halifax. More than 1900 people were killed instantly, and within a year more than 2000 had died. Around 9000 more were injured, many permanently, 1000 with eye injuries alone. Virtually all of north-end Halifax was destroyed. The impact of this incident focused the public's attention on the needs of those with physical disabilities.

The voluntary sector saw children as "innocent victims" and thus the only ones deserving of help. Public pressure to care for children led to the establishment of institutions such as the Toronto Hospital for Sick Children and, later, the Ontario Society for Crippled Children.

The World Wars

World War I had an enormous impact on the delivery of services to people with physical disabilities in Canada. For the first time in Canadian history many Canadians were faced with major physical problems, as soldiers returned from the front with a variety of serious illnesses and "**handicaps**," among them tuberculosis, blindness, mental illnesses, paralysis, and amputated limbs. The notion of who "deserved" help shifted. People with disabilities were no longer the unfortunate and the weak, but some of our "brightest and strongest"— our country's "hope for the future."

Because these disabilities had been incurred by our men in fighting for our country, the country felt an obligation to help them. And because, according to the *BNA Act*, the federal government was responsible for veterans, the federal government was obliged to take a leading role. Thus, help for people with disabilities took on a federal perspective in terms of government policy. Help also took on a federal perspective in terms of the voluntary sector: in 1918 both the Canadian Mental Health Association and the Canadian National Institute for the Blind were established.

Care for people with disabilities shifted from being merely the provision of food, shelter, and some educational services to the provision of rehabilitation services. The policy was to help veterans get into the labour market, and thus vocational training was seen as critical to the provision of care.

In 1915 the Military Hospitals Commission was created. Based on experience gained from World War I, a subcommittee of government workers and civilians was established shortly after war broke out in 1939 to develop a comprehensive plan for assisting veterans.

Another important result of the wars was the vast medical experience gained and the resulting innovations in **rehabilitation medicine**, including the development of "wonder drugs." After World War II, a group approach, now known as "the **rehabilitation team**" approach, was developed in Montreal to combat the many issues facing returning veterans. Team conferences and team planning are now standard practice in working with individuals who have disabilities, whether physical, mental, or intellectual. This approach recognizes that treating the effects of disabilities also includes the social aspects such as education, vocational training, housing, and employment and that professional expertise and access to a variety of services are needed.

CRITICAL THINKING BOX 6.1

In what way did World War I affect the public's view of people with disabilities?

The services developed in the war years for veterans were extended to include all Canadians. In 1948 national health grants were established by the federal government to assist all the provinces in providing rehabilitation services. These grants were also to be used for the training of medical personnel and for rehabilitation equipment. This initiative led to many services and facilities that we still have today, including Toronto's Variety Village, which was originally a school for children with disabilities and today offers a wide range of services including recreational activities for people with disabilities.

Rehabilitation Planning and the Labour Market

In the early twentieth century, the new **social movement** of organized labour pushed for protection of injured workers. This resulted in the Ontario *Workmen's Compensation Act* of 1914. At first this Act dealt with giving injured workers lost wages, but later it provided medical assistance and rehabilitation benefits as well. Today all provinces have such legislation, and in response to the position of women in the labour market, most such Acts have changed their wording from "workmen" to "workers."

A major breakthrough in the rehabilitation field was the 1951 Touchstone Conference. This national conference saw the provinces reassert their role in the field of rehabilitation, while at the same time encouraging a continuing presence of the federal government in planning and in coordinating a national rehabilitation program. The most significant outcome of the conference was the Federal–Provincial Vocational Rehabilitation of Disabled Persons (VRDP) initiative, which led to the *Vocational Rehabilitation of Disabled Persons Act* in 1961. The major tenet of the Act is that the federal government makes cost-sharing arrangements with the provinces for the provision of services to help people with disabilities enter or re-enter the workforce. The Act also requires that there be a special section in the federal and provincial employment services for placement in the work force of (primarily) people with physical disabilities.

Medicare

The federal *Hospital Insurance and Diagnostic Act* was passed in 1957. It provided people who have disabilities with free treatment and rehabilitation for insured services. In 1961

Saskatchewan established what has been called the first Medicare program in North America. This was followed in 1966 by the federal *Medical Care Act*, and with this legislation, a 50 percent cost-sharing arrangement for medical services was made between the federal government and the provinces. By 1971 all Canadians had medical coverage under this Act.

The *Canada Pension Plan Act* (1965) was another major breakthrough in this area. It stipulates that for those who have contributed to the plan and who are later deemed unlikely to be able to work because of a "severe" disability, a pension will be paid.

In 1964 a conference, similar in importance to the Touchstone Conference, was held for the "mentally retarded." Since the early 1960s there have been major breakthroughs for people with what are now called **developmental disabilities**. In 1963 a National Institute on Mental Retardation was founded together with York University in Toronto. Today, other such foundations exist at universities throughout Canada, which has greatly enhanced research and consultation in the field.

Parents of children diagnosed as having developmental disabilities have arguably had the greatest impact on care for any disabled group in Canadian history. The first such parents' council was formed in 1951; similar associations are in evidence throughout the country today, and there is a national association. These groups have successfully lobbied for services and for **antidiscriminatory** legislation. It is they who are largely responsible for the present-day inclusion, or mainstreaming, in many schools of children with special needs. Another major facilitator of changes in the treatment of those with developmental disabilities is the theory of normalization (to be discussed later in this chapter).

Human Rights Codes

Rehabilitation is not only an issue in Canada. Over the years the international community has put great emphasis on the prevention of various disabilities and on the integration of people with disabilities into society. This has manifested in a variety of ways, including international conferences such as the one dedicated to people with disabilities sponsored by the United Nations in 1981, the International Year of Disabled Persons. In part this was in reaction to lobbying by people with disabilities themselves, through a variety of self-help groups, in particular by Vietnam War veterans in the United States. Canada's response to the dedicated year was to table a special committee report entitled *Obstacles*.

In 1980, in Canada, a special committee was created to deal with issues affecting people with disabilities, including the effect of programs and services in the government and in the voluntary sector and the overlap and interlocking of such services. Perhaps most important, however, this committee addressed the issue of human rights. It strongly recommended that these people should have full and equal protection under the law.

Today, individuals with mental or physical disabilities are protected in human rights documents in Canada.

Care for the people with mental illnesses has developed along similar lines to those outlined for people with physical disabilities and for those with developmental disabilities. However, many would argue that the stigma is often greater for mental illness. The development of psychoactive drugs in the 1970s led to the discharge of vast numbers of patients from psychiatric institutions and allowed for care on an outpatient basis. These drugs did much to decrease the number of individuals getting custodial rather than rehabilitative care.

Advocacy

A major shift in the treatment of all individuals with disabilities has been "the consumer movement." No longer are people with disabilities unable to speak for themselves, and the 1980s trend toward self-help groups was critical in bringing about this change. This increased involvement is a result of several things, including better medical treatment and thus improvement in the mental and physical well-being of consumers; numerous improvements in assistive devices brought about by advanced technology; changes in expectations on the part of people with disabilities themselves and society as a whole; and increased access to and involvement in education and the workforce. To appreciate this change it is important to consider not only the historical changes that have occurred, but also the changes in theoretical perspectives.

THEORETICAL PERSPECTIVE

Three distinct models of disability have been developed, and each produces its own expertise and experts: (1) the biomedical model, (2) the economic model, and (3) the sociopolitical model. The operation of these models is reflected in the historical perspective, that is, throughout certain periods of Canadian history, implementation of one or the other model appears to have dominated.

Biomedical Model

The biomedical model emphasizes **impairment**, which the World Health Organization (WHO) in 1980 defined as "any abnormality of physiological or anatomical structure or function." Disablement is divided into respective varieties, and, according to Canadian lawyer and philosopher Jerome Bickenbach, social action concerns itself with issues of "prevention, cure, containment, pain management, rehabilitation, amelioration, and palliation."[1] This view largely resembles the medical model of treatment, and the individual is seen as a patient who is "sick" or hurt or, in some cases, a victim of bad luck. This model

---

BOX 6.1

Canadian Human Rights Act 1985

....

Section 2. Purpose

The purpose of this Act is to extend the laws in Canada to give effect, within the purview of matters coming within the legislative authority of Parliament, to the principle that every individual should have an equal opportunity with other individuals to make for himself or herself the life that he or she is able and wishes to have, consistent with his or her duties and obligations as a member of society, without being hindered in or prevented from doing so by discriminatory practices based on race, national or ethnic origin, colour, religion, age, sex, marital status, family status, disability or conviction for an offence for which a pardon has been granted....

(g)   Discrimination Based on Handicap

Handicap was added as a ground of discrimination in 1981 (S.O. 1981, c. 53, ss. 1, 2, 4: now ss. 1, 2, 5). While boards of inquiry had recognized an employer's duty to make reasonable accommodation of an employee's characteristics as a requirement of the Code, the 1986 amendments (S.O. 1986, c. 64, s. 18(15) introduced into section 23(2) (now s. 24(2)) an express reference to reasonable accommodation and a provision (s. 16(1)(a); now s. 17(2)) dealing specifically with the duty of accommodation in relation to the handicapped (S.O., 1986, c. 64, s. 18(10)).

Source: *Human Rights Legislation: An Office Consolidation.* Toronto: Butterworths, 1991.

---

lends itself to social goals that focus on accommodation, that is, society is obligated to provide a basic level of medical care and health services. This model also had a role to play in concerns about eligibility criteria and the emphasis on assessment in determining need. Much of the early history of disability in Canada and society's reaction to disability before World War I can be understood by using this model.

Economic Model

The economic model emphasizes the economics of disablement. How does one's impairment affect one's capabilities? This model is concerned with the effects of a disability not only on the individual, but also on society as a whole and on the individual's ability, or inability, to contribute to society. Concerns are framed as labour market issues. Any disability is significant in that it limits a worker's productive potential and skills. Using a cost–benefit analysis, people with disabilities are seen as an economic cost. Policies must take into account that people with disabilities may not be able to work to their full potential and thus not contribute fully to the labour market. These people are also a cost in terms of the provision of health and other services such as housing. This view of people with disabilities emphasizes the need to address any barriers that prohibit full participation of people with disabilities in the workforce, and it leads to the development of social policy that strives to fully integrate people with disabilities into the economic market.

The economic model can serve to explain the shift to rehabilitative services that occurred after World War I. Also, from this perspective many of the policies toward people with disabilities adopted by Canada in this century can be explained—for example, the establishment of vocational services, social insurance programs, and social assistance programs.

Sociopolitical Model

The third model is the one most representative of current trends in the area of disability policy. From this perspective, disability is viewed as a type of social injustice. This social injustice stems from the way people with disabilities are stigmatized in society and from the way they are treated, that is, from discriminatory practices. This sociopolitical model blends sociological theories and psychosocial theories about disability with an advocacy and civil rights perspective. It is society that determines disability; it is discriminatory social attitudes that become part of the social fabric, part of how institutions are organized and operated, and it is these institutions and their practices that often disadvantage and marginalize people with disabilities. In this model society disables people.

The sociopolitical model holds that disability needs to be destigmatized and that respect and rights must go hand in hand in shaping policy for people with disabilities. Thus, disability issues resemble other equality issues, such as racial discrimination and women's issues.

CRITICAL THINKING BOX 6.2

As a blind child today, how would your life be different from what it would have been in the 1980s?

The sociopolitical model is reflective of the rise of self-help groups and the increased participation of people with disabilities in the sociopolitical realm. The independent living movement stands as a clear example of a shift toward **empowerment**. This model is the one most concerned with reform.

As with most theories and models, social policy is often explained by a combination of models. The policies developed for people with disabilities are extremely diverse. Jerome Bickenbach cites fourteen policy areas for people with disabilities in his book *Physical Disability and Social Policy*. These include biomedical services (research, therapy, chronic care), independent living (group homes, the deinstitutionalization movement), employment issues, housing concerns, communication (media) issues, and human rights. In part because of the diversity of issues and concerns and because of the variety of disabilities (physical, mental, and intellectual), much of the policy development has been fragmented and is ad hoc in nature.

Obstacles (1981) discussed three goals sought by disabled individuals, and these individual goals have marked policy development in Canada for people with disabilities ever since. Individuals and groups representing disabled individuals have differed on which goal they want emphasized. Some goals have been emphasized more than others at particular times. Nevertheless, the three goals are as applicable today as they were in 1981. People with disabilities want

1. *to be treated with respect*. This includes the idea that people with disabilities should participate in decision making and in developing their own services and agencies.

2. *to have the same opportunities as other Canadians to participate socially, economically, educationally, recreationally, and in all other ways in the social life of the country*. Participation should not be limited by discriminatory acts or practices, and the means necessary to achieve this participation should be provided.

3. *services and assistance to ensure that their needs are met*. Environments, including the workplace, should accommodate people with disabilities so that full social participation can be achieved.

One issue that has complicated the development of consistent social policy in the area of disability is the conflict between programs that discourage people with disabilities from working with programs that encourage them to work. For example, is a person with a disability actually unable to work and thus in need and deserving of financial assistance? Or, could this disabled person work if certain accommodations were made in the workplace? The needs of people with disabilities are as varied as their disabilities, their capabilities, and their skills. Much of the confusion around policy stems from the various definitions of disability.

CRITICAL THINKING BOX 6.3

....

The sociopolitical model argues that society disables people. In what ways could society disable an individual?

Normalization Theory

A milestone in the treatment of people with disabilities is the "theory of **normalization**," developed in the 1970s. This theory led to the belief that all individuals are entitled to lives that are "as normal as possible." In many ways this theory explains the massive **deinstitutionalization** of those with developmental disabilities and mental illnesses. With the

---

BOX 6.2

Case Scenario

....

In an article entitled "Imprinting Our Image on the World," Judith Snow, a woman with disabilities who lives in Ontario, describes how society's view of people with disabilities and of their potential—and not her physical disability itself—sustained her disadvantages. Snow describes how after completing university, her world became limited by the practices of government and their institutions, who seemed insensitive to her needs as an individual.

Over a three-and-a-half-year period, Snow was bounced from one chronic care hospital to another because each facility was unable to provide her with the minimum five hours of daily attendant care that she required.

In an effort to preserve her mental health and to keep active and connected with life outside the institution, she continued to work four days a week at York University. However, Snow states, "The money I earned was used up in paying for a semi-private room, a private nurse in the mornings and my transportation ... my health began to break down because of the institution, its policies, atmosphere and staff. No matter how hard I worked to explain how I needed to be active, I was always pushing against the life of the institution."

Source: Judith Snow, "Imprinting Our Image on the World," in *An International Anthology of Women's Disabilities*, Diane Driedger and Susan Gray, eds. (Charlottetown: Gynergy, 1992), pp. 81–82.

---

move of many individuals with disabilities from institutions and asylums to group homes and other forms of independent living, people with disabilities are better able to participate in the daily social life of society. Deinstitutionalization has allowed many people with disabilities to have more participatory lives, but some argue that the real impetus behind this normalization was to save public money. Governments often moved people with disabilities out of institutions without providing them with adequate community programs and financial resources. Especially in urban areas, this policy has led to many people, particularly those with mental illnesses, becoming homeless.

Inherent in the theory of normalization is that "normal" is a desired outcome and that it is possible to determine what normal is. If what is normal can be determined, it follows that we can also determine what is not normal. Sociologists have written at great length about how a dominant group regards its experience as "natural," as "normal," and experiences that differ from these are considered less than normal. Therefore, when it comes to disability, it is society that socially constructs the difference. Paul Higgins, in *Making Disability, Explaining the Social Transformation of Human Variation*, points out that **learning disability** is a new term for a condition that in earlier times was called "word blindness." This example illustrates how views of people with disabilities are ever changing and that the issue of disability is an ongoing one. The example also helps to remind us that throughout history, normal has been a narrow concept and because of that, society has been able to shut out many from the mainstream, be it an ethnic group, women, or people with disabilities. Individuals with disabilities have often said that it is not the physical, mental, or intellectual disability that represents the major obstacle in their lives, but the barriers that society creates.

WHAT ABOUT THE FUTURE?

Individuals with a variety of disabilities now take part in the day-to-day life of Canadian society. Much remains to be done, and some accomplishments are being threatened. The recent recessionary years have seen the cancellation of many programs that assist people with disabilities, as major cuts to government spending have occurred in all areas of

CRITICAL THINKING BOX 6.4

Think of a particular disability (physical, mental, or intellectual) and describe two obstacles that the person who has this disability faces because of the disability itself. Now think of three obstacles the person faces that represent barriers imposed by society.

health care. Unemployment rates have risen, and there is greater competition for fewer jobs. Employment equity legislation has been curtailed, for example, by the Conservative government in Ontario. It is difficult to determine what the consequences of such actions will be on the lives of people with disabilities in Ontario and in other provinces, as more and more groups are competing for limited government resources.

Nevertheless, great strides have been made in the way disabled individuals are viewed and in terms of increasing the participation of people with disabilities in decision making that affects their own lives (**self-determination**). The inclusion of individuals with disabilities in advertisement, although still minimal, would not have been thought of five years ago.

In the early years of Canadian history, as our pioneers fought for their very existence, no one thought much about any individual's—let alone any individual with a disability's—recreational needs. The history of sport and of the Olympics is a relatively new one, yet today, wheelchair athletes take part in the Paralympics.

As with many developments, change takes place when people are aware of and become involved in issues. As our population ages, more and more Canadians are going to face physical disability and this, in turn, will increase awareness of the needs of people with disabilities. Since women have a longer life expectancy than men do, the needs of disabled women likely will increase in disproportion to those of men (see Figure 6.1).

In 1989 in Ontario, the then Office for Disabled Persons engaged Environics Research Group Limited to conduct a survey of the needs and attitudes of disabled Ontarians. The major findings are representative of a significant number of individuals with disabilities and organizations serving them. Most of all, the survey provided people with disabilities with an opportunity to share their views. For most "clients" the issue of "equality of opportunity and access" remains uppermost (see Table 6.1). They cite income as the area in most need of improvement (see Table 6.2); it is important to note that Table 6.2 was derived before the recent recession. Table 6.3 gives further evidence that, although gains have been made, people with disabilities in Ontario are still disadvantaged in comparison with Ontario's "general population." It is also interesting to note that how a disability limits a person is related to the severity and to the type of disability (see Figure 6.2).

BOX 6.3

Wheelchair Racers Preview Olympic Dash

....

If yesterday's races at the Metro Toronto Wheelchair Challenge were any indication, the names Chantal Peticlerc and Cheri Becerra will be heard together a lot in Atlanta in the next few weeks.

In a pair of possible previews of the Olympics, Montreal's Peticlerc, and Becerra, of Nebraska City, Neb., ended up even.

In the afternoon's first major clash, Becerra edged out Peticlerc for the 100-metre final.

About an hour later, Peticlerc returned the favor, winning the 400 metres in a Canadian-record time of 56.65 seconds.

The rubber match and the real test comes in the 800 metres today.

"I knew what to expect. I've seen her race before and I was pretty impressed," Peticlerc said.

But Becerra wasn't quite as impressed by Peticlerc, predicting a U.S. sweep of the 800-metre medals in Atlanta.

The women's 800-metre wheelchair event, along with the men's 1500 metres, will be a demonstration sport in Atlanta. Peticlerc and Becerra will also take part in the Atlanta Paralympics, following the Olympics, for athletes with disabilities.

In earlier action yesterday, Brampton racer Jeff Adams cruised to victory in the men's 1500 metres, a distance in which he, unofficially, has the world's fastest time.

Source: Josh Rubin, "Wheelchair Racers Preview Olympic Dash," *Toronto Star*, 14 July 1996. Reprinted by permission—The Toronto Star Syndicate.

BOX 6.4

Atlanta Olympics Take Aim at Barriers to the Disabled

Call it an Olympic first. One hundred years after the Games began, the world's most prestigious athletic event is opening itself as never before to people with physical disabilities.

Spectators and athletes alike will find accommodations in design from the height of the counters at hot dog stands to sight lines at the two field hockey stadiums to the shape of faucets in restrooms, all re-engineered for state-of-the-art accessibility.

The 26th Summer Games are the first to come under the Americans With Disabilities Act, which makes ease of access in public places mandatory.

Organizers anticipate about 1.5 million people will attend Olympic events.... Following on Aug. 15, the 10th Paralympic competitions are expected to attract 3500 disabled athletes from 127 countries. Officials estimate that 10 per cent of the million spectators at the Paralympics and 2 per cent of those at the Olympics will have physical disabilities.

With such back-to-back events, the new facilities are destined to become highly visible proving grounds for the U.S. law's sweeping requirements.

New U.S. Law Makes Accessibility Mandatory
Already, a potential winner has been identified. "The (Olympic) Stadium is the most successful, physically accessible stadium anywhere in the country," declares Jim Cherry, an Atlanta lawyer specializing in civil rights of people with disabilities.

The scope of the design project and its timing have tested the architects involved. The Americans With Disabilities Act came into effect in January 1993, just as early drawings were being produced. Any facility not yet completed had to comply, so architects and consultants set about redesigning such megastructures as the 83,000-seat stadium.

In the end, it will be the only site with swing-away chairs—200 of them—plus triple-seat units on casters, which can be removed when extra wheelchair spaces become necessary.

(cont'd)

In addition to seating, such issues as ramp slopes and lines of sight were tackled at every venue.

Among them are the stadium (home of the Atlanta Braves as of next year), two new stadiums for field hockey, the aquatic centre at Georgia Tech and the tennis centre at Stone Mountain, the International Horse Park equestrian centre and bleachers for viewing cycling, shooting and kayaking.

More challenging, and less successful in the eyes of some activists, are installations for rowing events at Lake Lanier, where spectators must descend a steep hill to reach viewing stands. Caught between the demands of the new law and environmentalists wishing to preserve the terrain, organizers decided in favor of the hill. Van service will be provided.

Not only concession stands must be accessible. Ticket booths, restrooms, restaurants, parking lots, bank machines, water fountains and elevators also must be barrier-free.

Source: Patricia Dane Rogers, "Atlanta Olympics Take Aim at Barriers to People the Disabled," *Washington Post Writer's Group*, July 1996.

Figure 6.1 Characteristics of Ontarians with Disabilities

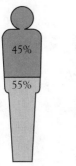

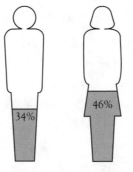
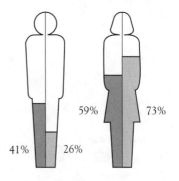

Proportion of men and women with disabilities by age group
- 15 to 64
- 65 and over

Percentage of men and women with disabilities living in households (all ages)

Percentage of men and women with disabilities aged 65+ living in households and institutions
- Living in households
- Living in institutions

Source: Adapted from Statistics Canada, *Adults with Disabilities, Their Employment and Education Characteristics*, Catalogue No. 82-554, 1991.

Table 6.1 Most Difficult Goal to Achieve

	Type of Client Disability					
	Responding Organizations (65) %	Mobility/ Agility (39) %	Emotional/ Mental (32) %	Hearing/ Speech (32) %	Vision (27) %	Multiple Disabilities (40) %
Ensure equality of opportunity and access	23	26	19	25	22	25
Help people with disabilities to integrate into communities	15	13	19	13	15	8
Ensure full range of services for people with disabilities	11	5	9	6	0	8
Help disabled persons enter and succeed in workforce	9	13	13	13	22	15
Help disabled persons to be independent	9	10	13	9	11	8
Make sure that people with disabilities receive a fair share of government services and funding	9	8	16	13	7	13
Promote acceptance of people with disabilities among the general public	5	8	3	9	7	8
Develop sense of community among those with similar disabilities	3	3	3	3	4	3

(cont'd)

Reach as many as possible who have same disabling conditions	3	5	0	0	7	3
Obtain parallel or separate services	2	3	0	3	4	3
Don't know or no answer	11	8	6	6	0	10

Note: Totals may not add to 100% because of rounding.

Source: Adapted from Statistics Canada, *Adults with Disabilities, Their Employment and Education Characteristics*, Catalogue No. 82-554, 1991, p. 87.

Table 6.2 Priorities for Improvement

Area of Priority	% of Respondents Who Chose Area
Income	29
Education	17
Accessibility	11
Recreation/Leisure Opportunities	9
Housing	7
Health Care	7
Assistive Devices	7
Transportation	6
Employment	3
Rehabilitation	2
Other	2

Note: Figures may not add to 100% because of rounding.

Source: Adapted from Statistics Canada, *Adults with Disabilities, Their Employment and Education Characteristics*, Catalogue No. 82-554, 1991, p. 62.

Table 6.3 Comparisons with the General Population

Characteristics (%)	Respondents with Disabilities (%)	General Population
Gender		
Males	39	49
Females	61	51
Ages (years)		
15–34	21	43
35–54	26	31
55–64	19	12
65+	32	14
Educational Attainment		
Elementary school	18	12
Secondary school	44	45
Some postsecondary	34	25
University	9	11
Employment Status		
Working full time	23	56
Working part time	9	10
Unemployment/looking for work	4	5
Students	5	11
Not in labour force	60	18
Annual Household Income		
< $10,000	14	12
$10 000–$20 000	22	16
$20 000–$30 000	17	16
$30 000–$40 000	10	17
$40 000–$50 000	8	14
> $50 000	10	25

Note: Totals may not add to 100% because of rounding.

Source: Adapted from Statistics Canada, *Adults with Disabilities, Their Employment and Education Characteristics*, Catalogue No. 82-554, 1991, p. 20.

Figure 6.2 Type and Severity of Most Limiting Disabilities

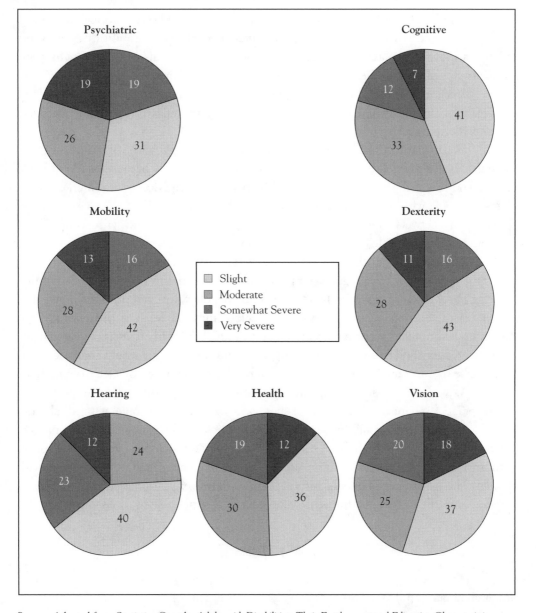

Source: Adapted from Statistics Canada, *Adults with Disabilities, Their Employment and Education Characteristics*, Catalogue No. 82-554, 1991, p. 17.

CHAPTER SUMMARY

The issue of disability is not a simple one, and the interplay of both historical events and theoretical perspectives affects the day-to-day lives of people with disabilities. As a society there is a move to greater empowerment of individuals with disabilities. Yet, in many ways, people with disabilities are still not accorded full participation in our society.

Wars, the labour movement, public disasters, epidemics, and the resultant changes in social policy and social programs have had an impact on policies that affect people with disabilities.

The initial institutional provider of services to people with disabilities was the Church. This responsibility shifted to the government, especially because of World War I and II. The rise of the voluntary sector and increased participation and awareness of the needs of people with disabilities among the Canadian public at large led to a sharing of responsibility between the government and the private sector. Now, with reduced government funding, the role of the voluntary sector is likely to increase.

A major trend in the past two decades has been for greater involvement in all aspects of social policy and programs for people with disabilities by people with disabilities.

Three models help to explain the direction of policy initiatives: (1) the biomedical model, (2) the economic model, and (3) the sociopolitical model. The theory of normalization has led to fuller participation of people with disabilities in all areas of everyday life (work, recreation, and housing), and yet this same movement, many would argue, accounts for there being vast numbers of individuals who need care and have no place to go for help.

As with other issues of equality, acceptance and attitudinal change must occur before practice changes. The needs, issues, and demands of people with disabilities resemble those of other groups in Canadian society who are disadvantaged or marginalized. There are parallels with the fight of people with disabilities for empowerment and equality with various Aboriginal and ethnic groups, with immigrants and refugees, and with women. The experience of people with disabilities, however, is unique in this country, as is reflected in the history and in the development of theories related to disability.

KEY TERMS

antidiscriminatory, p. 151

deinstitutionalization, p. 156

developmental disability, p. 151

disability, p. 146

empowerment, p. 155

handicaps, p. 149

impairment, p. 152

inclusive societies, p. 146

learning disability, p. 157

"mentally deficient," p. 148

DISCUSSION QUESTIONS

1. Compare and contrast three major theoretical perspectives about people with disabilities.
2. What accounts for the great changes in social policy toward people with disabilities that were brought about by the two world wars? In other words, why did the wars have such a great impact on the lives of people with disabilities?
3. From the perspective of the sociopolitical model, what effects might recent government cutbacks in the fields of health, education, and welfare have on the struggle for empowerment of people with disabilities?
4. What might be some negative consequences to the "theory of normalization"?

NOTES

1. Jerome Bickenbach, *Physical Disability and Social Policy* (Toronto: University of Toronto Press, 1993), p. 12.

Diversity and Conformity: The Role of Gender

Leslie Butler

I now see the women's movement for equality as simply the necessary first stage of a much larger sex role revolution.... What had to be changed was the obsolete feminine and masculine sex roles.... It seemed to me men weren't really the enemy—they were fellow victims, suffering from an outmoded masculine mystique that made them feel unnecessarily inadequate when there were no more bears to kill.

— Betty Friedan, *The Feminist Mystique*

God created men and women different—then let them remain each in their own position.

— Queen Victoria

Objectives

After reading this chapter, you should be able to

- define gender identity and gender spheres

- describe the different spheres men and women occupy

- give social and biological explanations for why men and women choose or are channelled in different life directions

- discuss the ways in which gender divisions are positive or negative for individuals and society

- form opinions about what, if anything, to do about the gender issues raised in this chapter

INTRODUCTION

The differences between men and women are perhaps the most celebrated of all human diversities. Poets and philosophers have probed the mysteries of love and the wonders of sexual difference for centuries, but only recently have sex and gender become the subject of scientific study. These studies confirm what many might already have known intuitively: your sex and gender influence every aspect of your life. Whether you are born a boy or a girl will affect everything from what kinds of jobs you will have and how frequently you want sex with your partner, to whether you are likely to be poor and how long you might live. Our masculinity or femininity is a physical and psychological lens that filters our very perception of reality. Knowing something about how sex and gender influence our personal and social lives can help us to better understand our experiences. But first, we need to understand what these terms mean.

To begin with, sex and gender are two different things, even though the terms are sometimes used interchangeably. Your **sex** is determined at conception and refers to the reproductive organs you are born with and your hormonal makeup. Your **gender** is a social role governed by how your culture defines masculinity and femininity. Sex is therefore something unchangeable, whereas gender changes as cultures evolve. (Twenty-first-century Canadian women wearing suits or playing sports would seem terribly unfeminine to their nineteenth-century counterparts.) This distinction between sex and gender is important because if we want to build a fair and equal society, we need to have the wisdom to know what we can change and what we cannot.

WHAT IS GENDER?

Gender Identity

Despite the many changes of the twentieth century, there are still clusters of traits we designate masculine and feminine. These clusters of traits make up our conception of masculine and feminine **gender identity,** or what it means to be a man or a woman. In North American culture, a truly masculine person is, above all, competent. He is physically strong and sexually virile, aggressive, logical, unemotional, decisive, and protective. A feminine person is, above all, warm and nurturing. She is physically "soft," intuitive, emotional, indecisive, and in need of protection. Women talk, men act; women conciliate, men confront. These associations are powerful determinants of how we feel and how we act as men and women. Some feminists have pointed out that masculine and feminine traits are not valued equally, that society pays lip service to the value of nurturing and warmth but actually rewards masculine traits more concretely than feminine ones.

These clusters of traits are **gender stereotypes**, or generalizations, about the way most men and women are expected to behave. Individuals certainly deviate from these stereotypes, and modern Canadian society tolerates a much wider range of opposite gender behaviour than in the past. However, despite the many social changes of this century, statistical evidence shows there is a surprisingly high degree of conformity to traditional roles.

It is tempting to believe we are unaffected by stereotypes, that we are free to look and behave as we choose. But think of the penalty a man pays for being effeminate and a woman pays for being "butch." Penalties such as ridicule, ostracism, and workplace discrimination are called **social controls**, and they help enforce rigid gender behaviour codes. When men are feeling emotional or vulnerable, they may feel conflicted about feeling "feminine" and may suppress those feelings for fear of being ridiculed. Women may similarly suppress their masculine side. Enforced by social controls, the gender stereotype becomes a self-fulfilling prophecy. Biology, too, may limit our freedom to choose our gender identity. We will discuss the social and biological influences on gender in more detail later in this chapter.

Diversity or Conformity?

It is interesting to note here that because gender is a social role and controls are in place to make sure most people play the right role, gender may actually enforce conformity rather than encourage diversity. In other words, gender may limit rather than liberate us.

Consider for a moment the expected attitude of men and women toward sex. Men are expected to (and do) initiate sex, to want it frequently, and to value sex over other kinds of intimacy; women are expected to value love over sex, to desire sex less frequently, and to see love as a prerequisite for sex. Because our very identity as men and women includes these messages about sex, these role definitions may profoundly affect and perhaps limit our sexual freedom. Women may feel unfeminine, and thus uncomfortable, if they are sexually aggressive; men may feel unmasculine, and thus uncomfortable, if they prefer submissive roles in sexual interplay. Women may feel guilty or conflicted about having purely sexual relationships that do not have emotional commitments. It is finally okay for women to want sex, but they must not want it too much for fear of being labelled "easy" or a slut. There is simply no male equivalent in our language for slut. Apparently, only women can be too easy and are far more likely than men to feel the guilt or shame associated with sexual promiscuity. Alternatively, men who are anything less than obsessed with sex may find themselves ridiculed or questioning their own masculinity. These powerful messages about appropriate sexual feelings and behaviour are one example of how gender identity may be restrictive rather than liberating.

Challenges to Traditional Gender Identity

It has become more commonplace to see people openly challenging these behaviour codes. **Transvestites** are those men and women who adopt the dress and behaviour of the opposite sex. Their refusal to behave in a gender-appropriate way challenges cultural definitions of masculinity and femininity. The often harsh reaction to transvestites is a measure of how deeply ingrained is the idea that women should behave like women and men like men. **Transsexuals** are genetically of one sex but have a psychological urge to belong to the opposite sex. Some transsexuals seek surgery to modify their sexual organs to bring their biological self in line with their psychological self. Gay sexuality has become so openly expressed in North American society that early tentative attempts to portray homosexuality in a sensitive rather than denigrating ways (movies such as *The Kiss of the Spider Woman* and *The Crying Game*) have been followed by mainstream sitcoms such as *Will and Grace*.

Although the challenges to rigid gender identity continue and even move into the mainstream of our culture, they are still the exception rather than the rule. The strict definitions of masculinity and femininity persist, along with the expectation that most people will adopt the "right" kind of behaviour. And, in fact, the vast majority do.

Gender Patterns

Both your sex and gender have a powerful influence on the kinds of experiences you will have in your life. When parents gaze at their children, for example, they may not know that compared with her brother, their daughter is more likely to

- live longer and be widowed
- earn less
- live in poverty
- marry younger
- be a single parent

Their son, on the other hand, is more likely than his sister to

- commit suicide
- be a victim of violence
- remarry if divorced
- lose custody of his children in divorce
- get cancer or AIDS

BOX 7.1

Feminist and Feminine?

In her groundbreaking work of the early 1960s called *The Feminine Mystique*, Betty Friedan chronicled women's struggle to break out of the confines of their domestic straightjacket. But Friedan also argued that the new role of women didn't mean they had to hate men or give up fulfilling romantic and sexual relationships with men. Much of the backlash against feminism in the past thirty years has centred on feminists as man-haters. Some believe being a feminist means women have to hate men or give up on marriage. Others say simply that the idea of romantic love is so entwined with traditional gender roles that it dies when those roles change and overlap. Still others say men react to the feminist challenge with a powerful backlash that includes violence. Friedan herself believed that feminism was not incompatible with romantic love and that the liberation of women would lead to the liberation of men.

Canadian statistics continue to bear out these facts. A woman can expect to live to age 81, whereas a man can only expect to live to age 75. At all ages Canadian women are more likely to be widows than men, and when women reach age 80, two thirds will be widows compared with just less than half of men aged 80. Half of elderly women who live alone live below the poverty line.[1] Women who work full time continue to earn only 70 percent of what full-time male workers earn,[2] and when women have children, the wage gap widens further. Women have part-time jobs much more often than men, and they continue to shoulder a greater share of the childcare and domestic work.[3] In Canada, women head four out of every five single-parent households,[4] and 56 percent of those households headed by single women have incomes that fall below the poverty line.[5]

It may surprise some readers to know that North American men are more likely to experience violence than women are, especially in light of our heightened awareness of abused women. In the United States, men are three times more likely to be killed than women.[6] Men of all ages commit suicide more frequently than their female counterparts, and when men reach age 80, they are five times more likely to commit suicide than women.[7] Although more women than men are entering Canadian universities, men are still far more likely than women to get higher degrees.[8] This underrepresentation of women with advanced degrees mirrors women's tendency to be shut out of high-level jobs, which is sometimes called the **glass ceiling.**

Individual men and women will not always follow these patterns. Nevertheless, there is striking consistency in the kinds of experiences men and women can expect to have. Let's look at some in more detail.

WHAT ARE GENDER SPHERES?

Because people conform to fairly well-defined notions of masculinity and femininity, patterns of male and female behaviour emerge. These patterns create what we might call **gender spheres**. By this, we simply mean there are areas of work, school, and play in which men dominate and areas in which women dominate. Although there has been a lot of social change in Canada, these traditional divisions between what men and women do are surprisingly persistent.

Occupational Spheres

In the area of work, men still dominate in administration, technology, the professional fields, and jobs requiring physical strength. Women still find themselves dominating in the "caring" professions such as nursing, social work, and teaching. Women also predominate in the clerical and service sectors. Table 7.1 is based on data from the year 2000 and compares the number of men and women employed in selected industry sectors. The data show clearly that men and women still find themselves in predictable male and female occupations.

Educational Spheres

Like the workplace, education also has its gender spheres. We might expect this because educational institutions feed the labour market and as such are a kind of gate that young men and women pass through on their way to jobs. If men and women self-select or are selected out (through biased hiring standards) of certain educational programs, then the gate to jobs requiring that training will close. Data from 1998 show that in Canadian community colleges, men are far more likely than women to study architecture, engineering, and applied sciences. Women predominate in secretarial, community and social services, nursing, and the humanities.[9] Distinct patterns also exist in universities, where women significantly outnumber men in education, health professions, social sciences, and the humanities; men are far more likely than women to enter engineering, mathematics, and physical science.[10]

Table 7.1 Employment by Industry and Sex, 2000

Industry/Sector	Men (n)	Women (n)
Manufacturing	1 644 500	635 700
Construction	727 200	88 400
Management, administration	292 200	254 000
Agriculture	259 800	112 800
Forestry, fishing, mining, oil	238 500	44 500
Health care, social assistance	288 700	1 237 700
Education services	343 200	631 600
Accommodation and food services	317 390	570 100

Source: Statistics Canada, "Employment by Detailed Industry and Sex," from *Labour Force Historical Review*, Catalogue No. 71F0004XCB, March 2001.

Leisure Spheres

Men and women have different amounts of free time, and they often choose to spend it differently. Although men spend more time than women doing paid work, they have slightly more free time than women because women do more unpaid work such as child-care and housework.

As the gender stereotype would predict, men are more physically active at all ages than women. In 1998, 44 percent of Canadian men reported that they regularly partici-pate in sports, compared to only 26 percent of women.[11] Men are far more likely than women to choose competitive and physically rough sports such as football and hockey; women are more likely to choose swimming, cross-country skiing, and bowling.[12]

To summarize, men and women continue to choose or be forced into separate work, school, and leisure activities. Figure 7.1 is compiled from 1998 data and gives a clear illustration of where masculine and feminine spheres remain separate and where they have begun to overlap.

The Issue of Equality

Once we recognize that men and women occupy different occupational and educational spheres, it is natural to wonder whether these spheres are separate but equal, or separate but unequal. In fact, the issue of equality is central to most questions surrounding sex and gender, and we will return to it several times in this chapter.

CRITICAL THINKING BOX 7.1

....

Superiority in Sports

Is male superiority in athletics a result of nature or nurture? Consider how women have closed the gap in record time for the Boston Marathon: In 1964 the men's marathon record time was 1 hour and 13 minutes faster than the women's record. In 2001, only 13 minutes and 2 seconds separated the men's record from the women's. With more women participating, better training for women, and larger monetary rewards, will women one day close the gap altogether?

Figure 7.1 Gender Spheres

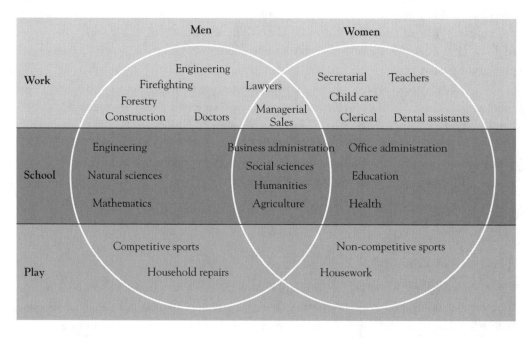

Source: Compiled from Statistics Canada, *Employment Income by Occupation*, Catalogue No. 93-332, April 1993; *The Daily*, Catalogue No. 11-001, May 11, 1993; and *Canadian Social Trends*, Catalogue No. 11-008, Spring 1995.

It is hard to ignore the economic inequality between the sexes in Canada: women simply do not get an equal share of the pay rewards, whether they work outside the home or inside. The work of raising children and maintaining a household goes unpaid. Women's occupations—childcare, clerical work, nursing, service jobs—for the most part pay less than men's—business, manufacturing, and professional jobs. Is it just a coincidence that women's work is less valued than men's? Is childcare, for example, inherently less valuable than janitorial work? Did men simply take an unfair share of the material rewards? Or, does having a pool of cheap and even unpaid (female) labour simply benefit employers? (Wages are kept down when there is a reserve army of labour ready and waiting to fill jobs.) A stark example of economic inequality between the sexes can be found in Table 7.2, which shows that even in female-dominated professions such as teaching, nursing and secretarial work, the few men who do enter those fields tend to make much more money than their female colleagues.

If women are the losers in the economic sphere, there is strong evidence that men are losers in the interpersonal sphere. As breadwinners forced to be absent from the home, they are more likely to forgo close relationships with their children. Confined by rigid definitions of masculinity, many men may be unable to achieve emotional and intellectual intimacy with their partners. Men rarely get sole custody of their children in divorces and often play a secondary role in raising children after divorce (see Box 7.2). For many men,

Table 7.2 Wage Gap in Selected Occupations

Occupation	Average Salary ($) Men	Average Salary ($) Women	Difference
Doctor	111 251	73 071	38 180
Lawyer	86 108	50 012	36 096
Engineer	52 154	37 838	14 316
Dental hygienist or assistant	49 938	25 764	24 174
Elementary-school teacher	45 471	37 694	7 777
Firefighter	44 883	32 439	12 444
Sales manager	44 592	26 921	17 671
Secretary	33 839	23 880	9 959
Childcare worker	20 897	13 252	7 645

Source: Statistics Canada, "Major Fields of Study of Male and Female Trades and Other Non-University Certificate Holders, 1991," from *The Daily*; Catalogue No. 11-001, 11 May 1993.

BOX 7.2

Child Custody Awards

....

A 1998 survey of 5000 Canadian divorce cases showed women get sole custody of children in 80 percent of Canadian divorces. Men get sole custody only 8.4 percent of the time. Some would say this is concrete evidence of gender discrimination against men. Intentionally or unintentionally, the courts may assume that men are unsuited for nurturing and raising children, leaving men with the pain of losing their children. Men's rights groups and Web sites devoted to promoting men's interests in custody awards have proliferated in recent years.

Source: Lorne D. Bertrand, and Joseph P. Hornick, "The Survey of Child Support Awards: Preliminary Analysis of Phase 2 Data," presented to the Special Joint Committee on Child Custody and Access (October 1998–May 1999).

---

the stress of having the family's material well-being thrust on their shoulders results in mental and physical health problems. The bare fact is, men die younger than women, and more men than women suffer from chronic stress-related diseases such as heart disease and alcoholism. Being valued as a meal ticket is probably every bit as confining for men as being valued as sex object or mother figure is for women. A picture of two solitudes continues to emerge with men cast in the role of provider and women in the role of caregiver.

Sexual Politics

Women who have historically found themselves on the short end of the economic stick have nonetheless achieved some degree of equality through what might be called sexual politics. This is the delicate, usually unacknowledged, power struggle between men who desire, or appear to desire, sex more than their female partners, who have the power to give or withhold sex. The fact that men have a greater sexual appetite than women, or at least a more openly acknowledged sexual appetite than women, is evident in sex trade statistics. The job market for female prostitutes, strippers, exotic dancers, and pornographic subjects far exceeds the demand for their male counterparts. This apparent difference in the sex drives of each gender has caused many feminists to observe that the only two professions in which women are able to out-earn men are prostitution and fashion modelling.

CRITICAL THINKING BOX 7.2

···

Sexual Politics

How real is the issue of sexual politics in most relationships between men and women? Do women use men's more openly acknowledged desire for sex to get some of the things they want out of a relationship (i.e., financial security, help around the home)?

Whether men hire prostitutes, exchange their paycheques for regular sex in marriage, or merely use money (along with flattery and favours) when courting and wooing, men's apparently greater need for sex gives women some leverage in negotiating with their partners. Before women could advance themselves in paid work outside the home, they could improve their socioeconomic standing by being sexually desirable to a wealthy man. Today, the process of sexual negotiation is much more subtle, and may even be invisible to those involved in it. But in the day-to-day give and take of male–female relationships, sexual politics continues to play an often unacknowledged role in determining who gets what out of the partnership.

The Myth of Progress

It may surprise some of you to see such stark evidence of persisting gender spheres. After all, aren't the bad old days gone? The days when women were prevented by law from entering politics, and when no man would choose to be a secretary or nurse for fear of total ostracism are gone. Much *has* changed. Economic imperatives like the need for two-income families have resulted in real changes in the workplace and the home. Attitudes about what is acceptable for men and women have also changed. Women now have professional hockey and basketball leagues. Some men choose to be nurses and secretaries. But the majority of men and women are still channelled into "acceptable" roles by powerful social controls. It may be that our liberated attitudes toward gender have changed much faster than social reality has.

We may have trouble accepting that gender spheres persist because deeply ingrained in our consciousness is the notion of progress. Our worldview is dominated by the idea that things are getting better and that this inexorable force will march ever forward and never backward. So even though there may not be equality between the sexes now, we assume there will be equality some time in the not-too-distant future. But the number of women in politics, for example, goes up and down. There were significantly more women in the Ontario legislature in the Bob Rae government of the early 1990s than there were in the Mike Harris government. It is clear that gains made by women into the traditionally male bastion of politics can also be lost. But so strong is our notion of progress that some people think that very little should actively be done to eliminate the inequalities between the sexes because things will gradually just get better.

WHY GENDER SPHERES EXIST

Nature and Nurture

Once we recognize that gender spheres exist, and that men and women do find themselves playing fairly predictable roles, it is natural to wonder why. Do we behave as men and women because we were born that way or because we learned how to behave? When a man is masculine, is he strong, aggressive, and unemotional because of biological factors or social factors? Does testosterone make him so? Or is he merely conforming to rigidly maintained social definitions of masculinity? Does a woman's biological makeup lead her to be nurturing, emotional, and conciliatory? Or does she learn there will be penalties if she behaves in an unfeminine way? You will recognize this as the **nature/nurture** debate central to most questions about human behaviour. The debate rages on. Although the nature/nurture debate is not likely to be resolved any time soon, it is worth looking at because it reveals some interesting ideological alignments and helps us understand how politically charged is the issue of sex and gender.

Progressivism and Conservatism

Biological explanations for why men and women seem to behave differently and occupy different social roles have a **conservative ideology** because nothing can be done to change the *status quo* (the way things are). Taken to its extreme, the biological argument would say there is little point in trying to make men more nurturing, compassionate, and conciliatory because men are driven by their biology to adopt exactly the opposite behaviour. Similarly pointless are attempts to make women more aggressive, logical, and decisive. Going a step further in the conservative position, most men will be less effective than women if they move into occupations such as child rearing and nursing that require traditionally feminine nurturing qualities. Women who move into politics and business will be hampered by their emotional nature. It is therefore sensible, when we are building our social world, to exploit the natural abilities of men and women rather than trying to buck the natural trend.

Social explanations for why men and women seem to behave differently demonstrate a **progressive ideology** because they include the possibility that the *status quo* can be changed. In other words, if behaviour is learned and not forced on us by unchanging laws of biology, then we can simply learn differently and change will happen. If we want to broaden the range of acceptable masculine and feminine behaviours, we can change the social environment in which we raise boys and girls: Dolls for boys and trucks for girls.

It is, however, unlikely that very many people side wholly on the nature or nurture side of the question (and are therefore neither entirely progressive nor entirely conservative). This is probably because in reality, we know people with both masculine and feminine traits. There is a widely held notion, probably based on the work of psychologists such as Carl Jung, that all men and women have both a masculine and a feminine side to their psyche. This mixing of masculine and feminine traits is what probably leads many people to conclude that a combination of biological and social factors shape human behaviour. Therefore, most people probably lean toward one side or the other rather than believing entirely in either nature or nurture.

It is worth noting here that whether you lean toward the nature or nurture side of the debate may depend more on self-interest than on how logical you find the arguments of the side you choose. For example, women who are dissatisfied with rigid role definitions that they perceive have relegated them to low-status, low-paying jobs may align themselves with the progressive nurture position. At least hope for change exists there. Similarly, men who like their positions of relative prestige and power might align themselves with the conservative nature position and believe that they are merely living out an inevitable role thrust on them by laws of nature. Alternatively, men who find themselves limited by the social dictate that they should be strong, unemotional breadwinners may also find themselves looking to break down rigid gender roles through social change.

Two Theories about Gender Spheres

Sociologists have also pondered why gender spheres exist. They tend to examine the behaviour of men and women in groups, rather than as individuals, and they look primarily to the social world not the biological world for explanations. The two theories that follow reflect two common divisions in the way people explain why men and women occupy distinct spheres: (1) gender spheres either result naturally and provide a useful way to organize our social world, or (2) they result from one group trying to maintain advantage over the other.

Structural–Functionalist Theory

The theory that says that gender spheres evolved naturally because of the fact that men and women had different biological strengths and weaknesses is called **structural–functionalism.** Men hunted because of their physical strength and women could not hunt because they were tied to the children by their capacity to bear and breastfeed them. As societies became more complex, male and female roles grew out of this fundamental division of labour: women at home, men out hunting and protecting the family. This perspective stresses that the roles played by men and women are natural and serve to help society function more or less smoothly. Men and women have clear roles and those roles stay the same over time. The idea is that societies, like organisms, evolve to survive. Social structures evolve to serve different purposes in the functioning of society. Structural–functionalists would point to the fact that it makes sense, from a group survival standpoint, to have men do dangerous work like hunting, firefighting, or mining because they are reproductively expendable. (We only need one man to produce twenty babies in a year if he impregnates twenty women, but we need all twenty women to produce twenty babies.)

For structural–functionalists, the exclusion of women from paid work or the devaluing of women's work also serves a useful function in distributing wealth fairly. At first glance this may seem absurd, but consider that the family is the basic unit and each family has a male breadwinner. Paying only the men makes it more likely that each family will have access to at least one of the scarce good jobs. When both men and women can take the good jobs, it is easier for families to "hog" wealth by taking two good jobs. This phenomenon is evident today when a male doctor marries a female lawyer.

Conflict Theory

In contrast, another sociological theory takes a different view of gender spheres. **Conflict theory** sees society as consisting of many different groups that have competing, or con-

---

CRITICAL THINKING BOX 7.3

Reverse Discrimination?

Do employment equity laws now give women an unfair advantage over men in the employment sphere? Or do these laws merely level the playing field for men and women?

flicting, interests. Each group is busy pursuing its self-interest even if it means disadvantaging or even exploiting another group. Conflict theorists would say that having clear male and female spheres and excluding women from the paid work sphere effectively cuts the competition for good jobs and monetary rewards in half. This was no doubt good for men, who used every means to maintain this advantage. But as economic necessities brought women into the workforce in large numbers, the competition for good jobs intensified. Much of the backlash against feminism in North America results from the fact that males today face much greater competition from females than their fathers faced. If you are male, you may face nearly twice the competition for jobs that your father did.

Because men benefited from limited competition, they would naturally use any means at their disposal to maintain the status quo. Conflict theorists might look at the means by which men maintained their advantage over women historically. These means are called instruments of social control and are seen not as natural but as "man"-made phenomena. Laws that prevented women from owning property, for example, were an important means by which men kept women out of the competition. Because owning property was a necessary criterion for just about any political or economic activity, women were effectively excluded from anything that shaped society. For conflict theorists then, the law becomes a social institution that does not benefit all equally, but rather an instrument used by one group to gain advantage over another.

It is vital to point out here that conflict theorists do not see gender as the only, or even the most important, distinction in understanding who dominates whom. Equally important are differences in social class. When women's work is undervalued, it is not necessarily men controlling women, but rather people with power and money (the ruling class) controlling those without power and money (the working class). An underemployed man earning a fraction of a professional women can more directly relate to class

CRITICAL THINKING BOX 7.4

....

The Disappearance of Men's Work

Since men have occupied the sphere of hard physical work, what will happen to men as the physical work in society increasingly is done by machines or disappears altogether? Will men lose their traditional territory as blue-collar jobs disappear and white-collar jobs—which women are equally or better qualified for—make up the majority of work?

difference than gender difference. Employers can be, and are increasingly, women. These women may even benefit from sexual discrimination against their sisters.

Conflict theorists might similarly identify ways women benefited from gender division of labour and used their biological childbearing roles to exert power over men. Some feminist scholars have unearthed evidence of ancient matriarchal societies in which women's central role as procreator put them in the position of power over men. A concrete modern example of how men are excluded from childrearing is seen in the disproportionate number of child custody suits that are won by women (see Box 7.2).

So, gender spheres may simply serve a function in the smooth operation of society by ensuring that jobs get done by those best equipped to do them, or gender spheres may be evidence of an ongoing battle of the sexes and social classes.

Merit versus Social Connections

Whether gender spheres evolved to help society function or because of conflicting gender interests, why do they persist, especially in a society that prides itself on providing equal opportunity for all? If people are free to choose their destiny, if they can truly be whatever they want to be, why do men and women mysteriously want to choose gender-appropriate activities? Why do they behave so predictably? Or could it be that people are not as free as they think, that strong social, economic, legal, and psychological controls steer men and women into predictable destinies?

If you believe that people are free to choose their path in life, that individual character and hard work can help women overcome barriers preventing them from entering a male sphere and men from entering female spheres, then you believe in a **meritocracy.** This simply refers to the idea that people get their rewards in life based on their individual merits (say, talents, skills, or intelligence). In a meritocracy, these skills and talents are rewarded fairly and equally regardless of factors such as gender, race, or social class. Therefore, women who manage to acquire the talents and skills necessary to do a job will ultimately get that job. Along this line of reasoning, it would be foolish and ultimately self-defeating for employers to turn away well-qualified women just because they are women. Therefore, if women find themselves ghettoized in low-paying, low-status jobs, the way out is to get the skills and education necessary for better jobs. Those skills will be rewarded. Similarly, men who are barred from female spheres also need to get the right qualifications to compete equally with women. Therefore, those who buy into the idea that we have a meritocracy would say gender spheres persist because individual men and women have not applied themselves to getting the right kinds of qualifications.

Others, however, doubt that a meritocracy can or does exist. They believe that the competition for jobs, money, and status is not a fair one at all and that the rewards are not given out to those with the most merit but instead to those with social connections to the group that controls hiring. Therefore, if women control the selection of candidates for early childhood education in schools, men will be excluded by virtue of their sex. Women simply will not value the kinds of qualities men bring to the job. Those who doubt we have a meritocracy tend to believe that women and men are prevented from entering some fields of education and occupation because of often invisible **systemic barriers**, not because they lack the skills or talents. These barriers are built right into the system in the form of laws, discriminatory practices, and psychological deterrents.

Laws

An example of how law works as a built-in barrier preventing women from entering the male sphere can be seen in the fact that women are still prohibited from combat roles in the military. History is crammed with examples of laws that prevented women from entering male spheres. For example, in the early twentieth century, women were not defined as persons under the law in Canada and therefore could not hold political office.

Discriminatory Hiring

Discriminatory hiring practices might include a host of subtle or not-so-subtle ways to screen out the wrong gender. An experienced male primary-school teacher in Ontario was privately told by the principal to stop applying for the Kindergarten job at his school because parents were simply not ready to have a man take their daughters to the washroom.

Gender-biased hiring standards can be another form of discrimination in hiring. Recently, women have challenged the high value placed on height or physical strength in screening applicants to police academies, arguing that the vast majority of police work requires skills such as mediation, conciliation, and communication (feminine strengths). To the men who created the tests, the gender bias would probably not even be visible, and they may see any attempt to change the standards as "lowering" the standards for women.

Psychological Barriers

Psychological barriers are less tangible but may be no less powerful in preventing men and women from being free to choose their path. Girls and boys may never even want to do nontraditional jobs because of powerful messages given to them about what is an appropriate activity for males and females. Education officials may wonder why social work still attracts very few males, and they may even institute a program to attract more male applicants to social work programs. But if boys sense that social work, with its emphasis on interpersonal skills and its relatively low pay reward, is an inappropriate activity for them, no amount of "affirmative action" will bring more men into the programs.

WHY IT ALL MATTERS AND WHAT TO DO ABOUT IT

Individual Choice

We know that men and women are different, that they are expected to and do behave differently, and as a result they occupy different spheres in our social world. We might even have some ideas about why gender divisions exist and persist. The logical next question is: Why does it matter?

It matters to individuals because men and women suffer when they are forced into rigid masculine and feminine roles that limit their potential or simply do not fit them. Stereotypes about how people should behave restrict people's freedom to act the way they want to and to pursue their real interests and strengths. Men who want to take a secretarial job and who have no desire for promotion or further responsibility are deterred from doing so by a disapproving society. (Does he have enough testosterone?)

It is difficult to overstate the profound infringement this is on a person's individual liberty. If the state were to pass a law prohibiting men from staying home to raise children, for example, Canadians would be outraged and challenges to the *Charter of Rights and Freedoms* would abound. But we quietly tolerate a powerful set of social controls that virtually guarantee men and women will "self-censor" their activities and conform to society's expectations. Although challenges to accepted gender roles have always existed and may over time change our conceptions of masculinity and femininity, they are still peripheral and cause the challengers much pain.

But conforming to society's expectations might cause as much pain as challenging them. Feminist scholars are now looking at the high rate of mental illness among women historically as evidence that some women literally lost their minds when they were prevented from using their talents in the world outside the home. Some were brilliant women who were forced into mundane domestic chores for which they were wholly unsuited.

Men, too, have suffered terribly because the masculine stereotype left them unable to communicate their emotions or achieve intimacy. Literature has many examples of emotionally crippled men who are isolated from their loved ones because they cannot communicate their feelings.

Constructing a Fair Society

On a societal level, our construction of society along rigid gender lines may not be as functional as we think it is, nor may it be very fair. What a waste of talent and potential we have created if we exclude talented men and women from certain jobs simply because they are men and women! It is an even greater waste if they exclude themselves by never even wanting to do other than what men and women have always done. What should we do to try to open up opportunities for individuals and to ensure that society uses its human resources to the best potential? How do we stop gender from limiting our life choices?

Education

One popular notion about how to break down gender barriers is to educate people. The assumption is that education will erase many gender stereotypes that restrict human potential. If we teach people that men and women have a very broad range of skills and talents that often do not conform to traditional male and female stereotypes, we may liberate the potential of men and women alike. An enlightened population is presumably more open to change than an unenlightened one.

Equity Laws

Another way to remove gender barriers is to simply cut to the chase and engineer the result we want through laws and regulations (see Box 7.3). If we want more men in secretarial fields or childcare, simply establish hiring quotas. If we want women to enter firefighting or engineering, make rules forcing educational institutions and employers to bring in more women. This is, of course, very controversial. In Canada, we have not gone as far as establishing quotas, but we have had employment equity legislation at both the federal and provincial levels. These laws promote the hiring of not just women but also minorities and people with disabilities by requiring employers to set their own hiring targets and to meet them. The debate about equity laws can be inflammatory at times. Some believe laws are necessary to balance out existing systemic barriers and overt discrimination against these groups. Others believe these laws cause reverse discrimination by excluding qualified males and lowering hiring standards. Those who favour employment equity also argue that gender stereotypes and the psychological barriers that prevent people from choosing nontraditional roles will be broken down most effectively when young children see male daycare workers and female engineers as role models.

Proportional Representation

Along these same lines, another way to eliminate gender spheres is to have proportional representation of women (and other disadvantaged groups) on hiring committees and educational selection committees. This approach admits that consciously or unconsciously, we will value the attributes of those most like ourselves. Proportional representation (i.e., the number of women on any committee should mirror the percentage of women in that community) would then lead to more qualified women being selected for employment or postsecondary programs. If women help define hiring standards, it might also lead to less gender-biased selection processes. In the case of police academies, this could lead to a higher valuing of communication and mediation skills and a deemphasis on physical strength. If women made up 51 percent of the Canadian House of Commons, women's concerns would be more urgently addressed by government. Proportional representation would also help open the doors for men in fields where they have suffered systemic discrimination.

Chickens and Eggs

Employment equity and proportional representation raise an interesting point that divides many people about how change happens. Those who want to cut to the chase with hiring quotas and proportional representation believe that you have to change reality first and then changes in people's attitudes and behaviour will follow. In other words, only *after* people see that women can be aggressive decision makers and men can be excellent nur-turers will gender stereotypes break down. This view stresses that our attitudes are shaped in response to what we see around us. The opposite view stresses that we must change people's attitudes first, and then social change will follow. This view stresses the role of education in social change. If we teach boys and girls to be open-minded about gender and to question traditional stereotypes, then those attitudinal changes will lead to the kinds of real changes contemplated by employment equity.

The Wisdom to Know the Difference

There may be some facts about gender that we simply cannot change, or we cannot change any time soon. Perhaps we need to find the wisdom to know what they are. For example, we know women must bear children, and they suffer economic penalties as a result. We know men pay dearly in health and longevity for their role as primary bread-winners. Whether gender divisions are caused by biological or social forces, we may want to build a society that accommodates these facts about gender rather than a society that denies them. For example, society could accommodate women's childbearing imperative by requiring all employers to have decent maternity leave programs, job-sharing provi-sions, and fewer pay and promotion penalties for women who have interrupted careers. Similarly, measures for men such as more frequent vacations, voluntary unpaid leaves, and flex-time working hours might help reduce the incidence of stress-related diseases such as alcoholism and heart disease that men suffer and die of.

CONCLUSION

Do gender divisions help society function smoothly or do they lead to conflict between the sexes? How you answer this question probably depends on the kinds of experiences you have

---

BOX 7.3

Why We Need Employment Equity Laws

....

Employment equity laws are designed to engineer changes in our workplaces to ensure that certain groups (women, people with disabilities, racial minorities, and Native people) are fairly represented in Canada's workplaces. But some people believe hiring quotas will cause reverse discrimination against qualified white males and could lead to unqualified women and minorities getting jobs. Advocates of equity laws counter by saying there are plenty of well-qualified women and minorities and there is no need to lower hiring standards.

---

had as a man or woman. The existence of a strong feminist movement throughout most of the last century in Canada may be evidence that some women find gender restrictive. Men, too, may want to free themselves from restrictive male stereotypes.

If we want to make changes, we must begin to understand how gender affects men and women individually and in groups. Only then can we make the kinds of changes that will enable men and women to live out their destinies as freely and as fully as they can.

CHAPTER SUMMARY

Despite many changes in Canadian society, men and women are still encouraged to adopt a fairly rigidly defined masculine or feminine gender identity. Gender identity is a socially

CRITICAL THINKING BOX 7.5

....

Emancipation of Women

There are more divorces, fewer children, and more people living alone in Canada today than in almost any other time in our history. How do you account for this? Have women's gains in the economic sphere resulted in "losses" in the domestic sphere? Is this good or bad? For whom is it good and bad?

defined role for men and women. When men and women consistently adopt traditional male and female roles, gender spheres are created. Gender spheres are simply areas of work, school, and play that tend to be dominated by either men or women.

Whether gender identity and the resulting gender spheres are created mostly by unchangeable biological factors or by changeable social factors is still hotly debated. Also at issue is whether the creation of male and female territories helps society to function smoothly overall or whether it creates conflict between the sexes. Some people believe men and women are free to choose their gender identity. Others believe it is forced on them by powerful social controls that reward proper masculine and feminine behaviour and penalize nonconformity.

Issues of freedom of choice and social equality are central to the gender question. Is individual freedom severely limited by rigid gender stereotypes and the social controls that enforce them? Do women lose out in the economic sphere when women's work is undervalued? Do men lose out in the interpersonal sphere when they are barred from nurturing roles? As you further your education and life experiences, you will form your own views on these important gender issues.

KEY TERMS

conflict theory, p. 182

conservative ideology, p. 180

gender, p. 170

gender identity, p. 170

gender spheres, p. 174

gender stereotypes, p. 171

glass ceiling, p. 174

meritocracy, p. 184

nature/nurture, p. 180

progressive ideology, p. 181

sex, p. 170

social controls, p. 171

structural–functionalism, p. 182

systemic barriers, p. 185

transsexuals, p. 172

transvestites, p. 172

DISCUSSION QUESTIONS

1. In small groups, discuss the gender roles of men and women in the culture your family originated from. How do the roles differ from culture to culture? How are they the same? Consider some other cultures, such as Afghanistan and the Taliban's laws regarding women.

2. Discuss the question of how rigid our gender roles are. Would the men you know be turned off by a sexually aggressive, dominant woman who works in a construction job?

Would the women you know be attracted to or turned off by a submissive man who loves his secretarial job and has no desire to move up the ladder?

3. Do you agree with employment equity laws? Why or why not?

4. Parents frequently remark that their male and female children were different from the moment they were born. Despite their attempts to treat their boys and girls the same, the children seem to follow predictable patterns of male and female behaviour. Which is more significant in forming our gender identity, nature or nurture?

5. Discuss some of the penalties people pay for violating society's expectations of them as men or women. Consider minor deviations such as men wearing long hair and major ones such as transsexualism.

6. Do you think the ability of men and women to form happy, lasting relationships is made more difficult by the gender inequalities in our society?

NOTES

1. Statistics Canada, *Women In Canada 2000: A Guide to Understanding the Changing Roles of Women and Men in Canada*, Cat. No. 89-503-XPE, available online at <www.statcan.ca/english/ads/89-503-XPE/hilites.htm>, accessed 19 February 2002.

2. Statistics Canada, *Average Earnings by Sex and Work Pattern,"* Survey of Labour and Income Dynamics* (Income Statistics Division, 2001).

3. *Women In Canada 2000*.

4. John Robert Colombo, ed., *The 1994 Canadian Global Almanac* (Toronto: Macmillan Canada, 1994), p. 82.

5. *Women In Canada 2000*.

6. Tom Biracree and Nancy Biracree, *Almanac of the American People* (New York: Oxford, 1988), p. 54.

7. Statistics Canada, *Suicides and Suicide Rate by Sex, by Age Group*, Cat. No. 82F0075XCB: 1997, available online at <www.statcan.ca/English/Pgdb/People/ Health/health01.htm>, accessed 19 February 2002.

8. Elaine Carey, "Women Still Two Steps Behind Men," *Toronto Star*, 9 August 1995, A15.

9. Statistics Canada, *Community College Diplomas in Career Programs*, Cat. No. 81-229-XIB, available online at <www.statcan.ca/English/Pgdb/People/Education/educ19.htm>, accessed 19 February 2002.

10. Statistics Canada, *University Qualifications Granted by Field of Study, by Sex*, CANSIM cross-classified table no. 00580602, available online at <www.statcan.ca/English/Pgdb/People/Education/educ21.htm>, accessed 19 February 2002.

11. Statistics Canada, "Sports Involvement," *General Social Survey 1998*, available online at <www.statcan.ca/English/Pgdb/People/Culture/arts18.htm>, accessed 19 February 2002.

12. Statistics Canada, "Most Popular Sports," *General Social Survey 1998*, available online at <www.statcan.ca/English/Pgdb/People/Culture/arts18.htm>, accessed 19 February 2002.

Sexuality: Evolution and Variation

Brigitte Guetter

It is a good thing to know something of the customs and manners of various peoples in order to judge of our own more objectively and so not think everything which is contrary to our ways is ridiculous and irrational, as those who have seen nothing are in the habit of doing.
— René Descartes

Nothing in life is to be feared. It is only to be understood.
— Marie Curie

Objectives

....

After reading this chapter, you should be able to

- describe new insights from the historical perspective of sexual evolution among major cultures

- identify the important scientific sexual research initiatives and their contributions to the understanding of human sexuality

- compare and contrast humans with other species of animals in terms of comparable sexual activities to examine what is natural

- consider Kinsey's and Storms's models of sexuality and discuss classic and recent findings relating to possible influences on adult sexual orientation

- examine diverse sexual practices among several modern cultures and evaluate possible conclusions about the universality of human sexual behaviour

TWENTY THOUSAND YEARS OF SEXUAL EVOLUTION

What Exactly Is Sexuality?

What does the word **sexuality** make you think of? Take a moment right now, put down this book, and list the ideas that come to mind.

Okay, did you do it? Did you think sexuality means sex, and sex means intercourse between two people, a male and a female? Or did you think of the various ways of performing sex? Did the ancient Hindu *Kamasutra* come to mind with its descriptions and full-colour illustrations of sexual positions? Or do you prefer the more scientific approach of someone like Legman, who calculated that there are 3870 possible positions? Did Freud, Kinsey, Masters and Johnson, or Hite come to mind? Did you think of love, hugging, kissing, breathing, sweating, or of pain, jealousy, and suffering? Did you think of marriage, of babies? Did you remember hearing about an African spider that has twelve legs and twelve penises? Or did you think of equipment, whips, chains, collars, and unthinkable gadgets?

Perhaps your thoughts included few or none of the above, but the possibilities for such a list are many and complex. (You might now want to check your current knowledge about sexuality by answering the questions in Box 8.1.) And yes, sexuality includes more than sexual intercourse.

BOX 8.1

Sexual Understanding Survey

....

Check your current understanding of some sexual issues by choosing either true (T) or false (F) for the following statements.

T   F   1.   Sexuality refers primarily to techniques of sexual intercourse.

T   F   2.   People became aware of the male's role in reproduction around 9000 B.C.E.

T   F   3.   Prehistoric societies behaved sexually "natural" and generally observed no incest taboo.

T   F   4.   The ancient Hebrews had a law that required an unemployed husband to have sexual intercourse with his wife every day.

(cont'd)

T   F   5. Adolescent homosexual experience among boys of ancient Greece caused most to become adult homosexuals.

T   F   6. The word "fornicate" comes from the Latin *fornix*, which refers to the arched doorways in which ancient Roman prostitutes would service their customers.

T   F   7. The ancient Chinese were sexually repressed, much as they are today.

T   F   8. The ancient Hindus of India cultivated sexual pleasure as a spiritual ideal and a religious duty.

T   F   9. Religion never dictates sexual behaviour but only reinforces what is "good."

T   F   10. The sexual repression of the Victorian age in the nineteenth century reflected Queen Victoria's own approach to sex.

T   F   11. Fertilization of a human ovum by a human sperm was not directly observed until the twentieth century.

T   F   12. During the nineteenth century, sexual acts that did not have reproduction as their goal were labelled "deviant" and seen as mental diseases.

T   F   13. Sigmund Freud, at the beginning of the twentieth century, proposed that the sexual instinct provides the energy source for the life instinct.

T   F   14. Henry Havelock Ellis, at the turn of the twentieth century, continued to link masturbation with insanity.

T   F   15. Modern scientific researchers, such as Kinsey and Masters and Johnson, were encouraged and supported by a world eager to receive information about human sexuality.

T   F   16. Nonhuman animals are similar to people in their sexual behaviours, including homosexuality, foreplay, masturbation, and rape.

T   F   17. Sexual orientation always dictates sexual behaviour in both humans and other species.

T   F   18. The imbalance of adult sexual hormones is the most frequent cause of homosexuality.

T   F   19. People are either heterosexual or homosexual.

T   F   20. Some homosexual males have certain brain structures similar to heterosexual females.

(cont'd)

BOX 8.1 *(cont'd)*

T	F	21.	The sexual apparatus of people of the South Pacific is quite different from that of North Americans, both in appearance and function.
T	F	22.	One of the few generalizations that can be made is that most couples engaging in sexual activity prefer to do so in more public places because of the increased arousal this provides.
T	F	23.	It is physically impossible for a woman to rape a man.
T	F	24.	Relative gender roles for men and women are the same the world over, varying only in degree.
T	F	25.	Married couples of Inis Beag, a small island off the coast of Ireland, have sex in the dark with their underwear on.
T	F	26.	In some societies women almost never have orgasms, and in other societies women virtually always do.
T	F	27.	Some societies initiate boys into manhood by deeply slitting the top of their penis along the entire length.
T	F	28.	In China today, couples receive monetary bonuses for second and third children in an effort to rebalance the dwindling birth rate of recent decades.
T	F	29.	In Japan, Christmas Eve is referred to as "Hormone Day" and celebrated with dinner, entertainment, limousine service, overnight stay in a fancy hotel, and work early the next morning.
T	F	30.	Teenagers in Sweden and Holland are much less knowledgeable about and more embarrassed to discuss sex than are teens in North America.
T	F	31.	In North America, young single people have sex more than three times as often as married couples.
T	F	32.	Vaginal intercourse is the most preferred sexual activity for North American couples.
T	F	33.	Anal intercourse ranks a close second to vaginal intercourse.
T	F	34.	Masturbation by married people is usually related to lack of sex with their partner.
T	F	35.	Genes and hormones primarily determine human sexual behaviour, and experience is relatively unimportant.
T	F	36.	There is no need to concern ourselves very much with sex because it is only one area of our lives and can and should be kept separate from the rest of it.

(cont'd)

Answer Key

T = True   F = False

1. F	10. F	19. F	28. F
2. T	11. T	20. T	29. T
3. F	12. T	21. F	30. F
4. T	13. T	22. F	31. F
5. F	14. F	23. F	32. T
6. T	15. F	24. F	33. F
7. F	16. T	25. T	34. F
8. T	17. F	26. T	35. F
9. F	18. F	27. T	36. F

Note: Detailed explanations for each question can be found throughout the chapter.

Our sexuality is an essential part of ourselves whether we have or will ever engage in sexual intercourse or in sexual fantasy, or even if we lose the capacity to function sexually because of injury or disease. Sexuality is the totality of the ways in which we experience and express ourselves as sexual beings. Like water to fish, sexuality is so much a part of our ongoing daily thoughts and activities that we hardly notice how much we are steeped in it.

In this chapter we will explore sexuality from the point of view of diversity, of variation. We will investigate the ways in which sexuality was and is experienced and expressed differently at different times, in different places, by different people in order to, as the French philosopher René Descartes said, "judge of our own more objectively."[1] We will investigate known and probable factors that may contribute to such differences. We will reflect on the various perspectives of different disciplines when appropriate—biology, psychology, sociology, anthropology, and spirituality. And whereas it is not the task of science to decree morality, it is always an intricate aspect of all our behaviours, and especially our sexual behaviours, and must therefore be taken into account. Let us then start at the beginning.

The Stone Age: Nature, Mystery, and Taboo

Why look back? you may ask. Why bother to find out what people did 20 000 years ago? One answer might be that knowing how a thing developed tells us much more about what it is now. We want to know not only that we are pregnant, but also understand how we

CRITICAL THINKING BOX 8.1

....

Thinking Critically ... about Critical Thinking

Critical thinking involves a set of thinking skills that include thoughtful analysis and probing of claims and arguments—your own or those of others. It uses careful observation, asking questions, seeing connections among ideas, and evaluating the evidence on which arguments are based and the logic of conclusions. Now consider how critical thinking skills can be applied to the study of the diversity of human sexuality. Why not simply accept the findings of the experts?

got that way. The Arunta of Central Australia, for example, still believe the cause of pregnancy to be spirits travelling in sandstorms. And they have reasons to think that they are right. Why do you suppose they think that? Which piece of "knowledge" do you prefer, theirs or yours? Why?

Now, back to our prehistoric folk. Some primitive statues and cave drawings portray women with round hips, voluptuous breasts, and prominent sex organs. Most theorists interpret them as fertility symbols and suggest that women's ability to bear children was worshipped by ancient civilizations, who very likely were ignorant of the male's role in reproduction. This, however, changed when people developed herds of livestock instead of only hunting animals for food and clothing. Such proximity to animals gradually developed in people an awareness of the male's role in reproduction, probably by about 9000 B.C.E. Out of this knowledge grew **phallic worship**, the worship of the penis as possessor of creative powers. Ancient cultures of Egypt, Greece, and Rome revered phalluses in art by representing them as swords, axes, and ploughs, and sometimes as necklaces, rings, or with wings. In an ancient Roman parade honouring Venus, the goddess of love, a gigantic phallus was proudly carried like a float along the path.

The first human taboo to appear was probably the **incest taboo**, the prohibition against sexual activity between close blood relatives, such as a brother and a sister. All human societies seem to have some form of this taboo, although it varies in terms of strictness. Marriage between brother and sister was permitted among the "divine" rulers of Egypt, for example, and within Hawaiian and Inca royal families. Ancient Egypt even permitted father–daughter marriages among royalty and aristocracy. Such marriages would have kept wealth, power, and, where applicable, divinity, in the family. Commoners had no such need and consequently no exemption from the incest taboo.

Ancient Hebrews: Be Fruitful, Multiply, and Enjoy

For the ancient Hebrews, the people of the Old Testament of the Bible, the divine injunction to "be fruitful and multiply" formed the backdrop against which sexuality unfolded. The emphasis was procreation. Childlessness, for example, was grounds for divorce. Homosexuality was strongly condemned because the divine injunction could obviously not be observed.

The Hebrew Bible did permit **polygamy**, the practice of having more than one spouse at a time, especially when, say, the second wife was added for noble reasons such as childlessness of the first wife. **Monogamy**, one spouse at a time, however, was clearly preferred. After all, God created Adam and Eve, not Adam and Eve and Charlotte. Sex, within marriage, was perceived and promoted as pleasurable. In fact, Jewish law prescribed the minimum frequency of sexual intercourse required of husbands:[2]

- No occupation: once per day
- Labourers: twice per week
- Ass drivers: once per week
- Camel drivers: once per month
- Sailors: once per six months

What do you think the rationale is behind these numbers? How would minimum frequencies look if we instituted such a law today (see Table 8.1)? Who would benefit most? Would you vote for it?

Hebrew women were expected to be good wives. They were seen as the chattel (property) of their husbands and could be divorced on a whim. Being a good wife included possibly sharing her husband with a second or third wife or even with a concubine. Adultery with a married woman, however, invited harsh penalties, especially for her, such as being stoned to death.

Ancient Greeks: Healthy Mind, Healthy Body, Graceful Sexuality

The classical golden age of Greece is between 500 B.C.E. and 300 B.C.E., the era during which philosophers such as Socrates, Plato, and Aristotle lived. Like the ancient Hebrews, the ancient Greeks valued family life but expressed sexual interests much more openly. They admired beautiful, well-developed bodies and understood the healthy mind–healthy body connection. Graceful sexuality was valued rather than reproductive capacity. The Greeks and their gods all were voracious in their pursuit of sexual variety, and the gods were said even to seduce mortals.

Table 8.1   Suggested Minimum Legal Frequencies of Sexual Intercourse for Modern Western Couples

People Affected by the Law	Never	Once a year	Every six months	Once a month	Once a week	Twice a week	Once a day	Three times a day	Other
Dentists									
Prime ministers									
Poets									
Your father									
Priests									
Queen Elizabeth II									
Lawyers									
Jurors (sequestered)									
Prisoners									
Retired people									
Your mother									
Prince Charles									
Professors									
School librarians									
Unemployed people									
Couples wishing to become parents									
You									

Now examine your choices. Is there a recognizable pattern? Have you grouped certain people together? If so, do you know the reason for your grouping? Do your choices look similar to those of your classmates? Discuss.

Both men and women were seen as **bisexual**. Homosexuality was considered normal, although exclusive long-term homosexual relationships were tolerated only as long as they did not threaten family life—for soldiers on campaigns, for example. Although sex between men and prepubescent boys was illegal, sex between men and adolescent boys (**pederasty**) was generally accepted, especially if the man was young himself, prominent, and could be construed as a teacher. Aristotle, however, disagreed with this and considered such practice depraved.

Prostitution flourished in ancient Greece. There were refined courtesans skilled in the art of love, who danced, played instruments, and were able to intelligently discuss current political issues. Their clients tended to be affluent nobles, who were not denounced for their visits to courtesans. There were also prostitutes and streetwalkers from and for lower society. They often lived in gaudy brothels and displayed wooden or painted penises outside the door.

Women were treated as chattels of relevant males. They were chaperoned when going outdoors. A husband could divorce his wife without cause. A wife, however, was permitted to divorce her husband only in the most extreme circumstance, which did not include adultery or pederasty.

Ancient Romans: Orgies, Sexual Excess, and Family Life

A real double standard existed between the ancient Roman ruling class and the people. Sexual excesses were rampant among emperors and their guests. Their orgies included sadomasochistic activities and bestiality, and Julius Caesar, for example, was reputed to be bisexual. The average Roman, however, saw homosexuality as a threat to the family, and family represented the source of strength of the Roman Empire. Although women were still considered the property of their husbands, they were more likely than Greek women to participate in social life with their husbands.

Several of our modern terms originated from Roman customs. **Fellatio** derives from *fellare,* which in Latin means "to suck." **Cunnilingus** comes from the Latin *cunnus,* meaning "vulva" and *lingere,* "to lick." **Fornicate** is a derivation of the Latin *fornix,* which means "arch" or a vault with a dome-shaped ceiling. These arches referred to the dark arch-shaped doorways around public arenas and near theatres where Roman streetwalkers would service their customers.

Early Christians: Grace and Salvation through Celibacy

Little is known about Jesus' views on sex. He taught love, tolerance, and forgiveness, and when he rescued Mary Magdalene from certain death by stoning for acts of adultery, he did remind her to "sin no more." It was probably in response to the decadent Roman culture where fornication and adultery were prevalent that the early Christians began associating sex with sin. They began rejecting pagan values and restricting sex to marriage. St. Paul, on his conversion in the first century, saw celibacy as the highest value, yet allowed that it was better to marry than to burn (with passion)—but he urged men to love their wives with restraint.

Other values were the continued demand that brides be virgins and the grievous sinfulness of homosexuality, masturbation, oral–genital contact, and anal intercourse. Later, in the fourth century, St. Augustine said that lust and shame were passed down from Adam and Eve and that all sex, even sex within marriage, was intrinsically evil and sinful. Only through celibacy was grace and salvation possible.

Eastern Religions: Sexuality as Spirituality

To the ancient Chinese, sexuality was akin to spirituality, a form of worship to lead to immortality. Around 200 B.C.E. the Chinese produced the first detailed sex manual. A man was to prolong intercourse as long as possible and bring his wife to **orgasm**, an intense, pleasurable sensation that occurs at the peak of sexual arousal and is followed by release of sexual tensions. The woman's pleasure, however, was incidental and the clear purpose was for him to absorb more of her *yin*, her natural feminine essence, to enhance his masculine *yang*. Oral–genital contact and anal intercourse were permissible as long as the man did not squander his yang by ejaculating. Spilling his seed was considered wasteful, which therefore ruled out masturbation, at least for men. For women it was permitted.

The ancient Hindus of India saw sexual pleasure as a spiritual ideal, a religious duty, not as a source of shame and guilt. Dating from either 677 B.C.E. or 350 C.E., the *Kamasutra of Vatsayana*, the most influential sex manual ever, was developed. It describes and colourfully illustrates many sexual positions, offers recipes for aphrodisiacs, and gives "subtle recipes for kissing, touching … leaving tooth and nail marks in the right places, conning your neighbour's wife, and salving your own conscience."[3] Although generally seeing sex as natural and good, after about 1000 C.E., Indian society gradually grew more restrictive toward sexuality.

Islam, the dominant religion in the Middle East, was founded by the Prophet Muhammad (570–632 C.E.), born in Mecca, a city in today's Saudi Arabia. Muhammad decreed that marriage was the only road to virtue, and sexual fulfillment within marriage was to be treasured. Celibacy was discouraged, but premarital intercourse was shameful and invited social condemnation, even death. Women were permitted only one husband, although men could take as many as four wives. Also, women in most Islamic societies had to keep their heads and faces veiled in public and avoid all physical contact, even shaking hands, with men other than their husbands.

Middle Ages: Cultural and Intellectual Stagnation

Medieval times, from about 500 to 1500 C.E., earned the term "the dark ages" because of cultural and intellectual stagnation and decay. The Roman Catholic Church's growing influence could be seen in the two dominant and conflicting views of women. On the one hand, women represented Eve, the original temptress, the "bad" girl, and on the other hand, women's hope of redemption lay in the concept of the Virgin Mary, the virtuous, pure, "good" girl. Can you think of a well-known performer who makes quite successful efforts at representing both concepts? Why do you think that might be appealing to men? to women?

Out of this view then grew, especially among the upper classes, the idea of courtly love, love that was pure and dignified, elevated from carnal sex, and focused on chivalry and romance.

Protestant Reformation: From Sex as Love to Anesthesia

Toward the end of the dark ages, Martin Luther (1483–1546) and John Calvin (1509–64) broke away from the Roman Catholic Church and formed their own communities, today's Protestant churches. Luther, having fallen in love, believed that marriage is as natural as eating and drinking and that priests should be permitted to marry and have children. Calvin emphasized functions of sex in marriage beyond procreation, such as the strengthening of the love bond and the relief of stresses of daily life. The Protestant Reformation took a more accepting and complex view of sexuality but continued the strict edict that it be expressed only within marriage. Severe penalties were promised for premarital or extramarital sex, including being exposed to public scorn by being held in the pillory or the stocks, wooden contraptions with holes for neck, hands, and/or feet. Flogging or even branding was in store for adulterers. Perhaps you will recall the adulteress Hester Prynne who was branded with the letter A in Nathaniel Hawthorne's novel *The Scarlet Letter*.

Reformation values continued through the reign of Queen Victoria of England (1837–1901), with renewed emphasis on repression and sin. Sex was to be strictly confined to marriage, and many wives saw sex as their duty to satisfy their husbands' needs or for procreation. Many believed that women were born with **sexual anesthesia**. But sex was problematic for men as well because ejaculation was said to drain men of their natural vitality. Sexual intercourse was recommended no more than once a month. The Reverend Sylvester Graham combined help for the overstimulated with good business sense by creating the Graham cracker, a plain food made with whole-grain flour to help control sexual appetite. This was, of course, intended to be especially beneficial for young men.

In this sexually repressed atmosphere, prostitution flourished. Men probably thought they were doing their wives a favour, and at one time there were as many as one prostitute to every twelve men in London.[4] Women's notorious sexual anesthesia, however, was in fact contradicted by anonymous surveys wherein most women admitted to experiencing pleasure from sex and reaching orgasm. Even Queen Victoria is reputed to have had a virile lover most of her life.

Scientific Approaches to Sexuality

It was against this backdrop of religious understandings of sexuality that the scientific study of sex began in the late nineteenth century. The discovery of sperm swimming in human semen was made by the Dutch microscopist Anton van Leeuwenhoek (1632–1723). In 1875 Oscar Hertwig first observed the actual fertilization of the egg by the sperm in sea urchins, although human fertilization was not directly observed until the twentieth century. The assumption that masturbation caused various maladies continued well into the twentieth century. It represented a transformation of the religious equation of sexual pleasure with sin into the medical idea that losing sperm produces disease.

Richard von Krafft-Ebing

Possibly the most influential medical proponent of these ideas was Richard von Krafft-Ebing (1840–1902), considered during his lifetime one of the world's leading psychiatrists. His major work, *Psychopathia Sexualis* (1882) reflected the dominant theme of the time—sex as disease. It described more than two hundred individuals with sexual deviations such as sadomasochism, bestiality, and necrophilia. The thread running through all the variations documented was masturbation and hereditary degeneracy. The work reflected the concern of the times about "deviant" sexuality, which included all sexual acts that did not

CRITICAL THINKING BOX 8.2

....

Thinking Critically … about Modern Beliefs, Myths, and Practices

All of life is an ongoing process of adjustment, change, and evolution. Which of our current beliefs, myths, and practices do you think evolved from earlier sexual values and customs?

have reproduction as their goal. Krafft-Ebing viewed sexual deviations as mental diseases that might be treated by medical science.

Sigmund Freud

A major advance in the scientific understanding of human sexuality came with the work of the Viennese physician Sigmund Freud (1856–1939), founder of psychoanalysis and psychiatry. It is important to recognize the cultural context in which Freud and other early sex researchers began their work. Victorian cultural norms about the taboo subject of sex were extremely rigid and oppressive. Historian Peter Gay said that Freud's world was

> a devious and insincere world in which middle-class husbands slaked their lust by keeping mistresses, frequenting prostitutes, or molesting children, while their wives, timid, dutiful, obedient, were sexually anesthetic and poured all their capacity for love into their house-keeping and their child-rearing.[5]

Freud developed a comprehensive theory of human behaviour, and he emphasized sex as the central aspect of human development and the principal motivating force in our lives. In his *Three Essays on the Theory of Sexuality* (1905), Freud traced for the first time the course of development of the sexual instinct, the energy source of the life instinct, in human beings from infancy to maturity. He outlined six psychosexual stages of development from birth to adulthood and emphasized early experiences as determinants of adult personality. Successful negotiation of each stage, said Freud, is necessary to produce a healthy adult personality and to prevent the formation of a **fixation** that would lead to a **neurosis**. His theories were highly risky and revolutionary, but Freud did persist through the early torrent of criticism, and psychoanalysis became one of the most influential and persevering theoretical frameworks of the time.

Henry Havelock Ellis

Another great, though not so well known, early contributor to the scientific study of sexuality was Henry Havelock Ellis (1859–1939), a physician in Victorian England. He compiled a veritable encyclopedia of sexuality. The first six volumes of his *Studies in the Psychology of Sex* were published between 1897 and 1910. A remarkably objective and tolerant scholar, Ellis tried to broaden the spectrum of normal sexual behaviour to include homosexuality. He argued that homosexuality was inborn and thus neither a vice nor a moral choice. It was, he said, simply a variation from the statistical norm, heterosexuality. Ellis also attacked the view that linked masturbation with insanity. Instead of being a malignant vice, he thought it was inevitable and to be expected. In fact, he suggested that most of the major forms of sexual deviations are **congenital** (present at birth) and related in some way to a normal sexual life.

Until the mid-twentieth century, most of our knowledge of sexual behaviour came from systematic observation of nonhuman animal sex, of sexuality in non-Western, nonindustrialized populations, or of "crazy" sex, that is, of psychologically disturbed people. Most of Freud's theories, for example, were based on the experiences of his emotionally disturbed patients. During the late nineteenth century, physicians considered it improper for a doctor to see a woman's genitals even while delivering babies. Midwives were generally employed for the task. Physicians would graduate from medical college without ever having seen a maternity case.

Alfred Kinsey

Now you might assume that such extreme attitudes are relics of the nineteenth century, but even in the mid-twentieth century, scientists who studied human sexuality still paid a price, both professionally and personally. Alfred Kinsey (1894–1956) probably would have lived longer but for the emotional toll he suffered because of the extremely hostile reception of his first two publications, even though they eventually became bestsellers. In 1948 Kinsey published *Sexual Behavior in the Human Male*, followed by his 1953 sequel *Sexual Behavior in the Human Female*. Both books grew out of Kinsey's need for information for a marriage-and-family course he was asked to teach at Indiana University in the mid-1930s. The shortage of scientific information about the sexual aspects of marriage prompted him to do his own research. He began with questionnaires to his own students and later, together with his colleagues, expanded to the larger population, interviewing thousands of Americans about their sexual experiences and behaviours. Kinsey and his colleagues were repeatedly warned about the dangers involved in collecting sexual histories. Threats of legal action and political investigation hounded them. Criticism from scientific colleagues harassed them. There were attempts to persuade Indiana University to stop the research, prevent or censor publication of the results, and ultimately to fire Kinsey. The university's administration, however, defended the Kinsey group's right to do scientific research, even though to say that it was not considered politically correct at the time would be a gross understatement. The claim was made that Kinsey's work undermined the moral fibre of the nation, making the country more vulnerable to Communist takeover. Nonetheless, Kinsey persisted, published, and, three years later, died. Kinsey's group helped pave the way for subsequent researchers. They broke the ice, and William Masters, of Masters and Johnson fame, gave them credit for making his subsequent work possible.

Masters and Johnson

The research and studies of Masters and Johnson are probably the best known and most cited of all sex-related data. William Masters, a gynecologist, and his colleague, Virginia Johnson, a psychologist, were the first to observe people's sexual behaviours in a laboratory setting rather than to question them on what they did sexually, as the Kinsey group had done. Of the 1273 original volunteers who applied, 694 participated in the research. The group consisted of 312 men and 382 women, 18 to 80 years old, of whom 552 were married couples, 106 unmarried women, and 36 unmarried men. They were observed through one-way glass. Married couples engaged in sexual intercourse and various forms of mutual stimulation such as manual and oral stimulation of the genitals. The single female subjects participated in studies of sexual arousal in response to insertion of a transparent artificial penis containing photographic equipment (a "**coition machine**") to record physiological changes in internal sexual organs. Unmarried males engaged in masturbation to ejaculation. Most of Masters and Johnson's findings related to physiological responses to sexual arousal that had never before been measured or documented. Their major and generally accepted finding was the occurrence of what they termed the **human sexual response cycle**, which is present in both sexes in four phases, always in the same order: excitement, plateau, orgasm, and resolution.

Masters and Johnson, however, worked at a time when society was unprepared to talk openly about sex, let alone to observe people engaged in sexual activity, even if it was in a laboratory. Accusations of immorality, voyeurism, and various other evils were directed at the researchers. In the late 1950s the team was subjected to direct sabotage. Parts of their equipment disappeared, and personal attacks, mainly directed at their children, followed. They were labelled sex-mongers and were socially ostracized. After publication of *Human Sexual Response* in 1966, the hate mail they received was unbelievable—the "drop-dead" category was about 90 to 95 percent.[6] But Masters and Johnson persevered, and their research now serves as the basis for modern therapy, counselling, and education. Both professionals and nonprofessionals can discuss sexual function and experience more knowledgeably. Although hostility to sex research is far from behind us, currently research is being carried out into every conceivable aspect of sexuality. So many articles and books are being published that it is almost impossible to keep up to date. What this research demonstrates is that sexuality is not the simple matter it was once thought to be but rather a highly complex area of life that is influenced by many factors.

Sexual Behaviour in Nonhuman Species

Taking a wider perspective of sexuality in evolution and adding to this many scientific findings suggests that sexuality does in fact evolve and is modifiable. It appears not to be a capacity or process that is decreed hard and fast, once and for all, for each and every one of us. Some people, however, prefer to classify sexual behaviours as *natural* or *unnatural* depending on whether other species do or do not engage in those behaviours. Humans, for example, are definitely not the only species to masturbate. Many species of mammals do it, but the female porcupine is possibly the most inventive; her technique is to hold one end of a stick in her paw and to walk about while straddling the stick. As the stick bumps against the ground, it vibrates against her genitals.

Masturbation is particularly common among primates (monkeys and apes). This activity is not necessarily the result of the loneliness and frustration of zoo animals, as was once believed, because free-roaming animals also engage in it. Monkeys and apes might even be considered to have an advantage over humans; their bodies are so flexible that they can perform oral–genital sex (fellatio or cunnilingus) even on themselves. Mouth–genital stimulation in fact seems quite natural, judging from the behaviour of other species. Observations indicate that although in nonhuman species it is less common for the female to stimulate the male's genitals with her mouth, it is quite common for the male chimpanzee to apply his mouth to a female's genitals. This is in part because the **pheromones** (sex scents) she produces stimulate sexual behaviour in him. The female seems to receive pleasure from this practice, as suggested by Bingam's observations of chimpanzees, our nearest evolutionary relatives:

> Wendy was turning so that her face was away from Billy and her posterior parts were turned conspicuously towards him.... Billy showed interest in the protruding genitalia [and] ... gradually the manipulations of his free hand became directed more and more [toward them].... He picked at them with his fingers and several times took them in his lips. Shortly after his manipulation began it became apparent that Wendy was sexually stimulated. The clitoris became noticeably erect, and I could detect occasional surges as though she were voluntarily increasing the erection.[7]

Such foreplay is probably of particular importance for Wendy and Billy because once chimps get around to actual intercourse, it's all over in less than thirty seconds. Rhinoceroses, on the other hand, are in no hurry. They mate continuously for one-and-a-half hours. The male usually ejaculates numerous times with his half-a-metre-long penis. Many other analogues of human sexual behaviour can be seen in many nonhuman species (see Box 8.2).

Homosexual behaviour also is found in many species. In fact, observations of other species suggest that our basic mammalian heritage is bisexual, a view supported by Kinsey's view of sexuality as representing a continuum between exclusive heterosexuality and exclusive homosexuality (more on that later). Konrad Lorenz, for example, reported a long-term homosexual relationship between two male ducks, a species that usually forms long-term bonds.[8] Male porpoises in captivity have been seen repeatedly attempting to insert their penis into the anus of another male even though females were available.[9] Successful anal intercourse has been documented in some male primates.[10] But females also attempt to copulate with other females. Hyde reported such behaviour in her own two female dogs, who, she said, "delight in mounting each other, particularly when company is present."[11]

HUMAN SEXUAL ORIENTATION

The general trend, as we move from lower species such as birds, fish, or rodents to higher species such as primates, is for **sexual behaviour** to be less directly controlled by hormones and instinct and more by the brain. Experience and learning, that is, environmental influences, are much more important in shaping sexual behaviour as we move up the evolutionary ladder. Sexual behaviour, however, is not the equivalent of **sexual orientation**. Sexual orientation refers to one's erotic attraction toward, and interest in developing loving relationships with, members of the opposite or one's own sex. Sexual behaviour refers to the activities chosen in the pursuit and nurturance of such a relationship.

BOX 8.2

Sexual Behaviour in Nonhuman Species

....

If sexual behaviours were classified as *natural* or *unnatural* depending on whether other species engaged in them, would our own human repertoire become larger or smaller? Consider these examples:

1. The male sea otter with amorous intentions will bite the female on the nose until she bleeds. This causes her to ovulate.[a]

(cont'd)

BOX 8.2 *(cont'd)*

2. The male mouse will gently nibble at his partner's neck to put her in the mood for love.[b]

3. Outbursts of attack and flight are part of the courtship of many species such as sea gulls and three-spined stickleback fish. Many Siamese fighting fish end up dead, slaughtered by their suitors.[c]

4. The male turtle, as foreplay, may massage his mate's head with his claws, take it into his mouth, and then later suck on her feet, one at a time.[d]

5. The male desert tortoise nips the female's legs and head until she withdraws into her shell. Then he mounts her from the rear, grunting, stamping his feet, and banging on her back with his front feet.[e]

6. Before mating, the male porcupine will thoroughly drench the female with his urine.[f]

7. The male moose makes a depression in the ground, then urinates in it and wallows around in the mud he has created. Then he pushes the female toward this "wallow," mounts her, and in about three minutes, the sexual act is completed.[g]

8. During copulation, the female praying mantis turns around, bites off, and devours her partner's head. His thrusting, now disconnected from the regulation by his brain, goes into high gear.

9. Minks will copulate for up to eight hours before the male withdraws.[h]

10. Ferenuk antelopes copulate while in motion, and the act lasts only a fraction of a second.[i]

11. Female orgasm in animals, although somewhat more elusive than male orgasm, has been documented in monkeys and other primates of many species. Observable signs include the "clutch reflex," a spasmodic arm movement back toward her partner; "copulation calls," a series of staccato grunts; lipsmacks; trancelike expressions; rhythmic contractions of the vagina and uterus; a sudden increase in heart rate, possibly accompanied by a round-mouthed *ejaculation face* (a term borrowed from the male's expression during ejaculation).[j]

12. Swans, wolves, and beavers generally have one mate for life. Most mammals, however, such as bears, wildebeests, dogs, and cats, have an unlimited number of mates throughout their sexual lives.

And where do we humans fit in? Is *natural* a practical measure when it comes to sexuality? What exactly is *natural*?

(cont'd)

Notes:

a. W.L. Witters and P. Jones-Witters, *Human Sexuality: A Biological Perspective* (New York: D. Van Nostrand, 1980).

b. J.S. Nevid, L. Fichner-Rathus, and S.A. Rathus, *Human Sexuality in a World of Diversity*, 2nd ed. (Needham Heights, Mass.: Allyn and Bacon, 1995), p. 22.

c. Beverley A. Drinnin, *Instructor's Manual for Rathus, Nevid, Fichner-Rathus Human Sexuality in a World of Diversity* (Needham Heights, Mass.: 1993), p. 14.

d. Ibid.

e. J.P. Scott, "Animal Sexuality," in *The Encyclopedia of Sexual Behavior*, A. Ellis and A. Abarbanel, eds. (New York: Hawthorn Books, 1961), pp. 132–44.

f. Drinnin, *Instructor's Manual*.

g. Scott, "Animal Sexuality."

h. C. Ford and F. Beach, *Patterns of Sexual Behavior* (New York: Harper and Row, 1951).

i. J. Geer, J. Heiman, and H. Leitenberg, *Human Sexuality* (Englewood Cliffs, N.J.: Prentice-Hall, 1984).

j. Sarah Hardy, "A Disputed Legacy," in *Culture and Human Sexuality*, D.N. Suggs and A.W. Miracle, eds. (Pacific Grove, Calif.: Brooks/Cole, 1993), pp. 19–37.

Determining Sexual Orientation

Determining a person's sexual orientation would at first glance seem to be a simple matter. We could just ask people about their inclinations or observe them in their choices of mates. For those who have always been and still are exclusively **heterosexual** or **homosexual**, that method might suffice. But what about people who have had a few same-sex experiences, perhaps experimenting in childhood or when they were teenagers? What about those who have had mostly same-sex attractions, but have attempted and even sometimes enjoyed relationships with the other gender? What about long-term prisoners who find themselves in situations where human warmth and contact can only come from a same-sex partner? What about those who reject such relationships and prefer loveless isolation? What about people who marry, have children, and perhaps many years later, much to their surprise and even dismay, find themselves in love with a same-sex partner? What about those who "knew all along"? What about **gays** (homosexual males) and **lesbians** (homosexual females) who may feel occasional **heteroerotic** attractions (attraction to members of the opposite sex), and heterosexuals who experience sporadic **homoerotic** interests (attraction to members of the same sex)? In Bell and Weinberg's 1978 study, for example, about 50 percent of one sample of lesbians reported that they are sometimes attracted to men.[12]

Kinsey's Seven-Point Continuum of Sexual Orientation

It would appear that people may have varying degrees of heterosexual and homosexual feelings and experiences. Kinsey and his colleagues recognized the blurry boundaries and proposed a continuum of sexual orientation rather than the previously accepted mutually exclusive and opposite poles (see Figure 8.1). This seven-point continuum ranges from zero, exclusive heterosexuality, to six, exclusive homosexuality, and includes five graded levels in between, the midpoint being bisexuality. This new system of categorization produced, as you can imagine, very different percentages of people classified as either heterosexual or homosexual.

Accurate reporting of sexual orientation is further complicated by many other factors such as the nature of the study sample—that is, which countries were represented, whether the samples were randomly selected and representative of their respective groups, whether both men and women were surveyed, and which age groups were included and reported. Further confounding may come from how the questions were phrased, whether

Figure 8.1 Two Models of Sexual Orientation

1. Original Two-Point Typology

Heterosexual ◄─────────────── or ───────────────► Homosexual

The typology model places heterosexuality and homosexuality on polar opposites and mutually exclusive points.

2. Kinsey's Seven-Point Continuum

0	1	2	3	4	5	6
Exclusively heterosexual experience	Mostly heterosexual, with incidents of homosexual experience	Primarily heterosexual, with substantial homosexual experience	Equal amounts of heterosexual and homosexual experience	Primarily homosexual, with substantial heterosexual experience	Mostly homosexual, with incidents of heterosexual experience	Exclusively homosexual experience

Kinsey's model proposes a continuum between heterosexuality and homosexuality. People in category 0, who accounted for the majority of Kinsey's subjects, were considered exclusively heterosexual. People in category 6 were considered exclusively homosexual.

Source: A.C. Kinsey, W.B. Pomeroy, and C.E. Martin, *Sexual Behavior in the Human Male* (Philadelphia: Saunders, 1948). Reproduced with the permission of the Kinsey Institute for Research in Sex, Gender, and Reproduction, Inc.

the questionnaire was mailed anonymously or whether a face-to-face interview was used, and the gender and attitude of the interviewer.

You can imagine how you might respond differently in the following two situations. In the first, you are asked in a printed questionnaire mailed anonymously to your home, "Over the past five years, how often have you had voluntary sexual contact with a member of your own gender?" Enclosed is the promise to share results with you when available if you want, as well as a postage-paid envelope. In the second situation you may be at the shopping mall to pick up a few things for dinner at the end of a tiring and frustrating day, and the opposite-sex person with the clipboard intercepts you with the question, "Over the past five years, have you engaged in any sexually deviant acts?" Although researchers into human sexuality have generally developed greater sensitivity and awareness of the possible **response bias** (a tendency toward a particular mode of responding) involved, there still exists significant variation in results reported by the numerous studies currently being done, and no consensus has yet been reached in the scientific community. It is, however, reasonable to assume that about 80 percent of men and 90 percent of women are exclusively heterosexual. About 2 percent of men and 1 percent of women are exclusively homosexual. The remaining group have had varying amounts of both heterosexual and homosexual experience.[13]

Although in classifying sexual orientation Kinsey did take psychological reactions, that is, fantasies and feelings, to people of the same or the other gender into account, he emphasized behavioural criteria. In contrast, some other psychologists, in creating their own definitions of homosexuality, have not been much concerned with whether physical intimacy with a person of the same sex ever occurred. The noted psychoanalyst Anna Freud (born 1953), daughter of Sigmund Freud, maintained that the crucial determinants of homosexuality are one's thoughts and images when masturbating. If fantasies are about people of the same gender, then the person is homosexual. A man, for example, who becomes sexually aroused by homosexual fantasies while making love to his wife, would be classified as homosexual even if he has never engaged in homosexual behaviour.[14] This erotic attraction then defines, in essence, the sexual orientation, and the behaviour is the physical activity that may be in response to one's orientation or in contradiction to it.

Storms's Two-Dimensional Model of Sexual Orientation

Social psychologist Michael Storms postulated a somewhat different model (Figure 8.2). He argued that heterosexuality and homosexuality are independent dimensions, similar to masculinity and femininity. Some people, males and females, may be extremely masculine, some extremely feminine, and others may be psychologically **androgynous**—that is, they possess both masculine and feminine traits. Furthermore, Storms argues that one can be high or low on both dimensions at the same time. He argues that there are separate dimensions of responsiveness to heterosexual stimulation (heteroeroticism) and homosexual stimulation (homoeroticism). Bisexuals here would be high in both dimensions, and asexual people would be low in both, a view that has been supported by some studies.

Origins of Sexual Orientation

Now the inevitable question, "Can homosexuality be changed?" needs to be addressed. In 1973 the American Psychiatric Association (APA) voted to remove homosexuality from its listing of psychiatric disorders in its authoritative *Diagnostic and Statistical Manual of Mental Disorders* (DSM). The notion that the homosexual was sick or maladjusted no longer had official professional recognition. We may now want to reconsider our original question and at least add, "Do we want to change homosexuality?" Here we need to consider some causes or origins of sexual orientation.

The psychoanalytic view suggests that homosexuality results from a fixation at an immature stage of psychosexual development and a persisting **negative Oedipus complex**, the wish to possess the parent of one's own sex and the view of the opposite-sex parent as one's rival. Freud himself believed the efforts to change homosexual orientation to be largely futile and strongly recommended against it.

Figure 8.2   Storms's Two-Dimensional Model of Sexual Orientation

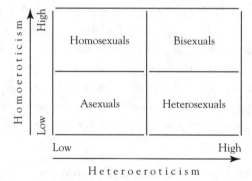

Storms's model deals with heterosexuality and homosexuality as independent dimensions. One could therefore be high on one and low on the other but also high or low on both dimensions at the same time.

Source: From "Theories of Sexual Orientation," by Michael D. Storms, 1980, *Journal of Personality and Social Psychology*, 38, pp. 783–92. Copyright 1980 by the American Psychological Association. Used by permission of the author.

Learning theorists point out that the sex drive at birth is undifferentiated, as Freud would agree, and that it becomes channelled through reinforcing (rewarding) and/or punishing experiences into heterosexuality or homosexuality.

Storms's interactionist theory proposes that homosexuality results when one's sex drive matures early, say before age 12, when the young preadolescent is still primarily in same-sex social groups.[15] Heterosexuality results when the sex drive matures later and heterosexual dating and friendships have emerged and have begun to eroticize heterosexual experiences. The sex drive of males in general matures earlier than that of females, and Storms's theory may provide one explanation why there are more homosexual men than women.

Sociologists emphasize the effects of **labelling**. If, for example, a young boy were called a "homosexual," he might consider this a derogatory term, respond with anger, anxiety, and embarrassment. This may motivate him to prove the label wrong, or it may lead to a **self-fulfilling prophecy** and cause him to see himself that way, finally accept the label, and provide the behaviour. Sociologists also refer to the social roles we play. Homosexuality may be one role, like others, that is assumed for various practical purposes and then tends to shape the person acting out the role.

The biological explanations are currently gaining momentum. So far, research has failed to connect sexual orientation with reliable differences in existing (adult) levels of sex hormones. Prenatal sex hormones, however, have been shown to play a role in determining sexual orientation in animals such as rats and sheep. If fetuses were deprived of normal levels of their respective sex hormones during the critical period when their brains were sexually differentiating, offspring were more likely to show homosexual mating patterns as adults.[16] Recent evidence has shown that this process may hold for humans. Autopsies have revealed structural differences in the brains of homosexual men compared with those of heterosexual men, making them more similar to heterosexual women's brains. Considerable evidence from studies of twins shows that homosexuality tends to run in families. And although psychosocial factors do play an important role and tend to confound findings within families, genetic factors are emerging as possibly being significant. In 1993, researchers at the National Cancer Institute found evidence linking a region on the X-sex chromosome (inherited from one's mother) to a homosexual orientation in men.[17] Subsequent study of groups of gay brothers continued to support the connection. We do, however, need to treat these findings with caution because so far only a marker at a general location on the X-chromosome has been found, not the specific gene. Nor is it known just how such a gene or combination of genes might account for sexual orientation.

Although caution is advised in the research of biological origins of homosexuality, considering that findings may produce both positive and negative reactions, it seems that overall the positive side is gaining. Homosexuality is coming to be seen more as a biologically determined attribute rather than a personal choice that can be turned on or off like a light switch.

Diverse Sexual Customs around the World Today

Preindustrial Societies

We have examined sexuality to find what is natural. We have studied biological processes to try to explain variations in sexual behaviour. Yet we know that all humans share the same physiological response to sexual pleasure. The same hormones flow through the arteries of people all over the world. The capacity for sexual orgasm is universal. We can also assume that the genitals of males and females are constructed and function similarly for you, for me, for our neighbour, and for people in Sweden, China, Ireland, and the islands of the South Pacific. Nevertheless, societies, as we have already seen in our historical perspective, differ widely in their sexual attitudes, customs, and practices. If sexuality were completely or even predominantly determined by biology, we would not find the diversity, as we will see.

Among the few generalizations that can be made is that all societies regulate sexual behaviour in some way. The specific regulations, however, vary from one culture to another and are possibly designed to prevent social disruption. The incest taboo is nearly universal. Couples everywhere engaged in sexual activity tend to seek privacy. Most societies condemn forced sexual relations, such as rape.

Trobriand Island: Female Assertiveness

One exception to the disapproval of forced sex occurs among the people of Trobriand Island, off the eastern tip of New Guinea in the South Pacific. Here, contrary to what the gender roles of our own society would lead us to expect, women rape men. There are only a few societies in which the female generally initiates love affairs, for example, the Maori and the Kwoma of the South Pacific. But the Trobrianders take it a step further, and as the anthropologist Bronislaw Malinowski explains, if the women perceive a strange man from any village but their own passing within sight, they have a right to attack him, a right they exercise with great energy and zeal. He is fair game for sexual violence, obscene cruelty, and rough handling. As Malinowski described the practice:

> First, they pull off and tear up his pubic leaf, the protection of his modesty and, to a native the symbol of his manly dignity. Then by masturbatory practices and exhibitionism, they try to produce an

erection in their victim and, when their manoeuvres have brought about the desired result, one of them squats over him and inserts his penis into her vagina. After the first ejaculation he may be treated in the same manner by another woman.[18]

That may not be all. Some women may defecate and urinate all over his body. They are not at all ashamed, but regard the custom as a sign of their general sexual prowess. Any shame or embarrassment is considered to be appropriately the victim's.

You may doubt that such rape is physically possible. Let's examine the process. The sexual excitation response is a reflex action and therefore mediated by the spinal cord. It proceeds without input (permission) from the brain. Remember your (perhaps) involuntary response at the beach last summer? And this applies to both the male's erection and the female's lubrication. The brain is of course secondarily informed of what's going on, and it does have some inhibitory capability, but in the heat of the moment, it may well not be carrying out its normally expected control function.

Mundugumor and Arapesh: Aggression and Gentleness

The anthropologist Margaret Mead lived among several other tribes (on the island of New Guinea in the South Pacific) whose sex roles differ from what is generally found in our and other Western countries; and tribes differ in behaviour from each other.

Among the Mundugumor, a tribe of headhunters and cannibals, both men and women are aggressive and warlike and lack consideration for the rights and feelings of others. The women dislike bearing and caring for children because it interferes with their warring exploits into neighbouring villages. Sexual orgasm is considered a routine part of sex for them. By contrast, Arapesh women rarely experience orgasm. No concept of a female's sexual climax even exists for them. Both men and women of the Arapesh tribe are gentle, peaceful, and considerate, and both men and women enjoy caring for and playing with children.

Tchambuli: Role Reversal

Among the Tchambuli, however, Mead found a reversal of what we stereotypically consider our Western sex roles. Tchambuli men are sensitive, considerate, and carefully groomed. They spend much time artistically applying make-up and even more time caring for children. They tend to be emotionally unstable, given to gossiping, bickering, and haggling over prices. Tchambuli women, on the other hand, are stable and practical, keeping their heads shaven and disdaining ornaments. They are dominant and more highly sexed than men. They also bring home daily their catch of fish, the Tchambuli's staple diet.[19]

Inis Beag, Mehinaku, and Mangaia: Repression, Anxiety, and Pleasurable Sex

Another trio exhibiting remarkable diversity of approach to sexuality is the folk community of Inis Beag, a small island off the coast of Ireland; the people of Mehinaku, a village in central Brazil; and those of Mangaia, a Polynesian island in the South Pacific.

Anthropologist John Messenger[20] describes Inis Beag as probably one of the most naive and sexually repressed societies in the world. French kissing, mouth stimulation of the breasts, or hand stimulation of the partner's genitals, it seems, are unknown, much less fellatio, cunnilingus, or homosexuality. Masturbation and premarital sexual activity are decreed sinful, and the process of elimination is dirty. Mothers avoid breastfeeding their infants as it involves nudity, which is nasty. Only babies are bathed while nude. Adults wash, in strict privacy, only the parts of their bodies that extend beyond their clothing, that is, face, neck, hands, lower arms, feet, and lower legs. Married partners have sexual intercourse in the dark, both with their underclothes on. And this only infrequently because sex is considered draining to his health and a burden to be tolerated by the wife. The man ejaculates as quickly as possible to spare her, and she is not expected to and does not experience orgasm, which is considered deviant behaviour for females. He then turns over and quickly falls asleep, having done his duty for procreation. As you can imagine, there is a great deal of anxiety about sexuality on Inis Beag.

Our second group, the people of Mehinaku also have plenty of anxiety about sex, even though, unlike Inis Beag folk, they have plenty of sex. Anthropologist Thomas Gregor[21] describes this highly eroticized but gender-segregated people. There is an openness with children about sex, and children can easily name their parents' numerous extramarital lovers. Men are highly sexed and compete aggressively for women's sexual favours. Women, however, have much less of a sex drive, and there seems to be no recognition of female orgasm. In a generally nonviolent but gender-segregated culture, a woman may be dragged to the woods and gang-raped if she should enter the men's house and see forbidden things. The sexual anxiety of the people is reflected in dreams and myths wherein those who engage in extramarital sex typically die in fantastic ways.

Third in our trio, Mangaia, a Polynesian pearl of an island, lies in stark contrast to both Inis Beag and Mehinaku. Anthropologist Donald Marshall[22] relates that, from an early age, boys and girls learn about sexuality through folktales that contain detailed descriptions of sexual acts and anatomy and through watching provocative ritual dances. They are encouraged to get in touch with their own sexuality through masturbation and sexual play as early as age seven. At about age thirteen, Mangaian boys are initiated into manhood by the superincision ritual in which a slit is made along the entire length of the penis. The incision was traditionally made with a flake of semi-flintlike local stone, but now it is usually done with a straight razor. Excruciating pain is involved, and the youth runs directly into the sea or stream for relief, at the same time proclaiming in agony and exultation, "Now I am a man!" The same expert who performs the superincision also gives the boy sexual instruction. He shows the boy how to kiss and suck breasts, and how to bring his partner to orgasm several times before he has his own. About two weeks after the operation, the boy has sexual intercourse with an experienced woman. This removes the scab. She teaches him various positions and activities and trains him to avoid **premature ejaculation**. Above all, a Mangaian man's goal is to continue the sexual action—the longer the better. A good man is expected to continue steadily for fifteen to thirty minutes or longer. The girl receives sexual instruction from an older woman and is usually initiated by an experienced male relative. Apparently, all learn how to experience orgasm. Mangaians do not value virginity because, they say, virgins do not know how to provide sexual pleasure.

Properly initiated boys now practise their new techniques with girlfriends on secluded beaches and other out-of-the-way spots in nature. They will also visit girlfriends in the evening in the huts where the girls sleep with their families. Parents may listen for their daughter's laughter and gasping so that they will know that the daughter has reached orgasm with a visiting young man, called a sleepcrawler. They try not to interfere with courtship and pretend to be asleep so as not to diminish their daughter's chances of finding a suitable mate for marriage. The average nice girl will have three to four successive boyfriends between the ages of thirteen and twenty. The average boy may have ten or more girlfriends. By about age eighteen, Mangaians usually have sex most nights of the week, with about three orgasms per night. The really important aspect of sexual intercourse for the Mangaian male lover is to give pleasure to his wife or girlfriend, and he aims to have her achieve orgasm two or three times to his once. One could say then that Mangaians have plenty of sex and little anxiety about it.

Industrial Societies

But, you may be asking, how can I identify with these far-away and strange people in places I've never heard of? Fair enough. Let's take a brief look at some more familiar places.

China: Emergence from Repression

China was for millennia the ultimate sexually appreciative and open society, but beginning in 1949, when the Communists came into power, China was transformed into one of the world's most puritanical, sexually repressed societies, at least in public. Couples who have only one or no children are given monetary bonuses and other advantages, and there are heavy financial penalties for unauthorized pregnancies and for second and third children. In 1996, a 29-year-old Communist Party member and hospital administrator from southern

China said that family planning officials at her workplace, asserting that she had become pregnant before obtaining her permit to have her one and only child, stripped her of her job, stopped her paycheques, and held her down for a pelvic exam to check her fetus's age.[23] Still, about half the population report having engaged in premarital intercourse; a male college student was expelled from Beijing University in April 1990 when it became known that he had done so, and other students reported that this was typical punishment.[24]

In recent years, however, an experimental Family Planning Program is gradually being introduced in certain areas such as Beijing, Shanghai, whose population is shrinking anyway, and the wealthy seaboard region of northern Zhejiang Province. Here women no longer need approval to have their first child. The aim is to replace forced abortions or sterilizations with education and voluntary family planning to manage China's 1.26 billion population. Along with up-to-date advice on sex and contraception, newlyweds also receive a jarring reminder that if they have certain medical conditions—from schizophrenia to colon polyps to congenital hearing loss—that they are forbidden to have children.[25]

Japan: Private Sexuality

The Japanese seem content to keep their private lives private. There are few sexologists in Japan, and the last scientific survey is about eighteen years old. Yet for the Japanese, Christmas Eve (Eebu) is the sexiest night of the year. To celebrate Eebu, every unmarried person must have a date, whether it is an ongoing romance or a last-minute arrangement. Elaborate plans are made, which often cost more than a thousand dollars, paid entirely by the man. Many men save all year for the event. H-day (hormone day) includes special clothes, limousine rental, probably an expensive heart pendant for her, a fancy dinner for two, possibly a visit to the Tokyo Disneyland, an overnight stay at a ritzy hotel, and breakfast the next morning, just before the couple dashes off to work on Christmas Day.[26] Japanese groupism, the fear of being alone, and the need to be rooted in society, is probably behind this custom, rather than sexual need.

Sweden and Holland: Informed Permissiveness

Sexual behaviours in Sweden and in Holland are much like ours, but meanings might be quite different. In both countries a certain degree of permissiveness seems prevalent. Teenagers are more likely to be informed about sexuality, including contraception. The norm, especially in Holland, is for young people to say that they would not dream of having sex without protection, both males and females carry condoms at all times, and unwanted pregnancies are rare. Discussion about sexual matters with parents is common, and embarrassment seems virtually absent.

CRITICAL THINKING BOX 8.3

....

Thinking Critically ... about the Ethnocentrism of Sexuality

Ethnocentrism is the tendency to see your own ethnic group and its social and cultural standards as the basis for evaluative judgments about the practices of others—with the implication that your own standards are superior. Do you think ethnocentrism could interfere with students' willingness to learn about and accept cultural differences in sexual values and practices? Could such acceptance be desirable or is it preferable that each group think and do as they prefer?

North America: Information for Personal Choices

We in North America are also on the path to better sexual understanding. Knowledge generally seems to have the effect of promoting behaviour with more positive and pleasant results and fewer negative and painful consequences. Referred to as the most comprehensive and scientifically sound sex survey ever conducted in the United States, the *1992 Sex in America* study surveyed nearly 3500 adults, aged eighteen to fifty-nine.[27] It was found that people usually have sex with people who are remarkably like themselves—in age, race or ethnicity, and education. Few people wait until they marry to have sex. However, people who ended up marrying knew their partners longer before having sex with them than couples in short-term sexual relationships did. Students, in fact, who met their partners in college, were unlikely to have sex within the first month of meeting each other, which suggests that college students are not hopping from partner to partner, as is generally thought.

How about frequency? Here's the surprise: The people who have the most sex are not the young and footloose, but those who are married or living together. Married women are much more likely to have orgasms (75 percent) than never-married women or those not living with someone (62 percent). Single women have much higher rates of never climaxing (11 percent) than married or cohabiting women (2 percent). And no, men aren't always clued in to whether their partners climax.

Another surprise was how few sexual activities are seen as appealing. Vaginal intercourse has nearly universal appeal (96 percent women; 95 percent men). No other genital sexual activity even approaches this preference. Anal intercourse is way down near the bottom of the list. Another popular sexual practice is masturbation. And counterintuitively, the most sexually active people are also the most likely to masturbate, and married people are significantly more likely to masturbate than people who are living alone. Masturbation, it seems, is not a substitute for sexual deprivation, but an activity that is stimulated by and stimulates other sexual activities.

But perhaps the greatest surprise is how much trouble we North Americans have with our sexuality. Deluged as we are by movies and television where it would appear that the greatest daily dilemmas are deciding on which of our eager sexual partners to bestow our steamy favours, in which order, and for how long, well over one-third of us are plagued by significant sexual dysfunctions. A study published by the *Journal of the American Medical Association* in 1999 reports that of more than 3000 American men and women aged eighteen to fifty-nine, 43 percent of women and 31 percent of men said they had one or more persistent problems with sex. For women, lack of interest and regularly not wanting sex was the most common problem at 32 percent; another 26 percent said they regularly did not have orgasms; and 23 percent said sex was not pleasurable. For men, the most common problem, at 31 percent, was persistently climaxing too early; 18 percent said they felt anxious about performance; 15 percent lacked interest in sex; and 8 percent did not find sex pleasurable.[28]

Can you imagine? Clearly something is missing. The escalation of sexual openness since the 1950s has created a general belief that we are more sexual than ever before. But instead of being liberated, we are worried that everybody else is doing it and we are somehow missing the party. There is much stylized talking and much abstract writing about sex, but rarely do men and women actually talk to each other except in the language of seduction. We are only just beginning to understand the myths and half-truths of past decades and centuries. Rigorous scientific research and open, solution-motivated discussion will show us that sexual behaviour can be studied and understood in the same way other social behaviours such as choosing a college or finding a job can be understood. Yes, we can simultaneously take the mystery out of, and put the magic back into our sexual responses and interactions. What do you think?

CONCLUSION

Where, you might ask yourself now, do we fit in? Where are we now? Where should we be heading? How do we put it all together? The various historical and ethnic traditions and values we have discussed remind us that no single set of sexual attitudes and behaviours are the norm for everyone. Each society and culture has evolved its own unique value system as a functional adaptation to its particular social, political, economic, and religious environment. Because human sexual behaviour is determined more by learning

CRITICAL THINKING BOX 8.4

....

Thinking Critically ... about Attitude and Behaviour Change

Research has shown that after studying human sexuality, students' *attitudes*, in general, tended to become more permissive, but their actual *behaviour* did not show a similar change. Control groups were generally not used, and students' backgrounds and previous experiences were not evaluated. What might be the possible significance of these findings?

and less by genes and sex hormones than is the sexual behaviour of any other animal species, human sexuality is often said to be liberated or emancipated from genes and hormones. The great emancipators—culture and society—have taken us, by means of our cerebral cortex, to sexual choice: freedom or oppression, depending on what choices we make. Bronislaw Malinowski, after he had lived among Pacific Islanders, wrote: "Sex is not a mere physiological transaction ... it implies love and love-making; it becomes the nucleus of such venerable institutions as marriage and the family; it pervades art and it produces its spells and magic. It dominates in fact almost every aspect of culture."[29] What do you think?

CHAPTER SUMMARY

Sexuality is the totality of the ways we experience and express ourselves as sexual beings. It includes gender, anatomy, sexual identity and orientation, and sexual behaviour.

Throughout most of human history, religion was the main source of information concerning sexuality. Beginning in the late nineteenth century, however, important scientific contributions to the understanding of sexuality were made by Richard von Krafft-Ebing, Sigmund Freud, Henry Havelock Ellis, Alfred Kinsey, and William Masters and Virginia Johnson.

Critical examination of sexual behaviour over the past 20 000 years shows little evidence of universal trends. One generalization that does emerge, however, is that all societies regulate sexual behaviour in some way.

Nonhuman animal behaviour reveals similar variations in sexuality, including analogues of rape, oral sex, foreplay, and homosexuality. The question of what is natural is brought into focus.

Human sexual orientation and behaviour can be viewed from different perspectives. Kinsey found evidence of degrees of homosexuality and heterosexuality. Storms proposed that heterosexuality and homosexuality may be separate dimensions rather than polar opposites. Evidence is also accumulating of other contributing factors such as life experiences and learning, genetics, and prenatal hormone effects.

The modern cross-cultural perspective, given the great variations represented, provides further insights into the evolution of sexuality and supports the view that experience and learning play possibly the most important roles in shaping human sexual behaviour. The evidence points to the absence of universality in sexual matters and to the influence of individual, immediate, and adaptive factors in the development of unlimited diversity of response.

KEY TERMS

androgynous, p. 213

bisexual, p. 201

coition machine, p. 207

congenital, p. 206

cunnilingus, p. 201

fellatio, p. 201

fixation, p. 205

fornicate, p. 201

gays, p. 211

heteroerotic, p. 211

heterosexual, p. 211

homoerotic, p. 211

homosexual, p. 211

human sexual response cycle, p. 207

incest taboo, p. 198

labelling, p. 215

lesbians, p. 211

monogamy, p. 199

negative Oedipus complex, p. 214

neurosis, p. 205

orgasm, p. 202

pederasty, p. 201

phallic worship, p. 198

pheromones, p. 208

polygamy, p. 199

premature ejaculation, p. 219

response bias, p. 213

self-fulfilling prophecy, p. 215

sexual anesthesia, p. 203

sexual behaviour, p. 209

sexual orientation, p. 209

sexuality, p. 194

DISCUSSION QUESTIONS

1. Trace the evolution of sexuality over the ages, across time, cultures, and religions, with a focus on the sexual behaviours of the various groups discussed in this chapter.
2. List the major scientific research studies of human sexuality, and assess their contributions to our current understanding of it.

3. Consider the similarities and differences in sexual behaviour of humans and other species, and compare and contrast behaviour in terms of masturbation, oral–genital stimulation, and homosexuality.

4. Distinguish between Kinsey's and Storms's models of sexuality, and evaluate the possible advantages and disadvantages of each for various relevant groups.

5. Discuss findings relating to influence on sexual orientation of experiences and learning, genetics, prenatal hormones, adult sex hormone levels, and differences in brain structure.

6. Critically appraise the possible value of understanding the diversity of sexual behaviour around the world, and consider whether it is reasonable to conclude that there may or may not be universality of human sexual behaviour.

NOTES

1. René Descartes, *Discourse on Method and The Meditations*, trans. by F.E. Sutcliffe (Markham, Ont.: Penguin, 1968), p. 30.
2. J. Telushkin, *Jewish Literacy* (New York: Morrow, 1991), p. 616.
3. Eric Berne, *Sex in Human Loving* (New York: Pocket Books, 1970), p. 18.
4. R. Tannahill, *Sex in History* (Briarcliff Manor, N.Y.: Stein and Day, 1980).
5. Peter Gay, *The Bourgeois Experience: Victoria to Freud* (New York: Oxford University Press, 1984) p. 6.
6. William H. Masters and Virginia E. Johnson, *Human Sexual Response* (Boston: Little, Brown, 1966).
7. H.C. Bingam, "Sex Development in Apes," *Comparative Psychology Monographs*, vol. 5 (1928) pp. 98–99.
8. Konrad Lorenz, *On Aggression* (New York: Harcourt, Brace, Jovanovich, 1966).
9. A.F. McBride and D.O. Hebb, "Behavior of the Captive Bottlenose Dolphin," in *Tursiops Truncatus, Journal of Comparative and Physiological Psychology*, vol. 41 (1948), pp. 111–23.
10. J. Erwin and T. Maple, "Ambisexual Behavior with Male-Male Anal Penetration in Male Rhesus Monkeys," *Archives of Sexual Behavior*, vol. 5 (1976), pp. 9–14.
11. Janet Shibley Hyde, *Understanding Human Sexuality* (New York: McGraw-Hill, 1990), p. 18.
12. A.P. Bell and M.S. Weinberg, *Homosexualities: A Study of Diversity among Men and Women* (New York: Simon and Schuster, 1978).
13. Hyde, *Understanding Human Sexuality*, p. 434.
14. Anna Freud, *The Ego and Mechanisms of Defense* (New York: International Universities Press, 1953, orig. pub. 1936).
15. Michael D. Storms, "A Theory of Erotic Orientation Development," *Psychological Review*, vol. 88 (1981), pp. 340–53.
16. L. Ellis and M.A. Ames, "Neurohormonal Functioning and Sexual Orientation: A Theory of Homosexuality-Heterosexuality," *Psychological Bulletin*, vol. 101 (1987), pp. 233–58.

17. D.H. Hamer, et al., "A Linkage Between DNA Markers on the X Chromosome and Male Sexual Orientation," *Science*, vol. 261 (16 July 1993), pp. 321–27.
18. Bronislaw Malinowski, *The Sexual Life of Savages* (New York: Harcourt, Brace, 1929).
19. Margaret Mead, *Sex and Temperament in Three Primitive Societies* (New York: Morrow, 1935).
20. J. Messenger, "Sex and Repression in an Irish Folk Community," in *Human Sexual Behavior: Variations in the Ethnographic Spectrum*, D. Marshall and R. Suggs, eds. (Englewood Cliffs: N.J.: Prentice-Hall, 1971).
21. T. Gregor, *Anxious Pleasures: The Sexual Lives of an Amazonian People* (Chicago: University of Chicago Press, 1985).
22. D.S. Marshall, "Sexual Behavior on Mangaia," in *Human Sexual Behavior: Variations in the Ethnographic Spectrum*, D. Marshall and R. Suggs, eds. (Englewood Cliffs, NJ: Prentice-Hall, 1971).
23. Elisabeth Rosenthal, "China Rethinks Iron Hand for One-child Policy," *Sunday Herald*, 1 November 1998.
24. D. Sutherland, "Limited 'Sexual Revolution' Seen in China: Nationwide Survey Shows More Liberal Attitudes Developing in Conservative Society," *Washington Post*, 27 May 1990.
25. Elisabeth Rosenthal, "China Rethinks Iron Hand," 1 November 1998.
26. T.R. Reid, "Snug in Their Beds for Christmas Eve: In Japan, Dec. 24 Has Become the Hottest Night of the Year," *Washington Post*, 24 December 1990.
27. CSG Enterprises, Inc., Edward O. Laumann, Robert T. Michael, and Gina Kolata, *Sex in America: A Definitive Survey* (Boston: Little, Brown, 1994).
28. Edward O. Laumann, Anthony Paik, and Raymond C. Rosen, "Sexual Dysfunction in the United States," *Journal of the American Medical Association*, vol. 281, No. 6 (February 10, 1999): pp. 537–44.
29. Malinowski, *The Sexual Life of Savages*, p. xxiii.

The Myth of the Traditional Family: Diversity in Canadian Families

Geoff Ondercin-Bourne

There is no golden age of family life to long for, no past pattern that, if we only had the moral will to return to, would guarantee us happiness and security. Family life is always bound up with the economic, demographic, and cultural predicaments of specific times and places.
— Arlene Skolnick, *Embattled Paradise*

Family: from the Latin, familia "the slaves of a household"
— *Random House Dictionary of the English Language*

Objectives

After reading this chapter, you should be able to

- define family in a way that accounts for the many variations of families in Canada today

- critically assess the underlying assumptions of the "traditional family"

- compare several theoretical approaches used to understand the evolution of families and relations among family members

- describe recent changes in Canadian families

- link the changes in familial structures and relationships to broader changes in society

INTRODUCTION

The family, we are told, is an institution in crisis. News headlines mourn the decline of the "traditional" family. We hear that modern society has turned its back on the family. Governments have undermined its authority through intruding social services such as Children's Aid and laws such as those restricting the use of corporal punishment. So-called special interest groups lobby governments on behalf of nontraditional families such as single parents or gays and lesbians. It is suggested that even the courts are making decisions that erode the position of the traditional family in our society.

If the family is now "under siege," then presumably there was a golden age when the traditional family thrived. This golden age was represented on television in the 1950s and early 1960s by such programs as *Leave It to Beaver, Father Knows Best*, and *Ozzie and Harriet*. Arlene Skolnick opened her recent book on the family with a prologue called "Who Killed Ozzie and Harriet?" This title suggests the apparent deterioration of modern family life, a "Paradise Lost," if you will. More recent television families such as shows as *My Wife and Kids* and even, in its own inimitable way, *Married with Children*, provided more up-to-date versions of family life that nonetheless conform with a particular view of what constitutes a family.

As the title of our book implies, society can best be understood through its diversity. In this diversity the very notion of the family is misleading at best. Families are evolving, as they always have, in response to social, political, and economic change. Consequently, to answer Skolnick's tongue-in-cheek question, no one killed Ozzie and Harriet because, for the most part, they never existed. The traditional family is an idea, not a fact.

In this chapter we will (1) provide some definitions of families and outline the difficulties of doing so; (2) explain some theoretical approaches to the study of families, making a key distinction between what we describe as unification theories and liberation

CRITICAL THINKING BOX 9.1

You can still see *Leave It to Beaver* on "oldies" TV stations. Compare the family life portrayed in that show with that portrayed in your favourite current TV show. How have family relationships on TV changed since the 1950s? In what ways have they remained the same?

theories; and (3) look at how families in Canada have changed, as well as the challenges facing Canadian families in the twenty-first century.

DEFINING FAMILY

Traditional Definitions

Definitions of family have generally been based on the inclusion or exclusion of individuals from the group; either you are in, or you are out. An example is George Murdock's definition that is quoted in many sociological studies of family. According to Murdock, family can be defined as "a social group characterized by common residence, economic cooperation, and reproduction. It includes adults of both sexes, at least two of whom maintain a socially approved sexual relationship, and one or more children, owned or adopted, of the cohabiting adults."[1] A more recent definition, by Rose Laub Coser, is clearly influenced by Murdock: "[The family] finds its origin in marriage; it consists of husband, wife, and children born in their wedlock, though other relatives may find their place close to this nuclear group, and the group is united by moral, legal, economic, religious and social rights and obligations."[2]

The traditional definitions highlight the importance of the biological function of families. Families that consist of a mother, a father, and their children are called **nuclear families**. However, does such a definition adequately describe the modern family? Can there be families that are not based on producing children?

Some critics see many limitations with the traditional concept of the nuclear family. For example, by defining family in biological terms, we seem to legitimate the notion of family as a "natural" unit. The implication here is that any relationship or grouping that falls outside this exclusive definition is necessarily "unnatural," whether or not it is generally accepted in society as a family. Among those excluded are childfree couples, single-parent families, commuting families, and remarried families. In addition, relationships such as gay and lesbian couples, which have gained some legal ground in the past decade, are most definitely excluded from the mainstream of Canadian family theorists.

Finally, let's look at the definition used in Canada's census, which, although more inclusive than the traditional definitions, is still heavily influenced by them. According to Statistics Canada, "census families include married couples and common-law couples with or without never-married children living at home, as well as lone-parent families."[3] As we shall see, this definition still omits many living arrangements that also lay claim to the name "family."

Two further issues raise questions about traditional definitions of family. For one, cultural differences are not factored into them. To what extent, for example, do North American Aboriginal families meet the criteria of the nuclear family? Does the structure of families immigrating from all over the world resemble that in the definitions of Murdock and Coser?

If we accept a definition of family based on the nuclear family, we may be marginalizing the impact of the **extended family** in many cultures, including our own. An extended family comprises two or more nuclear families joined together through blood ties. The classic example of an extended family is a husband and wife, their unmarried children, their married children, and the spouses and children of their married children. By focusing solely on the nuclear components that make up an extended family, the analysis ignores the unique character of that particular set of relationships. Based on these examples, it is hard to imagine a realistic "one size fits all cultures" definition of family.

The second issue is the changing nature of family. How applicable are the definitions of nuclear family to the families of the past? Consider the assumption of parents and children living under one roof. In Canada, this has not always been the case for everyone. For example, in the middle of the eighteenth century, many children in New France, some as young as five or six, were forced to work as live-in household servants. Were these children no longer part of a nuclear family?

The point is that uniform, fixed definitions of family are incomplete, and even misleading. The idea is gaining ground that "the family is a social construct."[4] The mutability of the structure of family must be an important component of its definition. Later in this chapter, we will discuss the ways that the Canadian family has adapted to its changing socioeconomic environment.

Eichler's Dimensions: An Inclusive Approach to Understanding Family

If the traditional definitions of family are incomplete, how do we at least determine some key characteristics of "family"? Margrit Eichler has emphasized the variations among families, using what she referred to as internal "dimensions."[5] We will focus here on five of these: the procreative dimension, the socialization dimension, the residential dimension, the economic dimension, and the emotional dimension. Box 9.1 describes some of the main elements of each.

This list is by no means complete, but even the five dimensions included here do provide a framework for analyzing the diversity of Canadian families. When we compare Eichler's dimensional approach with the all-encompassing definitions offered by Murdock, Coser, and even Canada's census, we see an important distinction: Eichler viewed families as a set of relationships, whereas Murdock and Coser defined them as a

BOX 9.1

Eichler's Five Internal Dimensions of the Family

....

Procreative Dimension
- Does the couple have children?
- If so, are they from the current relationship or a previous one?

Socialization Dimension
- Are both parents, one parent, or neither parent involved in childrearing?

Residential Dimension
- Do all family members live under the same roof?
- Does one family member live in a separate dwelling only?
- Does one family member have an additional separate dwelling?

Economic Dimension
- Is one family member solely responsible financially for the other members?
- Do two or more family members share the financial responsibility for other members?
- Are family members financially responsible for themselves?

Emotional Dimension
- Is the positive involvement of family members mutual or one-sided?
- Is there a lack of involvement from family members?
- Is there mutual negative involvement?

Source: Margrit Eichler, *Families in Canada Today* (Toronto: Gage, 1983). Reproduced with permission of the author.

fixed set of characters. Eichler's perspective allows us to look at "the family" as a dynamic institution that can account for a wide range of configurations. We will therefore use a dimensional analysis to understand Canadian families and the changes they have undergone, particularly since the 1950s.

Next, we will examine some theoretical perspectives that sociologists have used to study families. These theories enable us to determine how families affect, and are affected by, other social institutions and social relationships.

THEORETICAL PERSPECTIVES ON UNDERSTANDING DIVERSITY IN FAMILIES

Why do we consider theory? Why not just "look at the facts" and forget about theoretical questions and debates? The answer is that theories are useful models that help us make sense of the complexities of the real world. As Emily Nett explained: "To omit theory would be to reduce knowledge about families to a series of simple statistics or journalistic accounts at one extreme, and a compendium of value judgements, like a sermon, at the other.... Theory relates concepts and provides a basis for asking questions, finding answers, or doing both."[6]

Having acknowledged the importance of theory, we are faced with a dilemma. Given the limitations of space, how do we cover the many theorists who have written about families? In fact, we cannot. As a result, we have selected some of the theories that have appeared consistently in the literature on the family.

In this chapter, we divide theories of family into two groups, based on the analysis by David Cheal, a family sociologist:[7] (1) unification theories emphasize the universality of family structures and the benefits of family over its costs; (2) liberation theories emphasize both the diversity of families and the limitations that families place on individual members, as well as the strategies used to overcome these constraints. The debate between unification theorists and liberation theorists is central to our discussion about the nature of family.

Unification Theories

Following World War II, sociological analysis in the United States and Canada, including analysis of the family, was dominated by several schools of thought that were all variations of the unification approach. Although some of these theories had appeared earlier in the twentieth century, it was during the prosperous decades of the postwar boom that they enjoyed immense popularity.

Unification theories of the family hold the view that the family is an adaptive unit mediating between the individual and society; the family meets the needs of individuals for personal growth, development, and physical and emotional integrity. To the extent that the family meets an individual's social needs, it is seen as "functional."

Since the 1960s, however, competing schools of thought have put forward alternative perspectives on family life that have generated a lively debate on the family and its role in modern society. We will describe in detail two of the predominant sociological perspectives within the unification school—structural–functionalism and general systems theory—and offer brief summaries of two other perspectives that have been used by unification theorists.

Structural–Functionalism

Talcott Parsons, G.P. Murdock, W.F. Ogburn, W. Goode, and B. Schlesinger are well-known and influential structural–functionalists who wrote about families. **Structural–functionalism** argues that the family is an important institution that maintains social stability. Family members have many and diverse normatively prescribed activities that become integrated into a dynamic system called family. That is to say, family members behave according to the prescribed family norms of the society in which they live. Talcott Parsons, the sociologist most closely associated with this theory, saw the family as performing three particular functions that contribute to social harmony and integration: reproduction, socialization of new members, and emotional support.

As society changes, institutions, including the family, adapt to new social realities. For example, before industrialization and urbanization, families played a central role in educating their own children. They performed as a "unit of production" as well as a "unit of consumption." These families grew much of their own food, produced some of the implements used in their daily lives, and in some cases built their own houses. With all these responsibilities, extended families were important for a family's well-being.

As industries grew and people moved off the land to the cities, families became essentially units of consumption only. Institutions such as schools began to take over some of the social functions of families. A highly mobile family unit meets industrial capitalism's need for a flexible workforce. Therefore, according to Parsons, the smaller nuclear family was ideal. The extended family declined in importance in favour of the more independent nuclear family. Fewer familial commitments, argued Parsons, meant that workers were less preoccupied with concerns of family members and more with productivity. Thus, the breakdown of the extended family, in structural–functional theory, served the needs and interests of the modern capitalist economy. The family adapted. The isolated **conjugal family**, which superseded the extended family, was based on marriage, and it included a "breadwinner," usually the father, a homemaker, usually the mother, and the children conceived from that marriage. In the view of the structural–functionalists, this family type became the norm. It was, to use their terminology, "functional."

If such a familial arrangement is seen as functional, however, then those arrangements that do not conform to this model, or attempt to alter it, must, by definition, be dysfunctional. Structural–functionalists have not dealt with conflict and change, nor have they considered the dynamic nature of interpersonal relations. Change is seen as disruptive, and individual opposition to social pressure as "deviance." But, regardless of the criticisms that have been levelled at it, structural–functionalism has played a major role in determining how we conceive of families in our society.

General Systems Theory

General systems theory, also referred to simply as systems theory, analyzes the family as a total system that has an impact on all its members. This theory became popular in the 1960s, and although some ideas associated with it have been severely criticized since the 1970s, it is still being used in psychiatry, psychology, and family therapy. Of the many sociologists who have made important contributions to family studies using systems theory, the most influential is Reuben Hill.[8] According to Hill four qualities make it possible to study the family as a system:

1. Family members occupy various interdependent positions, that is, a change in the behaviour of one member leads to a change in the behaviour of other members.
2. The family is a relatively closed, boundary-maintaining unit.
3. The family is an equilibrium-seeking and adaptive organization.
4. The family is a task-performing unit that meets both the requirements of external agencies in the society and the internal needs and demands of its members.

Qualities 3 and 4 illustrate some of the similarities between structural–functionalism and systems theory. With reference to the first quality, Maureen Baker explained the emphasis of systems theory on recurring behaviour that is triggered by similar and interdependent conditions or responses. Baker gave the example of the cyclical nature of family violence, pointing out that children who grow up in a violent home environment are more likely to be abusive when they are parents.[9]

With respect to the second quality, systems theorists do not universally accept the idea that a family is relatively closed, although there is agreement that it is a "boundary-maintaining unit." In a study by Montgomery and Fewer, it was argued that families differ along a continuum of "relative openness" and "relative closure" that acknowledges some diversity in family behaviour. A family's relative openness "refers to the degree to which a mindful system is receptive to information."[10] For systems theorists, then, the boundaries that families maintain are in most cases permeable.

Perhaps the most controversial belief of systems theorists is their rejection of the idea of "causes of behaviour." As Montgomery and Fewer explained: "In systems theory, there is no cause, since behaviour is interactional and processual and has no discernible beginning."[11] Rather than cause, systems theory looks at behaviour in terms of "fit." Causal explanations of behaviour are viewed as inadequate because of three assumptions they make: (1) there is only one possible response to a given action, (2) the receiver of a particular action is incapable of generating alternative responses, and (3) the receiver has no impact on the person who commits the action. This line of reasoning ignores other factors that have an impact on behaviour. The following example will illustrate this deficiency.

If Driver A is cut off by an aggressive and inconsiderate Driver B, Driver A might respond by giving Driver B "the finger," to use the vernacular. However, according to systems theory, Driver A has other options. He or she could simply ignore Driver B. (If they are driving on a freeway in Los Angeles, Driver A might pull out a gun and shoot Driver B, as has actually happened on occasion.) Driver A's response, however, is not caused simply by Driver B's action. The choice made by Driver A might be based on his or her own background and personality. Furthermore, Driver B's action might be prompted by something that Driver A has done, driving too slowly, for example. Behaviour is too complex to be attributed to a single cause.

As already mentioned, systems theory is applied regularly in family therapy, as well as in psychiatry and psychology. But, sociologists from other schools of thought have criticized this approach. For example, systems theory's approach to spousal abuse, as illustrated by Montgomery and Fewer, suggests that the abused are at least partly to blame for their own abuse, because there is no "cause" that can be attributed solely to the abuser. The "circular pattern" of behaviour identified with systems theory means that "a problem within a family is not attributed to one individual as its instigator, but rather the problem is seen as being sustained by a continuous, circular interaction process among all family members."[12] Consequently, the victim must accept some of the blame, which draws attention away from the abuser. As you can imagine, this analysis has drawn considerable fire from researchers and frontline workers dealing with the problem of abuse, usually that of women by men. We will refer to this problem when we discuss liberation theories.

Liberation Theories

Liberation theories of family emerged in the 1960s and 1970s as people became increasingly skeptical of perceived "traditional" family roles. This growing skepticism of the traditional family was part of the general demand for changes in many social institutions and values, changes that invariably meant more freedom from the restrictions of traditional norms and values.

Traditional family patterns are inherently restrictive for some family members, as liberationist theorists point out. If the family is functional, it is only to the extent that it helps maintain unequal relationships that are based on the power of some individuals, or classes of individuals, over others. Liberation theorists, therefore, question the assumption that the family merely adapts to social change in a way that meets the personal needs of individual members.

Another important distinction between the unification and liberation approaches is that sociologists of the latter school do not limit their analyses to the identification of inequalities in the family. Instead, they extend their theories to consider alternative strategies to overcome those inequalities, up to and including the establishment of new relationships. Diversity, then, becomes the norm in the study of family, which makes dimensional theories, such as the one used by Eichler, useful tools for the analysis of families. We will describe two approaches that dominate liberation theories: conflict theory and feminist theory.

Conflict Theory

Conflict theory had its beginnings in the writings of Karl Marx and Friedrich Engels. During the 1960s, Marxist and neo-Marxist analyses were increasingly used by sociologists to explain relations within families as well as the family's role in capitalist society. Many feminist theorists have been influenced by conflict theory, although as the discussion of feminism will show, Marxists and feminists differ in some respects on the reasons for the subordination of women in families and in society as a whole. Recent theorists associated with conflict theory include D. Smith, W. Seccombe, and E. Zaretsky.

According to Marx and Engels, the character of social institutions and relationships, including the family, are determined by the economic system, or **mode of production**. As a result, families have evolved throughout history to serve the economic needs of each historical period. These historical periods have been characterized by a class struggle between oppressors and oppressed, including that between slave owners and

---

BOX 9.2

Two Other Approaches to Unification Theory

....

Symbolic Interactionism
Interactionist theorists define the family as "a unity of interacting personalities" and believe that through the interactions of its members, a family develops a conception of itself. Proponents of this approach include E. Burgess, C. Cooley, G. Mead, and S. Stryker. Social psychologists have used this approach in small-group laboratories to study parent–child and husband–wife interactions.

Family Life Course Perspective
According to life-course theorists, most families pass through a series of four stages: (1) a childless couple, (2) a couple with children, (3) "empty nesters," when the children leave home, (4) a widow or widower. T. Hareven, G. Elder, and P. Uhlenberg are among the key proponents of this theory.

---

slaves, feudal lords and serfs, and capitalists and workers. Now let us illustrate the impact of the mode of production and class struggle on the family.

If we examine the evolution of the family from prehistoric times, two major transformations stand out. First is the gradual change from natural tribal societies where group marriages were the norm, and the entire community was considered a family, to an increasingly monogamous (single-partner) marital arrangement that led to a smaller, more independent family structure. Second is the rise of **patriarchal** cultures and the subsequent decline and virtual disappearance of **matriarchy** as the social and religious norm. Based on the literature and the archeological evidence, this fundamental shift is thought to have begun at approximately 2400 B.C.E. because of invasion and conquest.

In Roman times family had an entirely different connotation. Friedrich Engels explains that the Latin word *famulus* means "household slave," and the plural *familia*, refers to "the totality of slaves belonging to one individual."[13] Under the Romans, the family developed into an institution where the male had absolute power over the rest of the family. Such an arrangement allowed him to ensure that his inheritance was bequeathed according to his wishes, which were stated in his will. From Roman times until this century, a father's inheritance invariably went to his sons. Only in the latter part of the twentieth century was this custom successfully challenged in some societies.

Based on these two changes, from large natural families to small independent families, and from matriarchal to patriarchal families, Marx and Engels reached the conclusion that monogamy was the first family form based "not on natural but economic conditions, namely on the victory of private property over original, naturally developed common ownership."[14] They also concluded that monogamy led to the antagonism between men and women.

The antagonism in capitalist society can be illustrated by examining the dual role that the family plays in the service of industry. On the one hand, the family consumes the outcome of production, which is consumer goods, and on the other, it produces the workers employed by the industries that produce the goods. The patriarchal character of families results from the division of labour between men and women. As already discussed, women play a larger role in meeting the domestic needs of their families, a role for which they are not paid, and a role that often compromises their wage-earning capacity. Although there is evidence that women are playing a more significant role in the workplace, as we shall see later in this chapter, in domestic affairs women are still the main providers. Conflict theorists argue that this creates a relationship of dependence and is the basis of the antagonism between male and female within the family.

Ironically, there is a similarity between conflict theory and the structural–functionalism of Talcott Parsons. It was Parsons, after all, who decreed that the nuclear family was best suited to industrial capitalism. Marx would not disagree; particular family structures are tailored to meet the needs of the mode of production. However, the crucial difference between Parsons and conflict theorists is that whereas the former sees the ties between family and the economy as beneficial and positive, the latter see them as oppressive and conflictive.

Marx argued that the victory of workers over the ruling, or capitalist, class will lead to the elimination of other forms of oppression. Hence, with the disappearance of private property, the oppressive character of monogamy will also disappear, and a new monogamy, one based on mutual respect and equality, will emerge. This will result in a fundamentally different kind of family.

Sociologists from the feminist school who also identify the subordination of women with the present social order have utilized conflict theory. However, as we will see in the next section, some feminists see Marx's theory as incomplete because, although it demonstrates the inequality between male and female partners, it ignores the female's role as mother; Marx's focus is on "production," rather than on "reproduction." Consequently, there is a series of issues related to reproduction, the intervention of governments, for example, that conflict theory does not take into account. These differences have led to a feminist–Marxist dialogue that has clarified some important issues for both sides.

Feminist Theory

Feminist theory of the family differs from all other approaches, including conflict theory, because it uses gender, rather than the individual, the family unit, or class as the most important factor in analyzing families. For feminists, gender is not a concept to be taken for granted. Despite the biological differences between men and women, gender is regarded as a "complex social construction with multiple dimensions that bear on the dynamics of families and other institutions."[15] Gender shapes our individual identities that are played out in school and work, as well as in the family.

CRITICAL THINKING BOX 9.2

If economic hardship and exploitation were eliminated, how might familial structures and relationships differ from their present forms? Think of the kinds of conflicts that might be reduced. Are there some tensions you would expect to persist, even in a world where basic economic needs were met?

Gender is essentially about "power" as it determines what is expected of males and females. These expectations reinforce a patriarchal hierarchy of relations that are based on the domination and oppression of women by men and that play an important role in shaping "family norms." The family, in return, is the primary organizational institution for gender relations. It is "the place where the sex/gender division of labour, the regulation of sexuality, and the social construction and reproduction of gender are all rooted."[16]

To understand the concept of family, feminists argue that we must focus on aspects of familial relationships that in many ways challenge the idea of "harmony" associated with traditional family life. Feminist theorists draw four conclusions from their analysis of these relationships:

1. Families are "arenas" in which individuals struggle to pursue different social and economic interests.

2. Families are founded on relationships in which men dominate, hence, they are patriarchal systems.

3. Families are systems where women generally accept their subordinate position, resulting in the **ideological legitimation** of inequality.

4. The definition of families as unified groups promotes **familism**, an ideology that presupposes "traditional" family norms and values.

The first two conclusions are consistent with the views of conflict theorists, who also view families in terms of competing interests and power relationships. As stated earlier, according to Marx and Engels, the antagonism between male and female led to the first class oppression—that of men over women. Class conflict, then, can take on a patriarchal form. The second two conclusions raise an important distinction that merits further discussion, namely the distinction between the **ideology of the family** and the family as it exists in modern society. Here is how the sociologist Meg Luxton explains the distinction: "To understand 'the family' we have to differentiate between ideology and the actual ways in which people interact, co-reside, have sexual relations, have babies, marry, divorce, raise children, and so on. In other words, 'the family' exists in two quite different forms: as 'familism,' a widespread and deeply embedded ideology about how people ought to live; and as economic and social groups which in fact organize domestic and personal life."[17]

We have already discussed theoretical approaches that focus on how families "ought" to be structured. The patriarchal basis of the nuclear family dictates a "natural" structure where men dominate women and children and where men have an independent identity outside the family. However, by emphasizing the complementary functions performed by men and women in the family, we keep the power of men over women hidden or "obscured."

The ideology of family extends beyond the family itself to define women's "proper place" in the economy. Because motherhood is seen as women's primary vocation, their labour outside the home is assumed to be of secondary value to that of men, who traditionally have had the role of earning enough money to provide for their entire family. Furthermore, women are seen as most qualified for occupations that resemble their roles as wife and mother. "Suitable" careers for women include caring for and teaching the young, nursing, clerical and service work, as well as producing and selling food and clothing. As a result, familism has reinforced the economic exploitation of all women.

Another important element of familism is the belief that the family shelters us from an increasingly impersonal world. The harmony that characterizes nuclear families contributes to a more stable society. If we deviate from this model, we risk undermining social stability. Feminists, on the other hand, argue that such harmony is in many cases an illusion maintained by ignoring the gender and age basis of family violence. Traditional theorists sometimes view family violence "as a series of individual assaults or else a pathology of 'family systems.' These views ignore a crucial fact...violence runs along the lines of power, with adult men and women abusing children, and men abusing women, much more than the reverse."[18]

In response to their oppressive environment, feminists such as Marlene Mackie urge women to take action. First, women must examine more carefully the social basis of their roles in reproduction, parenting, and the gender division of labour. Next, they must reject the ideology that underlies the traditional model of family and begin to examine how familial relationships can be a source of conflict and violence, rather than of harmony. In the end, feminists believe, women will recognize that "family" is not experienced the same way by all family members and that its hierarchical divisions can produce conflict.[19] Only after such an examination will women be better able to create a more satisfying life for themselves, both inside and outside their families.

Feminists have also demonstrated an awareness of some of their own shortcomings by carefully examining some of their own biases. For example, the multicultural character of our society has led many feminists to be more conscious of their own white, middle-class assumptions. In addition, the demands of gays and lesbians to have their family experiences recognized and accepted has forced feminists to broaden their analysis of the social norms that determine the reproductive and childrearing choices permitted in society.

Such analysis leads to the conclusion that family patterns and structures are subject to social rules and constraints, not just to biological ones. Consequently, for feminists, as for liberation theorists in general, it is the diversity of families that enables individuals to engage in meaningful and fulfilling relationships.

We have described some of the most commonly used theoretical approaches to the study of families. Each theory provides at least a partial picture of the structure of families, the roles played by their members, and how they are related to society as a whole. We have also attempted to account for diversity in families from the various theoretical approaches. Next, we will examine how families in Canada have changed and the extent to which these changes reflect a growing diversity in what we call "families."

THE CHANGING PATTERN OF CANADIAN FAMILIES

Depending on your point of view, families are doing one of two things: they are either changing or deteriorating. For those whose image of family is still based on the white, middle-class family with two parents, married, and living together with 2.2 children, the growing diversity of family structures is a sure sign of the deterioration of the family and the traditional values associated with it. On the other hand, for those who see diversity as the starting point for the understanding of family, the current changes are evidence that the family is a dynamic institution that has known change throughout history and that will continue to evolve in spite of the protestations of the proponents of "traditional family values."

We will now identify some of the key changes that have taken place in contemporary family life, using Eichler's dimensions as a framework. Then we will present a brief summary of our conclusions.

Procreative Dimension

Childbirth: Not So Soon, Not So Many

Several important transformations have occurred in families that are related to procreation. One of the most dramatic is the decline in the birth rate since the 1950s. To say, "They don't make them like they used to" is no overstatement when we examine the changes illustrated in Figure 9.1. As you can see, the birth rate declined by approximately 60 percent between 1959 and 1997 (from 116 to 44). Notice that most of the decline occurred during the 1960s and early 1970s, after which the decline is not as dramatic. However, apart from a slight increase around the early 1990s, the downward trend in Canada's birth rate has continued.

One contributing factor to the lower birth rate is that women are choosing to have their children later in life. Table 9.1 shows that for women in their 30s, the birth rate has steadily increased in the past two decades; whereas for women in their 20s, the general trend has been downward. Because of these changes, families in Canada are becoming smaller, on average, than they have ever been, and the age gap between parents and their children is growing as families put off having children until later in life. Future studies may provide insights into the impact of this evolving family structure on relationships within families.

Figure 9.1 Births per 1000 Women Aged 15–49, 1921–1997*

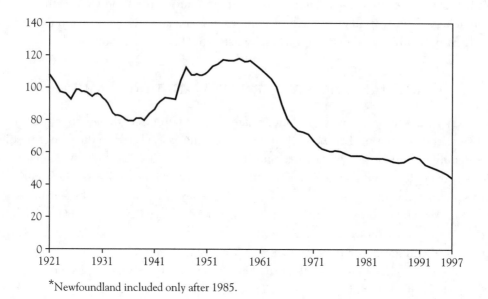

*Newfoundland included only after 1985.

Source: Statistics Canada, Chart 2.6, "Births per 1000 Women Aged 15–49," from *Births and Deaths*, Catalogue No. 84-210, May 1997.

Childfree Couples

So far in this section, our focus has been on families with children. However, some families either choose not to have children or are unable to have them. In addition, there are families whose children have grown up and left home, the so-called **empty nesters**. These make up a growing percentage of families in Canada. Table 9.2 shows the percentage of childfree families who are empty nesters versus those who never had children at all.

First, you can see that families without children make up approximately one-third of all families in Canada. Second, the percentage of empty nesters increased slightly between 1981 and 1991 and that of families who never had children declined during the same period. Since then, the percentage of families without children at home has remained stable at just under 35 percent.

The empty-nest stage of a family is the result of children becoming financially independent enough to leave home and in many instances start a family of their own. The departure of children is often seen as positive by the parents who gain a measure of freedom and independence for themselves once the responsibilities of childrearing are completed.

Table 9.1 Age-Specific Birthrates (per 1000 Women), 1961–1997*

| Year | Age Group | | | |
	20–24	25–29	30–34	35–39
1967	161.4	152.6	91.8	50.9
1977	102.9	125.5	65.4	20.2
1987	76.1	116.7	73.2	23.2
1997	64.1	103.9	84.4	32.5

* Newfoundland included only in 1997.

Source: Statistics Canada, Table 2.9, "Age-Specific Birth Rates, 1961–1997," from *Births and Deaths*, Catalogue No. 84-210, May 1997.

Unfortunately, the depressed economy of the 1990s led to a gradual increase in the number of children who either delayed leaving home or who returned after encountering financial difficulty. The "empty nest" became the "cluttered nest" in these circumstances. Consequently, as we learned from conflict theory, economic conditions play an important role in shaping the structure of families.

Increasing economic pressures on families, along with changing attitudes regarding the role of women in society, have led some couples to decide not to have children at all. Research by Rachel Schlesinger and Benjamin Schlesinger resulted in a profile of childfree families, as illustrated in Table 9.3. To use the vernacular, people who

Table 9.2 Percentage of All Families without Children and by Family Structure, 1981–1991

	1981	1991
All families without children	31.8	35.1
Empty nesters	54.2	59.4
Childfree	45.8	40.5

Note: Numbers may not add to 100 because of rounding.

Source: Statistics Canada, Table 3.2, "Families Without Children, by Family Structure, 1981–1991," from *Families: Number, Type and Structure*, Catalogue No. 93-312, 1991 Census of Canada.

choose this family structure are referred to as **"DINKs"** (double income, no kids). Most studies have indicated that there are four reasons for choosing to remain childless: Greater opportunity for self-fulfilment is first, followed by the desire for a more satisfying marriage. Tied for third place are female career and monetary considerations. However, as the sociologist Emily Nett[20] pointed out, there are no studies indicating the extent to which these goals are achieved. Nevertheless, the decision not to have children is one more example of Canada's diverse family culture.

Socialization Dimension

The socialization dimension in Eichler's model focuses on who in families is responsible for parenting. With a majority of women working outside the home nowadays, stereotyped attitudes toward raising children have changed. Traditional role differentiation, which cast men in the role of "breadwinner" and women in the role of "nurturer," has gradually been replaced by a recognition that both parents have a role to play both in the financial stability of families and in the nurturing of their young. However, this rethinking of male–female roles has not been accepted universally, or to the same degree, so that the process of change has been uneven.

On average, although men are playing a much more significant role in childrearing than they ever have before, in many families women are still spending more time than men as the family caregivers. In addition, despite men's increasing involvement in household chores, women devote more hours per day to **domestic labour** than their spouses do, whether they—the women or the men—work outside the home. Next, we will address the issue of childrearing itself and then the division of other forms of domestic labour.

Table 9.3 Voluntarily Childfree Couples: Some Research Findings

- The women are well educated, career oriented, and have a less traditional view of the female role.

- The women earn more than the average woman's salary, and this gives them a greater financial role in the marriage.

- The voluntarily childfree males have less stereotyped gender role attitudes than other males.

- Childfree families have a high degree of gender equality in their marital relationship.

- Women are usually the first to consider not having children.

Source: From *Canadian Families*, Rachel Schlesinger and Benjamin Schlesinger (Toronto: Canadian Scholars' Press, 1992), p. 35. Copyright ©1992, Canadian Scholars' Press. Reproduced by permission of the publisher.

Balancing Family Responsibilities with the Rest of Our Lives

Statistics Canada reported that in families with two working parents, women spend much more time on childcare than men do. Table 9.4 compares the daily time allocation of married women and men with and without children. One thing is for sure: children take their toll on men and women alike. Having children results in spending more time on unpaid work for both parents, and less time for sleep, free time, and paid work.

However, as the table shows, that impact is not distributed evenly between mothers and fathers. Women spend more than an hour and a half more on unpaid work than their partners, and that extra time appears to be at the expense of other areas of their lives. It is therefore clear that, despite the progress that has been made to date, equality between the sexes where family responsibilities are concerned is far from a reality. To further illustrate this point, only 20 percent of respondents to a national survey disagreed with the statement, "When children are young, a mother's place is in the home."[21]

Women's time allocation of unpaid labour naturally has an impact on the time they have to earn a living. In fact, the gap between women and men in the time devoted to unpaid labour is almost identical to that devoted to paid labour. That is, women work roughly one and a half hour less per day outside the home than their partners, 5.5 hours versus 6.9 for men.

Another important conclusion is that women in childless families still do more unpaid labour per day than their spouses do. Thus, having no childcare responsibilities does not necessarily equalize the workload at home. Thus, while men are doing more domestic chores than they did in earlier times, families still rely on the unpaid contribution of women's time more so than that of their male counterparts.

Gender roles have been transformed by changing economic conditions that have made two-income families the norm and by social values that have forced women and

Table 9.4 Time Allocation (Hours per Day) of People Aged 25–44 Employed Full-Time, 1998

	Married women without children	Married men without children	Married women with children	Married men with children
Unpaid work	3.2	2.3	4.9	3.3
Paid work	6.2	7.1	5.5	6.9
Sleep	8.0	7.8	7.8	7.5
Free time	4.3	4.9	3.6	4.2

Source: Statistics Canada, *Women in Canada 2000*, Catalogue No. 89-503, Table 5.12.

men to rethink their roles in day-to-day family life. Another factor that has an important impact on socialization within families is where family members actually live. In particular, the rise in the number of single-parent families and families formed from previous marriages has reshaped the way family members, particularly children, are socialized. Next, we will discuss the residential dimension.

Residential Dimension

For unification theorists, the nuclear family, with parents and children living under one roof, is assumed to be the norm and is considered one of the foundations of a stable, functional society. However, families can be characterized by an increasing diversity of living arrangements. This diversity is the result of two factors. First, a higher divorce rate has led to a larger number of lone-parent families and families where children spend time at the residences of both parents. Apart from divorce, the choice of single women to have children without getting married first has also contributed to the higher number of lone-parent families.

The Impact of Divorce

The liberalization of divorce laws through the 1968 *Divorce Act* and the revised *Divorce Act* of 1985 have had an enormous impact on the divorce rate in Canada. In 1968 there were 11 343 divorces, or 54.8 per 100 000 people. By 1987 it had peaked at 96 200, or 362.3 per 100 000. Since then it has fluctuated, peaking again in 1992 at 79 034 and dipping to 67 408 in 1997.[22] Regardless of the recent fluctuations, the increase since 1968 is enormous, almost 600 percent!

The number of lone parents has also risen dramatically, as Table 9.5 shows, making up 18.5 percent of the total number of families with children in 1996, compared with 9.0 percent in 1961. Of these lone-parent families, more than four fifths are headed by women, and this rate has not changed much between 1961 and 1996. This pattern of mostly female lone-parent families is reinforced by court custody decisions, whereby in 73.6 percent of the cases the children were awarded to the mother and in 11.8 percent to the father. In the remaining 14.3 percent of the cases, the decision was in favour of joint custody.

What effect do these figures have on the residential dimension of family life and the overall quality of that life? Carolyne Gorlick contrasted the traditional, or unification view of divorce with its reverse, what we are calling the liberation perspective. To the unification theorist, divorce is a deviant phenomenon, "characterized by stages of denial, mourning, anger, and readjustment."[23] Therapeutic and casework analyses, according to Gorlick, see divorce as a crisis, rather than as a necessary part of an adjustment period.

Those who disagree with the traditional family perspective argue that separation from a marriage that is not working can contribute to the individual's personal growth in

Table 9.5 Single-Parent Families, 1961–1996

	Families Headed by Women		Families Headed by Men		
	000s	As % of All Families with Children	000s	As % of All Families with Children	Women as % of Single Parents
1961	272.2	9.0	75.2	2.5	78.4
1966	300.4	9.0	71.5	2.2	80.8
1971	378.1	10.4	100.7	2.8	79.0
1976	464.3	11.6	95.0	2.4	83.0
1981	589.8	13.7	124.2	2.9	82.6
1986	701.9	15.5	151.7	3.3	82.2
1991	786.4	16.4	168.2	3.5	82.4
1996	945.2	18.5	192.3	3.8	83.1

Source: Statistics Canada, Table 2.6, "Lone-Parent Families, 1961–1996," from *Families: Number, Type and Structure*, Catalogue No. 93-312.

a way that was not possible during the marriage. First, it can create opportunities for widening the circle of family ties through remarriage and through new friendships that become possible in a different residential setting. Second, for family members leaving a nonsupportive family environment, divorce is a means of liberation from fear, anxiety, and physical and emotional abuse. Finally, the opportunities for family renewal are not necessarily dependent on remarriage. Lone custodial parents enjoy a measure of independence to make choices for themselves and their children that would not be possible otherwise. Particularly for parents fleeing domestic abuse, this is an important part of their liberation.

Women who choose to have children without getting married also enjoy this freedom. The number of women in this category has risen from 11.0 percent in 1981 to 24.2 percent in 1996.[24] These women have made a conscious decision that the traditional family structure is not the most suitable for them or their children.

Gorlick pointed out that neither perspective provides a complete picture of divorce and its impact on families. Separation initially creates stress for all family members, especially children who often cannot understand the complexities of divorce. With time, however, divorce can be seen as the beginning of a new life and a new family, not merely as the end of an old one. Diversity in residential patterns then has a positive impact on family growth and renewal.

Economic Dimension

Women in the Workforce

The most dramatic economic transformation in family life is the sharp increase in the number of two-income families. Duxbury and Higgins reported that in 1961, of all two-parent families in Canada, only 20 percent of them were dual-income. By 1981 that figure was close to 40 percent, and by 1991 it had climbed to 65 percent.[25] These figures mean that since 1961 there has been a more than threefold increase in the number of women in the workforce.

We have already discussed the impact of women working outside the home on the division of parental responsibilities in the areas of childrearing and domestic labour. The traditional "breadwinning" and "nurturing" roles are not adequate to characterize Canadian families in the early twenty-first century. This is a direct result of changes in the economy and the makeup of the workforce. For example, because the financial stability of families has become increasingly dependent on having two incomes, families have had to adjust to (1) both parents balancing both family and occupational responsibilities, (2) the growing need for external childcare, and (3) the emotional stress of job loss for both parents. In addition, lone parents are faced with the task of raising a family on only one income, as well as meeting childrearing and occupational responsibilities without the emotional and physical support of a spouse.

As families have become more dependent on two incomes, they have also become more dependent on external childcare, which has, in itself, added to the expense of family life. To demonstrate, in 1987, two-parent families with preschool children spent 4.4 percent of their income on childcare, a sizable sum. However, lone-parent families with preschool children fared much worse, spending 11.8 percent of their income on childcare.[26] The cost of childcare is just one of the pressures facing today's families in Canada. Next, we will focus on the broader issue of the financial pressures that are brought to bear on families.

CRITICAL THINKING BOX 9.3

Some people believe that we are simply too greedy, and that if families would make do with less, one parent could stay home with the children. As a result the "traditional family" would be preserved. Is this realistic, or have economic changes really had an impact on the structure of families?

Unemployment and Poverty in Canadian Families

One way that parents have adapted their jobs to their family responsibilities is by working part-time. However, in keeping with what we learned about the socialization dimension, women have been most often the ones to do the adjusting. According to Statistics Canada, 29.1 percent of women in two-parent families choose to work part-time because of the needs of the family, compared with 4.2 percent of men. For lone female parents, this figure drops to 20 percent because these women do not have a spouse with whom to share childrearing responsibilities.[27]

An obvious problem that affects a family's financial stability is unemployment. This is serious for all families, but the numbers indicate that it is particularly devastating for single-parent families. Statistics also indicate that considerably more female lone parents face unemployment than male lone parents. In 1992, for example, the unemployment rate for women who were single parents was more than double that of women in two-parent families, 19.2 percent versus 9.8 percent. That same year the figures for men were 13.9 percent and 8.3 percent, respectively.

Although the unemployment crisis of the 1990s improved by the end of the decade, poverty has persisted and the gap between rich and poor has increased. To measure the rate of poverty, the Canadian government uses a "low income cutoff" according to which any family that spends more than 58.5 percent of its income on food, shelter, and clothing is considered poor. By this standard, the percentage of Canadian families living in poverty has grown significantly in the past decade. The sociologist Alfred Hunter reported that "according to the current criterion, 14 percent (or 3 800 000) of Canadians were poor in 1991; this is up from 11.8 percent in 1986 and 12 percent in 1981."[28] This picture has not improved since 1991, and, given the current trend of government cuts to spending on welfare and other social services, the incidence of poverty in Canadian families can only increase.

Which family types are most vulnerable to financial stress? Table 9.6 gives a breakdown of the percentages of low-income families by category, including two-parent families, lone-parent families, and childfree couples. As you will see, lone-parent families, especially those led by women, are far more at risk of falling into the low-income category than other family types are. Also, Table 9.6 illustrates that the percentage of low-income families increases significantly during economic downturns such as that of the early 1980s and the 1990s. Next, we will examine the emotional dimension of family life.

Emotional Dimension

Any discussion of the emotional dimension of family relations inevitably leads to the issue of domestic violence. We will briefly describe the kinds of abuse that are most common and how the high incidence of domestic violence affects our perception of the family.

Table 9.6 Percentage of Families with Low Income, by Family Type, 1980–1997

	Non-Elderly Families[a]						
	Two Parent Families with Children[b]	Married Couples without Children	Other Couples[c]	Lone-Parent Families[b] Female Head	Male Head	Other Families	Elderly Families[d]
1980	9.6	6.8	4.1	56.7	24.7	25.0	18.8
1981	10.2	7.4	4.2	54.0	18.1	17.2	20.2
1982	11.9	8.9	4.8	59.8	26.5	18.8	14.8
1983	12.6	9.6	6.1	60.8	28.5	23.7	15.7
1984	13.2	10.0	6.2	62.4	27.2	20.0	16.5
1985	11.8	8.6	4.8	61.4	27.2	20.9	14.9
1986	11.0	9.1	4.4	57.7	22.7	17.1	14.2
1987	10.3	8.9	4.7	58.3	17.9	17.3	12.9
1988	9.2	7.8	3.3	55.1	23.1	18.3	12.7
1989	8.7	7.3	2.9	52.5	19.3	15.7	9.9
1990	9.9	8.2	3.3	59.6	25.3	18.2	7.5
1991	11.0	9.1	3.7	61.1	22.3	17.7	7.9
1992	10.7	8.6	5.6	57.2	20.9	20.4	8.5
1993	12.5	9.6	3.5	59.6	31.3	19.7	9.4
1994	11.5	9.4	5.5	56.4	32.3	19.3	7.1
1995	12.8	10.1	5.2	56.8	30.7	18.8	7.8
1996	11.8	10.0	5.3	60.8	31.3	17.8	8.7
1997	12.0	10.6	5.3	56.0	23.5	18.3	6.8

[a] Includes families with head under age 65.

[b] Includes families with children under age 18 living at home.

[c] Includes only families with children 18 years of age and over and/or other relatives.

[d] Includes families with head aged 65 and over.

Source: Statistics Canada, Table 6.7, "Percentage of Families with Low Income, by Family Type, 1980–1993," from *Families: Number, Type and Structure*, Catalogue No. 93-312, July 1992.

Violence against Female Partners

In 1999, according to Statistics Canada, of those women who reported incidents of violent spousal abuse, 26 percent had been victimized more than ten times in the past five years, while 10 percent had been victimized six to ten times, and 62 percent had been victimized at least once. Of those women, 25 percent reported being beaten by their spouses (versus 10 percent of male victims), 20 percent reported being choked (versus 4 percent of male victims), and 13 percent reported being threatened with a gun or knife (versus 7 percent of male victims). Men, on the other hand, were more likely to be slapped or have something thrown at them.

If we look at the most serious crime, homicide, we find that in 1998, 32.4 percent of female victims of solved homicides were killed either by their spouses or ex-spouses while another 25.6 percent were killed by other family members including parents and children.[29] Sadly, spousal abuse of all types is a well-documented fact of life in Canada today.

Although violence against women has been traced back as far as ancient Greece and Rome, it has not always been seen as a problem. Marion Lynn and Eimear O'Neill quote from *The Rules of Marriage*, from the fifteenth century, on what were considered at the time the merits of wife assault: "When you see your wife commit an offence, don't rush at her with insults and violent blows. Scold her sharply, bully and terrify her. And if this still doesn't work … take a stick and beat her soundly, for it is better to punish the body and correct the soul.… Readily beat her not in rage but out of charity … for [her] soul so that the beating will rebound to your merit and her good."[30]

This tolerance of wife assault was still common in nineteenth-century Britain, where a husband was permitted to strike his wife with any instrument no wider in diameter than his thumb. Thus, although today wife assault is illegal, for most of recorded history it has been accepted in patriarchal societies as a consequence of a man's authority over his wife and his children. (Remember the Latin origins of the word family, as quoted at the beginning of the chapter.)

Women are not the only victims of domestic violence. Children, too, bear the emotional scars of the dark side of family life. As Statistics Canada reports, "Of all violent crimes against children under 12 years of age and reported to police between 1988 and 1990, 41% were perpetrated by a member of their family: 24% involved a parent and 17% involved another family member."[31] What the statistics show is that some children have at least as much to fear from their families as they do from strangers.

Finally, although comparatively rare, assault against male partners is also acknowledged in studies of domestic violence. In 1991, 43 percent of female victims of violence and 3 percent of male victims had been assaulted or murdered by their partners.

Effect of Violence on Family Relations

The high incidence of domestic violence runs counter to the traditional view of the family as a refuge from a cold, heartless world. It cuts across class lines, although it tends to be more visible among lower income groups because people in these groups have more frequent interaction with relevant government departments, such as social services.

Feminist theorists have been at the forefront of research into the causes and outcomes of domestic violence. The subjects of their studies, be they women or children, are seen not only as victims, but also as "survivors." The pain suffered by victims is acknowledged, but so, too, is their capacity to overcome their circumstances through their adaptive capacities and strengths. Thus, the end of one negative family structure can lead to the emergence of a new positive one, although, of course, this does not happen without its own sacrifice and struggle. The emotional dimension, as Eichler concluded, "runs the gamut from the most tender, emotionally satisfying, positive involvements to the most frightening, abusive physically and mentally harmful relationships."[32] The diversity in these relationships must be the basis for further analysis of families.

FAMILIES IN THE TWENTY-FIRST CENTURY

We began this chapter with reference to what is decried in the media as the crisis of the "traditional family." What we have attempted to show is that "change" should not be confused with "crisis." Although the ideology of the family has come under attack, families themselves are doing what they have always done. They are responding to political and economic changes in society by changing themselves, becoming more diverse as they adapt to their new circumstances.

Perhaps the most controversial development in redefining *family* in the last few years has been the move toward recognition of **same-sex couples** as families. On 1 June 2001, this change was demonstrated clearly in the Nova Scotia legislature where Bill 75 was passed, allowing same-sex couples to legally register their relationships. According to *The Globe and Mail*, "Nova Scotia is the only jurisdiction to issue certificates formally recognizing homosexual couples as domestic partners."[33] Three key provisions of the bill are as follows:

1. entitlement to spousal benefits in the event that a relationship is terminated
2. protection under the *Matrimonial Act*
3. the right to examine partners' medical records and make emergency medical decisions

CRITICAL THINKING BOX 9.4

Can you think of any other "dimensions" that could be added to the ones used in this chapter? What would your additions to the list tell us about families? What forms of diversity would they demonstrate?

The Supreme Court of Canada paved the way for Bill 75 in 1999 when it ruled that same-sex couples were entitled to benefits such as

- claiming partners or children as dependents
- deducting childcare expenses
- taking advantage of income splitting
- gaining access to survivor benefits

Nova Scotia went even further on 9 July 2001 when a provincial Supreme Court judge ruled that it was unconstitutional and discriminatory to forbid same-sex couples from adopting children. This ruling means that gays and lesbians in Nova Scotia have the courts on their side in their struggle to gain equal status as families. For the moment, British Columbia is the only other province where the right to same-sex adoption is recognized by the courts. However, it is only a matter of time before the rest of Canada follows suit. What this dramatic change illustrates is that diversity will serve as the guiding principle to understanding Canadian families in the twenty-first century.

CHAPTER SUMMARY

This chapter began by attempting to reach a meaningful definition of the term family— one that is applicable to the wide variation in the structure of Canadian families. As the process by which the definition is developed is as important as the definition itself, the introductory section of the chapter also examined how we arrive at our definition. In attempting to reach a suitable definition, we discovered that the notion of the "traditional family" is incomplete at best, as it is unable to transcend the constraints of popular middle-class culture.

Next, we looked at how families have been studied from several theoretical perspectives, which are broadly divided into two categories: unification and liberation theories. Each approach has its own rationale for the nature of relations among family members and of family structure. No one approach gives a complete picture of family life or reasons for changes that have taken place in Canadian families, but some approaches are better equipped than others to explain the diversity of modern families.

Change has always been an essential characteristic of families. Consequently, we should not be surprised that what is referred to as the "traditional family" has always been more of an abstract idea than a reality. The statistics provided in this chapter have clearly demonstrated the kinds of changes that have taken place in Canadian families, particularly since the 1950s. They reveal a social institution that is evolving, as it always has, in response to other changes in our environment, be they social, political, or economic.

We addressed the issues of redefining *family*, in light of the recognition of same-sex couples as families. Nova Scotia is leading the charge in Canada as the only jurisdiction (at the time of writing) that allows same-sex couples to be legally recognized as domestic partners and the second (after British Columbia) province that allows same-sex partners to adopt children. These changes came about a year after the Supreme Court of Canada ruled that same-sex couples were entitled to various tax breaks and survivor benefits previously only awarded to heterosexual couples.

We conclude by acknowledging the enormous difficulties facing Canadian families and by contending that understanding the diversity of family life is essential if we are to address those challenges.

KEY TERMS

conflict theory, p. 236	ideological legitimation, p. 239
conjugal family, p. 233	ideology of the family, p. 239
DINKs, p. 244	liberation theories, p. 235
domestic labour, p. 244	matriarchy, p. 237
empty nesters, p. 242	mode of production, p. 236
extended family, p. 230	nuclear families, p. 229
familia, p. 237	patriarchal, p. 237
familism, p. 239	same-sex couples, p. 252
feminist theory, p. 238	structural–functionalism, p. 233
general systems theory, p. 234	unification theories, p. 232

DISCUSSION QUESTIONS

1. Choose a family from a television show you watch regularly that you believe conforms to the analysis of the unification approach. In what ways does it match the characteristics of family described in this chapter?
2. Choose another TV family that you believe illustrates the liberation approach. How does it match what you have learned from this chapter?
3. Canadian families are based on patriarchal authority. What would life be like in a family based on matriarchal authority? How would it differ from a patriarchal family?
4. Which of Eichler's dimensions do you think has the greatest impact on family relationships? Explain your answer.

5. Do you agree that "traditional" family patterns of authority create antagonistic relationships of dependence in families? Why or why not?
6. You are married and have a child. Both you and your partner work full time. Plan a schedule for a week that ensures that the domestic chores are divided equally.

NOTES

1. George P. Murdock, *Social Structure* (New York: Macmillan, 1949), p. 1.
2. Rose Laub Coser, *The Family: Its Structure and Functions*, 2nd ed. (New York: St. Martin's Press, 1974), p. xvi.
3. Statistics Canada, *A Portrait of Families in Canada* (Ottawa: Vanier Institute, 1994), p. 7.
4. Brigitte Kitchen, "Family Policy," in *Families: Changing Trends in Canada*, Maureen Baker, ed. (Toronto: McGraw-Hill Ryerson, 1990), p. 313.
5. Margrit Eichler, *Families in Canada Today* (Toronto: Gage, 1983), p. 8.
6. Emily Nett, *Canadian Families* (Vancouver: Butterworths, 1993), p. 24.
7. David Cheal, *Family and the State of Theory* (Toronto: University of Toronto Press, 1993), p. 4.
8. Reuben Hill, "Modern Systems Theory and the Family: A Confrontation," in *Social Science Information* 10:5 (1971), p. 12.
9. Baker, "Theories, Methods, and Concerns," p. 13.
10. Jason Montgomery and Willard Fewer, *Family Systems and Beyond* (New York: Human Sciences Press, 1988), p. 118.
11. Ibid., p. 21.
12. David Cheal, "Theoretical Perspectives," in *Marriage and the Family Today*, 2nd ed., G. Ramu, ed. (Scarborough: Prentice-Hall, 1991), p. 22.
13. Friedrich Engels, "The Origin of the Family, Private Property and the State," in *The Marx-Engels Reader*, 2nd ed., Robert Tucker, ed. (New York: W.W. Norton, 1978), p. 737.
14. Ibid., p. 739.
15. Barrie Thorne, "Feminism and the Family," in *Rethinking the Family*, Barrie Thorne and Marilyn Yalom, eds. (Boston: Northeastern University Press, 1992), p. 12.
16. Marlene Mackie, "Gender in the Family," in *Canadian Families*, Nancy Mandell and Ann Duffy, eds. (Toronto: Harcourt Brace, 1990), p. 50.
17. Meg Luxton, "Thinking About the Future," in *Family Matters: Sociology and Contemporary Canadian Families*, Karen Anderson et al., eds. (Toronto: Methuen, 1987), p. 238.
18. Thorne, "Feminism and the Family," p. 147.
19. Mackie, "Gender in the Family," p. 50.
20. Nett, *Canadian Families*, 1993.
21. Rick J. Ponting, *Canadian Gender-Role Attitudes* (Unpublished Manuscript, University of Calgary, 1986).
22. Statistics Canada, *Women in Canada 2000* (Ottawa: Minister of Industry, Cat. No. 89-503-XPE, 2000), p. 43.

23. Carolyn Gorlick, "Divorce: Options Available, Constraints Forced, Pathways Taken," in *Canadian Families*, Nancy Mandell and Ann Duffy, eds. (Toronto: Harcourt Brace, 1990), p. 212.

24. Statistics Canada, *Women in Canada 2000*, p. 43.

25. Linda Duxbury and Christopher Higgins, "Families in the Economy," in *Canada's Changing Families: Challenges to Public Policy*, Maureen Baker, ed. (Ottawa: Vanier Institute, 1994), p. 29.

26. Statistics Canada, *A Portrait of Families in Canada* (Ottawa: Minister of Industry, Science and Technology, Cat. No. 89-523E, 1993), p. 27.

27. Ibid., p. 29.

28. Alfred Hunter, "Social Inequality," in *Sociology*, Robert Hagedorn, ed. (Toronto: Harcourt Brace, 1994), p. 275.

29. Statistics Canada, *Women in Canada 2000*, pp. 182–83.

30. Marion Lynn and Eimear O'Neill, "Families, Power, and Violence," in *Canadian Families*, Nancy Mandell and Ann Duffy, eds. (Toronto: Harcourt Brace, 1990), p. 285.

31. Statistics Canada, *Families in Canada*, p. 54.

32. Eichler, *Families in Canada Today*, p. 13.

33. Brian Laghi, "Ottawa Introduces Same-Sex Benefits," *The Globe and Mail*, 12 February 2000.

III

Images of Diversity

PART III

Part III examines how diversity is treated in the media and is perceived in literature. Continuing with the house analogy, if Part I is the structure and Part II the interior, then Part III is how people view the house—that is, how they assess it, value it, and treat it.

Chapter 10 looks at how the media portray diversity. It begins with a definition and overview of the history of mass media. The primary purpose of this chapter is to help the reader to understand the impact of mass media, especially the U.S. mass media, on the world in general and on diversity in Canada in particular.

Chapter 11 provides an exciting journey through the field of Canadian literature. At a general level, it looks at how contemporary Canadian writing reflects this country's continually evolving culture and diversity. At a specific level, it examines how Canadian literature illustrates the diversities covered in this text.

10

The Medium Diversifies the Message: How Media Portray Diversity

Grant Havers

The medium is the massage.
— Marshall McLuhan

Technology is our fate.
— George Grant

Objectives

After reading this chapter, you should be able to

- explain the meaning and uses of "mass media"

- explain the four major stages in the history of mass media

- understand the rise of the global village

- understand the influence of television on attitudes toward diversity

- understand the impact of American media on the world

INTRODUCTION: MEDIA AND DIVERSITY

Media have had enormous influence on human culture and are as old as civilization. They disclose a great deal about the cultures that employ them and the rich diversity within and among human cultures. How do mass media portray diversity?

Since the beginning of the electronic age, many observers have wondered whether mass media can encourage awareness of cultural diversity or, in fact, hinder such awareness. Mass media present the possibility of bringing the world together in peace and tolerance, because of their power to beam the news of the entire world in the living rooms of each family in every nation. However, this achievement does not guarantee greater awareness of diversity but instead presents diversity through distorted lenses. Whatever the implications, there is no question that representation of diversity by the media has an enormous impact on how we all see diversity.

DEFINING MEDIA AND "MASS" MEDIA

Perhaps it is easier to understand the meaning of "medium" than of "mass medium." A medium (media is the plural form) is a technique of communication. Language is the oldest medium of all. However, a **mass medium** is more than the means by which people speak and write to each other. If we understand the world as a "mass" of people, the term "mass media" suggests that media have enormous impact on the entire world. Two elements are important here.

First, mass media usually have "mass" audiences. All cultures in history have used various media (see Table 10.1), but these have not always been "mass" media. A "mass" medium is available to most people and cultures. It connects different parts of the entire world together.

Second, mass media vary in purpose. They may be sources of entertainment, such as television; information, such as newspapers; communication, such as telephones; or a combination of all three, such as computers. But they must always be available to a wide audience.

Throughout this chapter considerable discussion will be devoted to how successful mass media have been in educating the world about its diversity. One useful rule of thumb to remember is that every medium has an impact on its environment. Mass media, as Marshall McLuhan pointed out, are not simply tools that perform simple functions of informing or assisting human beings. A medium is more than a useful artifact; it affects human behaviour itself. To quote McLuhan's famous saying, "The medium is the massage "[1] (see Box 10.1). This claim can be interpreted in numerous ways, but only one will be offered here: every medium shapes the content of what it is conveying. This means that books,

Table 10.1 Which Civilizations Use(d) Which Media

Civilization	Main Medium Used
Sumerian	Pictographs, stone (3500 B.C.E.)
Egyptian	Papyrus, hieroglyphics (3000 B.C.E.)
Indian	Script (2400 B.C.E.)
Greek	Parchment, stone (700 B.C.E.)
Roman	Papyrus, parchment, stone (50 C.E.)
Chinese	Paper, script (105 C.E.)
Mayan	Script (50 C.E.)
Aztec	Script (1400 C.E.)
English	Paper (1200 C.E.)

Notes: Dates suggest approximately when civilizations developed these media or made use of them. C.E. means "Common Era" and is the same time span as A.D. B.C.E. means "Before the Common Era" and is the same time frame as B.C.

newspapers, radio, and television all can influence (or massage) the message that is delivered to its audience. As any consumer knows, how advertising portrays the product is usually more important than the product itself. Given this fact, it is centrally important to understand how mass media have shaped and influenced the meaning of diversity, for good or for ill.

BOX 10.1

The "Prophet," Marshall McLuhan (1911–1980)

....

More than anyone else in this century, Marshall McLuhan understood the mass media. Born in Edmonton in 1911, he attended university in England in the 1930s, when he first studied the media. McLuhan became famous in the 1960s with his publications on the printing press, television, advertising, and technological change. *The Gutenberg Galaxy* and *Understanding Media* made him into a celebrity. It is ironic that by the time of his death in 1980, McLuhan himself had become a media phenomenon, appearing on the cover of major magazines, being asked for advice by politicians, and being hailed by many as a "prophet" for the television age.

A Brief History of Media and Mass Media

As already mentioned, throughout history civilizations of diverse origins have used media. People have always communicated with each other. But "mass media" have not always existed; that is, they have not always been available to large numbers of people. For example, writing was not always a mass medium; until the fifteenth century only elite groups in societies could write. By studying the history of media, we can begin to understand how media eventually became mass media.

The history of media can be divided into four stages (see Table 10.2), each of which marks a revolutionary turning point: (1) the oral stage, (2) the rise of the **alphabet** and writing, (3) the printing press, and (4) the electronic age, in which we now live.

The Oral Stage

The first stage was based on the condition of **orality**. Before the development of writing, the earliest human beings communicated almost entirely orally. Although human civilization has existed for perhaps six thousand years, the earliest writing appears to be not much more than five thousand years old. Until 3500 B.C.E. most people relied on the oral medium. It is estimated that the vast majority of languages spoken in human history have never been written down; little more than a hundred of them have a literature.[2] Human beings spoke words, sang poems, and gestured signals, but they did not write. Because they lacked any means of written communication, these oral cultures relied heavily on the constant memorization of their most cherished epics and folklore. It is important not to dismiss an oral culture as "primitive" based on its lack of writing. Indeed, oral cultures were extremely sophisticated in their use of memory, which was their sole way of recording stories. Ancient Greek, African, Middle Eastern, and Aboriginal storytellers resorted to the oral transmission of their cultures' tales. This process required poets of each generation to pass down stories to the next through the spoken word.

The Rise of the Alphabet and Writing

The second stage began to emerge when oral cultures initiated the long transition toward written language. Around 3500 B.C.E. the Sumerians in Mesopotamia (modern-day Iraq) developed the **pictograph**, which consisted of pictures representing words or utterances. Other peoples, such as the Babylonians and Assyrians of the Middle East, also developed elaborate systems of pictographs. Around 3000 B.C.E. the ancient Egyptians developed their own system of pictographs, known as **hieroglyphics**.

By 1500 B.C.E. the second period of media had taken hold in the Middle East, which greatly accelerated the transition to written language: the alphabet had been invented. Human beings could now communicate using a system of signs that had letters

Table 10.2   Important Dates in the History of Mass Media

3500 B.C.E.	Sumerians develop pictographs
3000 B.C.E.	Egyptians develop hieroglyphics, papyrus
2000 B.C.E.	Hebrew begins to develop
1500 B.C.E.	Phoenicians invent an alphabet
105 C.E.	Chinese invent paper
1455	Gutenberg invents the first printing press using movable type
1478	First printed ad appears
1702	First English daily newspaper appears
1741	First magazines appear in America
1844	First telegraph line operates
1873	Newspapers appear in the Middle East
1876	Telephone is invented
1877	Phonograph is invented
1887	Gramophone is developed
1895	Marconi develops the radio
1896	First public motion picture shown in America
1947	First TV news programs appear
1979	Walkman is introduced
1982	CD player emerges
1985	Personal computer is established
1990	Virtual reality becomes popular
1998	Universities, industry, and government begin planning for Internet2
2000	Napster file-sharing upsets music industry
2000	The Love Bug virus infects 45 million computers worldwide
2000	British virtual "newscaster" Ananova joins other virtual performers on TV and the Net
2000	Stephen King's novel *Riding the Bullet* becomes a best seller via Net downloads only
2001	Azerbaijan switches from the Cyrillic to the Latin alphabet

rather than symbols, as in the case of pictographs.[3] This invention also enabled people around the world to communicate with each other. Once it was discovered that materials such as papyrus could be employed to transmit the written word across great distances, various cultures became known to each other. The alphabet cannot be called a mass medium at this time, for until the invention of the printing press writing was still inaccessible to the vast majority of people.

Gradually, other cultures adopted the alphabet. The Phoenicians, a seafaring people of the Middle East, invented their alphabet about 1500 B.C.E. This reflected their desire to be able to trade goods using a flexible alphabet and enabled them to become independent of the dominant Egyptian culture of the time.[4] Eventually, the Greeks, in the eighth century B.C.E., took over the Semitic alphabet, which had twenty-two letters, and adapted it to their needs. One of the adaptations made by the Greeks was the introduction of vowels to the alphabet.[5]

As long as the alphabet remained the dominant medium, various ancient empires used it and expanded on it. Other cultures simply stuck to pictographs or combinations of symbols known as **script**. Whatever the type of medium used by a particular civilization, it reveals much about the priorities of that civilization. The Canadian historian Harold Innis shed light on these priorities by distinguishing **"time-oriented" media** from **"space-oriented" media**. Empires, such as Greece, that used durable media such as **parchment** (dried sheep or goat skin) put great importance on the preservation of time, the recording of their history on materials that would last. Other empires that used papyrus, like Egypt and Rome, and paper, like China, viewed the conquest of space (or linkages to the outside world) as central. As a result, they cultivated media that could be transported across vast distances.[6] Because media like stone and clay are impractical for transportation, it is clear that the empires that used papyrus, which is a very transportable medium, were most successful in acquiring knowledge about the rest of the world.

McLuhan introduced the idea that all technologies are "extensions" of human beings. Media "extend" a part of the human body by allowing that part to do something that it could not do by itself. For instance, print media—such as books and newspapers—are extensions of the eyes: they permit the eyes to see people, events, and cultures around the world that ordinary vision could not do by itself. Similarly, a computer extends the brain: the memory of the computer retains vast amounts of information that the brain cannot hold. The kinds of extensions that a culture uses reveal which parts of the body that culture considers most important (see Table 10.3). Given that certain cultures adopted an alphabet suggests that the eye was very important to them, for the alphabet extends vision.

Although not all nations developed an alphabet (for example, China did not), the alphabet became the dominant medium of Western Europe, Russian Asia, India, and sections of the Far East (see Table 10.4). It has been said that every alphabet in the world is based on the Semitic alphabet.[7] The effects of the alphabet on the world increased with the third stage in the history of media.

Table 10.3   Technology: The Extensions of Humanity

Technology	Part of Body It Extends
Club, hammer	Fist
Clothing	Skin
Knife	Teeth
Glasses, telescope, camera	Eyes
Writing, books, newspapers	Eyes
Refrigerator	Stomach
Wheel	Feet
Automobile	Whole body
Radio	Ears
Television	Eyes, ears
Computers	Brain
Virtual reality	Whole body

The Printing Press

The third stage of history of media began in 1455, when Johannes Gutenberg (1390–1468), in Germany, invented the printing press with movable metal type. This

Table 10.4   Some Major Alphabets of the World

Alphabet	Origin
Hebrew	Middle East
Ugaritic	Middle East
Greek	Mediterranean
Roman	Mediterranean
Cyrillic	Eastern Europe
Arabic	Middle East
Tamil	Southern India
Malayalam	Southwest India
Korean	Korea, East Asia

ushered in a wave of social change that continues to shake the world today. (Before this time, the Chinese had developed a printing technique for wooden type.) Before the printing press with movable metal type, reading in the Western world was restricted mostly to the learned scribes and elites of the ancient and medieval worlds. Gutenberg's invention made it possible for millions to become literate, because it enabled the mass production of inexpensive books. Thus, the alphabet became a mass medium. Indeed, the age of mass media had arrived. The printing press had two major effects on the meaning of diversity.

First, it made people greatly aware of their diversity. Now it was possible to produce literature on a mass scale for a mass audience. The various peoples of Western Europe became more aware of how different their cultures and languages are. The common, everyday languages or **vernaculars** of particular geographical areas could now be published using the printing press. Everyday French, German, and English people could now read the languages that they spoke. Nationalism, or love of one's nation, could not have developed without the printing press.[8] It made it possible for the various European peoples to read in their own languages. It also enabled them to develop languages that were truly "national," or common to all regions of a particular nation. Martin Luther translated the Bible into ordinary German by 1534. The different **dialects** (different versions of one standard language) of the various regions of Germany became one German language because the printing press could put out books teaching different Germans how to conform to one national, printed language. Soon after 1455 cultural influences that had largely been restricted to Europe spread across the world.

Second, the press encouraged homogeneity or mass sameness. Once the printing press was used as the way of standardizing the language of a culture, everyone had to learn the same language. There was no longer room for individuals to create their own vernaculars—all had to conform to one language now. There was no such thing as "bad grammar," until the printing press made it possible to force one "good" grammar on everyone.[9] Indeed, Gutenberg's creation made compulsory education possible. Thanks to the printing press, everyone could now become literate, because everyone could be educated in the same language.

Thus, the print media of the alphabet and the printing press opened up the distinctive possibilities of diversity and homogeneity. This two-headed and contradictory process accelerated even further with the emergence of electronic media in the nineteenth century.

The Electronic Stage

The fourth stage, the electronic stage, began in 1844 when Samuel Finley Breese Morse's **telegraph**, a device that transmitted messages via electric wire, was installed between

Baltimore and Washington, D.C. (see Table 10.5). Morse's first message on the telegraph was "What hath God wrought?"[10] It is not clear what Morse meant by this statement, but he may have been expressing surprise at the fact that his new invention had created a world whose diverse peoples could now communicate with each other almost immediately. The age of instantaneous communication through mass media had arrived.

Before the telegraph, messages and newspapers were transmitted as quickly as human beings could carry them—or move them—by horse. Now the telegraph could communicate messages across great distances in a relatively short time. The telegraph was the first of many inventions that were to be able to accomplish this feat: the telephone, radio, television, and computer followed in the twentieth century. All of these encouraged the instantaneous transmission of messages from one part of the globe to another, allowing everyone everywhere to be involved in everyone else's business. Thus emerged the **global village**. This achievement was entirely the result of the discovery of electricity. This village produced **"tribalism"** among the human species, a feeling that, because of the linkages established by electronics to the outer world,[11] all human beings are part of one big group making up the Earth.

Tribalism seems to foster awareness of diversity in an unprecedented manner. Thanks to electronic media, people around the world can now communicate with people in all the other parts, and they can do so instantaneously and effortlessly. For "space-

Table 10.5   Who Invented It?

Invention	Approximate Year	Who Got the Credit	
Printing press*	1455	J. Gutenberg	Germany
Telegraph	1844	S.F.B. Morse	United States
Telephone	1876	A.G. Bell	United States
Phonograph	1877	T. Edison	United States
Gramophone	1887	Emile Berliner	France
Radio†	1895	G. Marconi	Italy
Movies	1895	Lumière brothers	France

* This is the first printing press with movable metal type; the Chinese had invented presses with wooden type almost 700 years before Gutenberg.

† There is no single inventor of the radio: credit must also be given to Heinrich Hertz (1857–94), a German scientist, Reginald Aubrey Fessenden (1866–1932), a Canadian, who experimented with radio transmission of voices in the early 1900s, and to Lee de Forest (1873–1961), an American, who patented the vacuum tube in 1907.

oriented" cultures bent on developing linkages with the outer world, electronic media are a blessing, not a curse. But the question remains: Does this leap forward in communication translate into greater tolerance of diversity, or is the global village intolerant as well?

IS THE GLOBAL VILLAGE GOOD FOR DIVERSITY?

Television and Diversity

To answer the question "Is the global village good for diversity?" let us consider the effects of television, the dominant mass medium of our time and the technology credited as the most successful in expanding the global village. It is easy to observe why television is so successful, for it is one of the most widely available media of all time. Unlike print, television does not require the ability to read for it to be understood: No one requires special education to comprehend the messages of television. (Long before they pick up a book to read, three-year-olds, for example, want the toys advertised on television.)

Media affect our behaviour. They are not only tools that perform the functions of communication and information; media "massage" their audiences: they can affect people's behaviour without people even being aware of this influence. Observers are increasingly putting media under the spotlight in case these media ignore, insult, stereotype, and misrepresent ethnic minorities, for example.[12] In the global village, which consists of so many different cultures, how is life affected by the media? Four factors address this question.

First, television has encouraged many diverse communities and cultures to become aware of each other and themselves. Because television provides millions of people with access to a wider world, one of the effects has been to force many cultures to recognize their own isolation in the world. The feeling is that, if they do not show up on the nightly news, then they are not considered important. Although television has encouraged a feeling of isolation, it has also encouraged minorities and marginalized groups to demand an end to this isolation. Now that television can overcome the distances within the world, previously isolated groups want to be involved in the world's affairs. Having access to the world's information has encouraged this new demand. Indeed, it is significant that many political movements of minorities did not emerge until the television age.[13] Politics has been redefined in the media age (see Box 10.2).

Second, television has made it more difficult for the world to ignore the concerns and needs of these movements, especially when they have constantly appeared on the nightly news since, say, the 1960s. The plight of the poor around the world, for example, is increasingly difficult to ignore in the age of television exposure. The Live-Aid concert organized by various musicians to fight starvation in Ethiopia in the mid-1980s is an example of how mass media exposure can make a huge difference to the success of a cause or movement—it succeeded in raising millions of dollars.

Third, television often distorts the meaning of diversity to suit its own aims and purposes.[14] Whereas it is true that television responded to the political movements of the 1960s with unprecedented exposure, this coverage had less to do with informing its audience than with providing entertainment. For example, at first glance it would appear that the media coverage of the various African-American and Vietnam protest movements in the 1960s represented an informative response to newsworthy events. It was hoped that this coverage would dramatize the plight of the African-American poor in the ghettoes of the United States, as well as the concerns of the antiwar protesters. What happened instead, according to some observers, was that the media decided to focus on those members of the movements who could provide the most entertainment or "news value." Typically, the media focused on leaders who packed the biggest dramatic punch, entertained the audiences, and looked physically attractive. Those leaders who lacked a dynamic visual image were ignored in the media coverage, even if they were important to their movements.[15] This was a sobering lesson about television coverage, and it raised a disturbing question: Does television inform about the diversity of the global village, or does it simply entertain?

Fourth, the nature of television is that it favours entertaining, fast-moving imagery that grabs the attention of audiences. For this reason, many political movements around the world choose television as the medium best able to get across their message. As former U.S. president and Hollywood actor Ronald Reagan once commented, "Politics

---

BOX 10.2

The Politics of Mass Media

Mass media have influenced political movements for as long as politicians have existed. The printing press made possible the mass publication of pamphlets and newspapers, which are widely used by politicians.

Television debates can also make and break a politician's career. In 1960, when John F. Kennedy debated with Richard Nixon for the U.S. presidency, those who watched the debate saw Kennedy, with his cool charm, as the winner. Those who listened to the debate on radio thought Nixon won. Evidently, television won over radio that year, because Kennedy defeated Nixon in the election by a narrow margin.

CRITICAL THINKING BOX 10.1

....

Does TV Represent Diversity?

How often are characters from visible minority communities represented on your favourite television shows?

is show business." In the 1960s television provided political groups with an unprecedented opportunity to tell the world of their existence. Violence is a particularly attractive option to political movements or groups that are not well known to the world: violent scenes in time for the 6 o'clock news, which have proven to entertain audiences around the world, have also become a sure means of becoming recognized.[16]

Entertainment is far more important as an objective to the producers of television than is providing copious detail on a subject. For this reason, television cannot inform as well as books or newspapers can. Yet television does not simply entertain. It can also misrepresent the reality of diversity. Although in recent years television networks have become more attentive to the need to reflect the minority population of North American society, their attempts have often been misleading.

A greater effort has been made to bring more African-American characters onto the television screens and to make them more attractive role models for the young. This change is a significant difference from programming in the past, which either stereotyped minorities in degrading roles or ignored them altogether. Until recently, African-Americans were usually portrayed as criminal, immoral, or inferior, or were ignored altogether. Because millions of consumers in the United States are African-Americans, they are represented more on television than ever before. More shows are portraying African-Americans as part of the mainstream culture, rather than as members of a criminal subculture.

According to some observers, however, this new representation of African-American life on television is still biased. Most programming portrays families who have adopted the middle-class values of the dominant white society,[17] rather than portraying the real-life ghetto existence of many African-Americans. In short, American television still manages to ignore a fundamental reality of its largest minority group, even as it brings this group to the screen.

The same holds true for Canadian media. In the history of television in Canada, there have been very few shows documenting or describing the lives of minority and Aboriginal communities. The CBC has produced some fine documentaries on this subject, but very few visible minority and Aboriginal actors appear on dramas, comedies, and

---

CRITICAL THINKING BOX 10.2

···

Diversity and the News

When you watch new programs, how often do you find examples of ethnic or racial stereotyping on them?

---

the like. To make matters worse, visible minorities and Aboriginal peoples are often unfairly portrayed on the news as militant, violent, or unreasonable. This misrepresentation on television only serves to stereotype the Aboriginal and ethnic communities. It also results in coverage that is sorely lacking in information about the lives of these communities. For that matter, the media have only recently begun to employ women, as well as members of Canada's ethnic and Aboriginal communities, as journalists and broadcasters (see Box 10.3).

The Power of American Media

One related issue here is whether mass media can accurately convey diversity when so much of the control over mass media is not diverse. Most of the mass media in the world are controlled by American corporations whose aims may conflict with teaching about ethnic diversity. The United States has been accused of **"television imperialism,"** referring to the idea that it attempts to control other nations by using television as a means to dominate cultures.[18] In other words, it has been suggested that American media persuade people around the world to adopt American values by selling television shows and print media that portray American life, while paying little attention to life in other societies.

Certainly the United States has a huge role in media markets far beyond its borders: in almost thirty nations, including Canada, U.S. companies control 70 percent of the market for films, and they control 35 percent of the cable television market in Canada.[19] Moreover, U.S. movie corporations are the largest in the world. Using Innis's terms, the United States is a "space-oriented" culture that is intent on broadening its cultural and economic access. This effort on the part of the United States has many effects.

Indeed, the perception among many nations is that U.S. movies are subtle forms of political propaganda, aimed at flattering and spreading the influence of the United States.[20] Mass media often do celebrate the values and benefits of their country of origin, and American media are no exception here. McLuhan suggested that copies of American magazines and catalogues smuggled into the communist bloc posed a greater threat to its governments than any official political propaganda;[21] once the citizens of this bloc saw

---

BOX 10.3

Indigenous Peoples and the Media

....

Until recently, Indigenous peoples in Canada were represented either unfairly or incompletely by the mass media. They suffered stereotypes that depicted them as criminally oriented, alcoholic, or lazy. Or their stories and histories simply were not seen or heard in the media. In the past 15 years, because of an increased awareness of the Aboriginal contribution to Canada's history, TV shows have included some Aboriginal actors, and the Aboriginal People's Television Network was founded in the early 1990s. Yet news programs still often portray Indigenous peoples as violent and prone to conflict when airing stories about land claims and treaty negotiations.

---

what consumer goods the average Westerner enjoyed, the people challenged their governments severely. An U.S. movie that portrays ordinary people in possession of cars, stoves, and refrigerators may be a revolutionary message to the poor of the developing world. In this context, force is not needed to support the American way.

American media have at least two major effects on non-American nations. First, the flood of U.S. programming into other nations discourages the latter from creating their own programs that might better reflect their own national identities. Often the United States is accused of promoting **ethnocentrism**, a feeling of cultural superiority, through mass media. In short, it is believed that U.S. dominance over mass media has weakened attempts to strengthen ethnic diversity. The cultures of Latin America and the Middle East have constantly struggled to create programming alternatives that reflect their national identities.[22] Even nations such as France, which began this century dominating the film industry and the arts, have now fallen under the influence of U.S. media. It has reached the point where these nations are concerned about preserving their own culture and language. For this reason, both France and Canada have occasionally imposed tariffs to limit U.S. media imports.[23]

Second, some observers argue that the success of U.S. media throughout the world is difficult to challenge because these media can appear to convey and represent ethnic diversity so well. For example, the film directors, comedians, and dramatic actors featured in U.S. programming are increasingly coming from diverse ethnic backgrounds (e.g., Jewish, Italian, and African-American), reflecting the multicultural nature of U.S. society. These diverse elements may explain the broad appeal of American media to various parts of the world.[24] If this is the case, however, then this use of diversity is a new phenomenon, for American media have not always represented ethnic communities with the importance that they deserve. For example, one staple of American popular culture, the Western movie, still does not represent African-Americans in numbers reflecting their participation in the settlement of the West. Although one out of four cowboys was an African-American during the opening of the Western frontier, Hollywood Westerns still predominantly use white cowboy actors. Similarly, movies on Vietnam have still not fully represented the actual proportion of African-American troops who fought and died there.[25] The absence of characters belonging to minority groups on children's television programs has received comment.[26]

This inattention to diversity on the part of U.S. media poses a troubling question for those concerned with representing ethnic diversity through media: How can diversity be represented at all if U.S. media, which dominate the markets, pay so little attention to it? This problem is compounded by the fact that American media tend to be driven by profitability. That is to say, they tend to favour media and programming that provide revenue for advertisers over those that might inform the audience. Usually the more entertaining the particular program, the more profitable it is. Unfortunately, what entertains does not always inform. It is a fact that the most entertaining news shows on television provide far less news than a newspaper does. American news shows, which are supposed to inform their audiences first and foremost, often end up entertaining the audience with attractive images, without providing in-depth information about the subject.[27] Thus, it is dubious whether all media can be expected to provide serious data about the complexity of diversity when profits and entertainment are considered more important.

The Language of the Global Village

Another problem related to the representation of diversity in media is the dominance of the English language, which hinders non-English cultures from developing their own networks: English is the "media language."[28] This condition is becoming apparent on the Internet, too. Even though the Net has been described as an electronic, computerized global village (see Box 10.4 on page 276), the dominant language or *lingua franca* (the language spoken by all cultures in a given area of business) on the Net is English. Despite the fact that almost half of Internet users live outside North America, most computers cannot translate non-English into English. Fortunately, a North American consortium is now developing a universal translation code, known as Unicode, to allow computers on the Net to represent the letters and characters of virtually all languages.[29]

Unicode has been successful in international technology platforms, which should drive it into more environments. Unicode's continued success will rely on new computer operating systems, beginning with Microsoft NT, which are compatible with Unicode.

The dream of developing a truly multilingual World Wide Web is not a yet a reality, but it has moved much closer.

There is some additional reason to hope for change in this area. To be sure, a white Anglo-Saxon establishment has controlled the airwaves in the past: in addition, the vast majority of the world's media corporations are in the United States. But this establishment may not always have a monopoly. Historically, ethnic communities in Canada and the United States who feel ignored by the mainstream Anglo-Saxon press have taken to developing their own. Since the early twentieth century African-Americans have produced and directed films depicting the historical contributions of their community in American culture, as a way of counteracting the absence of African-American themes in Hollywood movies. African-Americans have found it necessary since the nineteenth century to create their own newspapers to respond to racist attacks and stereotyping.[30] In Canada, newspapers have been set up by Indian, Asian, Jamaican, and many other ethnic publishers to serve their own communities.

This trend toward greater ethnic participation in the industry continues. The rise of ethnic diversity in North America has led to the demand for hundreds of cable channel systems, divided by language and culture. For example, 107 languages are now spoken in Southern California, and the media industry has responded with videocassettes, disks, and computerized banking geared to the traditions and needs of these various ethnic groups. Canada's *Maclean's* magazine has recently introduced a special edition in Chinese. Women's television networks are gaining popularity in North America. There has even been discussion of setting up several television networks to serve the needs of distinctive ethnic communities, instead of placing network programming into the hands of only a few media companies.[31] Observers concerned about the "Americanization" of the world through mass media predict that nations as diverse as India, Egypt, Mexico, and Brazil will enjoy the benefits of the Anglo-American mass media while developing their own distinctive programming.[32] Since the 1960s, for example, India has ensured that an official radio network exists for each of its dozen most-spoken languages.

CRITICAL THINKING BOX 10.3

Diversity and Education

How many of your textbooks discuss in detail the history and culture of ethnic communities in Canada?

Surviving in the Global Village: Canada and Brazil

Canadians should take particular interest in those nations that have been able to maintain their ethnic identity against the onslaught of U.S. media. Canada has produced many influential thinkers on the subject of media technology and how it is a powerful support for American media.[33] Perhaps this is because Canada, more than any other nation, has been bombarded with U.S. programming ever since the rise of the media industry in the United States. The importation of American media into Canada has been seen by many Canadians as a threat to their identity. In a sense, this threat is serious: by 1900 Canadians read mostly American books, and the Canadian press was seen as modelled on American newspapers. Since the 1930s, the Canadian government has sometimes responded to this problem by creating agencies that favour Canadian broadcasting (such as the CBC) and by placing tariffs on U.S. magazines.[34]

Still, many Canadians are skeptical about the success of these efforts. George Grant argues that national identity cannot be reconciled with technological progress in the global village. In 1995 these concerns again became pressing, when Disney successfully acquired exclusive rights to use the symbols of the Royal Canadian Mounted Police (those rights have now reverted to the Mounted Police Foundation). It is simply impossible to maintain one's distinctive ethnic identity in an age driven by technical advancement.[35] In Canada, the Québécois want to maintain the language and culture of their French ancestors, and they also want to enjoy the benefits of U.S. technology and media. Some argue, however, that this effort is contradictory and doomed to failure, for the embrace of American technology and media might mean the disappearance of Québécois culture. Can a time-oriented culture survive in an age of space-oriented media?

The problem of keeping traditional cultures alive is compounded by the fact that modern mass media, especially television, tend to be so "present oriented." Media tend to focus simply on the present, at the expense of the past.[36] "There is no memory on TV," as the saying goes. In an age of instantaneous information achievable through electronic media, it is understandable that consumers would not want to study the past or tradition. Why focus on what is antiquated when the new is changing all the time? But there remains a problem for those concerned with the survival of diversity. Because our technological age tends to value the "new" or the most technically sophisticated as the "best," and the "old" as the inferior and irrelevant, can a traditional culture survive?

This last question is particularly important to the study of diversity, for if cultures cannot survive in the media age, how can diversity? Some thinkers, such as McLuhan, have contended that the lack of a strong national identity is advantageous in a deeply technological age. Because the rate of change is so great, it is not wise to develop an inflexible nationalism. Indeed, some praise Canada for its lack of such a strong identity,

---

BOX 10.4

Advertising and Consumerism

....

The mass media have always targeted the consumer through advertising. With the advent of the Internet, this process has accelerated rapidly; every good and service imaginable can be purchased around the world.

Yet consumerism teaches only one value—the desire to obtain the newest commodities; the new is heralded over the old. Some media observers (such as Benjamin Barber) have called attention to the triumph of "McWorld," or the transformation of the globe into one homogeneous consumer market, which threatens to undermine distinctive cultures and sacred traditions. Will the hunger for new and improved goods displace the need to preserve distinctive cultures, traditions, and roots?

---

adding that this limitation makes it better able to adjust to the pace of technological development.[37] Still, what if cultures and communities want to maintain their differences? Can this be done in the age of the global village, where Anglo-American media seem so dominant?

There is reason to hope for an optimistic response to these questions. Consider the example of Brazil. It has one of the largest television audiences in the world.[38] It also has wide access to U.S. programming. Yet there is no hard evidence to show that Brazilians are becoming "Americanized" because of this access. Indeed, despite the high level of violence in Brazilian society, there is no great demand for violent genres like the "slasher films," so popular in the United States. Indeed, according to one survey, Brazilians continue to admire the technological innovation represented by U.S. television, but they do not adopt the values of the United States.[39] Of course, Brazil has been

CRITICAL THINKING BOX 10.4

....

Canadian Content

Why do Canadian news stories show up so rarely on U.S. news programs?

able to enjoy these attitudes because its government is determined to maintain a high level of its culture's programming, to compete with the constant onrush of U.S. media.

As nations come to grips with the effects of television on their cultures, a new media revolution is already on its way. The emergence of virtual reality (computer-generated imagery that mimics reality) is said to herald this new era.[40] Can this new age of mass media create greater awareness of diversity? It will certainly accelerate the global village, for this age promises technologies that will link the world more instantaneously than ever before. The "teleputer," a combination of a computer and television that will permit a user to see, hear, and communicate with another user from a distant part of the globe, may also soon be online. The world will become "wired." Whether this new interconnectedness through computers, the Internet, virtual reality, or teleputers will create greater tolerance for diversity is another question. The record of mass media on this subject is mixed: television accelerated the global village, but this has not always produced greater harmony or understanding among cultures.

CHAPTER SUMMARY

Human beings have always employed techniques of mass communication. The use of mass media ranges widely from communication to information to entertainment. Mass media also affect our behaviour. They shape the message and content of what is being communicated to millions of people, especially the message and content of diversity.

In each of the four stages in the history of media, great changes in human behaviour have taken place. The oral stage demanded that people use their memories to "record" events; the rise of the alphabet extended the power of the eye, as ordinary people began to see what they were saying for the first time; the printing press encouraged nationalism; and the advent of the electronic age created the global village.

Electronic media have had by far the greatest impact on defining diversity in the modern world. Perhaps the most important effect of electronic media was turning the world into a global village, in which, because of the speed of communication via electricity, people of all nations feel interconnected. Since the emergence of the telegraph, this effect has only been strengthened by other electronic media.

Television, still the dominant medium in the world today, continues to accelerate this feeling of global interconnectedness. Whether television can represent diverse cultures in an accurate manner is an open question, for the success of television lies in focusing on the new, the entertaining, and the profitable. The record is mixed. Television can make people more aware of other cultures, but its presentation of diversity can be misleading and superficial.

BOX 10.5

Media Facts: Did You Know?

....

- Canadians watch on average twenty-five hours of television weekly.
- European TV networks start broadcasting in the afternoon.
- Africa has 2000 language dialects.
- The Chinese language has 40 000 characters.
- By age 20, the average North American has seen 800 000 commercials.
- There are 180 languages spoken in India.
- The average American has more TVs than bathrooms.
- Brazil has the fifth largest TV audience in the world.
- The best market for American movies (outside the United States) is Japan.
- The average American twelve-year-old has spent 13 000 hours in school and almost 20 000 hours watching TV.

To complicate matters further, most of the media markets are controlled by U.S. corporations. This control has led to the dominance of the English language in these markets, as well as the sustained influence of U.S. programs around the world, including Canada. Many nations have taken steps to control the influx of U.S. programming to protect their national identities.

One thing is certain. Mass media have changed every aspect of our world forever (see Box 10.5). There is no possibility of returning to an age when media technology was restricted to a privileged few, and people—the "masses"—knew little about other cultures in distant lands. For those concerned with emphasizing diversity, the permanence of mass media is ultimately a good thing. After all, even if the media in the global village do not always foster peace among its members, they certainly encourage the need to be aware of the various people who live in this village.

KEY TERMS

alphabet, p. 262

dialects, p. 266

ethnocentrism, p. 272

global village, p. 267

hieroglyphics, p. 262

lingua franca, p. 273

mass medium, p. 260

orality, p. 262

DISCUSSION QUESTIONS

1. Discuss five examples of commercials that illustrate how the "medium is the massage."
2. Discuss five efforts that can be made to make mass media more educational regarding diversity.
3. Is Canada being threatened by television imperialism? Compare the number of Canadian and U.S. TV shows on a typical programming day.
4. You have been asked to produce and direct a TV situational comedy that accurately portrays the multicultural makeup of our society. How do you do this?
5. The Canadian government has asked your advice on how to improve programming so that it reflects Canada's diversity but is also entertaining. What do you suggest?

NOTES

1. The title of Marshall McLuhan's book from which this quotation is taken is called *The Medium Is the Massage*, not "the message." McLuhan's point was that the form of the message (the medium) shapes (or massages) how the message is perceived. McLuhan's skill with language is evident in his choice of wording here.
2. Walter Ong, *Orality and Literacy: The Technologizing of the Word* (New York: Routledge, 1988), p. 7.
3. See Harold Innis, *Empire and Communications* (Toronto: Press Procépic, 1986), p. 32.
4. Ibid., pp. 38–42.
5. Ong, *Orality and Literacy*, p. 28.
6. Innis, *Empire and Communications*, p. 5.
7. Ong, *Orality and Literacy*, p. 89.
8. Innis, *Empire and Communications*, p. 128. See also Marshall McLuhan, *The Gutenberg Galaxy: The Making of Typographic Man* (Toronto: University of Toronto Press, 1962), pp. 218–19.
9. McLuhan, *Gutenberg Galaxy*, p. 231.
10. Morse, quoted in Neil Postman, *The Disappearance of Childhood* (New York: Delacorte Press, 1982), p. 68.
11. See Marshall McLuhan, *Understanding Media: The Extensions of Man* (New York: New American Library, 1964), p. 156.

12. See Augie Fleras and Jean Leonard Elliott, *Multiculturalism in Canada: The Challenge of Diversity* (Toronto: Nelson, 1992), pp. 233–48.

13. Joshua Meyrowitz, *No Sense of Place: The Impact of Electronic Media on Social Behaviour* (New York: Oxford University Press, 1985), p. 132.

14. Fleras and Elliott, *Multiculturalism in Canada*, p. 238.

15. See Todd Gitlin, *The Whole World is Watching: Mass Media in the Making and Unmaking of the New Left* (Berkeley: University of California Press, 1980), pp. 152–53.

16. Marshall McLuhan and Quentin Fiore, *War and Peace in the Global Village* (New York: Bantam, 1968).

17. See Conrad Philip Kottak, *Prime-Time Society: An Anthropological Analysis of Television and Culture* (Belmont, Calif.: Wadsworth, 1990), p. 63.

18. See Jeremy Tunstall, *The Media Are American: Anglo-American Media in the World* (London: Constable, 1977), pp. 38–63.

19. Tunstall, *The Media Are American*, p. 182; see also Mary Vipond, *The Mass Media in Canada* (Toronto: Lorimer, 1989), p. 134.

20. McLuhan, *Understanding Media*, p. 271.

21. Ibid., p. 152.

22. See Tunstall, *The Media Are American*.

23. Shirley Biagi, *Media/Impact: An Introduction to Mass Media* (Belmont, Calif.: Wadsworth, 1994), p. 472; see also Vipond, *Mass Media*, pp. 24–25.

24. Alvin Toffler, *Power Shift: Knowledge, Wealth, and Violence at the Edge of the Twenty-First Century* (New York: Bantam, 1990), p. 451.

25. Richard Slotkin, *Gunfighter Nation: The Myth of the Frontier in Twentieth-Century America* (New York: Atheneum, 1992), pp. 526–27.

26. Biagi, *Media/Impact*, p. 392.

27. Neil Postman and Steve Powers, *How to Watch TV News* (New York: Penguin, 1992).

28. Tunstall, *The Media Are American*, p. 126.

29. See Andrew Pollack, "Cyberspace's War of Words," *The Globe and Mail*, 10 August 1995, p. A15.

30. Biagi, *Media/Impact*, pp. 45–49.

31. Marshall McLuhan and Bruce R. Powers, *The Global Village: Transformations in World Life and Media in the Twenty-First Century* (New York: Oxford University Press, 1989), p. 88.

32. Tunstall, *The Media Are American*, p. 274.

33. Arthur Kroker, *Technology and the Canadian Mind: Innis/McLuhan/Grant* (Montreal: New World Perspectives, 1984).

34. Tunstall, *The Media Are American*, p. 104; Vipond, *Mass Media*, pp. 24–29.

35. See George Grant, *Lament for a Nation: The Defeat of Canadian Nationalism* (Ottawa: Carleton University Press, 1965), pp. 76–87.

36. See Postman and Powers, *How to Watch TV News*.

37. See McLuhan and Powers, *The Globe Village*, p. 165.

38. Kottak, *Prime-Time Society*, p. 12.

39. Kottak, *Prime-Time Society*, p. 93.

40. See Derrick De Kerckhove, *The Skin of Culture: Investigating the New Electronic Reality* (Toronto: Somerville House, 1995).

Perceptions of Diversity in Canadian Literature

Maureen Coleman

Literature ... binds one human being to the next and shortens the distance we must travel to discover that our most private perceptions are universally felt.
— Carol Shields

A country's literature is a crystal ball into which its people may look to understand their past and their present, and to find some foretaste of their future.
— Robertson Davies

Objectives

After reading this chapter, you should be able to

- understand how literature is the voice and mirror of a culture

- understand the evolution of diversity in Canadian society through its literature.

- appreciate the relationship between power and voice in Canada as revealed in the stories of Native Canadians, racial and ethnic minorities, immigrants, and refugees

- recall stories and other writing that reflects the diversity of cultures between, and within, the geographical regions of Canada

- appreciate how contemporary Canadian writing strongly gives voice to our continually evolving cultural diversity in society's perceptions of family, sexuality, and gender

INTRODUCTION

The Role of Literature in Recording and Defining a Culture

Every society has its shared and unique experiences, which are shaped by the storyteller into song, poem, drama, comedy, myth, and legend. Literature is the **voice** of a culture. This chapter will describe how the spoken and written record of Canadian life has evolved and was passed from generation to generation. The first and continuing stories of diversity in Canada were those of the "two solitudes" of English and French, with the resulting development of two distinct, parallel literatures each written in its own language (see Web site <diversity2e.nelson.com> for more detail). It will trace the changes in the story of Canadian society that came with the influx of people from many and various backgrounds and with the passage of time. We can see how these stories circulated within the Canadian community and combined with those of others to form a new vision. Perceptions of gender diversity can be found in the body of **feminist literature** that has filled an absence in the story of Canadian society. Northrop Frye referred to this "cross-pollenization" of cultures as a process that invigorates and strengthens.[1] We will also examine how Canadian writing found its way onto the world stage. We will see how the literature of and by Canadians provides a mirror that reflects our image, in all its complexity and diversity, not only to the world but also to ourselves. In her 1973 work *Survival: A Thematic Guide to Canadian Literature*, Margaret Atwood showed how Canadian stories present a new culture. It is one that is separate not only from the European motherlands of England and France, but also from our neighbours in North and South America. In the thirty years since *Survival's* publication, perceptions of diversity have changed dramatically as Canadian society continues to evolve. Acceptance and appreciation of the many people whose stories have blended continue to expand and reshape Canada's multicultural odyssey.

Literature has the power to personalize and humanize sociological data and historical events. The writer creates a character, living in a time and place, with that era's particular values and attitudes, through whose eyes we can view that world. By identifying with that person, the reader becomes actively engaged in that society; in a sense each writer freeze-frames a particular Canadian world for the reader to enter. As well, we begin to think about where each of us fits into the Canadian saga. Although it is true that our stories are shaped by the society we live in, so too is it true that the society is influenced by its stories. We can all identify with the **universal themes** explored in all literature from a uniquely Canadian viewpoint.

BOX 11.1

Culture and Story: A Changing Relationship

....

A comprehensive study of this revolution in thinking about the relationship between culture and story can be found in *The Empire Writes Back*, co-written by Bill Ashcroft, Gareth Griffiths, and Helen Tiffin of Australia. It has led to "**postcolonial writing** in cultures as various as India, Australia, the West Indies, Africa, and Canada,… [that] challenges the existing canon and dominant ideas of literature and culture … post-colonial texts … constitute a radical critique of the assumptions underlying Eurocentric notions of language and literature."[2]

CANADIAN LITERATURE: PART OF A POSTCOLONIAL GLOBAL TREND

Voices from the Margins Move to the Centre

Canadian stories, which are part of this international postcolonial body of writing, are those of Native Canadians, African-Canadians, immigrants, refugees, and women. Also included are those previously silenced because of physical and mental diversities. In Canada, as elsewhere in the world, the stories of marginalized individuals and groups within the society were often ignored or suppressed. However, with more positive attitudes toward diversity, this **absence of voice** is being overcome.

Perceptions of Native People: The Nature of Cultural Imperialism

Only in the last quarter of the twentieth century did Aboriginal peoples throughout the world have the freedom to tell their own stories. This is certainly true in Canada for Native Canadians. From all parts of the country, they struggle to overcome centuries of political and cultural imperialism. Separating myth from reality is a difficult task. In an article entitled "Seeing Red over Myths," Drew Hayden Taylor, writer, actor, and filmmaker of Ojibway heritage, discusses "the myth of pan-Indianism…. It reveals a persistent belief that we are all one people. Within the borders of what is now referred to as Canada, there are more than 50 distinct and separate languages and dialects. And each … has emerged from a distinct and separate culture."[3]

Best-Known Stories: Romantic Stereotypes

Initially, the European newcomers viewed Canada's Native peoples with a mixture of scorn and fear. Concerted efforts were made to impose European culture on the native populations. Little attention was paid or value attributed to Aboriginal cultures. However, from the middle of the eighteenth century, the literature reveals the romantic stereotype of the "noble savage." In John Richardson's novel *Wacousta*, "Pontiac, the real Indian chief, appears in dignity and power, more sympathetic a character than the English commander de Haldimar."[4] The attitude was that Natives were innocents, part of the pure natural world, victims of their own ignorance. Charles Mair, in his verse-drama *Tecumseh*, wrote:

> ...there lived a soul more wild than barbarous;
> a tameless soul—the sunburnt savage free—
> Free, and untainted by the greed of gain:
> Great Nature's man content with Nature's good.[5]

In *Survival: A Thematic Guide to Canadian Literature*, Margaret Atwood pointed out that our perception differs from the American good Indian/bad Indian viewpoint. The Canadian version was more of a victor/victim version, or, as Leonard Cohen expressed it in his novel by the same name, Native peoples were *Beautiful Losers*. The stories tend to end with the native willingly sacrificing his or her own ways to those of the newcomer.

Untold Stories: Realism and Legend, Big Bear, and Louis Riel

Canada has another untold story of poverty and the loss of self-respect that comes with being a "kept people." Generations passed before this picture in the Canadian family album was seen. In *The Temptations of Big Bear*, Rudy Wiebe tells of the only Cree chief, Big Bear, who resisted offers of the white man to give up native land for the railway and settlement.

Another dramatic story of the fight against the tide of western expansion is that of **Métis** leader Louis Riel. Riel's people were rejected by both whites and Natives and denigrated as "halfbreeds." Riel's story has become an integral part of Canada's myth and legend. Early tellings of the tale presented Riel as a reactionary, a fool resisting progress, and finally a lunatic who could not accept defeat. Later Riel's story would appear in many forms—poetry, drama, novel, documentary, and film, and in the rewriting or revision of history. In these Riel is renamed as a hero, a bold, courageous leader, a visionary willing to sacrifice his life for his people.

For generations, Riel and Big Bear were ghosts haunting the Canadian imagination and conscience. Literature was important in defining the place of the Métis in

Canadian culture, first by obscuring it, later by revealing its true nature. Maria Campbell's autobiography *Halfbreed* is one of the first books to do this. Both native and white societies had a strong traditional resistance to acceptance of the Métis, Canada's first people of mixed cultures.

Native Voices of Today Speak for Themselves

Native peoples maintained their strong oral tradition, and thus their stories were passed down through the generations. As we are drawn into the original story circle, it becomes a healing circle as well, one that is much needed by both groups—those whose stories they are and the rest of us. In 1990 Thomas King edited a collection, *All My Relations: An Anthology of Contemporary Canadian Native Fiction*, containing the writing of nineteen authors, including himself. That King is of Cherokee, Greek, and German descent is part of what is meant by "contemporary Canadian."

Most of these stories are influenced by various aspects of traditional native culture. Others centre on natives in a contemporary world, sometimes tracing journeys from the reservations to the cities and back again. Some speak of old injustices, like Harry Robinson's "An Okanagan Indian Becomes a Captive Circus Showpiece in England." Others, like Basil Johnston's "Summer Holidays in Spanish," refer to the more recent destructive consequences to native communities of residential schools. One of the contributors to King's anthology is playwright Tomson Highway, then artistic director of Native Earth Performing Arts in Toronto. His drama *The Rez Sisters* (1988) is a realistic study of seven women who live on a Manitoulin Island Reserve. Realism, mixed with traditional native storytelling and humour, is the style of Drew Hayden Taylor, playwright, journalist, actor, and director. Taylor's essay "Pretty Like a White Boy: The Adventures of a Blue Eyed Ojibway" is a funny but pointed look at the problems of identity that a person of mixed race has in dealing with people's cultural assumptions when one looks white but thinks Indian. This is also the theme of Carol Geddes's article "Growing Up Native." Geddes is of the Tlingit nation in Yukon. White teachers steered native children away

CRITICAL THINKING BOX 11.1

Discuss Taylor's challenge in understanding our assumptions about the diversity among Canada's first peoples. What other myths are widely held about Native peoples? What are the sources of these beliefs? Are they supported by fact?

BOX 11.2

Native Writers Tell Their Stories

....

Another comprehensive collection of writings by Native Canadian writers is edited by Daniel David Moses and Terry Goldie: *An Anthology of Canadian Native Literature in English* (1998). Included are stories from fifty-seven authors, representing twenty-eight different tribes, five traditional Inuit songs, and seven traditional orature from Southern First Nations.

---

from academic courses, under the assumption they did not have the intellectual capacity for them. Geddes speaks, too, of the irreversible change in lifestyle that began with the building of the Alaska Highway. Much of the change was destructive to both family and community. Jenine Dumont, a descendant of Gabriel Dumont, who fought with Louis Riel, wrote in her essay "I Didn't Know I Was Different" about the difficulties she had accepting that she was part Indian. Lee Maracle, a Métis woman from British Columbia, is another important voice. Her works include *I Am Woman*, *Bobbi Lee: Indian Rebel* (1990), and *Sojourners Truth and Other Stories*. Maracle also coedited *Telling It: Women and Language Across Cultures*, a record of and impressions from an international women's conference held in Canada.

Poet and Mi'kmaq from Nova Scotia Rita Joe wrote in the "Introduction" to her third book of poems, *Lnu and Indians We're Called:* "One way for native people to experience the positive parts of their culture is through spiritual productiveness. This is what I try to convey—there is a great need to tell our story in 1991, more than ever."[6]

Personal Voices Move Closer to the Social Centre

Some stories address the condition of being "colonized" on a more personal level. Perhaps the winning of *Funny Boy* by Shyam Selvadura of two literary awards in 1995, the Smith Books in Canada award for a first novel and the Commonwealth Prize for best first book published in the Caribbean and Canada, indicates both a cultural and literary maturity. The title contains a double irony. The protagonist, Arjie Chelvara Tuam, is a young man who is "funny" in two ways. First, he is of Sri Lankan background, and, second, he is homosexual. By veiling his true self in the clothing of clown and joker, Arjie tries to find his way and his place in a mostly Western, white, and heterosexual Canadian society. The acclaim given to this book is perhaps a strong indicator that as a society we are coming to the understanding that diversity is at the core of Canadian identity.

CRITICAL THINKING BOX 11.2

Is this official recognition a "coming out" from denial of our own ethno-centrism? Is it a hopeful sign that must always be balanced against ultra-conservatism and censorship on other fronts? What reasons may explain why the Canadian level of ethnocentrism is more or less than in another culture?

Stories of Race and Ethnicity: "Other" Voices Finally Heard

Black Voices

African-Canadians in Ontario and Nova Scotia have been part of Canadian culture since Loyalist times, and in some cases of shipwreck even before. Some voices from Nova Scotia now being heard include the following:

- poet Maxine Tynes (*Borrowed Beauty*, 1987)
- poet, playwright, critic George Elliott Clarke (*Whylah Falls*, 1990), edited *Eyeing the North Star: Directions in African-Canadian Literature* (1997) and *Execution Poems*, winner of the 2001 Governor General's Award for poetry
- filmmaker Sylvia Hamilton (*Black Mother, Black Daughter*, 1989)
- *a cappella* singing group Four the Moment

They are all artists whose works fill in the blanks in the history, near and distant, of their communities. They also celebrate their strength and survival against racism, unofficial and official (e.g., the destruction of Africville), along with their broadening roles in the communities of province, nation, and world.

Many writers have arisen among the black Canadians who have come from the English-speaking islands of West Indies mostly to Toronto and to Montreal from former French colonies. Ayanna Black, in her poetry collection *No Contingencies* (1986), writes of her colour in "A Sense of Origin," of being a woman in "Reflection," and of urban poverty and street people in "Bag Lady" and "In Memory of Lorraine" (a friend who died of a drug overdose).

Austin Clark, in "Canadian Experience" and in his many other stories, writes that immigration to Canada means more than a cultural and climatic adjustment; if you are a black person, it also means adjusting to a different, more subtle version of racism than the one left behind in Barbados. Rosemary Brown, social worker, politician, and international aid worker, writes of similar experiences in her autobiography *Being Brown* (1989).

Danny Laferriere is a writer from the Haitian community in Montreal whose books include *An Aroma of Coffee, A Drifting Year,* and *Dining With the Dictator.* Poet and short story writer Dionne Brand states that if you are absent from literature or the forms in which you are included are only negative, then you must "write yourself." To that end she fights stereotyping by creating complex characters. Brand is coauthor of *Rivers Have Sources, Trees Have Roots—Speaking of Racism* (1986).

Neil Bissoondath, a Trinidadian of East Indian ancestry, like some other writers mentioned here, came to Canada as a student. In an essay entitled "I'm Not Racist But…" Bissoondath defined the difference between racism born of hatred and that born of ignorance. Like Brand, he believes that the only way to change this is to write against stereotyping. Both of these writers have felt that Canada's multicultural policies might be contributing to this by focusing on the differences of various groups of Canadians, rather than on their similarities. In his recent book, *Selling Illusions: The Cult of Multiculturalism in Canada,* Bissoondath discusses these ideas, which have stirred up considerable controversy.

Countering the cultural imperialism of English language and literature is also an objective of Marlene Nourbese Philip, lawyer turned writer. In *Harriet's Daughter* (1988), her novel about a teenager growing up in Toronto, and in her poetry collection entitled *She Tries Her Tongue; Her Silence Softly Breaks* (1989), Philip consciously set out to explore and value all forms of language other than the imposed traditional ones. She edited *Frontiers*, essays on these topics.

Laurence Hill's books *Any Known Blood* and *Black Berry Sweet Juice: On Being Black and White in Canada* are told from the perspective of a mixed race family who moved from the United States in the 1960s.

CRITICAL THINKING BOX 11.3

Should a writer who does not belong to a particular cultural group be able to tell a story through the eyes of a character who does? Some writers who belong to particular cultural groups, women, blacks, natives, Asians, or people with physical disabilities, such as blindness or deafness, believe that such writing is not valid or honest. What are the arguments for and against this phenomenon, known as "appropriation of voice"?

Contemporary Writing Focuses on Diversity: Different Voices Break the Silence

Immigrant and Refugee Voices

When we read **immigrant and refugee stories,** and those of their children or grandchildren, we begin to understand not only the nature of Canadian diversity, but also how complex it is. The process of finding your place in a new culture is difficult, and in each case, different. For an immigrant or refugee this is especially true if it means learning a new language. Mary di Michele, who came from Italy in 1955, writes in her poem "Luminous Emergencies":

> That my tongue has been un-
> Mothered. That my tongue has thickened
> with English consonants and diphthongs,
> mustard and horseradish. That burning.
> That burdened.
> While on my lips Italian feels
> almost free, like wind in the trees
> when the window's sealed shut
> and you're inside playing Scrabble.
> No—English is not so cosy!
> It's hypothermic. It's haunted
> by ghost letters & gnomic.[7]

The state of being between worlds is written about often. Authors describe the relationship between giving up the language that names and contains the meanings of the place that has been left as the loss of part of themselves. Along with the difficulties of learning a new language come the feelings of powerlessness and frustration of being unable to communicate thoughts and feelings.

Eva Hoffman came to Canada at the age of fourteen from Poland. She now makes her living using her second language, English, as an editor for the *New York Times*. In her 1989 autobiography, *Lost in Translation*, Hoffman describes this complex process of loss and gain. Another story that explores the issue of the power of language is "A Class of New Canadians," by Clark Blaise. The main character, a teacher, is a new Canadian from the United States. He has a part-time job at night. The reader becomes uncomfortable with this teacher's paternalistic attitude toward his adult students, who, like him, have come to Canada (Montreal) to make a new life.

Himani Bannerji, born in Bangladesh and educated in India, arrived in Canada as a young woman in her late twenties. She teaches sociology at York University in

Toronto. In her story "The Sound Barrier," Bannerji analyzes the communication gulf between herself and her mother. She draws the reader from a Western culture into an understanding of what "mother" means to someone like her mother, from an Eastern culture. Bannerji shows how the sound barrier between her and her mother goes far beyond the language of the word "mother" to include thousands of years of cultural meaning. She compares this disparity to the gulf of understanding that exists between Canadians of Western backgrounds and those from Asian cultures. "Why My Mother Can't Speak English" is another story that asks and attempts to answer this same question. Written by Gary Engkent, who came to Canada from China in the 1950s, the story questions the relation of language to citizenship.

Final Decree (1981), by Hungarian-born George Jonas, is a mystery story based on culture shock. Josef Skvorecky was already a successful writer when he came to Canada from Czechoslovakia in 1969 after the Soviet invasion. Some of his works written in English are *The Cowards* (1970), *The Bass Saxophone* (1977), and *The Engineer of Human Souls* (1984). The stories by both Jonas and Skvorecky reflect the experience of refugees who have come to Canada because of losing their homes to war and violence. Civil and political justice are important concerns to them.

Evelyn Lau ran away from home when her parents, Chinese immigrants, refused to let her write. *Runaway: Diary of a Street Kid* (1989), is a factual account of her life on Vancouver's streets. It was followed by two novels, *Fresh Girls* (1993) and *Other Women* (1995). Her new work *Inside Out* continues her theme of reflection on her life, relationships, and identity as a writer.

Today in Canada it is easy to find a variety of writing and have access to readings, theatrical productions, and special events that tell the stories and experiences of our diverse peoples. All types and styles of works written out of the feminine experience are presented; however, this change occurred as recently as the last quarter of the twentieth century. Novels, such as the two mentioned below, with the lives of women or minority groups at the centre of the story were rare before then.

Carol Shields, in *The Stone Diaries* (1993), created a story around the unsettled life of Daisy Goodwell. Shields's novel is peopled with characters whose lives reveal differences in experiences of personal freedom, told from a woman's viewpoint. She writes of orphans, dysfunctional families, anti-Semitism, unfulfilled women, and the diversity in values of the societies, as well as the effects of moving back and forth across the Canadian–American border.

For immigrants who did not speak English, often it was the third generation before a storyteller's voice broke through the sound barrier into the mainstream culture. Some immigrants, like Michael Ondaatje, had the benefit of having come from a former British colony, where the second language was English. These writers understood well the

---

BOX 11.3

Stories of the Dislocations Experienced by Immigrants

....

- "An Immigrant's Split Personality," by Sun-Kyung Yi of Korean background
- "Rebirth," by Pablo Urbanyi, born in Hungary, grew up and worked in Argentina
- *The Sacrifice*, by Adele Wiseman, European Jewish background
- *The Apprenticeship of Duddy Kravitz*, by Mordecai Richler
- "A Holocaust Survivor's Story," by Miriam Rosenthal
- "A Minor Incident," by Robyn Sarah
- *Tamarind Mem* and *Hero's Walk*, by Anita Rau Bedami, East Indian background
- "Mancuso's and Sons," by Frank Paci, Italian background
- *Lives of the Saints*, by Nino Ricci

---

relationship of voice to power and numbers in a society, and this theme becomes a vital element in their novels. In Ondaatje's novel *In the Skin of a Lion* (1987), the construction of the Bloor Viaduct represents an important image and symbol of cultures mixing, clashing, and yet quite often and unpredictably, meshing. He portrays the frustration and isolation of the language barrier to these newcomers. With the attainment of the new language, the link to Canadian society, comes the inevitable loss of the old language and the culture it gives voice to.

THE INTERRELATIONSHIPS OF DEMOGRAPHICS AND STORY

The Great Canadian Experiment or the Micro-Global Village

Canada has been called the first international nation. Except for Native peoples, all of us are from somewhere else. We are, or are descended from, immigrants or refugees, who arrived here, at various times and from diverse points in the "global village." Anthropologists use the term low context to describe a culture where diversity is more common than similarity. Some who came to Canada planned the move to gain a better life for themselves and a more positive future for their children. For others it was a refuge from war, economic upheaval, or natural disaster. For still others flight from imprisonment, or other forms of repression for political reasons, was the impetus to move. We have among us people whose stories are as diverse as can be imagined (see Table 11.1).

One group of recent immigrants is the Hong Kong Chinese. They came to Canada in the face of unknown but definite change, when Communist China took over the former British colony in 1997. Their story presents some cultural similarities with their predecessors, people who came to find adventure and fortune in the "golden mountains" of British Columbia, who stayed to build, and who died building, the railways. However, their acceptance into Canadian society will be much smoother than it was for those who came from China in the nineteenth century. Those immigrants were exploited as cheap labour and then denied the right to bring their families to Canada. They were charged a prohibitive head tax, and they suffered greatly from the prevailing attitudes that

Table 11.1 Some Canadian Writers and Their Ancestry or Origins

Writer	Ancestry or Origin
Clark Blaise	American
Joy Kogawa	Japanese
Rohinton Mistry	Indian
Mary di Michele	Italian
Paul Yee	Chinese
Maxine Tynes	Black (Loyalist)
Drew Hayden-Taylor	Ojibway and English
Dionne Brand	West Indian
Lee Maracle	Métis/Salish
Alistair MacLeod	Scottish
Stephen Leacock	English
Gabrielle Roy	French
Morley Callaghan	Irish
Alberto Manguel	Argentinean
Michael Ondaatje	Sri Lankan
	Your cultural origins?

CRITICAL THINKING BOX 11.4

....

Is your part in the Canadian story represented in our literature? Is it part of an early and continuing chapter, such as that of the Acadians? Is it one with more contemporary immigrants or women, or perhaps both, at the centre? Perhaps it is a revised part of the story. If you are a Native person or a descendant of blacks, Japanese, or Chinese who have been Canadians for generations, how has your story evolved? Or is your chapter in the Canadian story yet to be told?

viewed them as the "yellow peril." Many years passed before word of this legalized racism was acknowledged.

One place where the acknowledgement did appear was in Sky Lee's powerful novel *Disappearing Moon Cafe* (1990), which tells this story from the point of view of a fourth-generation family member living in Toronto in 1987. Silence, both official and personal, kept this part of the Canadian story suppressed. It is symbolic of other omissions, denials, and neglects that signalled to third- and fourth-generation writers the need to revisit, uncover, and reveal the complete, true—and often difficult—tale of the evolution of Canadian culture. We learned belatedly, that it is the stories of those who are in power that are told. A more realistic picture can be found in the works of Wayson Choy, *Jade Peony*, *Paper Shadows: A Chinatown Childhood*, Evelyn Lau, and newer writers Denise Chong and Madeleine Thien and playwright Betty Quan.

LITERATURE LINKS REGIONALISM, SOCIAL INEQUALITY, AND STRATIFICATION

The Atlantic Region: The Geographical, Economic, and Sociopolitical Margins

Atlantic Canadian writers focus clearly on the poor working class. In many different styles, they describe this as the major difference between the Atlantic provinces in general and the Canada that is middle class. Pride of heritage, the power of the sea, and isolation are consistent themes. Atlantic Canada's people of French, English, Irish, and

---

BOX 11.4

Canadian War Stories: Changing Attitudes

....

Important works reflecting Canadian attitudes to war in the twentieth century include the following:

- WWI: Hugh MacLellan's *Barometer Rising*, Timothy Findley's *The Wars* (1977), Alden Nowlan's poem "Ypres: 1914"
- WWII: Gabrielle Roy's *The Tin Flute* (1945), Findley's *Famous Last Words* (1981), Roch Carrier's *La Guerre, Yes Sir!* (1968), Rudy Wiebe's *Peace Shall Destroy Many* (1962), "That Morning in Brussels" and "The Nest" poems by Raymond Souster, Farley Mowat's autobiographical *And No Birds Sang* (1979). *The Stone Carvers*, by Jane Urquhart, and *The Ash Garden*, by Dennis Bock, examine the aftermath of WWII from an international perspective, as does Michael Ondaatje's *The English Patient*.
- In *Anil's Ghost*, by Ondaatje, the Canadian protagonist is a civil rights investigator caught in the tension of a present day civil war in her former homeland of Sri Lanka.

Scottish descent have strong oral traditions, as do Atlantic blacks and native Mi'kmaq ("people of the dawn"). However, historically the latter two groups have been silenced.

Newfoundland

Our cross-country journey begins at Canada's most easterly point of land. We find ourselves wind-blown, perched on a cliff gazing into the north Atlantic through the eyes of E.J. Pratt, who in his poem "Silences" wrote:

> There is no silence upon the earth or under the earth like the
> silence under the sea;
> No cries announcing birth,
> No sounds declaring death.[8]

Then our gaze falls on an ominous presence. Pratt's poem "The Shark" describes it:

> He seemed to know the harbour,
> So leisurely he swam;
> His fin,

Like a piece of sheet-iron
Three-cornered,
And with knife-edge,
Stirred not a bubble
as it moved
With its base-line on the water.[9]

In our imaginations we can travel offshore about 400 km, back to 1912, and watch with horror as the ocean claims the *Titanic* and about fifteen hundred people. Pratt's epic poem "The *Titanic*" expresses the terrible power and beauty of the north Atlantic.

We turn away from the sea and go inland to learn the story of *The Rowdyman* (1973), written by Gordon Pinsent, a native Newfoundlander, who later wrote the screenplay and acted in the movie. The main character is Will Cole, whose life contains the elements of the stories of so many from Atlantic Canada. He works in a pulp mill in a one-industry town, with little chance of future improvements, unless he goes away to Toronto to work—like his girlfriend did. To leave or to stay is the big question for people from this area. Bernice Morgan explores these questions and other realities of life on "The Rock" in her novels *Random Passage* and *Waiting for Time*.

Literary works from Canada's east coast are populated with characters who made either, or sometimes both, of these choices, to stay or go, at different times. We witness the emotional wrench from family and community that is felt on both sides. We see the determination of those remaining not only to survive, but also to nourish the community and cultures of home. Wayne Johnston's family saga *Baltimore's Mansions* is about the conflicts caused in communities and families leading up to Newfoundland's decision to join Canada as the tenth province in 1949. Other policies of then Premier Joey Smallwood, particularly those involving uprooting whole communities from the isolated outports, became significant events in the story of Newfoundland. Derek O'Brien's exposé of sexual abuse of boys by priests and brothers, *Suffer the Little Children*, tells a tragic story with its far-reaching emotional, legal, and social scars on the whole island community.

Nova Scotia

In Nova Scotia a reader can begin with the historical stories of Hugh MacLennan, written after he had spent some time studying and working in England and the United States. *Each Man's Son* (1951) is set in the fictional "Broughton" (Glace Bay), a fishing and coal-mining town in Cape Breton. A deserted mother and son are helped by Dr. Alan Ainslie. The doctor is driven by his Gaelic Presbyterian guilt to work ceaselessly, caring for his community. Before reaching the story's dramatic ending, we have a strong sense of the economic and social forces that shaped these people's lives. Tension is created by attempts to preserve a way of life, when faced with economic exploitation and challenges from "outsiders." Readers understand how an attitude of suspicion and caution was bound to develop. *Each Man's Son* was set in 1913. Sheldon Currie's story "Glace Bay Miners' Museum" (and the film *Margaret's Museum*) is set in the 1940s and has the same theme. The story of the Westray mining tragedy of the 1990s will surely be written.

Alistair MacLeod's short story collection *The Lost Salt Gift of Blood* (1976) offers further insight into the minds and hearts of Cape Bretoners. "The Boat" focuses, with empathy and compassion, on one family, as its members struggle with the desire for personal freedom, set against a strong sense of family obligation. In the community context, when it comes to survival there is no question about risking civil disobedience and out-smarting the Mounties: "After all, they're trying to enforce a law that was made in Ottawa by some guy that was never out in a boat in his life." MacLeod's award-winning novel *No Great Mischief*, set in the present nationally and internationally, explores these themes further. The obligation and importance of loyalty to one's people, the conflicts that inevitably arise, and the many subtle and complex ways in which the human spirit responds are intricately examined in the story.

The Mountain and the Valley (1952), by Ernest Buckler, is another novel that reflects on the themes of outsiders and insiders, and connection and disconnection with the rest of Canada and elsewhere. Once again the themes of isolation, self-reliance, and the value of education are important in the characters' world. This time the tale is set in the rural Annapolis Valley. Don Shebib's classic Canadian film *Goin' Down the Road* tells this ongoing story of the culture shock that is inevitable when someone from the east coast has to go away to find work.

Three writers who give us a view of that world, from the vantage point of having "gone down the road" are novelists Ann-Marie MacDonald (*Fall on Your Knees*), Lynn Coady (*Strange Heaven, Play the Monster Blind*), and playwright Michael Melski (*Hockey Mom, Hockey Dad, Miles from Home*). Although the settings in each case begin with a Cape Breton influence, the themes are universal and the characters are social outsiders in some way. These stories include many diversities that were often taboo subjects in the past, such as mental illness, domestic violence, homosexuality, incest, and racism. All three writers portray the evolution of attitudes regarding sexuality, women's understanding of their roles in the parental home, in relationships with men, as mothers, in the community, and in the world. The changing roles of men as husbands and fathers are also realistically presented.

New Brunswick

Three authors whose writings are important in defining the culture of New Brunswick are Alden Nowlan, David Adams Richards, and Antoine Maillet. Maillet has become the voice of the Acadian people of New Brunswick, which since the Acadian cultural revival that began in the 1970s, is recognized as the only Canadian province that is truly bilingual. *La Sagouine* (1971), translated in 1979, and *Pélagie-la-Charette* (1979) were such great successes worldwide that she has dominated contemporary Acadian writing. Her many stories and characters give voice to the geography, history, and people of Acadia with a passion for life and a sense of humour about human nature. Maillet believes that to recognize her writing is to recognize the people from whom she is descended.

Alden Nowlan is considered the poet of the underprivileged. His poetry, novels, and short stories are motivated by his immediate community, especially the effects of poverty on the human spirit. In his best known poem, "Britain St.," and stories such as "A Christmas Visit" and "The Glass Roses," Nowlan writes of loneliness, violence, and despair with a gentle compassion. Nowlan was one of the first to write about unacknowledged social realities like family violence and the plight of the single mother. His poems and stories compel us to look at the hypocrisy of denial.

There is a much harder edge to the stories of David Adams Richards about the harshness of life in the Miramichi. The characters in *The Coming of Winter* (1974), *Blood Ties* (1976), and *Lives of Short Duration* (1981) inhabit a world where subsistence is the norm, where every form of deprivation exists, and where social structures have collapsed. Hope is as rare a commodity as diamonds. Life has become meaningless. Richards describes the moral decay that comes from consistent powerlessness as directly caused by economic exploitation of the land and its people, combined with general social breakdown. In *The Bay of Love and Sorrows* (1998), tension and rivalry are created "when the once-strong friendship between privileged Michael Skid, the young son of a judge from town, and farmhand Tommy Donnerall ends in bitter misunderstanding" and murder. In *Mercy Among the Children* a family becomes isolated, exploited, and abused because of the father's decision to never hurt another human being. His determination to rid himself of the legacy of an alcoholic father is unshakeable. The narrator is Sydney's twenty-five-year-old son, Lyle. He responds to the injustices to his mother, his sister, his grandfather (falsely imprisoned for arson), his father, and himself by becoming a tough and very angry young man.

Prince Edward Island

Canada's smallest and mostly rural province is Prince Edward Island. This is the setting for Lucy Maud Montgomery's prolific writing, especially her "Anne" and "Emily" stories. Perhaps because of Montgomery's idyllic descriptions of the island, PEI has become a refuge for many artists who come "from away" to work in peaceful surroundings.

The diversity of Alzheimer's disease is the subject of poet Hugh MacDonald's collection entitled *Looking for Mother*. The poem of the title begins "It wasn't till mother lost her mind that I saw what I'd lost." It is a moving and honest search for who his mother really was. He begins with childhood memories, interviews those who knew her best, and ends with her time spent in the Sacred Heart Nursing Home, lost even to herself.

Milton Acorn of PEI is known as "The People's Poet." The titles of his works give an idea of the topics he was concerned with in his life and writing: *In Love and Anger*, *Against a League of Liars*, *I've Tasted My Blood*, *Dig Up MY Heart*, *I Shout Love and Other Poems*, *Hundred Proof Earth*, and *The Island*.

Quebec: Cultural and Linguistic Isolation—Two Bodies of Literature Define the Two Solitudes

Quebec has produced a voluminous literature throughout its history and continues to do so. Québécois literature offers readers a picture both of how this region is different from the others and of the diversities found within Quebec culture. This outpouring of creativity, which is characteristic of all the arts in "La Belle Province," is directly related to its cultural and linguistic isolation. Six million Québécois live among three hundred million North Americans, including about thirty million Canadians. From earliest days there was an urgency and commitment among Quebeckers to tell, and record, their unique role in the evolution of Canadian culture, to tell their stories in their own language. (See the Web site for this book at <www.diversity2e.nelson.com>, Chapter 11, "The Politics of Story: The Relationship between Power and Voice" for more information.) Certain writers let the characters, setting, and plot reveal the nature of the world Quebeckers lived in. This might be said of Gabrielle Roy and Roch Carrier, whose stories include people and events reflecting both cultures. For others, such as Yves Thériault and Michel Tremblay, a political situation became the heart of the story. The authors use a personal or internal dichotomy as an analogy for the Canada–Quebec conflict. For Thériault it was the fact that he is Métis, as shown in the short story, "Akua Nuten: The South Wind." For Tremblay it was his homosexuality, evident in the play *Hosannah*.

The role of women in Quebec society until recently was only visible from the masculine perspective. This picture was limited by the strong patriarchies of church and state, particularly control over education, in what was a mostly rural society until after World War II. In Quebec society there used to be only two choices for a woman: she could be a wife and mother or a nun. This applied to girls and women of all classes. Anne Hébert, Marie-Claire Blais, and Gabrielle Roy are three writers who expanded and deepened that picture. For Hébert and Blais it meant distancing themselves from the society in which their stories are set. Poet and novelist Anne Hébert spent her adult life, after the age of thirty-three, in Paris. Her best-known novel is *Kamouraska* (1970), in 1973 made into a movie by Claude Jutra. Elizabeth, the main character, at her second husband's deathbed, reflects on how throughout her life she has not been able to escape this limited destiny. She went from a stifling childhood, to an unhappy marriage, to an affair with an American (with whom she plotted her husband's death), to a trial and acquittal, and retreat into a respectable second marriage to an older man. The themes of ridding oneself of guilt and struggling toward personal freedom are central to Hébert's poetry, too.

Marie-Claire Blais, considered a literary prodigy, wrote her first novel, *Mad Shadows* (*La Belle Bête*), in 1959 at the age of nineteen. The reader watches the spiritual and moral decay that develops in the young female narrator, as she must live with her mother's strong favouritism toward her brother, a very beautiful child with mental disabilities. A later novel entitled *A Season in the Life of Emmanuel* (1965) relates the story of the members of a family the year this sixteenth child is born into it. We see the diversity in the lives of the boys and girls, depending on their position in the family, especially regarding education and hopes for the future. The mother is a silent shadow working in the background. Her story is never told. Blais did much of her writing about Quebec from the vantage point of the United States.

Gabrielle Roy's novel *The Tin Flute* (1945), set in prewar Montreal, centres on the lives of a mother and daughter. The younger woman, Florentine, desperately tries to escape her mother's life of poverty, self-sacrifice, and subservience to family and faith.

The poems and stories of Irving Layton, Mordecai Richler, and Leonard Cohen speak of another diversity within Quebec society, the Jewish community, a minority within the English minority. Layton's poem "On Seeing the Statuettes of Ezekiel and Jeremiah in the Church of Notre Dame" gives a powerful feeling of what it's like to be in a cultural and religious minority. Cohen's poem "Genius" describes the continuing presence of anti-Semitism in the world. In addition to describing relationships within Quebec, all three of these writers have written about various aspects of contemporary Canadian life. In 1992, Richler published his controversial nonfiction work *Oh Canada! Oh Quebec! Requiem for a Divided Country*, on the matter of Quebec separation. These writers are considered international artists and their works are translated into many languages around the world.

Ontario: Largest and Richest, but Complex Internal Diversities

The vastness alone has led to diversity in stories about life in Canada's largest province, Ontario. They range from Morley Torgov's humorous stories of growing up Jewish in the steel town of Sault Ste. Marie, to Alice Munro's and Robertson Davies's differing portraits of conservative, small-town Ontario. The centres of power, political and business, Toronto and Ottawa, are settings for many good novels. Ontario's proximity to the pervasive American influence has also had an effect on the perceptions of Ontarians. It provides a theme for countless stories by Ontario writers.

Ontario's urban culture is the source of stories told from many viewpoints. Hugh Garner's *Cabbagetown* (1950) pictures Toronto life in the 1930s, in the poor neighbourhood where the Irish and other European newcomers lived. The world of the Irish Catholic minority in the white, Anglo-Saxon Protestant (WASP) Toronto of the 1930s, 1940s, and 1950s is found in Morley Callaghan's stories. Themes of social injustice, public and private morality, and strength of character are examined in *Such Is My Beloved* (1934), *More Joy in Heaven* (1937), *The Loved and the Lost* (1951), and other works. The perennial urban problems of the poor, the homeless, prostitutes, and racial discrimination were elements of life that Callaghan was very conscious of through his work as a reporter at the *Toronto Star*.

Margaret Atwood portrays the urban and suburban roles of women in both poetry and novels: *Edible Woman* (1969), *Lady Oracle* (1976), and the poetry collection *Power Politics* (1971) present a stinging, often humorous critique of a patriarchal society. The changes that have occurred in feminist issues have been part of her stories from the 1960s until the 1990s, as illustrated in *Bodily Harm*, (1981), *Handmaid's Tale* (1985), and *The Robber Bride* (1993). Her historical novel *Alias Grace* (1996) is based on a famous murder case in nineteenth-century Ontario. The story reveals not only attitudes to women, but the powerful prejudice against the Irish, how this affected the investigation and trial of Grace and her lover, the nature of their sentences, and the lives of women in prison.

Additional contemporary portraits of the lives of women can be found in the writing of Alice Munro, Marian Engel, Constance Beresford Howe, Margaret Gibson, Joan Barfoot, Katherine Govier, Jane Urquhart, Jane Findlay Young, and Gwendolyn McEwan.

The major concerns of national and global political and civil justice, poverty, and the nature and source of violence are those not only of Atwood but also of Ontario writers Timothy Findley, Michael Ondaatje, Dave Godfrey, Hugh Hood, Richard Wright, and Alice Munro. As a result the settings of most stories by writers based in Ontario (and elsewhere in Canada), although they may originate here, can and often do include characters, events concerned with global issues. This is especially true of authors who, as immigrants and refugees, write from a viewpoint influenced by their places and cultures of origin.

The Prairies: Manitoba, Saskatchewan, and Alberta

Certain images and themes are common to the literatures of Manitoba, Saskatchewan, and Alberta and different from the rest of Canada. These are closely linked to the prairie landscape. The sense of isolation and loneliness that pervades when you live in vast, open, wind-swept, and seemingly endless spaces of land and sky forms part of the background to stories from this region. This sensibility reaches into tales of town, city, forest, and north of the tree line onto the Arctic wasteland. Recently, concern for the environment has become an important theme in the story of the Prairie provinces. Determination, self-reliance, and independence have thus marked the character of the westerner.

Saskatchewan

The physical and emotional effects of this landscape are truly portrayed in the works of Saskatchewan writer Sinclair Ross, especially in the novel *As for Me and My House* (1941) and the short story "The Painted Door." Another, more humorous, but poignant picture of prairie life is Max Braithwaite's fictional *Why Shoot the Teacher?* (1965). It introduces us to the volatile brand of politics that developed in Canada's newer provinces. Our best guide to the world of small town Saskatchewan is W.O. Mitchell. Rudy Wiebe writes of the marginalized cultural groups in Saskatchewan, his own Mennonite community, the Cree (whose chief was Big Bear), and the Métis. In *Peace Shall Destroy Many* (1962), the central character, a young Mennonite, during World War II is torn between his community's pacifism and the desire to serve his country. Wiebe draws many parallels between the three marginalized groups and brings attention to how they are different from Saskatchewan's majority culture in language, values, and absence of voice.

Manitoba

The imaginary town of Neepewa, created by Margaret Laurence, and the setting of her five novels is our entry into the life of a small Manitoba prairie town. Laurence's novels and short stories give a compassionate but realistic view of the social stratification. The distinctions between rich and poor and the place of the outsiders are clearly drawn. We see the one ignored Chinese family and the Métis families on the edges—despised and degraded. However, it is the roles of women in that small town, and as they move out across Canada, that Laurence most clearly describes. She traces the changes through the Depression, the war years, up until the 1970s. Readers see the world through the eyes of women of all ages and stages of life, from 90-year-old Hagar in *The Stone Angel* (1964), to that difficult transition from girl to woman evoked by Vanessa MacLeod, the narrator in the short story collection *A Bird in the House* (1974).

In Adele Wiseman's novels *The Sacrifice* (1956) and *Crackpot* (1974), we learn of the Jewish immigrant experience in Winnipeg and about life in the city's north end. Gabrielle Roy wrote stories about the different cultural groups that populate rural northern Manitoba. W.D. Valgardson wrote of the Icelandic communities around Gimli, on Lake Winnipeg. Carol Shields's novel *The Stone Diaries* and other stories are imbued with the history, geography, and spirit of the west.

Alberta

Robert Kroetch, George Ryga, and Aritha Van Herk have all provided us with tales of Alberta. Three of Kroetch's books form his "Out West Trilogy": *The Words of My Roaring* (1966), *The Studhorse Man* (1969), and *Gone Indian* (1973). The trilogy investigates four decades of social change, including the Depression years, post–World War II dislocations, and the good years of cattle farming in the 1960s and 1970s. A later novel, *Badlands* (1975), has the reader accompany the main character, William Dawe, as he rafts up the Red Deer River into the heart of the Alberta Badlands in his obsessive search for dinosaur bones.

George Ryga was born in Alberta of Ukrainian background. He is best known for his play *The Ecstasy of Rita Joe* (1970), the story of a young Indian girl who, on the one hand, is incited to rebellion by the white society around her and, on the other, is a victim of bureaucratic indifference. The plight of the Native person is a continuing concern throughout Ryga's plays and novels.

In Aritha Van Herk's stories the women characters are determined, independent, and adventurous risk takers. They are modern women who challenge the stereotypes about femininity. In the 1978 novel *Judith*, the main character is fed up with urban living; she returns to the country to single-handedly operate a pig farm. Arachne, in *No Fixed Address* (1986), is a travelling saleswoman who weaves her way in and out of the small towns of Alberta and Saskatchewan selling her line of women's lingerie. The lives of these unconventional women, their relationships with neighbours, friends—male and female—and lovers are presented with energy and honesty.

British Columbia: The Pacific Coast, Gateway to the Orient

The unique placement of Canada's most westerly province, between the Rocky Mountains and the Pacific Ocean, has been an important factor in the shaping of its culture. The isolation and challenge of the mountains, as a metaphor for life, can be found in the poems of Earle Birney, particularly "Bushed" and "David." E.J. Pratt's narrative poem "Towards the Last Spike" presents the mountains as a barrier that must be overcome if Canada is to be united physically, and politically. Many books of fact (e.g., Pierre Berton's *The Last Spike*, 1971) and fiction have incorporated this event. However, the untold stories of the human cost of this achievement, especially the exploitation of Native peoples and Chinese immigrants, were cloaked in silence for decades.

The mountains are the setting for stories of the excitement and adventure of the gold rush days. Later, during World War II, the abandoned mining towns became the detention camps for Japanese-Canadians. Property was confiscated, and families were separated. All Japanese-Canadians were banished from their homes in Vancouver, along the coast, and in the Fraser Valley, on suspicion that they were spying for Japan. *Obasan* (1981), by Joy Kogawa, and its sequel, *Itsuka* (1992), reveal this tragic tale and its aftermath from the perspective of the Japanese-Canadian community. It was not until the publication of *Obasan*, forty years after enactment of this policy, that the complete story came out. A docudrama by Dorothy Livesay, entitled "Call My People Home," tells this story in poetry form.

British Columbia and its capital city, Victoria, are names indicating settlement by the British. But location also makes it Canada's gateway to the Orient. The Japanese and Chinese chapters of the Canadian story began on the shores of British Columbia. Sky Lee's novel *Disappearing Moon Cafe* (1990) takes us into the world of four generations of the Wong family. The first Wong arrived in the gold rush days and took part in the building of the railway. He, his wife, children, and grandchildren struggle to survive, and eventually build a successful business in Vancouver. It is the struggle of a community to form a Canadian identity despite isolation, racism, and culture clash. The main character is Kay, a Bay St. financial analyst and new mother. She revisits her family history, concluding that her forebears won a place for her and her son in Canadian society.

Swamp Angel (1954) and *Equations of Love* (1952), by Ethel Wilson, and *The Double Hook* (1959), by Sheila Watson, depict British Columbia society in the 1950s and 1960s. They speak of the dehumanizing and alienating effects of modern urban living. In *Intertidal Life* (1984), and other works, often set in the islands off the coast of British Columbia, Audrey Thomas carried these themes into contemporary times. These writers posed questions about relationships between men and women, women and women, and women and children.

The North: Yukon and the Northwest Territories—The Romance and Realism of the Last Frontier

Many Canadians were introduced to the distant north of Canada through the poems of Robert Service ("The Cremation of Sam McGee"), the animal stories of Jack London, or *Klondike*, Pierre Berton's 1958 narrative of the gold rush. Even more of us entered that northern world through the experiences of Farley Mowat, as described in *Never Cry Wolf* (1963) and *People of the Deer* (1952), through Yves Thériault's novel *Agaguk* (1963), and through *Windflower* (1970) by Gabrielle Roy. Besides awakening us to the north's natural beauties and the unique culture of the Inuit, we learned how these were endangered by intrusions from the south. Mowat's controversial works pointed out his environmental concerns for the wildlife but especially for the Native people whose whole pattern of existence was being destroyed with no thought for the consequences. The poems of Al Purdy give us wonderful snapshots of the area's unusual natural beauty in "Arctic

CRITICAL THINKING BOX 11.5

How have the following elements of Canadian society promoted the recognition and acceptance of diversity within our culture?

1. We are a relatively new democratic society, from its beginnings made up of diverse peoples.
2. By law, all children must receive an education.
3. We have the transportation and communication means—railroads, airlines, the Trans-Canada Highway, CBC Radio and TV, the National Film Board—to learn each other's stories, despite a vast geography and difficult climate.
4. We have developed a good standard of living.

Rhododendrons," and sombre reflections on its long history of isolation in "Lament for the Dorsets."

Inuit writer Alootook Ipellie's story "Frobisher Bay Childhood" describes a time when his isolated community (renamed Iqaluit) was in a time of transition. It began with the arrival of material goods from southern Canada, movies, and the establishment of an American military base nearby. In retrospect he can see it was the beginning of the erosion of a strong sense of community. Gradually, his people experienced the loss of independence that came with reliance on the traditional way of life.

THE ROLES OF FAMILY, GENDER, AND SEXUALITY IN CANADIAN LITERATURE

Diversity through a Child's Eyes

Brian from Who Has Seen the Wind?

Probably the best-known Canadian story about childhood is W.O. Mitchell's 1947 novel *Who Has Seen the Wind?* It is about Brian, a young boy growing up in a small Alberta town on the edge of the vast prairie. As Brian develops in awareness, he tries to understand the difference between himself and "the young Ben," who seldom goes to school and appears to be free of adult restrictions. Brian must face drastic change in his own family when first his grandmother and then his father dies. He begins to notice that the eccentric people like his entrepreneurial Uncle Sean, Saint Sammy the madman who lives on the prairie, and drunkard and bootlegger "the Ben," are met with varying attitudes. Some receive acceptance and help, others are rejected and scorned. Mitchell's 1940s radio series "Jake and the Kid" was made into a CBC television series. A later novel, *How I Spent My Summer Holidays* (1981), is a darker vision of childhood presenting a loss of innocence.

Anne *from* Anne of Green Gables

Some might argue that it is *Anne of Green Gables*, by L.M. Montgomery and set in rural Prince Edward Island, that is first among Canadian stories of childhood. Published in 1908, it has remained popular ever since, continuing to be sold all over the English-speaking world as well as in translation. The story has been made into a film, a play, and a television series. The biggest reason for its popularity is the character of Anne herself. Anne's charm and imagination capture our hearts as soon as we meet her. The second reason is that, for decades, it was one of the few Canadian stories that had a girl as its central character. Certainly Anne did not have a typical childhood. Her parents died when she was very young, and she was brought up in an orphanage. Anne's adoptive "parents" were not a conventional couple, but a brother (Matthew) and sister (Marilla), who had wanted a boy to help them out on their farm as they were getting older. Early twentieth-century ideas about children are illustrated clearly in this book. A reader can see that people were skeptical at best and often fearful about adoption. Madness or some terrible illness could be in the family background: "Although the island has no monopoly on sexist attitudes towards children, there is no question that male children are more useful, more cost-efficient and more welcome."[10] Anne is intellectually curious and straightforward in her manner, neither of which was considered a feminine characteristic. Even worse, Anne has red hair and the temper to go with it. Best of all, for her avid female readers, was that Anne earned better marks in school than her friend, Gilbert. However, Montgomery has to be true to her times in ending the story. Even though Anne won the scholarship to go to teachers' college, she willingly gave it up to remain at home and care for the ailing Marilla.

Morag *from* The Diviners

Twenty years later the experience of another orphan girl, Morag, in Margaret Laurence's *The Diviners* (1977), is significantly different from Anne's. Neither she nor her adoptive parents are accepted by the community: Christy is the town garbage man, his wife, Prin, is obese and depressed, and they all live in a poor shack on the edge of town. Morag is clever. She carefully plans her escape from the restrictive small-town environment. The choices Morag has to make about her education, friends, sexuality, and eventually marriage, motherhood, and work, are complex—and she must make them alone. In *The Diviners*, Laurence gives Morag the power to challenge and break the stereotypes about women that existed during the period her story is set in, from about 1925 to early 1970s. As Paula B. Jessop wrote:

> Laurence's rebellious Morag is a character who relentlessly, energetically rejects the limiting moral demands of society's mores while developing a moral strength that gives her much needed independence. She makes bold decisions about her life that break with tradition and forever prevent her from conforming to the superficial dictates of society. This is what gives her deep personal freedom.[11]

The reader travels with Morag through her childhood, her "coming of age," young adulthood, and maturity, as she reflects on the path her life has taken. As in all of her novels and short stories, Margaret Laurence examines the tensions that exist for all people, but especially for women, between the values of personal freedom and concern for others.

Missy *and* Ruby *from* From Bruised Fell

Jane Findlay Young's story is of two young sisters living at the end of the twentieth century in an uncertain world of constant change. Even though their parents are living, they feel orphaned. Family life is constantly disrupted by their mother's mental illness, the parents' divorce, moves back and forth to England, their father's remarriage, and another series of moves across Canada necessitated by his engineering work. They have only each other to turn to. The story is an honest and moving portrait of a family, which is not that atypical in contemporary life. How Missy and Ruby respond to all the change in their lives, and their love and protection of each other are at the centre of the story. Ruby, unable to accept the loss of her mother, finally succumbs to physical and emotional illness. The author depicts the inner lives and imaginations of these children in a sensitive and believable manner.

Literary Families Reveal the Diversity in Their Communities

The books and authors examined next are all about finding one's place in the world. Each story examines a different version of the patriarchal family.

Alice Munro's *Lives of Girls and Women* (1971) and Robertson Davies's *Fifth Business* (1970), are novels that begin in small-town Ontario. Jubilee is the name of the imaginary town created by Munro. *Fifth Business* is the first story of a trilogy set in the imaginary town of Deptford. The people in these towns are almost entirely white of Anglo-Saxon origins. The main differentiating feature is the type of Protestantism practised. Both authors are concerned with how childhood experiences affect the rest of our lives.

The most obvious difference is the gender of each author, which influences the gender of each text's central character. Munro wrote from the point of view of Del as a girl and a young woman, with the story ending the summer of high-school graduation. We are aware of her private inner self in a way that those in her everyday life are not. In *Fifth Business*, Dunny (Dunstable) Ramsay narrates his own tale. He is retiring from a lifelong career of teaching. Believing that people think his life has been dull and boring, he writes a story/letter to reveal the exciting secret life he led during holidays. The titles of these two books indicate that each is concerned about the roles we play in life and the opinions of others. Munro's title questions women's place in society as played out in small town Jubilee. It is a novel of the feminine experience. The meaning of the term "fifth business" is more obtuse, and therefore Davies prefaced the novel with a definition. Fifth business is a term used in theatre to refer to a character who acts as a catalyst in the progression of the plot; the person is not a main character, yet he or she is vital to the action.

In Munro's novel we see the world through the narrator's eyes as she tries to understand herself and other girls and women. Del thinks about her relationship with her mother, the differences between herself and her friends, and the behaviour of other women, especially regarding their interactions with the men in their lives. These reflections are all interwoven in the uneven process of Del's physical, emotional, intellectual, and spiritual growth. The development of Del's not always subtle, but decidedly female, sense of humour is an especially delightful aspect of the story. The importance of this novel, especially for women readers, cannot be overestimated. It was one of the first Canadian novels to outline the sexual awakening of a young girl within the context of the world of women. Female readers could only go so far in identifying with the experiences of male characters in stories of initiation into the adult world. In short story collections that followed, especially *Something I've Been Meaning to Tell You* (1974) and *Who Do You Think You Are?* (1978), Alice Munro expands on how attitudes regarding women began to change in the second half of the twentieth century. This happened partly because of stories like Munro's, which presented girls and women in a fuller light.

The setting in time is the second important difference between the two novels. *Lives of Girls and Women* provides an insightful analysis of the world of typical small-town Canadian women, over a wide age and social range, in the 1940s and 1950s. By contrast, Dunny grew up in pre–World War I days, when boys and men were constantly reminded of responsibilities to family and community. Another theme of Davies's novel concerned the effects of external events or forces—fate, accident, timing—on the human psyche. Davies, influenced by Jungian psychology, created and developed characters who cover the spectrum of human emotional possibilities.

Adele Wiseman's *The Sacrifice* (1954) is about a Jewish family, displaced from Russia by the new communist regime, that finds its way to Winnipeg, where its members try to adjust to life in Canada. In the process conflict between the generations develops. A serious rift unfolds in the family that is the undoing of its patriarch, Abraham. The idea for Wiseman's later work *Crackpot* germinated from her own experience as a teenager, born in Canada into an immigrant family. She felt shame and embarrassment, and later guilt, to be seen with her grandmother, who dressed in dark clothes, covered her head in a "babushka," and spoke broken English.

The Apprenticeship of Duddy Kravitz (1959), by Mordecai Richler, takes place in the community of St. Urbain St. in Montreal. In this case the family is split up. Duddy's mother has died, his father has opted out, and his brother is away at university. Duddy learns his survival skills from the street's unsavoury characters. His immigrant grandfather impresses on him the importance of owning land, and this becomes his driving ambition. Duddy succeeds at this, but realizes too late that his success was at the cost of betraying his girlfriend and friends and disappointing his grandfather.

Margaret Atwood is probably the best known among Canadian writers. In all of her work, she describes and analyzes how perceptions of women as objects change to views of women as subjects, worthy of consideration for their own sakes. Like other feminist writers, Atwood pointed out that, for this to happen, women themselves must be the first to change in the way they see themselves and their daughters. Women have to avoid being victims of their own press. The story of Joan in *Lady Oracle* (1976) is a complex tale that traces her journey from an unhappy childhood of resistance to her mother's rigid expectations, to a series of relationships with men for whom she tried to appear in their feminine image. For years Joan leads a double life. Finally she realizes that the only way to live is to tell the truth about herself. During this period Atwood's tone and style tended to be stark and unemotional. She made it her business to overturn expectations, to subject the reader to verbal shock treatment. The short poem that opens *Power Politics* had this effect:

> You fit into me
> like a hook into an eye
> a fish hook
> an open eye[12]

Atwood often wrote from the point of view of alienated individuals. Some other themes that Atwood has explored are (1) inauthenticity, which she especially relates to women, (2) the dangers of a colonial mentality, with the resulting uncertainty about Canadian identity, and (3) the need to define one's own space as separate while still being related to others.

In the later phase of her work, covering from the late 1970s through the 2000s, Atwood "does employ a greater range of style and topics. She is by turns more lyrical and personal" as in this excerpt from "Variation on the word sleep," as well as "more satirical and political":[13]

> I would like to be the air
> that inhabits you for a moment
> only. I would like to be that unnoticed
> & that necessary.[14]

In some cases the elders in families and communities are important voices in Atwood's stories, revealing different roles for older people, how they adapt to changes in themselves and the world around them.

Breaking the Silence about Matters of Gender and Sexuality

In Canada, as elsewhere, diversity was not accepted in certain areas of human life. It was hidden, denied, and unspoken. Injustice, oppression, and all forms of human suffering were the result. As the social climate changed, stories of these individuals came to light. Inevitably, discussion and often controversy during and after productions—in print or

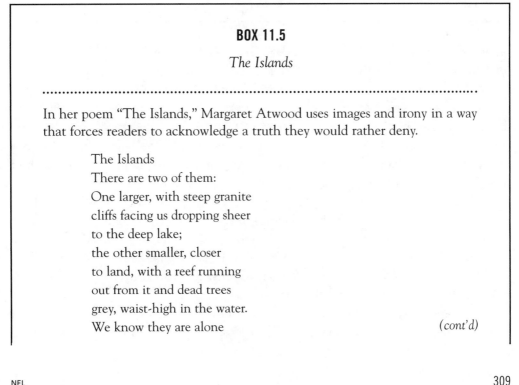

BOX 11.5

The Islands

In her poem "The Islands," Margaret Atwood uses images and irony in a way that forces readers to acknowledge a truth they would rather deny.

> The Islands
> There are two of them:
> One larger, with steep granite
> cliffs facing us dropping sheer
> to the deep lake;
> the other smaller, closer
> to land, with a reef running
> out from it and dead trees
> grey, waist-high in the water.
> We know they are alone

(cont'd)

BOX 11.5 *(cont'd)*

and always will be.
The lake takes care of that
and if it went,
they would be hills
and still demand
separateness
from the eye
Yet, standing on the cliff
(the two
of us)
on our bigger island,
looking,
we find it pleasing
(it soothes our instinct for symmetry, proportion
for company perhaps)
that there are two of them.

Source: Margaret Atwood, "The Islands" in *The Circle Game* (Toronto: House of Anansi, 1966). Reprinted with the permission of Stoddart Publishing.

other media—arises on such topics. Society's secrets such as incest, homosexuality, racism, religious intolerance, family violence, sexual discrimination, genocide, and war crimes are revealed. Even the most ancient fears, those surrounding mental and physical health, persist. As the twenty-first century begins, negative attitudes toward people with Alzheimer's disease and AIDS persist. Gradually, these issues have become subjects of literature in fiction and nonfiction. Recent television docudramas include *The Valour and the Horror* (about war and violence) and *The Boys of St. Vincent* (about pedophilia and breach of trust). The progress of acceptance has been uneven but steady.

Elly Danica's *Don't a Woman's Word* (1988) and Sylvia Fraser's *My Father's House* (1987) are biographical works about being subjected to incest. When this knowledge became conscious for Fraser, a journalist and writer, she not only understood her own life better but also characters and events in her novels. Fraser's allusions to sexual politics between children, and between children and adults, which had been noted earlier by readers and critics, took on new meaning.

Poems, plays, and stories on the subject of homosexuality, for example, Shyam Selvadurai's *Funny Boy*, are now generally accepted. Jane Rule, in an article entitled

---

BOX 11.6

The Voices of Experience

....

Some recent works focus directly on the themes of aging, illness, and death from the perspective of a central character in the novel. The diversity of responses to these universal experiences reveals much about human nature and society's attitudes and assumptions regarding the elderly. Hagar in *The Stone Angel* (1964), by Margaret Laurence, and Eve in *The Book of Eve* (1973), by Constance Beresford Howe, are two classic examples. More recent characters are Barney Panofsky from Mordecai Richler's *Barney's Version* (1998), William McKelvey in Matt Cohen's novel *Elizabeth and After* (1999), and the two grandfathers in Alistair MacLeod's *No Great Mischief* (2000).

"Lesbian and Writer: Making the Real Visible," discusses the conflicts that arise because of her honesty about her sexuality. The heterosexual community believes Rule's writing would gain greater acceptance if she played down her homosexuality. The gay community wants Rule to use her writing more as propaganda for their cause. Rule herself says, "I owe to my own art all the honesty and insight I have, not simply about homosexuals and artists, both of which I happen to be, but about the whole range of my experience as a member of a family, a community, a country."[15] Rule's best-known novel is *Desert of the Heart* (1986, which became the movie *Desert Hearts*). Gay and lesbian characters are part of Ann-Marie MacDonald's novel *Fall on Your Knees*, as is the matter of incest.

CHAPTER SUMMARY

Canada has a unique and complex culture, with diversity a defining characteristic. With literature as our vehicle, we can tour Canada's social landscape. Readers can be drawn into the stories of the country's first peoples, our parents and grandparents times, as well as the experiences of more recent newcomers. Each presents strong ideas and feelings about a particular society. We experience the internal diversity, gaining understanding about relationships within the whole of Canadian society. This applies equally to people who have been Canadians for generations and to newer members of the Canadian family.

In the first half of the twentieth century, literature reflected a changing Canadian society. It revealed regional diversities, differences and changes in rural, small-town, and

CRITICAL THINKING BOX 11.6

How has literature helped to change the way people think about diversity in Canada? Has it changed perceptions so that being different is viewed more positively that it was in the past?

urban life, and social attitudes to women and children. Both world wars caused us to recognize that Canada's story is separate and distinct from European culture and other cultures from which its people originated. Although some diversities, such as those between French- and English-speaking Canadians have persisted, others have diminished in importance. However, full acceptance of some cultural groups, such as Loyalist blacks, Chinese-, and Japanese-Canadians, for over a century was a struggle. Their voices were silenced or ignored until later in the century.

Canadian writers are now at the forefront of a reversal in the relationship between power and voice. In the second half of the twentieth century voices of the dispossessed, marginalized, and devalued, were acknowledged as telling the most vital stories being published in all parts of the world. In some societies, voices were stilled because of colonization and cultural imperialism, as with Canada's Native peoples. Feminist writings are also part of this global change. All of these diversities are part of the stories of Canada written to the world.

KEY TERMS

absence of voice, p. 283

feminist literature, p. 282

immigrant and refugee stories, p. 289

Métis, p. 284

postcolonial writing, p. 283

universal themes, p. 282

voice, p. 282

DISCUSSION QUESTIONS

1. How does literature personalize and humanize sociological data and historical events?
2. Explain how the focus on diversity by many contemporary writers is part of a global trend of postcolonial writing.

3. Trace how stories about Canada's Aboriginal peoples moved from their portrayal as "noble savages," to images of rebels and reactionaries, to realism with a decidedly negative slant. Contrast these versions with those written today as many native writers, both men and women, from communities, whether urban, small town, rural, or reservations, throughout the country speak in their own voices about past and present.

4. Explain how Canada's literary history (voice) is linked to its political and historical development (power). How did this phenomenon lead to the evolution of two distinct bodies of literature, one in English and one in French?

5. In stories set in the various regions of Canada, certain themes recur that reflect their social and economic realities. Identify the themes that are important for: (a) Atlantic Canada, (b) Quebec, (c) Ontario, (d) the Prairie provinces, (e) British Columbia, and (f) northern Canada (Yukon, Northwest Territories, and Nunavut).

6. Why is it that if you are a person of colour, if you speak a language other than English or French, or you have come to Canada from an Eastern culture, it is only within the past thirty years that you had a chance of finding yourself reflected in Canadian literature?

7. Omissions and silences have led to writings that explore the effects, on individuals and communities, of being treated differently. What questions are being explored in the stories by and of Canadians with (a) black, (b) Chinese, (c) Japanese and (d) certain European origins, as well as (e) in works written by more recent immigrants and refugees?

8. Some of the most controversial issues in Canadian society are directly related to the diversity of views regarding gender, sexuality, and the family. Discuss the differing viewpoints on one issue in each of these three areas of human diversity that have been written about in fact and fiction.

NOTES

1. Northrop Frye, "Northrop Frye's Canada," *Globe and Mail*, 15 April 1991, p. A13.
2. Bill Ashcroft, Gareth Griffiths, and Helen Tiffin, eds., *The Empire Writes Back* (London: Routledge, 1989), cover.
3. Drew Hayden Taylor, "Seeing Red Over Myths," *Globe and Mail*, 8 March 2001, p. A15.
4. Margaret Atwood, ed., *The New Oxford Book of Canadian Verse in English* (Toronto: Oxford University Press, 1982) pp. xxx–xxxi.
5. Charles Mair [n.d.], "Tecumseh," in Elizabeth Waterston, *Survey: A Short History of Canadian Literature* (Toronto: Methuen, 1977), p. 22
6. Rita Joe, *Lnu and Indians We're Called* (Charlottetown: Ragweed, 1991).

7. Mary di Michele [1955], "Luminous Emergencies," in Russell Brown, Donna Bennett, and Nathalie Cooke, eds., *An Anthology of Canadian Literature in English* (Toronto: Oxford University Press, 1990), pp. 706–10.
8. E.J. Pratt [1937], "Silences," in Sandra Djwa and R.G. Moyles, eds., *E.J. Pratt: Complete Poems, Parts I and II* (Toronto: 1989). Reprinted with the permission of University of Toronto Press.
9. E.J. Pratt [n.d.], "The Shark," in Sandra Djwa and R.G. Moyles, eds., *E.J. Pratt: Complete Poems, Parts I and II* (Toronto: 1989). Reprinted with the permission of University of Toronto Press.
10. Johan Aitken, *Masques of Morality* (Toronto: The Women's Press, 1987), p. 96.
11. Paula B. Jessop, "Teaching Tough Texts Truthfully," in David Hillen, ed., *indirections* (Toronto: OCTELA, Sept. 1994), p. 5.
12. Margaret Atwood, *Power Politics* (Toronto: House of Anansi, 1973), p. 1. Reprinted with the permission of Stoddart Publishing.
13. Russell Brown, Donna Bennett, and Nathalie Cooke, eds., *An Anthology of Canadian Literature in English*, p. 584.
14. Margaret Atwood [1981], "Variation on the word sleep," in *True Stories*. Copyright © Margaret Atwood, 1981. Reprinted by permission of Oxford University Press Canada.
15. Jane Rule, "Lesbian and Writer: Making the Real Visible," in Melita Schaum and Connie Flanagan, eds., *Gender Images* (Boston: Houghton Mifflin, 1992), p. 175.

Glossary

Absence of voice: The situation in which the stories of marginalized individuals or groups in a society are ignored, degraded, and suppressed. This creates a slanted, inaccurate, and incomplete picture of the society.

Age at first marriage: The average age at which men and women marry for the first time.

Age-specific marriage rate: The number of people marrying in different age groups.

Age-specific mortality rate: The number of people dying in different age groups.

Aggregating: Summarizing demographic observations or information.

Alphabet: A system of letters that permits languages to be written.

Androgynous: Having both masculine and feminine psychological or behavioural characteristics. The term also refers to people who have both male and female biological or physical characteristics, but who show sexual differentiation and can be labelled biologically, as either male or female.

Antidiscriminatory: Legislation or actions that attempt to ensure. That individuals or groups are not disadvantaged because of their gender, age, disabilities, race, or ethnicity.

Animate: A classification of nouns within Algonquian languages; it usually, but not always, refers to things that are alive.

Ascribed status: A characteristic that people are born with and over which they have little or no control. An ascribed status, such as race, sex, social class, and age, significantly influences people's lives, affecting their chances of achieving educational, occupational, and financial success.

Assimilation: The process whereby immigrants adopt the language, values, norms, and worldview of the host culture at the expense of their heritage culture.

Band: A native political entity, ultimately defined by the federal government.

Beringia: A continent-sized landmass that linked Siberia and Alaska (also called the Bering Land Bridge).

Bill C-31: An amendment to the *Indian Act*, passed in 1985, that enabled people who had lost their Indian status through marriage or through the marriage of their mothers to apply to be reinstated as registered Indians.

Bisexual: Sexual attraction to and preference for developing romantic relationships with members of either sex.

Capitalist class: Karl Marx's term for those who own the means of production-the land, machinery, factories, and so on-required for the production of goods and services.

Celibacy: The state of being unmarried.

Census: A list compiled by the government of every person who is in a population at a given point in time.

Civil registry: A list of births, deaths, or marriages compiled by a government.

Coition machine: A scientific measuring device consisting of a transparent tube containing photographic equipment, which is inserted into the vagina to measure and record physiological changes in internal sex organs.

Comparative method: A method used to evaluate the quality of demographic sources; it involves calculating trends of vital events based on information from adjacent districts.

Conflict theory: The perspective that sees society as consisting of many groups whose interests often conflict. The theory proposes that inequality stems from the exploitation and oppression of one section of society by another. Therefore, inequality should be reduced or abolished.

Congenital: Existing at or dating from birth and acquired during development in the uterus, rather than through heredity.

Conjugal family: A family whose members are linked by blood ties.

Conservative ideology: The belief that things are best left as they are. An example is the belief that biological causes determine male and female behaviour and, therefore, that attempts to change traditional gender spheres are futile.

Crosschecking the data: A process used to evaluate the quality of demographic information; it involves using a variety of sources linked to people in order to verify the information obtained about them.

Cross-sectional analysis: A method used to examine demographic patterns over the life cycle, involving dividing people into nonoverlapping age categories. Demographic patterns are then generalized to describe the demographic experience over a lifetime.

Crow's Index of Selection: A method used to measure the potential for natural selection in human populations; it takes into account both deaths and births (mortality and fertility).

Crude birth rate: The number of live births for every 1000 people in a population.

Crude death rate: The number of deaths for every 1000 people in a population.

Crude marriage rate: The number of marriages for every 1000 people in a population.

Cunnilingus: A sexual activity involving oral (mouth) stimulation of a female's genitals by a partner.

Decennial census: The census that is recorded once every ten years.

Deinstitutionalization: A movement to discharge people from institutional settings and to place them in the community.

Demography: The scientific study of human populations.

Department of Indian Affairs (DIA): The federal ministry or branch of the federal ministry responsible for native people.

Dependency ratio: The ratio of the number of people aged less than 15 and over 64 years to the number of people aged 15 to 64 years.

Developmental disabilities: Intellectual development that has been delayed; formerly referred to as mental retardation.

Dialect: A version of a language that is distinct from a standard version in terms of grammar, pronunciation, and vocabulary; it is usually restricted to a specific geographical area of a nation or territory whose regions share the same language.

DINKs: An acronym that stands for "double income, no kids." Applied to couples in which both partners work and they choose not to have children.

Disability: "Any limitation (resulting from an impairment) in the ability to perform any activity considered normal for a human being or required for some recognized social role or occupation," from the World Health Organization, International Classification of Impairments, Disabilities and Handicaps (WHO), 1980. Note that it has become common practice in Canada to use the term *disability* to represent the notion of disability, handicap, and impairment and that adjectives such as mental, intellectual, and physical are used with the term disability to denote which body part and/or function is affected.

Discrimination: The unequal or unfavourable treatment of people because of their perceived or actual membership in a particular ethnic group which restricts their full participation in the social, economic, and political life of Canada.

Disposable income: Income above that required for basic necessities, such as food, clothing, and accommodation.

Documentary method: A method of evaluating the quality of demographic sources by using the opinions of informed colleagues to assess the accuracy and completeness of the records.

Ecclesiastical registries: A list of births, deaths, or marriages compiled by religious groups.

Emigration: The movement of people out of a specific geographical area.

Emigration rate: The number of people leaving an area for every 1000 people in the population.

Empowerment: To have the resources, such as physical or financial means, to take control of one's own life.

Empty nesters: Parents whose children have left home to live on their own.

Equality of opportunity: When all citizens, regardless of their ascribed status, are provided the opportunity to succeed educationally, occupationally, and financially.

Ethnic group: A group of people who share norms, values, traditions, and ancestry and, thus, are considered distinct.

Ethnocentrism: Viewing or judging the world from the point of view of one's own culture. Two variations are the assumption that what is true of one's culture is true of other cultures and the belief that one's culture is superior to other cultures.

Evolution: A change either in physical form or in the frequency of certain genes over time.

Executive federalism: A term describing the fact that important and far-reaching political decisions in Canada are made by the prime minister, provincial premiers, federal and provincial cabinet ministers, and senior bureaucrats. Some believe this method of decision-making runs counter to democracy, or to the belief that citizens should be involved in government decision making.

Expectation method: A method used to evaluate the quality of demographic sources, which involves calculating expected proportions of vital events based on such factors as economic conditions, marriages, and migration.

Exploitation: Kart Marx's term for the situation where the capitalist class pays workers less than the real value of their work.

External migrants: Those migrants who move from outside a specific area. These areas can be defined at many different levels, such as a neighbourhood, province, or nation.

Familia: The total number of slaves in a household (Latin).

Familism: An ideology that promotes the traditional view of the family as the norm: working father, stay-at-home mother, and children. Also known as familialism.

Fecundity: The maximum number of children that a woman can produce during her lifetime.

Federalism: A system of governing a country that divides responsibilities between two levels of government. Each level is responsible for the same population and cannot abolish the existence of the other level.

Fellatio: A sexual activity involving oral stimulation of a male's genitals in which the partner's mouth is active while the penis remains relatively passive.

Feminist literature: Stories related from the point of view of women, where the feminine experience is central to the story and women's perceptions are differentiated from those of men. The stories often include issues and events omitted from previous literature.

Feminist theory: The view that women are disadvantaged in society and therefore must seek equality with men.

Feminization of poverty: A term indicating the growing percentage of women living in poverty.

Fertility: The number of live births in a population.

Fertility rate: The number of live births per 1000 women aged 15 to 44.

Fixation: The process by which one becomes excessively attached to (or fixated on) some object or person that was appropriate for an earlier stage of development. This condition is assumed to produce a variety of neurotic behaviours (see **Neurosis**).

Fornicate: A derivation of the Latin word *fornix*, which means arch; to have sex.

Gay: Homosexual orientation, particularly male homosexuality.

Gender: Cultural definitions of masculinity and femininity.

Gender identity: The social role a person assumes, usually but not always masculine for men and feminine for women.

Gender spheres: Areas of work, school, or recreation, which are dominated by one or the other gender (e.g., engineering for men and secretarial work for women).

Gender stereotypes: Generalizations about how men and women should behave, what their strengths are, and where they are best suited to work, learn, and play in society.

Genealogical analysis: Recreating family histories. This method can be used to calculate the amount of relatedness (inbreeding) among people in the population.

Genealogies: Family histories or trees.

General systems theory: A sociological approach that studies the family as a self-contained unit.

Glass ceiling: The invisible gender barrier that keeps women at the bottom of the occupational hierarchy and prevents them from winning promotions to positions of power.

Global village: A condition in which every part of the world is electronically connected to every other part, creating a feeling that each culture is involved in the affairs of all other cultures.

Golden Horseshoe: The narrow stretch of cities along Lake Ontario from Niagara Falls to Oshawa.

Gross migration rate: The number of people who enter and leave an area for every one thousand people in the population.

Handicap: "Any resulting disadvantage for an individual that limits the fulfilment of a normal role or occupation," from WHO, 1980. See **Disability**.

Heteroerotic: Having sexual, but not necessarily affectionate, attraction to members of the other gender.

Heterosexual: Preferring to develop romantic and sexual relationships with members of the opposite gender.

Hieroglyphics: The pictographic system used by the ancient Egyptians.

Homoerotic: Having sexual, but not necessarily affectionate, attraction to members of one's own gender.

Homosexual: Preferring to develop romantic and sexual relationships with members of one's own gender. (From Greek *homos*, meaning same, not from Latin *homo*, meaning *man*.)

Household: A group of people who live together.

Human sexual response cycle: Masters and Johnson's model of human sexual response, present in both males and females, which consist of four phases: excitement, plateau, orgasm, and resolution.

Ideological legitimation: An assumption or set of assumptions that attempts to justify a political, economic, or social relationship or system.

Ideology of the family: See **Familism**.

Immigrant and refugee stories: Stories that examine themes concerning leaving a familiar world, the risk and complexities of becoming part of an unknown and different society while accepting the inevitable losses involved. Challenges facing newcomers include coping with the distance from family and friends, learning a new language, adjusting to new political and social institutions. One theme that appears often in stories by and about refugees and immigrants is attitudes toward the role of women.

Immigration: The movement of people into a specific geographical area.

Immigration rate: The number of people entering an area for every 1000 people in the population.

Impairment: "Any abnormality of physiological or anatomical structure or function," from WHO, 1980.

Inanimate: A classification of nouns within Algonquian languages; it usually, but not always, refers to things that are not alive.

Incest taboo: The prohibition against intercourse and reproduction between close blood relatives.

Inclusive society: A society characterized by the involvement and participation of all of its members.

Income: The flow of money received over a specified period.

Indian Act: An act through which the federal government gave itself tremendous power over Native people in Canada.

Individual discrimination: Acts of discrimination that are carried out by individuals.

Infant mortality rate: The number of children dying under one year of age.

Institutional discrimination: Discrimination that limits the full participation of minority groups in the social, political, economic, and educational institutions of Canada. This type of discrimination may or may not be intentional.

Internal migrants: Those migrants who move within a specific area. These areas can be defined at many different levels, such as a neighbourhood, province, or nation.

Isonomy: A method used to estimate inbreeding by examining the frequency of marriages occurring between people who share the same surname.

Kinship coefficients: A method used to estimate inbreeding by examining the proportion of surnames within a population.

Labelling: Applying descriptive terms to people or their behaviours; labelling tends to produce the expected behaviour in the labelled person and in others, resulting in a "self-fulfilling prophecy."

Language family: A group of related languages.

Language isolate: A language that has no known related language.

Learning disability: A comprehensive term that describes limitations in one's capacity to learn.

Lesbian: Female with a homosexual orientation.

Liberation theories: Approaches to the study of family that see conflict as an essential characteristic of families and change and diversity as a means of freeing some family members from an oppressive family environment.

Life expectancy: The age to which most humans can expect to live (average age at death).

Life span: The maximum age that a human has ever lived.

Lingua franca: The common language used among cultures with different languages to communicate with each other.

Live births: Babies born alive.

Longitudinal analysis: A method used to examine demographic patterns over the life cycle involving following a birth or marriage cohort through time.

Mass medium: A medium available to and used by most people in the world.

Matriarchy: A type of family where authority is vested primarily in the female.

Means of production: The land, machinery, factories, and other resources required for the production of goods and services. In a capitalist society, the means of production are owned by a small percentage of the population.

Medicine wheel: A conceptual framework, teaching tool, and healing guide in Native culture based on the notion of the circle and the spiritual and symbolic significance of the four directions.

Meech Lake Accord (1987): The constitutional accord that was agreed to by the prime minister and the ten provincial premiers. The name of the accord was taken from the Meech Lake cottage where the meeting took place. The accord died when it failed to receive the appropriate approval from the Manitoba legislature.

Mentally deficient: A term used in the past to describe a person whose intellectual development was limited.

Meritocracy: A social system that rewards people in direct proportion to their merits (skills, talents, and abilities), rather than to their gender, race, or social connections. A meritocracy would remove all systemic barriers that block men and women from entering nontraditional spheres.

Métis: A person of mixed native and white genetic heritage (metis) or one who is a descendant of a particular people of French-Cree heritage (Métis).

Middle class: Those who own a small amount of wealth and are employed in relatively secure and high-paying occupations.

Migration: The movement of people into and out of specific geographical areas.

Mode of production: The means by which goods are produced in society; in Marxist theory, the defining characteristic of a society.

Monogamy: Marriage with one spouse in which neither engages in sexual activity with anyone else.

Morbidity: The number of people with a specific disease in a population.

Mortality: The number of people in a population dying in a given period.

Multiculturalism: The federal government's official commitment to promote the positive aspects of cultural differences and the English and French languages, thus furthering national unity.

Multiculturalism Act: Multiculturalism became officially sanctioned by the legislative act of the federal government, which became law on 21 July 1988.

National Policy (1879): A conscious attempt by the government of John A. Macdonald to build an economy based on manufacturing and to lessen Canada's dependence on resource exports.

Natural selection: The preferential survival and reproduction of individuals in a population by virtue of possessing a genetic characteristic that gives them an advantage.

Nature: Biological explanations for human behaviour and interaction. Sometimes referred to as biological determinism.

Negative Oedipus complex: A group of unconscious wishes, feelings, and ideas focusing on the desire to "possess" the same-gendered parent and to "eliminate" the opposite-gendered parent; it is a reversal of the positive Oedipus complex, in which the desire is to possess the opposite-sexed parent and to eliminate the same-sexed parent, a complex that in well-adjusted persons is to be resolved beginning at five to six years of age.

Net migration rate: The increase or decrease in the size of a population for every 1000 people based on the number of people who enter an area minus those who leave.

Neurosis: In classical psychoanalytic theory, neurosis is the symptoms produced by an affective fixation at an immature stage of development, such as an irrational attachment to people or objects, and an inability to form normal, mature relationships. Currently, the term neurosis is used as a generic cover term for any enduring mental disorder that is distressing, recognized by the individual as unacceptable and alien but where contact with reality is maintained. It is commonly identified with various anxiety disorders.

Nominative records: In demography, sources of demographic information that list a person's name.

Nonrandom mate selection: A distinct preference in the choice of a mate or marriage partner.

Normalization: The desire of people to live lives in as "typical" a way as possible or to function on a day-to-day basis in an average way.

Nuclear family: A household that includes a married couple and their children.

Nuptiality: Marriage.

Nurture: Social explanations for human behaviour and interaction. Sometimes also referred to as social determinism or social beaming theory.

Orality: The technique of communication that relies solely on the spoken or gestured word.

Orgasm: Intense, reflexive, physiological, and pleasurable release of sexual tension following sexual stimulation and the buildup of sexual arousal during intercourse or any other sexual activity. It is the third and shortest of the four phases described by Masters and Johnson.

Paleodemography: The study of prehistoric populations based on their physical remains.

Parchment: The dried skin of sheep and goats, used by the ancient Greeks for writing material.

Patriarchy: A family type where authority is vested in the male.

Pederasty: Sexual love between men and adolescent boys. The term is currently also used to include prepubescent boys.

Phallic worship: Worship of the penis and its symbolic representations as possessor of creative powers, especially in ancient cultures, as the role of the penis in reproduction came to be understood.

Pheromones: Chemical substances used as means of communication among members of a species. Pheromones may serve such functions as signalling sexual receptivity and alarm and marking territory.

Pictograph: A system of pictures that represent various sentences or utterances.

Pipe carrier: A person who has been given a pipe, as a sign of respect, to use for the purposes of peace and harmony.

Pluralism: The belief that ethnic conflict will always be a central part of modem, industrial societies and that ethnicity will always be a vital component of individual and group identity.

Political power: The degree to which a person or a group can enforce its demands.

Polygamy: Marriage in which a man has more than one wife or a woman has more than one husband.

Population: A group of people who live within a specific geographical or political boundary, who are genetically similar (interbreed), and who share a cultural heritage during a particular time frame.

Postcolonial: The period after colonization has ended. In reference to literature, many writers have emerged in the West Indies since the islands gained independence from European colonisers.

Powwow: A festival that, when open to the public, usually involves drumming, competitive dancing, traditional costumes and foods, and the sale of crafts.

Prejudice: The attitude of judging people on the basis of statements, ideas, and beliefs that do not hold up under critical scrutiny.

Premature ejaculation: A sexual dysfunction in which a male regularly reaches orgasm sooner than he or his partner would prefer because of an inability to recognize and control the sensations occurring just before ejaculation.

Progressive ideology: The belief in using social change to improve society. For example, under the assumption that social causes determine male and female behaviour, changing how society raises children will liberate people from restrictive gender spheres.

Race: An arbitrary system of classification that divides humans into different categories (races) based on differing physical characteristics, such as skin colour and eye shape. Biologically, humans all belong in the same species (race). Sociologically, however, physical traits are important symbols.

Racism: Discrimination based on race and assumed behavioural and mental similarities or deficiencies. Racism usually takes the form of the belief in the superiority of one race to another.

Regionalism: An attitude of the citizens of a particular region that they have not been given adequate recognition for their part in building Canada and have been penalized by the federal government in favour of another region.

Registered or status Indian: Someone who is "legally" an Indian, according to the federal Indian Act.

Rehabilitation medicine: A field in medical science that aims to return or to restore people to a former state of health or well being. This term now also refers to helping people to participate to their fullest potential in society by achieving the highest level of well-being possible.

Rehabilitation team: The professionals, such as nurses, doctors, physiotherapists, and social Sex: workers, who work toward restoring people to former states of health.

Representation by population: The principle that allocates seats in the House of Commons to each province according to its share of the national population. For example, a province that has 10 percent of the population receives 10 percent of the seats.

Reserve: An area of land that has been reserved for Native peoples' use.

Residential schools: Church-run boarding schools for Native children; these lasted from 1910 to the 1960s.

Response bias: A preference for making one particular response over others where the preference is not related to the issue, such as the preference to say "yes" rather than "no" or to answer in a way to reflect favourably upon oneself rather than to be truthful.

Royal commission: An information-gathering device used by the federal government to investigate issues deemed important to Canada. The commission travels across Canada, headed by people appointed by the federal government. A royal commission can only advise government, it cannot implement policy.

Same-sex couples: a familial partnership comprises two members of the same sex (i.e., two men or two women).

Script: A system of combined symbols for words.

Self-determination: Making free choices and acting without outside interference.

Self-fulfilling prophecy: When things turn out just as one expected or prophesied, likely because one behaved in conformity with the expected outcome.

Sentencing circle: An innovative Native justice forum based on traditional concepts of restorative justice that involves community members and not just legal professionals and that provides ways of dealing with people who are charges with crimes that are alternatives to the choices usually available in the Canadian legal system.

Sex: A man or a woman's biological sexual characteristics. The reproductive organs and the hormonal system a person is born with.

Sexual anesthesia: A reduction or absence of sexual feelings or enjoyment.

Sexual behaviour: The activities chosen in pursuing or nurturing a sexual relationship with a chosen partner, independent of one's sexual orientation.

Sexuality: All those aspects of constitution and behaviour that are related to sex, including disposition toward love and deep affection, sexual dysfunctions, the quality of being sexual, and gender.

Sexual orientation: One's erotic attraction toward and interest in developing loving relationships with members of either the other or one's own gender, independent of one's sexual behaviour.

Social controls: The means society uses to ensure that men and women behave in gender-appropriate ways. These controls may include laws, ridicule, and discrimination.

Social inequality: The degree to which people have access to and control over valued resources, such as money, wealth, status, and power.

Social movements: Major historical changes in the day-to-day lives of groups resulting from concerted social action. Examples include the women's movement and the civil rights movement.

Sociopsychological dimension to regionalism: Concerned with how people living in different regions feel and act toward each other, their community, and the federal government.

Space-oriented media: Media that facilitate delivery and communication of information across vast distances of territory or space.

Stereotype: A collection of generalizations about a group of people, which are negative, exaggerated, and unable to be maintained when subjected to critical analysis.

Stratification: A society is stratified when it is made up of groups of people who have differing degrees of access to and control over valued resources.

Structural–functionalism: 1. A theory proposing that inequality serves a positive function by ensuring that the most functionally important occupations are carried out by the most talented people, thus preserving the stability and proper functioning of society. An example is the idea that strict divisions of labour between men and women reduce role confusion and ensure that necessary jobs are done by those best equipped to do them. **2.** A sociological approach that views the family as a stabilizing force for its members and for society as a whole.

Sweat lodge: A traditional structure used to create a sauna-like sweat bath from heated rocks with water poured on them; also a tradition-based practice in which people physically and spiritually cleanse themselves, often as part of their healing path and of (re)connecting themselves to their Native identity.

Systemic barriers: laws, discriminatory practices, and psychological roadblocks, which together construct a system to prevent men and women from entering non-traditional spheres.

Telegraph: A device invented in 1844 that transmits messages across distances using electric wire.

Television imperialism: A term used to describe the power of television over other media; the tendency for television to be the dominant medium in a culture.

Time-oriented media: Media sufficiently durable to preserve the history and tradition of cultures across vast amounts of time.

Transfer payments: The name given to the billions of dollars that the federal government gives to the provinces and territories to help them deliver services to their populations. The key types of transfer payments are Canada Assistance Plan (CAP) and Equalization and Social Welfare Assistance.

Transsexual: A person whose sex is the opposite of his gender identity. Some transsexuals use surgery to alter their sexual characteristics to match their gender.

Transvestite: A man or woman who adopts the dress and the behaviour of the opposite sex.

Treaty: A legal agreement signed between either the British or the Canadian government and one or more native nations.

Tribalism: The condition in which people are encouraged to act as members of a group, rather than as individuals.

Upper class: Those who own a considerable amount of income and wealth. In Canada, the upper class constitutes about 5 percent of the population.

Unification theories: Approaches to the study of family that see families as adaptive units that mediate between individuals and society.

Universal themes: Topics or subjects of a literary work that are common to all human beings, regardless of the work's setting in time or place or the nature of the society in which they live. Some examples include good and evil, family relationships, loyalty, a sense of belonging, and desire for a home.

Variable: A characteristic that differs or varies among groups.

Vernacular: A form of speech or a dialect that is characteristic of a particular region or nation.

Vital event: A demographic term referring to births, marriages, or deaths.

Voice: The expression of one's opinion and experience in spoken or written words, the opinion itself, and the right to express an opinion.

Wealth: The accumulation of assets, such as a house, savings, or a car.

Working class: Karl Marx's term for the vast majority of the population who must sell their labour in order to survive.

Selected Bibliography

Chapter 1

Bradfield, Michael. *Regional Economics: Analysis and Policies in Canada*. Toronto: McGraw-Hill Ryerson, 1988.

Brodie, Janine. *The Political Economy of Canadian Regionalism*. Toronto: HBJ, 1990.

Brym, Robert. "Canada's Regions and Agrarian Radicalism," in *Images of Canada: The Sociological Tradition*, James Curtis and Lorne Tepperman, eds. Scarborough: Prentice-Hall, 1990.

Conway, J.F. "Western Alienation: A Legacy of Confederation," in *Contradictions in Canadian Society*, John A. Fry, ed. Toronto: Wiley, 1984.

Davis, Jo, ed. *Not a Sentimental Journey: What's Behind the Via Rail Cuts, What You Can Do About It*. Toronto: Gunbyfield Publishing, 1990.

Dyck, Rand. *Canadian Politics: Critical Approaches*. Scarborough: Nelson, 1993.

Gibbins, Roger. *Conflict and Unity: An Introduction to Canadian Political Life*, 3rd ed. Scarborough: Nelson, 1994.

Harmer, Harry. *The Longman Companion to Slavery, Emancipation and Civil Rights*. Toronto: Pearson Education Ltd., 2001.

Hiller, Harry S. *Canadian Society: A Macro Analysis*. Toronto: Pearson, 2000.

Hurtig, Mel. *The Betrayal of Canada*. Toronto: Stoddart, 1990.

Lithwick, N.H. "Is Federalism Good for Regionalism?" in *Federalism in Canada*, Garth Stevenson, ed. Toronto: McClelland and Stewart, 1989.

Mathews, Ralph. *The Creation of Regional Dependency*. Toronto: University of Toronto Press, 1983.

Morton, Desmond. *A Short History of Canada*. Edmonton: Hurtig, 1983.

Phillips, Paul. *Regional Disparities*. Toronto: Lorimer, 1978.

Qualman, Darrin. *The Farm Crisis and Corporate Power*. Ottawa: Canadian Centre for Policy Alternatives, 2001.

Savoie, Donald J. *The Canadian Economy: A Regional Perspective*. Toronto: Methuen, 1986.

Swan, Neil, and John Serjak. "Analysing Regional Disparities," in *Social Inequality in Canada: Patterns, Problems, Policies*, 2nd ed., James Curtis, Edward Grabb, and Neil Guppy, eds. Scarborough: Prentice-Hall, 1993.

Wien, Fred. "Regional Inequality: Explanations and Policy Issues," in *Social Inequality in Canada: Patterns, Problems, Policies*, 2nd ed., James Curtis, Edward Grabb and Neil Guppy, eds. Scarborough: Prentice-Hall, 1993.

Chapter 2

Abu-Laban, B. "Arab Immigration to Canada," in *Two Nations, Many Cultures: Ethnic Groups in Canada*, J.L. Elliott, ed. Scarborough: Prentice-Hall, 1979.

Bilson, G. *A Darkened House: Cholera in Nineteenth-Century Canada.* Toronto: University of Toronto Press, 1980.

Bourbeau, R., and J. Légaré. *Évolution de la mortalité au Canada et au Québec, 1831–1931. Essai de mésure par génération.* Montreal: Les Presses de l'Université de Montréal, 1982.

Brookes, A.A. "The Golden Age and the Exodus: The Case of Canning, Kings County." *Acadiensis*, 11 (1981), 57–82.

Brunger, A.G. "Geographical Propinquity Among Pre-famine Catholic Irish Settlers in Upper Canada." *Journal of Historical Geography*, 8 (1982), 265–82.

Cavalli-Sforza, L.L., and W.F. Bodmer. *The Genetics of Human Populations.* San Francisco: W.H. Freeman, 1971.

Charbonneau, H. "Jeunes femmes et vieux maris: la fécondité des mariages précoces." *Population*, 35 (1980), 1101–22.

Charbonneau, H., and A. LaRose, eds. *The Great Mortalities: Methodological Studies of Demographic Crises in the Past.* Liege: Ordina Editions, 1979.

Connell, K.H. *The Population of Ireland 1750–1845.* Oxford: Clarendon Press, 1950.

Crawley, R. "Off to Sydney: Newfoundlanders Emigrate to Industrial Cape Breton 1890–1914." *Acadiensis*, 17 (1988), 27–51.

Cressy, D. "The Seasonality of Marriage in Old and New England." *Journal of Interdisciplinary History*, 16 (1985), 1–21.

Crow, J.F. "Some Possibilities for Measuring Selection Intensities in Man." *Human Biology*, 30 (1958), 1–13.

Crow, J.F., and A.P. Mange. "Measurement of Inbreeding from the Frequency of Marriages Between Persons of the Same Surname." *Eugenics Quarterly*, 12 (1965), 199–203.

Darroch, A.G., and M.D. Ornstein. "Family and Household in Nineteenth-Century Canada: Regional Patterns and Regional Economies." *Journal of Family History*, 9 (1984), 158–77.

Dixon, R.B. "Explaining Cross-Cultural Variation in Age at Marriage and Proportions Never Marrying." *Population Studies*, 25 (1971), 215–33.

Dobzhansky, T. "Natural Selection in Mankind." *The Structure of Human Populations*, G.A. Harrison and A.J. Boyce, eds. Oxford: Clarendon Press, 1972.

Donnelly, F.K. "Occupational and Household Structures of a New Brunswick Fishing Settlement: Campobello Island, 1851," in *Labour in Atlantic Canada*, R. Chanteloup, ed. Saint John: University of New Brunswick, 1981.

Elder, G.H., and R.C. Rockwell. "Marital Timing in Women's Life Patterns." *Journal of Family History*, 1 (1976), 34–53.

Elliott, J.L. "Canadian Immigration: A Historical Assessment," in *Two Nations, Many Cultures: Ethnic Groups in Canada*, J.L. Elliott, ed. Scarborough: Prentice-Hall, 1979.

Fogel, R.W., S.L. Engerman, J. Trussel, R. Floud, C.L. Pope, and L.T. Wimmer. "The Economics of Mortality in North America, 1659–1910: A Description of a Research Project." *Historical Methods*, 11 (1978), 75–108.

Gaffield, C.M. "Boom and Bust: The Demography and Economy of the Lower Ottawa Valley in the Nineteenth Century." *Canadian Historical Association, Historical Papers*, (1982), 172–95.

Gee, E.M.T. "Early Canadian Fertility Transition: A Components Analysis of Census Data." *Canadian Studies in Population*, 6 (1979), 23–32.

Gibson, J.R. "Smallpox on the Northwest Coast, 1835–1838." *BC Studies*, 56 (1982), 61–81.

Gossage, P. "Absorbing Junior: The Use of Patent Medicines as Abortificants in Nineteenth-Century Montreal." *The Register*, 3 (1982), 1–13.

Hajnal, J. "Age at Marriage and Proportions Marrying." *Population Studies*, 7 (1953), 111–36.

Harney, R.F. "Men Without Women: Italian Migrants in Canada 1885–1930." *Canadian Ethnic Studies*, 11 (1979), 29–47.

Harrison, G.A., and A.J. Boyce., eds. *The Structure of Human Populations*. Oxford: Clarendon Press, 1972.

Henry, L. *Population: Analysis and Models*. New York: Academic Press, 1976.

Kaprielian, I. "Immigration and Settlement of Armenians in Southern Ontario: The First Wave." *Polyphony*, 4 (1982), 14–27.

Katz, M.B., M.J. Doucet, and M.J. Stern. "Population Persistence and Early Industrialization in a Canadian City: Hamilton, Ontario, 1851–1971." *Social Science History*, 2 (1978), 208–29.

Kaye, V.J., and C.W. Hobart. "Origins and Characteristics of the Ukrainian Migration to Canada," in *Persistence and Change: A Study of Ukrainians in Alberta*. C.W. Hobart et al., eds. Toronto: Ukrainian Canadian Research Foundation, 1978.

Keyes, J. "Marriage Patterns Among Early Quakers." *Nova Scotia Historical Quarterly*, 8 (1978), 299–307.

Kussmaul, A. "Time and Space, Hoofs and Grain: The Seasonality of Marriage in England." *Journal of Interdisciplinary History*, 15 (1985), 755–79.

Landry, Y. "Mortalité, nuptialité et canadianisation des troupes française de la guerre de Sept Ans." *Social History*, 12 (1979), 298–315.

Lavoie, Y. *L'Émigration des Québecois aux États-Unis de 1840 à 1930*. Quebec: Editeur officiel du Québec, 1979.

Li, P.S. "Immigration Laws and Family Patterns: Some Demographic Changes Among Chinese Families in Canada, 1885–1971." *Canadian Ethnic Studies*, 13 (1980), 58–73.

Li, P.S. "Chinese Immigrants in the Canadian Prairie, 1910–1947." *Canadian Review of Sociology and Anthropology*, 19 (1982), 527–40.

Lloyd, S. "The Ottawa Typhoid Epidemics of 1911 and 1912: A Case Study of Disease as a Catalyst for Urban Reform." *Urban History Review*, 8 (1979), 66–89.

Matwijiw, P. "Ethnicity and Urban Residence: Winnipeg, 1941–1971." *Canadian Geographer*, 23 (1979), 45–61.

McGinnis, J.D.P. "The Impact of Epidemic Influenza: Canada, 1918–1919." *Canadian Historical Association, Historical Papers*, (1977), 121–40.

McKeown, T. *The Modern Rise of Population*. London: Edward Arnold, 1976.

McLaren, A. "Birth Control and Abortion in Canada, 1870–1920." *The Canadian Historical Review*, 59 (1978), 319–40.

McQuillan, K. "Economic Structure, Religion, and Age at Marriage: Some Evidence from Alsace." *Journal of Family History*, 14 (1989), 331–46.

Medjuck, S. "The Social Consequences of Economic Cycles on Nineteenth-Century Households and Family Life." *Social Indicators Research*, 18 (1986), 233–61.

Model, J. "The Timing of Marriage in the Transition to Adulthood: Continuity and Change, 1860–1975." *Turning Points: Historical and Sociological Essays on the Family*, J. Demos and S. Boocock, eds. Chicago: University of Chicago Press, 1978.

Nam, C.B., and S.O. Gustavus. *Population: The Dynamics of Demographic Change*. Boston: Houghton Mifflin, 1976.

Norris, D.A. "Household and Transiency in a Loyalist Township: The People of Adolphustown, 1784–1822." *Social History*, 13 (1980), 399–415.

Osborne, B. "The Cemeteries of the Midland District of Upper Canada: A Note on Mortality in a Frontier Society." *Pioneer America*, 6 (1974), 46–55.

Parker, W. "The Canadas." *Studies in Overseas Settlement and Population*, A. Lemon and N. Pollock, eds. New York: Longman, 1980.

Roth, E. "Historic Fertility Differentials in a Northern Athapaskan Community." *Culture*, 2 (1982), 63–75.

Roychoudhury, A.K., and M. Nei. *Human Polymorphic Genes: World Distribution*. Oxford: Oxford University Press, 1988.

Sharna, R.D. "Premarital and Ex-nuptial Fertility (Illegitimacy) in Canada 1921–1972." *Canadian Studies in Population*, 9 (1982), 1–15.

Shryock, H.S., and J.S. Siegel. *The Methods and Materials of Demography*. San Diego: Academic Press, 1976.

Statistics Canada's Internet Site, <www.statcan.ca>.

Statistics Canada. *1996 Census Handbook*. Ottawa: Industry Canada, 1997.

Statistics Canada. *1996 Census of Canada*.

Statistics Canada. *Births and Deaths, 1996*. Ottawa: Industry Canada, 1999.

Statistics Canada. *Marriages, 1996*. Ottawa: Industry Canada, 1999.

Swedlund, A.C. "Historical Demography: Applications in Anthropological Genetics." *Current Developments in Anthropological Genetics*, Vol. 1. J.H. Mielke, and M.H. Crawford, eds. New York: Plenum Press, 1980.

Veevers, J.E. "Age Discrepant Marriages: Cross-national Comparisons of Canadian-American Trends." *Social Biology*, 31 (1984), 118–26.

Weaver, J.C. "Hamilton and the Immigration Tide." *Families*, 20 (1981), 197–208.

Willigan, J.D., and K.A. Lynch. *Sources and Methods of Historical Demography*. New York: Academic Press, 1982.

Wrigley, E.A. "Family Limitation in Pre-industrial England." *Economic History Review*, 19 (1966), 82–109.

Wynn, G. "Ethnic Migrations and Atlantic Canada: Geographical Perspectives." *Canadian Ethnic Studies*, 18 (1986), 1–15.

Chapter 3

Allahar, Anton L., and James E. Cote. *The Structure of Inequality in Canada.* Toronto: James Lorimer and Company Ltd., 1998.

Clement, Wallace. *The Canadian Corporate Elite: An Analysis of Economic Power.* Ottawa: Carleton University Press, 1986.

Grabb, Edward G. *Theories of Social Inequality: Classical and Contemporary Perspectives.* Toronto: Holt, Rinehart, and Winston, 1990.

Hunter, Alfred A. *Class Tells: On Social Inequality in Canada.* Toronto: Butterworths, 1981.

Turner, Bryan S. *Equality.* London: Tavistock, 1986.

Chapter 4

Barrett, Ralph V. "Pedagogy, Racism and the 'Postmodern Turn.'" *The College Quarterly*, 1 (Fall 1994).

Berger, Peter, and Brigitte Berger. *Sociology: A Biographical Approach.* New York: Basic Books, 1972.

Berton, Pierre. *Why We Act Like Canadians.* Markham, Ont.: Penguin, 1987.

Elliott, Jean Leonard, and Augie Fleras. *Unequal Relations: An Introduction to Race and Ethnic Dynamics in Canada.* Scarborough: Prentice-Hall, 1992.

Fleras, Augie, and Jean L. Kunz. *Media and Minorities: Representing Diversity in a Multicultural Canada.* Toronto: TEP, 2001.

Fleras, Augie, and Jean Leonard Elliott. *Multiculturalism in Canada: The Challenge of Diversity.* Scarborough: Nelson, 1992.

Gould, S.J. *The Mismeasure of Man.* New York: W.W. Norton, 1981.

Government of Canada. *The Canadian Multiculturalism Act: A Guide for Canadians.* Ottawa, 1990.

Haas, Jack, and William Shaffir. *Shaping Identity in Canadian Society.* Scarborough: Prentice-Hall, 1978.

Hawkins, Freda. *Canada and Immigration: Public Policy and Public Concern.* Kingston and Montreal: McGill-Queen's University Press, 1988.

Henry, Frances. *The Caribbean Diaspora in Toronto: Learning to Live with Race.* Toronto: UTP, 1994.

Henry, Frances, Carol Tator, Winston Mattis, and Tim Rees. *The Colour of Democracy: Racism in Canadian Society*, 2nd ed. Toronto: Harcourt Brace, 2000.

Hill, Daniel G. *Human Rights in Canada: A Focus on Racism*. Ottawa: Canadian Labour Congress, 1977.

Hiller, Harry H. *Canadian Society: A Macro Analysis*. Toronto: Prentice-Hall, 2000.

James, Carl E. *Seeing Ourselves: Exploring Race, Ethnicity and Culture*. Toronto: TEP, 1999.

Kalbach, Madeline A., and Warren E. Kalbach. *Perspectives on Ethnicity In Canada: A Reader*. Toronto: Harcourt Brace, 2000.

Kelley, Ninette, and Michael Trebilcock. *The Making of the Mosaic: A History of Canadian Immigration Policy*. Toronto: UTP, 1998.

Kennedy, K.A.R. *Human Variation in Space and Time*. Dubuque, Iowa: Brown, 1976.

Li, Peter S. *Ethnic Inequality in a Class Society*. Toronto: Wall and Thompson, 1988.

Montagu, A., ed. *The Concept of Race*. London: Collier-Macmillan, 1964.

Palmer, Howard. *Immigration and the Rise of Multiculturalism*. Toronto: Copp Clark, 1975.

Chapter 5

A good place to begin a search for information on Native culture is the local Native Friendship Centre. These are found in most Canadian cities. Other good sources of information are the Native Studies departments found in some community colleges and a few universities.

Barman, Jean. "Aboriginal Education at the Crossroads: The Legacy of Residential Schools and the Way Ahead," in *Visions of the Heart: Canadian Aboriginal Issues*, D.A. Long and O.P. Dickason, eds. Toronto: Harcourt Brace, 1996.

Bergman, Brian. "Dark Days for the Inuit." *Maclean's*, 4 March 1996, p. 67.

Dickason, Olive P. *Canada's First Nations: A History of Founding Peoples from Earliest Times*. Toronto: McClelland and Stewart, 1997.

Francis, Daniel. *The Imaginary Indian: The Image of the Indian in Canadian Culture*. Vancouver: Arsenal Pulp Press, 1992.

Frideres, James S., and Rene Gadacz. *Aboriginal People in Canada: Contemporary Conflicts*, 6th ed. Toronto: Prentice-Hall, 2001.

Henslin, James, Dan Glenday, Ann Duffy, and Norene Pupo. *Sociology: Canadian Edition: A Down-to-Earth Approach*. Toronto: Allyn and Bacon, 2001

Knockwood, Isabelle. *Out of the Depths*. Lockeport, N.S.: Roseway Publishers, 1992.

LaRoque, Emma. "Three Conventional Approaches to Native People," in Brett Balon and Peter Resch eds., *Survival of the Imagination: the Mary Donaldson Memorial Lectures*. Regina: Coteau Books, 1993, pp. 209–18.

Purich, Donald. *The Metis*. Toronto: Lorimer, 1988.

Rice, Brian, and John Steckley. "Lifelong Learning and Cultural Identity: Canada's Native People," in Michael J. Hatton ed., *Lifelong Learning: Policies, Practices, and Programs Toronto, School of Media Studies, Humber College* (APEC pub. #97-HR01.5), 1997, pp. 216–29.

Smith, Donald. *Le Sauvage*. Ottawa: National Museum of Man, 1974.

Steckley, John, and Bryan Cummins. *Full Circle: Canada's First Nations*. Toronto: Prentice-Hall, 2001.

No author. *Indian Treaties and Surrenders*, Vol. 1. Toronto: Coles Publishing (reprint of federal government publication), 1971.

Chapter 6

Alford, Glen, ed. *The Advocate*. Toronto: Ontario March of Dimes.

Bickenbach, Jerome. *Physical Disability and Social Policy*. Toronto: University of Toronto Press, 1993.

Bowland, A., C. Nakatsu, and J. O'Reilly, eds. *The 1995 Annotated Ontario Human Rights Code*. Toronto: Carswell, 1995.

Canadian Human Rights Act, R.S.C., 1985.

Driedger, Diane, and Susan Gray, eds. *Imprinting Our Image: An International Anthology of Women's Disabilities*. Charlottetown: Gynergy, 1992.

Eisenberg, Myron G., Cynthia Griggins, and Richard J. Duval, eds. *Spring Series on Rehabilitation: Vol. 2. Disabled People as Second-Class Citizens*. New York: Springer, 1982.

Findley, Timothy. *The Piano Man's Daughter*. Toronto: Harper Collins, 1995.

Higgens, Paul. *Masking Disability: Exploring the Social Transformation of Human Variation*. Springfield: Charles C. Thomas, 1992.

Human Rights Legislation: An Office Consolidation. Toronto: Butterworths, 1991.

Ministry of National Health and Welfare: Disabled Persons in Canada. Ottawa: Ministry of National Health and Welfare, 1981.

Office for the Disabled Persons. *The Needs and Attitudes of Disabled Ontarians*. Toronto: Environics Research Group, 1989.

Rioux, Marcia, and Michael Bach, eds. *Disability Is Not Measles: New Research Paradigms in Disability*. North York, Ont.: Roeher Institute, 1994.

Rogers, Patricia. "Atlanta Olympics Take Aim at Barriers to the Disabled." *Toronto Star*, 16 July 1996.

Rubin, Josh. "Wheelchair Racers Preview Olympic Dash." *Toronto Star*, 14 July 1996.

Special Committee on the Disabled and Handicapped, First Report (Obstacles). Ottawa: 1980.

Chapter 7

Baker, Maureen. "Gender and Gender Relations," in *An Introduction to the Social World*, R. Jack Richardson and Lorne Tepperman, eds. Toronto: McGraw-Hill Ryerson, 1987.

Bly, Robert. *Iron John: A Book About Men*. Reading, Mass.: Addison-Wesley, 1990.

Carey, Elaine. "Women Still Two Steps Behind Men." *Toronto Star*, 9 August 1995, p. A15.

Colombo, Robert. *The 1994 Canadian Global Almanac*. Toronto: Macmillan Canada, 1994.

Fillion, Kate. *Lip Service: Challenging the Sexual Script of the Modern Woman*. Toronto: HarperCollins, 1995.

Friedan, Betty. *The Feminine Mystique*. New York: Dell, 1974.

Jones, Charles, Lorna Marsden, and Lorne Tepperman. *Lives of Their Own: The Individualization of Women's Lives*. Toronto: Oxford University Press, 1990.

Lorenz, Konrad. *On Aggression*. New York: Harcourt Brace and World, 1966.

Mackie, Marlene. *Exploring Gender Relations: A Canadian Perspective*. Toronto: Butterworths, 1982.

Miles, Rosalind. *The Women's History of the World*. Paladin: London, 1989.

Tannen, Deborah. *You Just Don't Understand: Men and Women in Conversation*. New York: Ballentine, 1990.

Wolf, Naomi. *The Beauty Myth*. Toronto: Random House, 1990.

"Women's Ranks Thin in Politics." *Toronto Star*, 28 August, 1995, p. A3.

Chapter 8

Barash, David P., and Judith E. Lipton. *Myth of Monogamy: Fidelity and Infidelity in Animals and People*. W.H. Freeman & Co., 2001.

CSG Enterprises, Inc., Edward O. Laumann, Robert T. Michael, and Gina Kolata. *Sex in America: A Definitive Survey*. Toronto: Little, Brown, 1994.

The Good Sex Guide. TVOntario, Ontario Educational Communications Authority, 1993.

Hatfield, Elaine, and Richard L. Rapson. *Love and Sex: Cross-Cultural Perspectives.* Toronto: Allyn and Bacon, 1996.

Gottman, John M., and Nan Silver. *The Seven Principles for Making Marriage Work.* Crown, 1999.

Herold, Edward S. *Sexual Behaviour of Canadian Young People.* Markham, Ont.: Fitzhenry and Whiteside, 1984.

LeVay, Simon. *Queer Science: The Use and Abuse of Research into Homosexuality.* Massachusetts: MIT Press, 1997.

Nevid, Jeffrey S., with Fern Gotfried. *Choices: Sex in the Age of STDs.* Toronto: Allyn and Bacon, 1997.

Pines, Ayala M. *Romantic Jealousy: Causes, Symptoms, Cures.* Routledge, 1998.

Rathus, Spencer A., and Susan Boughn. *AIDS: What Every Student Needs to Know.* Toronto: Harcourt Brace Jovanovich, 1993.

Ridley, Matt. *The Red Queen: Sex and the Evolution of Human Nature.* Penguin U.S.A, 1995.

Suggs, David N., and Andrew W. Miracle. *Culture and Human Sexuality.* Pacific Grove, Calif.: Brooks/Cole, 1993.

Waite, Linda J., and Maggie Gallagher. *The Case for Marriage: Why Married People Are Happier, Healthier, and Better off Financially.* Doubleday, 2000.

Chapter 9

Anderson, Karen, et al. *Family Matters: Sociology and Contemporary Canadian Families.* Toronto: Methuen, 1987.

Baker, Maureen, ed. *Canada's Changing Families: Challenges to Public Policy.* Ottawa: Vanier Institute, 1994.

Baker, Maureen, ed. *Families: Changing Trends in Canada*, 2nd ed. Toronto: McGraw-Hill Ryerson, 1990.

Cheal, David. *Family and the State of Theory.* Toronto: University of Toronto Press, 1993.

Eichler, Margrit. *Families in Canada Today.* Toronto: Gage, 1983.

Hagedorn, Robert, ed. *Sociology.* Toronto: Harcourt Brace, 1994.

Mandell, Nancy, and Ann Duffy, eds. *Canadian Families.* Toronto: Harcourt Brace, 1995.

Montgomery, Jason, and Willard Fewer. *Family Systems and Beyond.* New York: Human Sciences Press, 1988.

Nett, Emily. *Canadian Families*. Vancouver: Butterworths, 1993.

Ramu, G., ed. *Marriage and the Family Today*, 2nd ed. Scarborough: Prentice-Hall, 1991.

Schlesinger, Rachel, and Benjamin Schlesinger. *Canadian Families in Transition*. Toronto: Canadian Scholar's Press, 1992.

Statistics Canada. *A Portrait of Families in Canada*. Ottawa: Minister of Industry, Science and Technology. Catalogue no. 89-523E, 1993.

Statistics Canada. *Women in Canada 2000*. Ottawa: Minister of Industry, 1995.

Thorne, Barrie, and Marilyn Yalom, eds. *Rethinking the Family*. Boston: Northeastern University Press, 1992.

Tucker, Robert, ed. *The Marx–Engels Reader*, 2nd ed. New York: W.W. Norton, 1978.

Chapter 10

Biagi, Shirley. *Media/Impact: An Introduction to Mass Media*. Belmont, Calif.: Wadsworth, 1994.

Barber, Benjamin R. *Jihad vs. McWorld: How Globalism and Tribalism Are Reshaping the World*. New York: Ballantine Books, 1996.

De Kerckhove, Derrick. *The Skin of Culture: Investigating the New Electronic Reality*. Toronto: Somerville House, 1995.

Fleras, Augie, and Jean Leonard Elliott. *Multiculturalism in Canada: The Challenge of Diversity*. Toronto: Nelson, 1992.

Innis, Harold. *Empire and Communications*. Toronto: Press Procépic, 1986.

Kottak, Conrad Philip. *Prime-Time Society: An Anthropological Analysis of Television and Culture*. Belmont, Calif.: Wadsworth, 1990.

Kroker, Arthur. *Technology and the Canadian Mind: Innis/McLuhan/Grant*. Montreal: New World Perspectives, 1984.

McLuhan, Eric, and Frank Zingrone, eds. *Essential McLuhan*. Concord, Ont.: Anansi Press, 1995.

McLuhan, Marshall. *The Mechanical Bride: Folklore of Industrial Man*. New York: Vanguard, 1951.

McLuhan, Marshall. *The Gutenberg Galaxy: The Making of Typographic Man*. Toronto: University of Toronto Press, 1962.

McLuhan, Marshall. *Understanding Media: The Extensions of Man*. New York: New American Library, 1964.

McLuhan, Marshall, and Quentin Fiore. *War and Peace in the Global Village*. New York: Bantam, 1968.

McLuhan, Marshall, and Bruce R. Powers. *The Global Village: Transformations in World Life and Media in the Twenty-First Century.* New York: Oxford University Press, 1989.

Meyrowitz, Joshua. *No Sense of Place: The Impact of Electronic Media on Social Behaviour.* New York: Oxford University Press, 1985.

Ong, Walter. *Orality and Literacy: The Technologizing of the Word.* New York: Routledge, 1988.

Postman, Neil. *The Disappearance of Childhood.* New York: Delacorte Press, 1982.

Postman, Neil, and Steve Powers. *How to Watch TV News.* New York: Penguin, 1992.

Tunstall, Jeremy. *The Media Are American: Anglo-American Media in the World.* London: Constable, 1977.

Vipond, Mary. *The Mass Media in Canada.* Toronto: Lorimer, 2000.

Chapter 11

Aitken, Johan Lyall. *Masques of Morality.* Toronto: Women's Press, 1987.

Ashcroft, Bill, Gareth Griffiths, and Helen Tiffin, eds. *The Empire Writes Back.* London: Routledge, 1989.

Atwood, Margaret, ed. *The New Oxford Book of Canadian Verse in English.* Toronto: Oxford University Press, 1982.

Atwood, Margaret. *Survival.* Toronto: McClelland and Stewart, 1972.

Atwood, Margaret. *Power Politics.* Toronto: McClelland and Stewart, 1971.

Atwood, Margaret. *Lady Oracle.* Toronto: McClelland and Stewart, 1976.

Atwood, Margaret. *Bodily Harm.* Toronto: McClelland and Stewart, 1981.

Atwood, Margaret. *The Handmaid's Tale.* Toronto: McClelland and Stewart, 1985.

Atwood, Margaret. "What Do Canadians Want?" in *Canadian Content,* Sarah Norton and Nell Waldman, eds. Toronto: Holt Rinehart and Winston, 1988.

Beresford-Howe, Constance. *The Book of Eve.* Toronto: Macmillan, 1973.

Beresford-Howe, Constance. *The Marriage Bed.* Toronto: Macmillan, 1981.

Braithwaite, Max. *Why Shoot the Teacher?* Toronto: McClelland and Stewart, 1974.

Broughton, Kathryn MacLean, ed. *Heartland.* Toronto: Nelson, 1983.

Brown, Russell, Donna Bennett, and Nathalie Cooke, eds. *An Anthology of Canadian Literature in English.* Toronto: Oxford University Press, 1990.

Callaghan, Barry. "Canadian Wrye," in *Canadian Content*, Sarah Norton and Nell Waldman, eds. Toronto: Holt Rinehart and Winston, 1988.

Campbell, Maria. *Halfbreed*. New York : Saturday Review Press, 1973

Choyce, Lesley, ed. *The Cape Breton Collection*. Porter's Lake, NS: Pottersfield Press.

Davies, Robertson. <www.iccs-ciec.ca/blackwell.html>, *Canadian Studies: A Guide to Sources*.

Djwa, Sandra, and R.G. Moyles, eds. *E.J. Pratt: Complete Poems, Parts I and II*. Toronto: University of Toronto Press, 1989.

Fowke, Edith. *Folklore of Canada*. Toronto: McClelland and Stewart, 1976.

Geddes, Gary, ed. *15 Canadian Poets* x *2*. Toronto: Oxford University Press, 1988.

Geddes, Gary, and Phyllis Bruce, eds. *15 Canadian Poets*. Toronto: Oxford University Press, 1970.

Goh, Maggie, and Craig Stephenson, eds. *Between Worlds*. Oakville: Rubicon, 1989.

Henry, Frances, Carol Tator, Winston Mattis, and Tim Rees. *The Colour of Democracy*. Toronto: Harcourt Brace, 1985.

Hébert, Anne. *Kamouraska*. Toronto: Moussen, 1973.

Herberg, Dorothy Chave. *Frameworks for Cultural and Racial Diversity: Teaching and Learning for Practitioners*. Toronto: Canadian Scholar's Press, 1993.

Holman, Hugh C. *A Handbook to Literature*. Indianapolis: Bobbs-Merrill, 1983.

Hutcheon, Linda. *The Canadian Postmodern*. Toronto: Oxford University Press, 1988.

Hutcheon, Linda, and Marion Richard, eds. *Other Solitudes*. Toronto: Oxford University Press, 1990.

Karpinski, Eva C., and Ian Lea, eds. *Pens of Many Colours*. Toronto: Harcourt Brace Jovanovich, 1993.

Keefer, Janice Kulyk. *Under Eastern Eyes*. Toronto: University of Toronto Press, 1987.

King, Thomas, ed. *All My Relations*. Toronto: McClelland and Stewart, 1990.

Kroetch, Robert. *Badlands*. Toronto: New Press Canadian Classics, 1975.

Lai, David Chuenyan. "A 'Prison' for the Chinese Immigrants," in *The Asianadian*, Vol. 2, No. 4, 1983.

Lecker, Robert, and Jack David, eds. *The New Canadian Anthology*. Toronto: Nelson, 1988.

Montgomery, L.M. *Anne of Green Gables*. Boston: L.C. Page, 1908.

Moses, Daniel David, and Terry Goldie, eds. *An Anthology of Canadian Native Literature in English*, 2nd ed. Toronto, Oxford University Press, 1998.

Munro, Alice. *Lives of Girls and Women*. Toronto: McClelland and Stewart, 1971.

Munro, Alice. *Who Do You Think You Are?* Toronto: McClelland and Stewart, 1978.

Norton, Sarah, and Nell Waldman, eds. *Canadian Content*. Toronto: Holt Rinehart and Winston, 1988.

Pinsent, Gordon. *The Rowdyman*. Toronto and New York: McGraw-Hill Ryerson, 1973.

Reaney, James. *The Donnellys: Sticks and Stones, The St. Nicholas Hotel, and Handcuffs*. Victoria and Toronto: Press Porcépic, 1983.

Reid, John G., and Mark Lescarbot. *The Canadian Encyclopedia*, 2nd ed. Edmonton: Hurtig, 1988.

Schaum, Melita, and Connie Flanagan, eds. *Gender Images*. Boston: Houghton Mifflin, 1992.

Shields, Carol. *Swann*. Toronto: Viking Penguin, 1990.

Shields, Carol. *The Stone Diaries*. Toronto: Viking Penguin, 1994.

Sullivan, Rosemary, ed. *Poetry by Canadian Women*. Toronto: University of Toronto Press, 1989.

Taylor, Drew Hayden. "Seeing Red Over Myths." *The Globe and Mail*, 8 March 2001.

"Post-Survival Canada: 12 Writers in Search of a Paradigm." *The Globe and Mail,* 30 June 2001, p. D2.

Thériault, Yves. *Aguguk*. Montreal: L'Actuelle, 1971.

Waterson, Elizabeth. *Survey*. Toronto: Methuen, 1973.

Weaver, Rovert, ed. *Canadian Short Stories*. Toronto: Oxford University Press, 1960.

Wiebe, Rudy, ed. *The Story Makers*. Toronto: Gage, 1987.

Williamson, Janice. *Sounding Differences: Conversations with Seventeen Canadian Women Writers*. Toronto: University of Toronto Press, 1993.

Biographies

Paul U. Angelini is the operations coordinator for the General Arts and Science Program at Sheridan College in Brampton, Ontario. He has developed and delivered curriculum at Sheridan since 1988 in the fields of politics, sociology, human diversity, and philosophy. Paul completed his master's degree in political studies at Queen's University and his combined honours bachelor of arts in political science and sociology at McMaster University.

Michelle A. Broderick completed her Ph.D. in Biological Anthropology at the University of Toronto. Since graduating in 1994, she has taught a variety of courses at Sheridan College, McMaster University, and the University of Toronto. Michelle is currently working in Institutional Research at the University of Toronto.

Leslie Butler has been a community college professor for eleven years. She has taught English and general education courses, including social work, journalism, and graphic design. She received a master's degree in English from the University of Waterloo and a master's degree in journalism from the University of Western Ontario.

Maureen Coleman is a writer, reviewer, and book club leader. She is recently retired from Sheridan College where she taught English and General Education courses, the latter focusing on cultural diversity through Canadian and international literature. She holds bachelor's degrees in history and education from St. Francis Xavier University and a master's degree in teaching English from the University of Toronto.

Eddie Grattan is currently an elementary-school teacher. He has formerly taught at Sheridan College, Brock University, and McMaster University. He is presently completing his doctoral dissertation on social class, sports, and the media.

Brigitte Guetter has developed and taught courses in human sexuality, personality, abnormal, and social psychologies; sociology; cultural diversity; critical thinking; and communications since 1989 at George Brown College, Seneca College, Nova Scotia Community College, and Sheridan College. She is currently with The Multicultural Council of Windsor and Essex County. She received her bachelor of science and bachelor of education degrees from the University of Toronto.

Grant Havers received his Ph.D. in Social and Political Thought from York University in 1993. He is currently assistant professor of Philosophy at Trinity Western University in British Columbia. Grant's current research involves a study of political ideologies in the postmodern age.

Nancy Nicholls is a professor in the Social Service Worker program at Centennial College and was the 2000 recipient of the Board of Governor's Award for Excellence in Valuing Diversity. She holds a master's degree in social work from the University of British Columbia and an honours bachelor of arts from York University.

Geoff Ondercin-Bourne has taught global issues, Canadian politics, sociology, literature, communications, and ESL at Sheridan College for fourteen years. He also teaches communications and literature at Mohawk College. Geoff received a master's degree from McMaster University and an honours B.A. from the University of Guelph.

John Steckley has been teaching at Humber College since 1983 and has taught Anthropology at Memorial University of Newfoundland and at Trent University, and Native Studies at Laurentian University. He recently published *Beyond Their Years: Five Native Women's Stories* (1999). With Bryan Cummins, he has co-authored *Full Circle: Canada's Native People* (2001) and *Aboriginal Policing: A Canadian Perspective* (in press, 2002). His areas of specialization are Native languages (primarily Huron) and Native history. John has a master's degree in anthropology from Memorial University of Newfoundland and is currently completing his doctorate in postsecondary education at OISE at the University of Toronto. He was adopted into the Wyandot tribe of Kansas in 1999 and given the name *Tehaondechoren* ("He splits the country in two").

Index